UNITED STATES TAX COURT PRACTICE AND PROCEDURE

UNITED STATES TAX COURT PRACTICE AND PROCEDURE

Lester M. Ponder

PRENTICE-HALL, INC.
ENGLEWOOD CLIFFS, NEW JERSEY

Prentice-Hall International, Inc., *London*
Prentice-Hall of Australia, Pty., Ltd., *Sydney*
Prentice-Hall of Canada, Ltd., *Toronto*
Prentice-Hall of India Private Ltd., *New Delhi*
Prentice-Hall of Japan, Inc., *Tokyo*

"This publication is designed to provide accurate and authoritative information in regard to the subject matter covered. It is sold with the understanding that the publisher is not engaged in rendering legal, accounting, or other professional service. If legal advice or other expert assistance is required, the services of a competent professional person should be sought."

—From the Declaration of Principles jointly adopted by the Committee of the American Bar Association and a Committee of Publishers and Associations.

Library of Congress Cataloging in Publication Data

Ponder, Lester M
United States Tax Court practice and procedure.

Includes bibliographical references and index.
1. United States. Tax Court. I. Title.
KF6324.P6 343'.73'040269 76-6455
ISBN 0-13-938688-2

Printed in the United States of America

To my dear Sallie—her patient understanding and steady encouragement have made the writing of this book pleasant and possible.

A Word From the Author

THE UNITED STATES TAX COURT justifies a practice and procedure treatise at this significant juncture in its history. The issuance of new comprehensive and definitive rules, for the first time embracing the concept of discovery, and also declaratory judgment jurisdiction, obviously called for a new book on the Court's practice and procedure. The achievement of its golden anniversary in 1974, when it also moved into its first building, has added an historic milepost.

Despite its fifty-year history and its tremendous volume of federal tax litigation (over 10,000 new cases filed annually), this irreplaceable tribunal has been virtually ignored, compared to other, less important, courts.

With the rapid recent growth of tax controversy, it has become the forum for ultimate judicial resolution of these disputes between citizens and their government, in perhaps ninety percent of all trial, court-docketed tax cases, the remainder being divided, of course, between the district courts and the United States Court of Claims. Creation of its Small Claims Division in 1971 has added a new dimension by permitting individual taxpayers to plead their own small cases.

This book has been written to provide a practical working tool for the general practitioner and a worthy refresher for the veteran tax litigator, as well as a text and source book for the law student. The author has drawn upon his 35 years of experience in Tax Court practice, first as counsel for the Commissioner of Internal Revenue, and, since 1951, as counsel for taxpayers, resulting in his participation in between 800 and 1,000 cases, of which about 100 have resulted in trials.

The author also gained close first-hand insight into the Rules, during the period of their preparation, in his capacity as American Bar Association Taxation Section Council Director to its Committee on Court Procedure, from August 1971 to August 1973. This Committee was privileged to respond to the Court's request to study the draft Rules and to advise the Court of views of private practitioners thereon, just as the Chief Counsel's Office of the Internal Revenue Service received a similar invitation. In fact, these two groups held meetings jointly to consider the draft Rules and thus the better to advise the Court.

This book first explains the origin and history of the Court and the pros and cons of its choice as a litigating forum. The extremely important subject of jurisdiction is next considered, followed by the subject of parties before the Court, pleadings including motion practice, disposition of cases without trial, as on summary judgment, the intertwining of settlement negotiations with trial preparation, and then trial preparation itself, including discovery, depositions, actual trial of a case considering the effect of the new Federal Rules of Evidence, post-trial aspects, appeals and small cases. In short, with this book the practitioner may confidently tackle a Tax Court case from the statutory notice to final decision, carrying it through to a satisfactory conclusion.

Chapter 6 should be of special help to the practitioner as "bread and butter" advice and suggestions in the realities of working with the Appellate Division of the Internal Revenue Service and Regional Counsel's Office, both in the settlement and the trial preparation aspects of a case. The stipulation of facts process is strongly emphasized, as it is the most important phase of a Tax Court case.

In addition to the text, a number of forms are included in the appendix, most of which are from actual docketed cases. It is earnestly hoped that these forms will be truly helpful to the practitioner in drafting sound pleadings and then going forward with the subsequent necessary steps in effectively presenting his client's position.

The full text of the Rules of Practice and Procedure with blank Tax Court forms have also been included, in a separate appendix, retaining the explanatory Notes provided by the Court.

All statutory references are, of course, to the Internal Revenue Code of 1954.

Lest the reader wonder why a more recent decision has not been cited, July 1, 1975, was mandated as the basic citation cutoff date for publishing reasons, with only a few rare exceptions.

I am grateful to the Court for making available copies of all decisions and orders on procedural issues promptly upon their release. I am also especially appreciative to the Court for access to all unpublished procedural memorandum sur orders which are cited and analyzed herein.

My sincere appreciation to my two dedicated secretaries who did the bulk of the typing—Mrs. Violet Humfleet until March 1975, and

Mrs. Joy Balzerick thereafter—as well as Miss Georgia Lord and Mrs. Debbie Lynch. My appreciation also to Miss Mary Ann Roman and Mrs. Stephanie Penrod for technical assistance.

In retrospect, writing this book has been pure joy—the attainment of a long-time dream. In prospect, my high hopes that this book will fill a real need and will help many to understand the Tax Court better and to be more effective advocates therein. If this prospect is achieved, my writing effort will have been adequately rewarded.

Lester M. Ponder

CONTENTS

UNITED STATES TAX COURT PRACTICE AND PROCEDURE

CHAPTER 1

History and Organization— Choice of Forum

Section 1.01—Origin

THE ADOPTION OF THE SIXTEENTH AMENDMENT to the Constitution in 1913 was a revolutionary event in the history of our federal tax system with its institution of the income tax law. Because the early rates were so low, it is unlikely that either taxpayers or governmental officials realized just how revolutionary and far-reaching would be its results, one of which was the necessity for development of a litigating process by which taxpayers could have redress from unlawful or improper assessment of taxes by the sovereign. The later enactment of a far-reaching estate tax law and also a gift tax law intensified the necessity for such taxpayer relief.

Prior to the adoption of the Sixteenth Amendment, taxpayers had already been permitted to sue for refund of taxes erroneously and illegally collected, in either the appropriate United States District Court or the United States Court of Claims. Such suits, of course, were permitted for income tax refunds thereafter. Within a short time, it clearly became apparent that the refund suit procedure was inadequate to protect all taxpayers who had meritorious causes for resisting the government's assessment of additional taxes, but who for one of several reasons were unable to pay the assessed additional tax and sue for refund without great hardship and, in many cases, were simply not able to pay at all to obtain this remedy.

At first the administrative technique of further reviews by higher officials in the Internal Revenue Service was instituted by the establishment of an Advisory Tax Board of six members to act for two years, its duties being to pass upon questions of interpretation and administration if desired by the Commissioner and if requested by the taxpayer. Soon realizing the inadequacy of this first administrative relief mechanism, the Commissioner next attempted to grapple with this tax prepayment problem by creating a Committee on Appeals and Review to consider the merits of taxpayers' cases prior to assessment. This administrative group in the Internal Revenue Service organization considered appeals lodged by taxpayers on a protest procedure, very similar to that presently in existence using the Appellate Divison (formerly the Technical Staff), with a major difference that it functioned only in Washington, not in field offices throughout the country. While this Committee endeavored to carry out its duties as fairly as possible, it was still only another arm of the governmental agency which had originally initiated the assessment. Taxpayers and their representatives had a natural feeling that this Committee would be reluctant to reverse the Commissioner's position, especially since only the taxpayer, and not the Government, might contest an adverse decision of this Committee in a later suit for refund.

Further, by this time the tax rates were increasing and the volume of cases was likewise growing, making it quite difficult for this Committee to stay on top of its work load. Pressure began to build in the Congress for the creation of some type of agency or tribunal which would be independent of the Commissioner and which would have jurisdiction of appeals from the Commissioner's decision prior to paying the asserted additional tax. In short, the urgent need was for a litigate first–pay later, independent adjudicating tribunal. Hence, in the Revenue Act of 1924 the United States Board of Tax Appeals was created to provide taxpayers with such a forum in which tax liabilities could be litigated without being required to resort to the complicated and often inequitable process of payment first–litigate later. This legislation contained no provision for appeal from a Board decision. Hence, a taxpayer's remedy in the event of an adverse decision by the Board was to sue in a federal district court, from which, of course, an appeal could be taken to the appropriate court of appeals, with the district court having to re-try *de novo* issues of fact that had been presented to the Board. Within a very short time after the creation of the Board, both Government officials and taxpayers became aware that this was an unnecessary duplication of procedure, being further complicated and unduly expensive. The Congress immediately acted in the Revenue Act of 1926 by providing for a direct appeal from the Board to the appropriate court of appeals.

Under the 1924 and 1926 Revenue Acts, the Board was established as an independent agency in the executive branch of the Government, not as a court, and so remained until 1969. Until 1942 its descriptive title of "Board" and the enabling language which failed to describe it as a "Court" were sources of confusion and even embarrassment for this tribunal, Government tax officials and taxpayers and their representatives, because for all practical purposes it functioned as a judicial tribunal operating in the federal judicial system. The first step toward changing its technical image from administrative to judicial was taken in the Revenue Act of 1942 when its name was changed to The Tax Court of the United States. Other than this change in name, however, there was no provision in the 1942 Revenue Act or any subsequent legislation prior to 1969 which changed its basic characteristics. The change in name alone did seem to give greater judicial appearance, if not standing, to this tribunal.

Section 1.02–The "Court" Becomes a Court

During the years of its development, the Tax Court followed judicial rules of procedure and evidence and in every way except statutory was considered and treated as another branch of the federal judiciary rather than simply an independent executive agency as the statute provided. For many years, therefore, leading up to 1969, consideration had been given by the Congress to a legislative amendment which would do by statute what was already done in practice, that is, cause this important tribunal to become *de jure* what it had already become *de facto,* a legally constituted *tax court.* Hence, by Section 951 of the Tax Reform Act of 1969, approved December 30, 1969, The United States Tax Court was established as a court of record under Article I of the Constitution. The ramifications of this 1969 enactment are, of course, most important and will be noted throughout this book. But it should always be remembered that even prior to 1969 the Tax Court did function as a court of record, albeit without the specific statutory authority. For all practical purposes it was already a judicial tribunal operating in the federal judicial system, but it was not a "Court" within the true meaning of the term until the 1969 enactment.

Even though it is now a court of record under Article I of the Constitution, its jurisdiction is still limited to that provided by the Internal Revenue Code. Jurisdiction attaches with the filing of a timely petition and jurisdiction ends when the decision of the Court becomes final, but while a case is lodged in the Court it has the same powers with respect to contempt, the carrying out of its writs, orders, etc. that Congress has previously given to the district courts. The key point here is that the Tax Court's jurisdiction is strictly limited to the provisions of the Internal Revenue Code, and general equitable principles cannot be applied. This is not to say that the Court is unmindful of equities between the parties but technically such equities cannot affect a decision of the Court.

Section 1.03–Membership

The Court consists of 16 members, known as the Chief Judge and the Judges of the Tax Court, appointed by the President with the advice and consent of the Senate "solely on the grounds of fitness to perform the duties of the office." No individual shall be a judge of the Court unless he is appointed to that office before attaining the age of 65. The term of office of any judge of the Court shall expire 15 years after he takes office. Judges are eligible for reappointment and usually are reappointed. In fact, for many years all interested judges have been reappointed.

Presently there are also special trial judges (until January 1, 1976, known as commissioners), who hear Small Tax Cases and such other cases as may be assigned by the Chief Judge, with review by the Chief Judge or another judge before issuance of the Court's opinion.

Section 1.04–The Chief Judge

Perhaps too little attention has been given to the important role played by the Chief Judge in the life and history of the Court. Since its inception the Court has biannually elected a Chief Judge in odd-numbered years to serve the succeeding two fiscal years beginning July 1. Traditionally, each elected Chief Judge has been reelected for at least one term, sometimes for two.

The Chief Judge's task is to perform the normal duties of the chief judge of any Court, but also additional duties because of the special nature of the Court. His regular duties include presiding over many of the regular Wednesday Motions Calendars, presiding over the conference sessions of the full Court, appearing before the appropriate committees of the Congress as the Court's spokesman and handling top-level personnel matters. His special duties include deciding which cases shall be reviewed by the full Court; deciding which cases shall be issued as regular opinions, which as memorandum opinions and which as memorandum *sur* orders, as well as assigning judges and special trial judges to trial sessions. To attain decisional uniformity to the extent possible is also a very important responsibility of the Chief Judge. When it is realized this involves sensitive dealings with the 15 other judges, as well as several other retired judges who are hearing cases on a recall basis, the enormity and difficulty of his task are apparent.

He is ably supported by his own legal staff, headed by his chief law assistant, who assists in the preliminary review of all proposed opinions as prepared by the individual judges and submitted to the Chief Judge for review. Although his chief law assistant might recommend appropriate action on a proposed opinion, such as publication as a regular decision, the buck stops only on the Chief Judge's desk, where the final decision must be made. For example, if the Chief Judge disagreed with a proposed opinion, he would presumably note the case for review by the Court, especially if he deemed it of precedential importance. Thus, the Chief Judge has great power over the direction of the Court and its flow of cases. Fortunately, the Court has been blessed with strong, but courteous and even-handed, Chief Judges throughout its existence, one of the chief factors in the attainment of its present high stature in the world of American jurisprudence.

As indicated, the full Court holds frequent Friday conferences on a regular basis for consideration of cases chosen by the Chief Judge. On occasion, the judge presiding at the hearing of a case finds himself in the minority and may actually write a dissenting opinion, with the opinion of the Court being written by another judge.

In deciding which cases will be issued as official, "regular" opinions or as memorandum opinions, the Chief Judge will be guided by the importance of the case, its complexity, its novelty, but chiefly its precedential value. Hence, memorandum opinions are considered of slight precedential value and usually are cases turning primarily on fact questions.

When the phrase–"Reviewed by the Court"–appears after the Court's decision at the end of its opinion, the case has been the subject of a Friday conference and bears the imprint of all 16 judges. For an attorney to find such an opinion in his favor is obviously a pearl beyond price, carrying, as it does, the full weight of the Court's view, but alas, the opposite also holds true.

In rendering its opinions, the Court has announced a policy of following the rule of law laid down by the court of appeals of the circuit to which appeal would be likely in a particular case. Now known as the *Golsen* rule, from the case reported at 54 T.C. 742 (1970), it supersedes prior policy under which the Court felt that, as a national court, it was constrained to follow its own precedents if it continued to believe them correct, regardless of its reversal by the court of appeals which would hear the case if appealed. This change of policy represents but one of the several efforts of the Court in recent years to follow a realistic, understandable course of action to the benefit of taxpayer and the Government alike.

Section 1.05–The Court's Judicial Conference

The Court has instituted a most helpful policy of holding judicial conferences, usually biannually in May, with designated judges meeting with selected counsel from both the private tax bar and the Government.

The Section of Taxation, American Bar Association, has been the designating agency for the private bar and the Chief Counsel of Internal Revenue Service for the Government. Problems of mutual interest are discussed, all points of view are welcome and worthwhile results are accomplished. Such topics as the new Rules and obtaining courtrooms are recent examples of the agenda.

Section 1.06–The Clerk

Any consideration of the Court's operations would be incomplete without an understanding and appreciation of the highly critical role played by the Clerk of the Court. As with the role of the Chief Judge, the smooth functioning of the Clerk's office is vital to the Court's success, yet only when malfunctioning occurs do the parties appreciate how seldom this happens. In the vast majority of cases, the Clerk's office functions smoothly and efficiently.

It should be noted that the Clerk has a much more difficult task than clerks of many other courts. He must serve *all* papers, unless a party chooses otherwise, and the extent of service by the parties in the future will likely be quite small, leaving this heavy burden almost entirely on the Clerk. Further, he must prepare all orders and docket entries, unless a judge sees fit to do so, contrary to the practice in most other courts, including federal district courts, where the attorneys must perform these chores.

When it is considered that in recent years the annual incoming volume of new cases has been approximating 10,000, the Clerk's staggering work load is readily apparent. The critical importance of his work is illustrated by the many disputes over the timeliness of petition filing, where the record in the Clerk's office is crucial to that awesome decision.

Section 1.07–Organization

A system of judicial retirement has been provided but retired judges may be recalled by the Chief Judge with their consent. This practice has been rather prevalent within the last 15 or 20 years and bolsters the working personnel of the Court so that its case loads may be more expeditiously handled. Recalled retired judges have been a boon to the Court and many handle a large complement of cases.

Traditionally, a fairly well-balanced geographical selection has prevailed in the selection of judges, although there is no such statutory requirement.

Although the Code provides that the Chief Judge may divide the Court into divisions of one or more judges, assign the judges of the Court to divisions and designate the chiefs of division, in actual practice hearings are held before one judge; to assign multiple judges to a division would unduly delay the work of the Court because of its heavy case load. Division hearings decide any proceeding instituted before the Court and any motion assigned to the division by the Chief Judge.

When a judge has died after having heard a case, but before rendering his opinion, such case is reassigned to another judge for decision unless one of the parties objects after notice being given, which has rarely, if ever, occurred. The same rule applies when a judge becomes disabled or for any other valid reason is not able to decide the case expeditiously. The Chief Judge makes the reassignment.

Reports of the Tax Court and all evidence received by it "including a transcript of the stenographic report of the hearings" are public records open to the inspection of the public. The reports of the Court are required to be published and are printed by the Government Printing Office. Thereby they become competent evidence of the reports of the Court in all courts of the United States and the several states without further proof or authentication.

The principal office of the Court is in the District of Columbia, but the Court or any division thereof may sit at any place within the United States, which in practice has encompassed all principal cities in the United States, including, of course, the far-flung states of Alaska and Hawaii.

Thus, through necessity, the Court has become the only continuous federal circuit-riding forum because of the location of its headquarters in Washington D.C. It affords ample advance notice to the parties of its hearing dates and places. It will grant a taxpayer's request for place of hearing except in rare cases. If the taxpayer fails to request a place of hearing, the Government will do so. This circuit-riding situation has caused complaints from both parties from time to time, but on balance the Court has overcome most of the disadvantages inherent in the unavailability of the Court in a local city for ready reference as problems arise in the handling of a case. Its ability to overcome these disadvantages has been largely achieved by virtue of maximum cooperation between the Government representatives (Appellate Division and Regional Counsel's Office of the Internal Revenue Service) on the one hand and taxpayer's representatives on the other. The parties have thus been able to resolve most procedural and even substantive questions on their own without Court participation, whereas in the federal district courts and the Court of Claims such matters are usually resolved before the court itself, or a magistrate, either on pre-trial motions or similar procedure.

These solutions have been hammered out over the years so as to enable the Court to handle its large work load without stationing a judge in any city other than Washington, D.C., but instead sending the judges and deputy clerks throughout the length and breadth of the land to hear cases when they accumulate sufficiently to warrant a trial calendar in a particular city.

Except in Small Tax Cases, the proceedings of the Court must be conducted in accordance with the Court's rules and in accordance with the Rules of Evidence applicable in trials without a jury in the United States District Court for the District of Columbia.

Section 1.08–Choice of Forum

The Congress has provided three trial forums for tax controversies:

(1) the United States Tax Court;

(2) the United States district courts, and

(3) the United States Court of Claims.

The threshold question in every litigable tax controversy is which of these forums should be chosen for actual trial. Certain absolute rules may eliminate one, or even two, of the forums, thus providing the choice without consideration of the discretionary factors. In other matters, however, no absolute rule controls and all three forums may remain possibilities down through the final moment of choice, leaving little advantage in any of the three, thus causing the trial lawyer to make the final choice based on technical and sometimes subtle distinctions. In the most difficult cases, the choice may become almost a matter of intuition for the experienced practitioner.[1]

At the outset, the practitioner is normally met by the prepayment-of-tax test, since the district courts and the Court of Claims require advance payment of tax in order to secure their jurisdiction. If advance payment is difficult or impossible at the time of choice, obviously the Tax Court remains the sole possibility. This situation undoubtedly causes a great number of cases to be lodged in the Tax Court that otherwise would be filed in one of the other courts.

If the particular tax controversy involves other than income, estate, or gift taxes, it can be filed only in the district courts or Court of Claims, which have jurisdiction over all federal taxes, whereas the Tax Court jurisdiction is limited to the three above named. Since most tax controversies involve "the big three," this point is usually of small importance.

If a jury trial is desired, a district court suit must be chosen. In particular types of cases, such as valuation of property, intention of the parties, or contemplation of death transfers, jury trials may be more advantageous than court trials, particularly if local knowledge is an important factor.

If a taxpayer wants to make sure that his case may be appealable to a court of appeals, he must choose either the Tax Court or a district court. On the other hand, since the Court of Claims now functions in effect as a trial court at the trial judge level, followed by the right of appeal to the full court, this intramural appellate procedure has many of the aspects of appeals from the Tax Court or a district court to a court of appeals. The great advantage here in the Court of Claims is that if the

---

[1] The extensive literature analyzing the factors involved in selecting the proper tax forum include the following: Ferguson, "Jurisdictional Problems in Federal Tax Controversies," 48 Iowa L. Rev. 312 (1963); Garbis & Frome, "Selecting the Court for the Optimum Disposition of a Tax Controversy," 27 J. Taxation 216 (1967); Gannett, "Pre-Trial Strategy in a Tax Case: Choice of Forum: A Checklist of Points to Consider," 22 N.Y.U. Inst. on Fed. Tax 75 (1964); Ash, "Factors in Selecting the Forum in Which to Litigate," 12 N.Y.U. Inst. on Fed. Tax 935 (1954); Lane & Hamovit, "The Preparation of Tax Refund Cases in the District Courts and the Court of Claims," Joint Committee on Legal Educ. of American Law Inst. & American Bar Ass'n. (1964); Smail, "Traps in Refund Suits," 39 Taxes 639 (1961); Holzman, "Should You Use a Jury?" 36 Taxes 301 (1958); Walston, "The Use of Juries in Federal Civil Income Tax Cases," 39 Taxes 144 (1961); Cusack, "Federal Tax Procedures: Refund Claims and Suits," 12 Prac. Law 45 (1966); Miller, "Tax Litigation in the Court of Claims," 55 Geo. L.J. 454 (1966); Pavenstedt, "The United States Court of Claims as a Forum for Tax Cases," 15 Tax L. Rev. 1 (1959); Beaman, "When Not to Go to the Tax Court: Advantages and Procedures in Going to the District Court," 7 J. Taxation 356 (1957); Groman & Zarky, "Rules of Evidence in the Tax Court of the United States," 1958 So. Calif. Tax Inst. 603; Lore, "When Should a Tax Case Be Taken to Court: The Many Costs of Litigation," 3 J. Taxation 2 (1955).

taxpayer can find favorable precedent in that court, he will be assured that it cannot be reversed by a court of appeals, and that the only possible reversal is by the Supreme Court if it grants a writ of certiorari, which rarely occurs.

If a taxpayer is willing and able to pay the asserted tax, the next step requires careful research to determine whether any applicable decisions favor the taxpayer or the Government. Such research entails careful and detailed analysis of the reasoning of the opinions as well as the final result in each applicable case. Since tax cases, like most court controversies, frequently turn on very fine factual distinctions, the practitioner must be skilled in analyzing the applicable decisions to see which ones come closest to his particular fact situation. There will usually be a welter of cases in the Tax Court on the familiar types of controversy, such as reasonableness of compensation, which means that the practitioner must sift and scrutinize these cases and arrive at those which most nearly approximate his own. As for Court of Claims cases, they will usually be found in fewer numbers on any particular issue than in the Tax Court because the Court of Claims hears fewer tax cases. As for district court decisions, they will usually not be as important in deciding whether to sue in a particular district court, as district courts are regional rather than national. Further, since district courts frequently hear jury tax cases, rather than court tax cases, there are fewer court cases to study than even in the Court of Claims.

After reviewing the decisions of the three courts, it will also be necessary to review those of the circuit court which will have appellate jurisdiction of the potential Tax Court or district court case. Since the Tax Court does not always follow the first, or even second or third, reversal by a court of appeals, the fact that a Tax Court case has been reversed will not necessarily mean its demise, except in the reversing circuit, under the so-called *Golsen* rule.[2] With respect to district court cases, a reversal by its court of appeals sounds the death knell for that particular district court decision.

In conducting the necessary research for choice of forum, it should also be noted that, if there are no decisions directly in point by any of the three courts, some assistance may be obtained from decisions in related areas, for example, in construing the intention of the parties. If one of the three trial courts has taken a view favorable to a taxpayer, such as accepting the oral testimony of the taxpayer as to his intention on a certain issue, then that forum may well be chosen in a case involving the taxpayer's intention on another issue.

---

[2] *Golsen*, 54 T.C. 742 (1970), *aff'd.* 445 F.2d 985 (1971), *cert. denied*, 404 U.S. 940 (1971).

As for the burden of proof, it is placed on the taxpayer in all three courts in the usual situation, with statutory exceptions including transferee liability, fraud, and cases involving omissions of more than 25 percent of gross income. In the district courts and the Court of Claims, the Treasury may assert equitable defenses of recoupment and setoff to rebut proof of an overpayment.

In one particular area, that involving asserted unreasonable accumulation of earnings under Section 531, the Tax Court is the sole jurisdictional choice if the taxpayer desires to invoke Section 534, which exclusively permits that Court to enter an order that the taxpayer has shifted the burden of proof to the Government on the question of reasonableness of the accumulation.

It is generally considered that because the Tax Court hears only federal income, estate, and gift tax cases, it possesses more tax expertise than either the district courts or the Court of Claims. This may be either an advantage or disadvantage for a taxpayer, depending on the nature of his particular case. If the issue is highly technical and it is believed that a thorough understanding of the technicalities will favor the taxpayer, then the Tax Court might well be chosen. On the other hand, if the issue is broadly factual in nature, or requires a mixed finding of law and fact to reach the decision, such as the proper accumulation of earnings or the valuation of property, which depends to a great extent on overall judgment of the fact-finder and his prior experience in many fields, not alone in the field of taxation, then the district courts or the Court of Claims may seem preferable. Any generality in this area is dangerous and again involves an element of intuition which requires many years of experience to achieve, if at all.

One of the factors to be considered in any litigated matter, be it tax or otherwise, is the speed with which a final decision may be obtained. This is a two-edged sword, since taxpayers may be found on either side in different cases. When all is said and done, if a practitioner desires to expedite final litigation of his case, there is much that he can do by speedy preparation and constant contact with the Government lawyer to expedite its procedures in all three courts.

CHAPTER 2

Jurisdiction

Section 2.01—Basic Jurisdictional Requirements

AS PREVIOUSLY POINTED OUT, the Court is one of limited jurisdiction by the provisions of the Internal Revenue Code.[1] Hence, a considerable volume of litigation has arisen involving jurisdictional questions.[2] Until the enactment of the Tax Reform Act of 1969, the Court's jurisdiction since its creation in 1924 had been limited to cases in which the Commissioner or his delegate had determined a deficiency in income, estate or gift tax; in short, all Chapter I, Subtitles A and B, taxes, or transferee liability with respect to such determined tax deficiencies. (The Court's jurisdiction over the renegotiation of government contracts was effectively terminated in 1971 and, therefore, is not within the scope of this book.) The statutory requirements must be strictly met. Jurisdiction cannot be conferred by stipulation of the parties.

The Court must decline to take jurisdiction on its own motion even though the Commissioner fails to raise the jurisdictional ground.[3] Obviously, the Court will ordinarily decide all jurisdictional questions before a case is reached on its merits, but it is "never too late" for jurisdiction to be denied.

A jurisdictional plea may be raised at any time because of the Court's limited jurisdiction. The Court either has it or it doesn't—there is no gray area here. The "no such thing as a little bit pregnant" principle

---

[1]*Johnson,* 19 B.T.A. 840 (1930), *aff'd,* 56 F.2d 58 10 AFTR 1264 (5th Cir., 1932), *cert. denied,* 286 U.S. 551 (1932); *Tyson v. Comm'r,* 66 F.2d 160 12 AFTR 950 (7th Cir., 1933). Sec. 6212-6214 contain the basic jurisdictional provisions.

[2]*Eastman Gardiner Naval Stores Co.,* 4 B.T.A. 242, 245 (1926).

[3]*Ruby,* 2 B.T.A. 377 (1925); *Beacon,* T.C. Memo Op. Docket 3987 (1945), ¶45,172 P-H Memo T.C.; *Wheeler's Peachtree Pharmacy, Inc.,* 35 T.C. 177 (1960).

applies and failure to properly plead will not confer jurisdiction.[4] Although the Court has no equitable jurisdiction,[5] it "must consider all matters necessary to the proper exercise of that jurisdiction,"[6] as would a court of equity having jurisdiction of the ultimate subject matter.

A notice of deficiency or transferee liability, generally referred to as the "90-day letter", must be timely mailed to the taxpayer at his last known address.[7] All essential facts to establish jurisdiction must be clearly stated in the petition.[8] If not so stated, the Court may dismiss the appeal on its own motion so as not to improperly extend its jurisdiction.

The authority of a duly licensed attorney, admitted to practice before the Court, to act for the petitioner he purports to represent, may not be questioned by the Court so as to require proof that he has authority to file a petition.[9] As in all other respects, with specified exceptions, the burden of proving that the Court has jurisdiction rests upon the petitioner.[10]

In short, therefore, two factors are critical for the Court to have jurisdiction of any case: (1) the Commissioner or his delegate must *determine* a deficiency, and (2) he must send a notice of his determination to the taxpayer.[11] Nothing less will suffice.

Section 2.02—Last Known Address

There is a large volume of litigation defining what constitutes the "last known address of the taxpayer."[12] The basic rule which emerges is that if the Commissioner has used due diligence in ascertaining the last

---

[4] *First National Bank of Wichita Falls,* 3 T.C. 203 (1944); *Goldstein,* 22 T.C. 1233 (1954). *See also Stanton,* 34 B.T.A. 451 (1936), *aff'd,* 98 F.2d 739, 21 AFTR 796 (7th Cir., 1938), *cert. denied,* 305 U.S. 650 (1938).

[5] *Comm'r v. Gooch Milling & Elevator Co.,* 320 U.S. 418, 31 AFTR 764 (1943); *Rothensies v. Electric Storage Battery Co.,* 329 U.S. 296, 35 AFTR 297 (1946).

[6] *Fidelity Trust Co.,* 4 B.T.A. 411 (1926). The Court is unable to allow equitable recoupment based upon an overpayment or underpayment in a tax year other than the one for which a deficiency has been determined in a proper notice of deficiency.

[7] *Jones,* 62 T.C. 1 (1974). The statutory notice has been popularly called a "Tax Court ticket." *Corbett v. Frank,* 293 F.2d 501, 8 AFTR 2d 5223 (9th Cir., 1961). *See also* Rules, Title XXI.

[8] *Nibley-Mimnaugh Lumber Co.,* 37 B.T.A. 617 (1938); *Shingle,* 34 B.T.A. 875 (1936); *Penn Mutual Indemnity Co.,* 32 T.C. 653 (1959), *aff'd,* 277 F.2d 16, 5 AFTR 2d 1171 (3rd Cir., 1960).

[9] *Communist Party of the U.S.A. v. Comm'r,* 332 F.2d 325, 13 AFTR 2d 1167 (App. D.C., 1964), *rev'g* 38 T.C. 862 (1962).

[10] *National Committee to Secure Justice in the Rosenberg Case,* 27 T.C. 837 (1957).

[11] *McCue,* 1 T.C. 986 (1943); *Forest Glen Creamery Co.,* 33 B.T.A. 564 (1935); *cf. Taylor,* 36 B.T.A. 427 (1937), where the Comm'r filed a return for the taxpayer, who had failed to file, after which the Comm'r unsuccessfully sought dismissal. *See also* Rules, Title XXI.

[12] *Zaun,* 62 T.C. 278 (1974).

known address for mailing purposes, there has been compliance with the jurisdictional requirement.[13]

As a practical matter, the subordinates of the Commissioner who have investigated a tax return and have proposed a deficiency notice, usually have had sufficient contact with the taxpayer or his representatives to ascertain whether the address shown on the return in question is correct or whether the taxpayer has removed to another address since that time. It should be noted, however, that in the vast majority of cases the notice of deficiency is simply mailed to the address shown on the tax return without any investigation by the Commissioner or his subordinates as to its accuracy. This can lead to disastrous consequences if the taxpayer has removed to a new address since he filed his return because under postal regulations little, if any, effort is made to locate the taxpayer for purposes of delivering the notice to him, even though the Commissioner mailed the notice by registered or by certified mail with return receipt requested. In former days the postal authorities apparently made more diligent efforts to locate the taxpayer where the notice was undeliverable because the taxpayer had moved, but at the present time a great many notices of deficiency are never delivered to the taxpayer because he has moved from the address shown on his return. If his representative has filed a power of attorney with the Service, a copy of the notice will, of course, be mailed to the representative, but in many instances no such power of attorney has been filed and the notice simply is returned to the Commissioner as undeliverable and the Commissioner makes no effort to track down the taxpayer. In such situations, obviously, the 90-day period will expire without the filing of a Tax Court petition and the taxpayer is placed in the dilemma of being forced to pay the tax, file refund claim and suit for refund thereafter, with its probable attendant hardship.

This problem teaches practitioners that they should place a power of attorney on file at the earliest possible date in order to insure that they will receive a copy of the notice of deficiency, but if this is impossible, they should contact the appropriate office of the Service to ascertain the mailing date of a notice when this comes to their attention. It may be possible to obtain a copy of the notice prior to the expiration of the 90-day period if the representative moves quickly after learning of its issuance.

Obviously, a taxpayer can waive an incorrect mailing address by filing a timely petition since he has suffered no damage and lost no legal right as a result of this error,[14] but on the other hand, if the mailing address does not meet the requirements of the "last known address" rule,

---

[13] *Goldstein,* 22 T.C. 1233 (1954); *Graham,* T.C. Memo 1975-59, ¶ 75,059 P-H Memo T.C.

[14] *Zaun,* 62 T.C. 278 (1974); *Comm'r v. Stewart,* 186 F.2d 239, 40 AFTR 53 (6th Cir., 1951), *rev'g* T.C. Memo Op. Docket 19056 (1949), ¶ 49,274 P-H Memo T.C.

the taxpayer will be protected for an untimely filed petition.[15] As previously noted, it will be a question of fact in each case as to whether the Commissioner may reasonably believe that the mailing address of the notice was the address to which the taxpayer wished the notice sent.[16] In short, the phrase "last known address" should be the address, within the knowledge of the Commissioner, where mail is most likely to reach the addressee, or where he reasonably believes the addressee wishes it sent.[17] Although the statute requires mailing by registered or certified mail, if the notice is sent by ordinary mail and is actually received by the taxpayer, it has been held that the notice is valid, but a *caveat* would be to apply this holding with considerable caution.[18]

There is no easy answer to this "last known address" problem because the Court will not place an undue burden on the Commissioner by holding that he must absolutely ascertain the correct present address of a taxpayer since that is virtually impossible as a practical matter. In our mobile society, where one out of every five persons is said to move from one address to another within a given year, this would place a crushing burden on the Commissioner in the light of his issuance of many thousands of deficiency notices each year.

It is believed that this problem has not reached significant proportions because in most deficiency cases, the taxpayer has had sufficient contact with the Service to properly advise the Service of his correct address, but even in such situations the taxpayer may neglect to advise the Government representative that he has moved to a new address since filing the return in question. In such cases, mailing the notice to the address shown on the return will give the Court jurisdiction.[19] Vigilance is the answer because once burned, it would be too late to obtain Tax Court jurisdiction.

Even if a proper power of attorney has been filed with the Service, the failure of the Commissioner to send a copy of the notice to counsel designated therein does not affect the time within which the taxpayer must file his Tax Court petition if a proper notice has been sent to the taxpayer at his last known address.[20] This points up the necessity

---

[15] *Shelton,* 63 T.C. 193 (1974); *Heaberlin,* 34 T.C. 58 (1960); *Carbone,* 8 T.C. 207 (1947).

[16] *Degill Corporation,* 62 T.C. 292 (1974); *Estate of Hurd,* 9 T.C. 681 (1947); *Estate of Clark v. Comm'r,* 173 F.2d 13, 37 AFTR 984 (2nd Cir., 1949), *aff'g* 10 T.C. 1107 (1948).

[17] *Bergfeld v. Campbell,* 290 F.2d 475, 7 AFTR 2d 1355 (5th Cir., 1961), *aff'g* 188 F. Supp. 505, 6 AFTR 2d 5479 (1960); *Marvin,* 40 T.C. 982 (1963); *Berger v. Comm'r,* 404 F.2d 668, 22 AFTR 2d 5889 (3rd Cir., 1968), *aff'g* 48 T.C. 848 (1967).

[18] *Rosewood Hotel, Inc. v. Comm'r,* 275 F.2d 786, 5 AFTR 2d 1012 (9th Cir., 1960), *vacating* unreported Tax Court dismissal order.

[19] *Luhring v. Glotzbach,* 304 F.2d 556, 9 AFTR 2d 1812 (4th Cir., 1962), *aff'g* 9 AFTR 2d 376 unreported D.C. decision (1961).

[20] *Allen,* 29 T.C. 113 (1957); *Houghton,* 48 T.C. 656 (1967); *Berger,* 48 T.C. 848 (1967).

of careful preparation of the power of attorney, because the Service has announced that it will follow the rule that where a taxpayer files a power of attorney authorizing a designated person to receive *all* communications concerning his tax matters for a particular tax year and requests that they be mailed to the attorney at the latter's address, it will constitute the taxpayer's last known address for deficiency notice purposes.[21] In short, the statutory notice must be mailed to the taxpayer, not his duly authorized representative, unless the Commissioner is so instructed.

Section 2.03–The Notice of Deficiency

The statutory notice of deficiency is the only notice which gives a taxpayer the right to appeal, but the statute has no specific requirements for any special form of notice.[22] An appeal will not lie from a 30-day letter,[23] or any other kind of preliminary letter from the Service,[24] such as a letter of explanation to taxpayer's counsel[25] or from any other type of Service communication which does not constitute a determination.[26] In essence, if the notice starts with the phrase "The Commissioner has determined a deficiency," it is probable that a valid deficiency notice has been issued and the taxpayer must appeal by filing a petition within the 90-day period, which stays any assessment or collection proceeding throughout the Court's retention of jurisdiction.

The Court has consistently refused to deny jurisdiction because of an inadequate or incorrect explanation of the computation of the deficiency as set forth in the notice, or even failure of the notice to contain any explanation at all.[27]

---

[21]Rev. Proc. 61-18, C.B. 1961-2, 550; *Houghton,* 48 T.C. 656 (1967). This ruling (Rev. Proc. 61-18) does not bind the Comm'r if the original notice is issued to the taxpayer, *Berger,* 48 T.C. 848 (1967), *aff'd,* 404 F.2d 668, 22 AFTR 2d 5889 (3rd Cir., 1968).

[22]*McCue,* 1 T.C. 986 (1943); *Eversole Estate,* 39 T.C. 1113 (1963); Rule 13(a). *See also* Rules, Title XXI.

[23]*Mohawk Glove Co.,* 2 B.T.A. 1247 (1925); *Frost Superior Fence Co.,* 1 B.T.A. 1096 (1925).

[24]*Fidelity Insurance Agency,* 1 B.T.A. 86 (1924); *Nichols,* 14 B.T.A. 1347 (1929); *Moyer,* 1 B.T.A. 75 (1924); *Musser,* 1 B.T.A. 278 (1925).

[25]*Penrose,* 3 B.T.A. 329 (1926), *and see Livingston Worsted Co.,* 1 B.T.A. 991 (1925).

[26]*Wattington,* 2 B.T.A. 153 (1925); *Gould,* 1 B.T.A. 846 (1925). *See also Lyeth,* 41 B.T.A. 186 (1940); *Lerer,* 52 T.C. 358 (1969). The Court may consider the entire background of the communication to decide if the Comm'r has made a valid determination. *Scofield Estate v. Comm'r,* 266 F.2d 154, 3 AFTR 2d 1054 (6th Cir., 1959), *aff'g rev'g and rem'g* 25 T.C. 774 (1956).

[27]*Eversole Estate,* 39 T.C. 1113 (1963); *Revell, Inc. v. Riddell,* 273 F.2d 649, 5 AFTR 2d 455 (9th Cir., 1959), *aff'g* 2 AFTR 2d 6247 unreported D.C. decision (1958); Mertens, *Law of Federal Income Taxation,* Sec. 50.18.

This state of the law has engendered considerable dissatisfaction on the part of taxpayers' attorneys, who have been outspoken in their criticism of a taxpayer receiving a deficiency notice which really tells him little, if anything, about the Commissioner's theory of the determined deficiency. It is difficult, if not impossible, for an attorney to prepare an adequate petition if he is first employed upon the receipt of the statutory notice without prior background knowledge of the views of the examining agent or other subordinates of the Commissioner who initiated the deficiency proceeding, and yet who must prepare a meaningful petition setting forth the relevant facts in support of the taxpayer's appeal from the statutory notice. In effect, the attorney in this situation is working in the dark to a great extent, although of course he can consult with the taxpayer and the taxpayer's certified public accountant, if available, to obtain as much information as possible about the Government's theory of the case, if they themselves have such knowledge.

It is still true, however, that in a great many instances a "shot gun" statutory notice is issued, for example at the last moment to toll the running of statute of limitations on assessment of a deficiency, without specific knowledge on the part of the attorney as to the Government's real position in the case. This state of affairs has caused much dissatisfaction in the ranks of the Section of Taxation, American Bar Association, to such an extent that in 1966 at its Annual Meeting in Montreal, a legislative recommendation was adopted to the general effect that the Commissioner must assume the burden of proof in any Tax Court case where the deficiency notice explanation was inadequate or incomplete. The Congress has taken no action on this legislative recommendation and in view of the passage of several years since its adoption in 1966, the prospects of its enactment would appear to be very slight.

In defense of the Commissioner's dilemma, it was pointed out at the Montreal meeting that perhaps as many as 100,000 statutory notices are issued annually and that it would be a monumental burden to require the Commissioner to carefully draft each notice so as to fully apprise the taxpayer of the Government's legal position and theories, especially since a very low proportion of all statutory notices are appealed to the Tax Court. This may come as a surprise to many, but when it is considered that a statutory notice of deficiency must be issued to each taxpayer before a deficiency may be assessed, unless he signs an agreement or one of the other exceptions applies, such as jeopardy assessment, it will be readily recognized that most statutory notices are issued to taxpayers who have simply failed to reply to earlier communications from the Service indicating that a deficiency is due and owing and will be assessed unless the taxpayer responds promptly. When such response is not received, then the Commissioner has no recourse but to issue a statutory notice of deficiency in order to assess the deficiency thereafter, if the taxpayer fails to timely appeal to the Tax Court.

This will always be a vexing question, because in many other situations the office of the Service which is preparing the statutory notice, whether the Audit Division or the Appellate Division, the only two Service offices which perform this function, has prior knowledge that the taxpayer intends to appeal to the Tax Court upon issuance of the statutory notice. This is especially true where the amount of the proposed deficiency is quite large, such as $100,000 or more. In those cases most taxpayers prefer not to pay the tax and pursue their litigation remedy by refund suit, but instead to use the Tax Court petition procedure and thus avoid the immediate payment of the deficiency. Perhaps the Commissioner could use such a rule of thumb and thereby more adequately explain his theory or theories in statutory notices where the case is likely to be appealed. This would also be true in fraud, transferee and other complex cases.

Likewise, it is well established that the Commissioner may issue inconsistent statutory notices to different taxpayers without undermining the efficacy of each such statutory notice.[28] "Inconsistency in determinations, when they are not made in bad faith, does not equate with an absence of the statutorily required determination, as the taxpayers suggest."[29] The filing of a petition for redetermination of a deficiency has been held to constitute conduct inconsistent with a later claim that the deficiency notice was legally insufficient.[30]

In summary, the Court has always taken a broad view of what constitutes a valid notice of deficiency under the statute and properly so, because the Commissioner is charged with the protection of the revenues. When this awesome responsibility of the Commissioner is considered in context, to require him to follow certain straight-jacketed rules in preparation of a valid statutory notice would lead to a crippling of the flow of revenue to the national treasury, a result to be avoided if at all possible. This is not to say that the statutory notice should generally tell the taxpayer little more than that a deficiency of a certain amount has been determined against him. But it should also be noted in defense of the Commissioner that most of the statutory notices in substantial or

---

[28] *Freeport Transport, Inc.*, 63 T.C. 107 (1974) and cases there cited, including *Harrison,* 59 T.C. 578, 592 (1973) and *Schmitz,* 51 T.C. 306, 313 (1968).

[29] *Goodall Estate,* 391 F.2d 775, 781-4, 21 AFTR 2d 813 (8th Cir., 1968), *aff'g and rev'g* 51 T.C. 775 (1969).

[30] Mertens, *op. cit.,* Sec. 50.11, note 12, and cases there cited.

complicated cases are carefully prepared and do inform the taxpayer of the Commissioner's legal position, perhaps not in the depth that many taxpayers and their attorneys would prefer, but certainly in sufficient detail to permit the taxpayer's petition to be meaningful and informative. This trend has been accentuated during the last few years by the more frequent review of statutory notices by the Office of Regional Counsel before issuance by the Audit Division, which formerly had no legal review prior to issuance, as have Appellate Division notices for many years. Regional Counsel tries to make sure that each statutory notice it reviews is adequate in every respect, and on the whole, the statutory notices it reviews do adequately inform taxpayers of the Government's position.

In a recent case on this question, the petitioner argued that the deficiency notice not only improperly advised it of the Commissioner's theory, but also caused it to be misled in preparing for trial.[31] The statutory notice disallowed the deduction for officers' compensation referring to Section 162 in support of this determination. Petitioner assumed that the Commissioner would rely on the statutory language relating to the unreasonableness of salaries paid. At the trial, however, the Commissioner took the position that bonuses paid were actually disguised, taxable dividends, which was sustained by the Court. In affirming, the appellate court held that, because petitioner was notified in the statutory notice that Section 162 was involved, it could not have been deceived. The appellate court also pointed out that a statutory notice is not required to detail the Commissioner's entire theory, but that the deficiency requirement is met if the taxpayer is informed of a disallowance on his return, especially when a reason therefor is also given in the notice.

Where a statutory notice is vague as to the ground for the Commissioner's determination, it should be curable by an adequate opening statement, especially if counsel for the Commissioner is able to affirm that his opening statement theory has previously been communicated to petitioner or his counsel.

Under Rule 31, notice pleading has been officially enunciated by the Court for the first time. The purpose of notice pleading is to streamline the pleadings procedure so that parties are apprised of their opponent's general contentions and arguments.

The Court does not have jurisdiction with respect to additions to taxes under Section 6651 and Section 6654 unless a statutory notice of deficiency has been issued determining a deficiency in taxes for the same

---

[31] *Nor-Cal Adjusters,* 503 F.2d 359, 34 AFTR 2d 74-5834 (9th Cir., 1974), *aff'g* T.C. Memo 1971-200, ¶ 71,200 P-H Memo T.C.

years as those to which the additions are proposed.[32] Such failure of jurisdiction does not deprive a taxpayer of fundamental due process and equal protection of the laws.[33] Likewise, the Court has no jurisdiction of questions relating solely to the assessment of interest.[34]

Section 2.04–The "Deficiency"

What is a deficiency? This is a critical term since a notice of deficiency is the foundation of the Court's jurisdiction. In essence, a deficiency is the total amount of tax liability determined by the Commissioner in the notice in excess of "the amount shown as the tax by the taxpayer upon his return."[35] The Court's jurisdiction is limited to the tax year, or years, for which the deficiency notice is sent.[36]

The Commissioner has no authority to determine a deficiency for a fractional part of a taxpayer's correct taxable year, and if the Commissioner does attempt to so determine a deficiency for an unauthorized period of time, there is no deficiency within the meaning of the Code.[37] The Court has no jurisdiction over any period other than that covered in the deficiency notice, which would be true even though the return covered an incorrect period and the Commissioner determined a deficiency based upon such incorrect return.[38] An exception to this rule would be that when the period on which the Commissioner's determination is based covers the taxpayer's final tax period, it is a valid determination for that period so as to give the Court jurisdiction.[39]

---

[32] *Johnston,* 52 T.C. 792 (1969).

[33] *Fendler v. Comm'r,* 441 F.2d 1101, 27 AFTR 2d 71-1296 (9th Cir., 1971), *aff'g* unreported D.C. order of dismissal; Mertens, *op. cit.,* Sec. 50.10.

[34] *Schuster v. Comm'r,* 312 F.2d 311, 11 AFTR 2d 1766 (9th Cir., 1962), *aff'g* 32 T.C. 998 (1959) *and rev'g* 32 T.C. 1017 (1959); *Coddington,* T.C. Memo 1960-95, ¶60,095 P-H Memo T.C.

[35] Sec. 6212(a); *Hannan,* 52 T.C. 787 (1969).

[36] *Jones,* B.T.A. Memo Op. Docket 106613 (1942); *Difco Laboratories, Inc.,* 10 T.C. 660 (1948); *Dial,* 24 T.C. 117 (1955); *Iverson Estate,* 27 T.C. 786 (1957); *Harris,* T.C. Memo 1970-331, ¶70,331 P-H Memo T.C.

[37] *Scofield Estate,* 25 T.C. 774 (1956).

[38] *Gooding v. Comm'r,* 310 F.2d 501, 10 AFTR 2d 5994 (4th Cir., 1962), *aff'g* T.C. Memo 1961-299, ¶61,299 P-H Memo T.C.; *Columbia River Orchards, Inc.,* 15 T.C. 253 (1950); *Berry,* 26 T.C. 351 (1956), *rev'd and rem'd* 254 F.2d 471, 1 AFTR 2d 364 (9th Cir., 1957); *California Brewing Association,* 43 B.T.A. 721 (1941), petition for review *dismissed per curiam,* 129 F.2d 321, 29 AFTR 836 (9th Cir., 1942).

[39] *Harvey Coal Corp.,* 12 T.C. 596 (1949); *Edwards,* T.C. Memo Op. Docket 24909 (1953) ¶53,344 P-H Memo T.C., supplemental opinion T.C. Memo 1955-263, ¶55,263 P-H Memo T.C. *aff'd,* 242 F.2d 142, 50 AFTR 1802 (5th Cir., 1957).

Section 2.05—Who Is the "Taxpayer"?

The statute provides that any "taxpayer" may file a petition,[40] but even this simple wording has resulted in considerable controversy, especially in connection with reorganized or dissolved corporations, estates and trusts. Who is the "taxpayer"? Certainly citizens, residents of the United States, nonresident aliens, and domestic and foreign corporations qualify as "taxpayers" for this purpose.

Generally, a deficiency notice is invalid if sent to someone other than the taxpayer; specifically, if it is not sent to the taxpayer. Likewise, a petition filed by someone other than the taxpayer or a fiduciary legally entitled to initiate the case on behalf of the taxpayer is ineffective to confer jurisdiction on the Court.[41] Hence, the rule emerges that an appeal must be filed by the taxpayer or his duly authorized representative if the Court is to have jurisdiction.[42] Sad, but true, are many instances of invalid filing of petitions by the wrong person—not the person to whom the deficiency notice is addressed.[43] Examples are that one stockholder may not file a valid appeal for other stockholders even though similarly situated;[44] a partnership may not file an appeal for the partners;[45] nor may a shareholder file a valid appeal for a corporation.[46]

A single joint notice of deficiency may be issued where a joint income tax return has been filed by husband and wife.[47] If the Commissioner has been notified by either spouse, however, that separate residences have been established, then, instead of a single joint notice,

---

[40]Sec. 6212(a).

[41]Rule 13(a); *Nibley-Mimnaugh Lumber Co.,* 37 B.T.A. 617 (1938). But a more liberal judicial definition of "taxpayer" is indicated. *See National Bank of Commerce,* 34 B.T.A. 119 (1936) and cases cited; Mertens, *op. cit.,* Sec. 50.25, n. 6.

[42]*Harrison v. Comm'r,* 107 F.2d 341, 23 AFTR 882 (6th Cir., 1939), *rem'g* unreported B.T.A. dismissal order; *Powers,* 20 B.T.A. 753 (1930).

[43]*Lowrance,* 23 B.T.A. 1055 (1931); *Eversole Estate,* 39 T.C. 1113 (1963); *Hanify,* 21 B.T.A. 379 (1930).

[44]*Stange,* 1 B.T.A. 810 (1925), *rev'd,* 43 F.2d 593, 9 AFTR 127 (3rd Cir., 1930); *Powers,* 20 B.T.A. 753 (1930).

[45]*Taylor Bros.,* 9 B.T.A. 877 (1927). *Cf. Thalhimer v. Comm'r,* 62 F.2d 703, 11 AFTR 1354 (4th Cir., 1933), *aff'g* unreported B.T.A. dismissal. *See* sec. 701. The partners have been allowed to amend by filing separate petitions. *Bankers Realty Syndicate,* 20 B.T.A. 612 (1930). *See Sack,* 36 B.T.A. 595 (1937) involving whether a partnership is an association taxable as a corporation.

[46]*Ennis,* 21 B.T.A. 406 (1930).

[47]*Eversole Estate,* 39 T.C. 1113 (1963).

duplicate originals must be sent to each spouse.[48] It also should be noted that the Commissioner might issue a single joint notice at his peril, even though the names of a husband and wife appear on a joint return since one spouse, usually the wife, might successfully contend that her name was placed on the joint return through forgery or duress.[49] Further, the Commissioner may send separate notices of deficiency to one of two spouses who have filed a joint return when the other spouse is not entitled to a notice of deficiency.[50]

The Court has held that the filing of a timely petition by the wife, to whom a separate notice has been issued under Section 6212(b)(2), may not be treated as a petition filed on behalf of the husband.[51] If a husband and wife have filed separate returns, however, they may not file a joint petition.[52]

When there are two or more affiliated corporations, a notice of deficiency must be sent to each one, since a notice to only one such corporation would not meet the statutory requirements for a valid notice to the other and does not authorize the filing of an appeal with the Court by the corporation to which no notice has been issued,[53] even though their officers may be identical.[54] With respect to an affiliated group of corporations which are qualified to make a consolidated return, although the regulations provide that only the parent may file a petition,[55] the Court has held that other members of the group may be proper petitioning parties.[56]

Section 2.06–Timely Filing of the Petition

It is critical that a petition be *timely* filed, that is, within 90 days generally, or within 150 days if the notice is addressed to a person

---

[48]Sec. 6212(b)(2). If in doubt, better practice to file a joint petition in the name of husband and wife. Rule 32.

[49]*Bauer v. Foley,* 408 F.2d 1331, 23 AFTR 2d 69-1119 (2nd Cir., 1969), modifying 404 F.2d 1215, 23 AFTR 2d 69-307 (2nd Cir., 1968), *rev'g and rem'g* 287 F. Supp. 343 (1968), 21 AFTR 2d 1517.

[50]*Dolan,* 44 T.C. 420 (1965), overruling *DuMais,* 40 T.C. 269 (1963); *Griebel,* T.C. Memo 1965-210, ¶65,210 P-H Memo T.C.

[51]*Joannou,* 33 T.C. 868 (1960). *See also Manton,* 11 T.C. 831 (1948) and *Davenport,* 48 T.C. 921 (1967), Sec. 6013(d)(3).

[52]*Held, Jr.,* 20 B.T.A. 863 (1930).

[53]*Crocker First National Bank of San Francisco,* 26 B.T.A. 1078 (1932); *Central Market Street Co.,* 25 B.T.A. 499 (1932); *Furniture Exhibition Building Co.,* 24 B.T.A. 1279 (1931).

[54]*Phoenix National Bank,* 14 B.T.A. 115 (1928).

[55]Reg. Sec. 1.1502-16(A).

[56]*Community Water Service Co.,* 32 B.T.A. 164 (1935).

outside of the states of the Union and the District of Columbia.[57] The Court has construed this last provision as meaning that the taxpayer should have 150 days within which to file the petition if the person to whom the notice was addressed, was outside the United States and that it did not refer to an address outside the United States. This construction was affirmed by the Second Circuit, which stated, however, that the Tax Court erred in holding that the Code grants the 150-day period only to persons outside the designated area "on some settled business and residential basis, and not on a temporary basis."[58] A majority of the Tax Court now appears to agree with this interpretation by the Second Circuit.[59]

Even though far distant from the continental United States, Alaska and Hawaii are now governed by the 90-day, rather than the 150-day, rule.[60] The period is computed, of course, without counting Saturday, Sunday, or a legal holiday in the District of Columbia as the last day.[61] Calendar days, not business days, are counted.[62]

The 1954 Code enacted a most helpful relief provision for computation of the filing period by providing that a petition shall be deemed to be filed on the mailing date, which can be proved by the date of the postmark stamped on the "cover" in which the petition is mailed.[63] Since there has already been considerable controversy as to whether a postmark date was stamped on the cover, the safest procedure is to mail petitions by certified mail at the post office so as to obtain a stamped certificate of mailing, which will avoid any controversy as to timeliness. In short, date of registration of certified or registered mail will be accepted as the postmark date.[64]

The statutory provision will not control, however, unless the following mailing and delivery requirements are met:[65]

(1) The petition must be contained in an envelope or other appropriate wrapper, properly addressed to the Tax Court;

---

[57]Rule 13(b); Sec. 6213; Reg. Sec. 301.6213.1.

[58]*Mindell,* 200 F.2d 38, 42 AFTR 907 (2nd Cir., 1952), *rev'g per curiam* unreported Tax Court dismissal order.

[59]*Krueger,* 33 T.C. 667 (1960).

[60]Reg. Sec. 301.6213-1(a).

[61]Sec. 6213(a).

[62]*McGuire,* 52 T.C. 468 (1969).

[63]Sec. 7502; *Perry Segura & Associates, Inc.,* T.C. Memo 1975-80, ¶75,080 P-H Memo T.C., holding that where intervening acts of the U.S. Postal Service cause destruction of the postmarked envelope in which the petition was mailed, a taxpayer may present extrinsic evidence to establish timely mailing. *Cf. Lindemood,* T.C. Memo 1975-195, ¶75,195 P-H Memo T.C.

[64]Sec. 7502(a) and (b).

[65]Sec. 7502; *Perry Segura & Associates, Inc.,* T.C. Memo 1975-80, ¶75,080 P-H Memo T.C.

(2) It must be deposited within the described time in the mail in the United States with sufficient postage prepaid;

(3) If the postmark on the envelope or wrapper is made by the United States Post Office, such postmark must bear a date on or before the last date, or the last day of the period, prescribed for filing the petition;

(4) If the petition, however, is sent by United States registered or certified mail, the registration shall be *prima facie* evidence that the petition was delivered to the office to which it was addressed, and the date of registration is deemed the postmark date; and

(5) The petition must be delivered to the Tax Court; however, if the petition is sent by registered or certified mail, proof that the petition was properly registered or certified and that the envelope or wrapper was properly addressed to the Court, constitutes *prima facie* evidence that the petition was delivered.

Since certified mail has been accepted generally as performing the same service as registered mail where matter is mailed which has no intrinsic value, the 1954 Code was amended by the 1958 Act to qualify certified mail for treatment similar to that of registered mail for these purposes.[66]

Again, it cannot be stressed too often that the petitioner should obtain a certified mail receipt showing postmark thereon and not rely simply on mailing by certified mail without postmark. If questioned, a petition will not be considered as timely filed unless the taxpayer can produce a certified mail receipt properly and timely postmarked as required by the regulation.

Since the Rules provide that any document to be filed must be filed in the office of the Clerk of the Court in Washington during business hours,[67] the postmark must be "within the prescribed period or on or before the prescribed date for the filing of the [petition],"[68] indicating that the exact hour when the petition is postmarked might be important in the case of a petition mailed on the last day for filing.

"Business hours" at the Clerk's office in Washington, D.C., are from 8:45 a.m. to 5:15 p.m., except Saturdays, Sundays and legal

---

[66]Sec. 7502(c).

[67]Rule 10(d).

[68]Sec. 7502(a)(2).

holidays.[69] Although mailing is the normal method of filing, a taxpayer may still file a petition by hand-delivering it to the office of the Clerk in Washington during business hours.

Until 1969 there was no permissible deviation from the strict requirement that a petition must be filed within the specified 90-day or 150-day period. 1969 and 1974 statutory amendments have introduced new concepts in the running of the time for filing a petition. By the 1969 amendment, the statutory period is suspended for any period during which the Government has extended the time allowed for making corrections under the applicable statutory sections.[70] Similarly, the 1974 amendment extends the time for filing a petition under prescribed circumstances involving a prohibited transaction by a non-qualified person.[71]

The Tax Court, as a body of limited jurisdiction, has consistently refused to accept jurisdiction of cases in which the petition was not timely filed, regardless of the merits of extenuating circumstances. Occasionally a circuit court has liberalized the Tax Court's rigidity, as in a 1951 case where the Seventh Circuit held that where a statutory notice of deficiency was addressed to the taxpayer's former residence but returned by the postal authorities undelivered, and then remailed to the taxpayer in care of the company with which he was employed, the 90-day period within which to file the petition did not begin to run until the date of the second mailing.[72] Also the Ninth Circuit has held that, where a taxpayer never received the deficiency notice (which was properly addressed and mailed), the subsequent personal service of a copy of the notice on the taxpayer started a new 90-day period.[73]

Section 2.07—Miscellaneous Jurisdictional Matters

There is no restriction on the number of deficiency notices the Commissioner may send the taxpayer until the taxpayer files a timely petition, to the first or a later notice, but when he does so, subsequent

---

[69] Rule 10(d).

[70] Sec. 6213(e), added by Sec. 101(f)(3) of the Tax Reform Act of 1969, Public Law 91-172.

[71] Sec. 4971(c)(3), added by Public Law 93-406.

[72] *Eppler v. Comm'r,* 188 F.2d 95, 40 AFTR 361 (7th Cir., 1951), *rev'g* unreported Tax Court dismissal order.

[73] *Tenzer v. Comm'r,* 285 F.2d 956, 7 AFTR 2d 450 (9th Cir., 1960), *rev'g* unreported Tax Court dismissal order.

notices are invalid.[74] It has been held that a notice sent to the taxpayer's last known address and then remailed by registered mail after it was returned undelivered is "mailed" when originally sent and the 90-day period should be computed on this basis.[75]

Although a deficiency in tax must be determined by the Commissioner for the Court to have jurisdiction, in redetermining a deficiency the Court may decide that the taxpayer has overpaid his tax liability and so order.[76] The Court is concerned *only* with the correct amount of the liability, not its collection.

In redetermining a deficiency in income or gift tax for any year, the Court may consider facts with respect to other years to the extent necessary to redetermine such disputed tax liability although it cannot determine whether the tax liability for the other year, or years, has been overpaid or underpaid.[77] In short, once the Tax Court has obtained jurisdiction on account of a deficiency determination, it has authority to determine all facts to enable the proper computation of the tax liability for the period in dispute, whether it be deficiency or overpayment.[78]

Where a single notice determines deficiencies for several taxable years, the taxpayer may limit his appeal to a particular year, or years, not necessarily all the years for which deficiencies have been determined in the notice.[79] In such situations the Court will have jurisdiction only as to that year, or years, as to which the taxpayer has assigned errors in the petition although, of course, the Court has jurisdiction to consider facts in other years in order to determine the correct deficiency, or overpayment,

---

[74] *Harvey Coal Corp.*, 12 T.C. 596 (1949); *McCue*, 1 T.C. 986 (1943).

[75] *Marcus*, 12 T.C. 1071 (1949); *Block*, 2 T.C. 761 (1943).

[76] *Peerless Woolen Mills v. Rose*, 28 F.2d 661, 7 AFTR 8203 (5th Cir., 1928); *Gooding*, T.C. Memo 1961-299, ¶61,299 P-H Memo T.C. *See Glowinski*, 25 T.C. 934 (1956), *aff'd per curiam*, 243 F.2d 635, 51 AFTR 156 (D.C. Cir., 1957).

[77] *Dobson v. Comm'r*, 320 U.S. 489, 31 AFTR 773 (1943); *Akeley Camera & Instrument Corp.*, 18 T.C. 1045 (1952); Sec. 6214(b).

[78] *Cf. The LTV Corporation*, 64 T.C. 589 (1975), where respondent conceded consolidated net operating losses for 1968 and 1969 sufficient to eliminate the deficiencies determined by respondent for 1965 and 1966, but disagreement continued over the amount of the pre-carryback deficiency for 1965 and 1966, the precise amount of the consolidated net operating loss attributable to 1968 and 1969, and the amount of the 1968 and 1969 losses which must be used to eliminate the deficiencies for 1965 and 1966. The Court held that respondent's concession did not deprive the Court of jurisdiction under section 6214 to resolve the issues raised in the pleadings. In an apparent Pyrrhic victory for petitioner, the Court further held that, since respondent's concession was accepted, there were zero deficiencies for 1965 and 1966, and a decision was entered for petitioner, stating that a resolution of the continuing controversy would not affect the decision in the years before the Court, and would simply provide an advisory opinion declarative of the size of a deduction petitioner might be able to use in some future years.

[79] *State Farming Co., Inc.*, 40 T.C. 774 (1963); *Motors Securities Company, Inc.*, T.C. Memo Op. Docket 31656 (1952), ¶52,316 P-H Memo T.C.

for the period in question.[80] A taxpayer may file a single timely petition appealing from multiple notices.[81]

For the Court to have jurisdiction the notice must be timely mailed, that is, within the statutory period for assessment of additional tax against the taxpayer. Thus, the notice must be mailed either within the normal three-year period of limitations, or within the period of limitations as extended by agreement of the taxpayer and the Service; within the six-year limitation period when more than 25 percent of gross income is omitted, or within the additional limitation period of one year where transferee liability is determined.[82] In cases where the fraud penalty has been determined, or where no return has been filed, no period of limitations applies for issuance of a timely notice.

Since the Court's jurisdiction is limited to the redetermination of deficiencies and overpayments, the Court has no jurisdiction to review the Commissioner's denial of a refund or credit claim.[83] Similarly, the Court has no jurisdiction with respect to internal matters of administrative or office procedure of the Service,[84] or questions of policy.[85]

The Court has no jurisdiction over interest, either on a redetermined deficiency[86] or a redetermined overpayment.[87]

It is now well established that the Court has jurisdiction with respect to constitutional questions.[88] As with all courts, however, a challenged provision of the internal revenue laws must be clearly unconstitutional before the Court can hold it unenforceable.[89] If there is substantial doubt, the law must be declared constitutional.[90]

---

80 See cases cited note 77.

81 *Egan*, 41 B.T.A. 204 (1940); *Bryant*, 33 T.C. 201 (1959).

82 Sec. 6512.

83 *U.S. ex rel. Girard Trust Co. v. Helvering*, 301 U.S. 540, 19 AFTR 507 (1937); *Epstein*, 34 B.T.A. 925 (1936); *Goodman*, T.C. Memo 1959-149; ¶ 59,149 P-H Memo T.C.

84 *Kerr*, 5 B.T.A. 1073 (1927).

85 *Greene*, 2 B.T.A. 148 (1925); *Levine Bros., Inc.*, 5 B.T.A. 689 (1926).

86 *Schuster v. Comm'r* 312 F.2d 311, 11 AFTR 2d 1766 (9th Cir., 1962); *Coddington*, T.C. Memo 1960-95, ¶ 60,095 P-H Memo T.C.; *Comm'r v. Estate of Kilpatrick*, 140 F.2d 887, 32 AFTR 192 (6th Cir., 1944), *aff'g* unreported B.T.A. order, Docket 107775 (1942).

87 *Fuller*, 20 T.C. 308 (1953), *aff'd*, 213 F.2d 102, 45 AFTR 1551 (10th Cir., 1954); *Shedd Estate*, 37 T.C. 394 (1961), *aff'd*, 320 F.2d 638, 12 AFTR 2d 6221 (9th Cir., 1963).

88 *Keusch*, 23 B.T.A. 216 (1931), *appeal dismissed*, 60 F.2d 481, 11 AFTR 767 (3rd Cir., 1932), *cert. denied*, 287 U.S. 641 (1932); *Fahnestock Estate*, 2 T.C. 756 (1943).

89 *Lattimore*, T.C. Memo 1962-75. A constitutional question must be raised by proper pleadings. *Solowey Estate*, 15 T.C. 188 (1950), *aff'd per curiam*, 189 F.2d 986, 40 AFTR 188 (2nd Cir., 1951), *cert. denied*, 342 U.S. 850 (1951); *Edelman Estate*, 38 T.C. 972 (1962).

90 *West Town State Bank*, 32 B.T.A. 531 (1935); *General Aniline & Film Corp.*, 3 T.C. 1070 (1944).

Once a taxpayer has invoked the jurisdiction of the Court, it will not consider the constitutionality of an Act under which the taxpayer has filed his appeal since he has waived his right of objection.[91] In short, one cannot claim the advantage of a statute and at the same time question its constitutionality.[92]

General allegations of unconstitutionality will not suffice; precise challenge is required.[93]

The Court has held that it has jurisdiction with respect to a timely appeal from a deficiency notice filed by a withholding agent, even though it might be questioned whether an agent is a "taxpayer" within the meaning of the statute.[94]

Section 2.08—Bankruptcy and Receivership

Perhaps no area has presented thornier jurisdictional and procedural problems for the Court than bankruptcy and receivership proceedings. If the adjudication or appointment occurs before a petition is filed with the Court, immediate assessment of the deficiency is permitted under Section 6871(a). This provision does not require the sending of a notice of deficiency. The Court is expressly prohibited from accepting a petition after the adjudication of bankruptcy, approval of the petition in bankruptcy or the appointment of a receiver.[95] Section 6871, however, does not deny the Court jurisdiction to redetermine deficiencies and additions to tax for pre-bankruptcy years for such deficiencies and additions to tax where neither assessed nor claimed in bankruptcy proceedings closed prior to the issuance of the deficiency notice.[96] The same rule applies to additions to tax for fraud which were not presented to the bankruptcy court for adjudication.[97] Section 6871(b) acts as a bar to the Court's jurisdiction only if the taxpayer has had an opportunity to litigate the asserted deficiency in the bankruptcy proceeding.[98]

---

[91] *Cappellini,* 14 B.T.A. 1269 (1929).

[92] *Bateman,* 34 B.T.A. 351 (1936).

[93] *Dillon,* 20 B.T.A. 690 (1930); *Isenbergh,* 31 T.C. 1046 (1959).

[94] *Houston Street Corp.,* 84 F.2d 821, 18 AFTR 224 (5th Cir., 1936), *rev'g* B.T.A. Memo Op. Docket 78528 (1935); *see also Capital Estates, Inc.,* 46 B.T.A. 986 (1942), *aff'd,* 138 F.2d 156, 31 AFTR 652 (3rd Cir., 1943).

[95] *Pollen,* 64 T.C. (No. 24)(1975). But the Regulations provide that a letter explaining how the deficiency was computed will be sent. Reg. Sec. 301.687(b)-1(c). *See also Ruby,* 2 B.T.A. 377 (1925) *and Wedeen,* T.C. Memo Op. Docket 521 (1944), ¶ 44,265 P-H Memo T.C.

[96] *Orenduff,* 49 T.C. 329 (1968).

[97] *Prather,* 50 T.C. 445 (1968).

[98] *Prather,* 50 T.C. 445 (1968); *King,* 51 T.C. 851 (1969).

If a timely petition is filed prior to the adjudication of bankruptcy or appointment of a receiver, the Court does not lose jurisdiction.[99] The Commissioner, however, may present the issues which involve the deficiency plus interest, as well as additions to the tax, to the bankruptcy or receivership proceeding tribunal even though a petition has been filed with the Court.[100] If the Court enters its decision redetermining tax liability in such a case, a copy of its decision must be filed with the bankruptcy or receivership court.[101] Even though the Tax Court may have jurisdiction, a determination by a bankruptcy court of the correct liability is *res judicata.*[102] Concurrent jurisdiction was first enacted by the 1926 Act and has been since retained in the same general form.

Some litigation has occurred with respect to whether a particular action validly constituted the appointment of a receiver so as to bar the later filing of a Tax Court petition. Such cases have occurred under the jurisdiction of the Maryland, New York, Oregon and Missouri statutes.[103]

Section 2.09—Jeopardy Assessments

In the case of a jeopardy assessment under Section 6861, the Code provides that the Court has jurisdiction to redetermine the entire amount of the deficiency and any and all amounts assessed at the same time in connection with the jeopardy assessment. Since jeopardy assessments are rare, the Court's jurisdiction in such cases is of limited importance.

Although rarely invoked, when jeopardy assessments are made, unusual jurisdictional questions may arise. A jeopardy assessment may be made *before* or *after* a deficiency notice has been sent and whether or not an appeal is made to the Court; if it is made after a Tax Court decision, it is limited to the amount of deficiency determined by the Court.[104] It may not be made after a Tax Court decision has become final or a petition

---

[99] *Monjar v. Higgins,* 132 F.2d 990, 30 AFTR 719 (2nd Cir., 1943), *aff'g* 39 F. Supp. 633 (1941), 28 AFTR 54; *Herman Walker Realty Co.,* B.T.A. Memo Op. Docket 74743 (1941).

[100] Sec. 6871(b).

[101] Reg. Sec. 301.6871(a)-1 and (b)-1.

[102] *Comas, Inc.,* 23 T.C. 8 (1954).

[103] Maryland—*see Financial & Industrial Securities Corp.,* 27 B.T.A. 989 (1933).
New York—*see Pink,* 38 B.T.A. 182 (1938).
Oregon—*see French & Co.,* 10 B.T.A. 665 (1928).
Missouri—*see Clifton City Bank,* 6 B.T.A. 643 (1927).

[104] Sec. 6861(b), (c), and (d).

for review has been filed with the appropriate circuit court of appeals.[105] If a jeopardy assessment is made before a deficiency notice has been sent, a deficiency notice is required to be issued within the required 60-day period.[106] The Commissioner is required to notify the Court of the amount of a jeopardy assessment if the petition is filed with the Court before the making of such an assessment or is subsequently filed.[107] In such situations, the Court has jurisdiction to redetermine the entire deficiency and all amounts which have been assessed in connection therewith.[108] Where the Court has been informed by the taxpayer of the Commissioner's statement of the amounts of the jeopardy assessment, the failure of the Commissioner himself to notify the Court directly of those amounts does not invalidate the jeopardy assessment, or deprive the Court of jurisdiction, including the authority to determine whether the interest assessment is correct.[109]

Since a jeopardy assessment is discretionary and not subject to review, the Court will not inquire into the reasons for the Commissioner's belief that jeopardy exists.[110]

Although jeopardy assessment jurisdictional cases are rare, the so-called "quick termination" of the taxpayer's tax year situations have engendered increased litigation in this area.[111] The Fifth Circuit has held that the tax liability which becomes immediately due and payable following a quick determination of the taxpayer's tax year is a deficiency, and a prepayment redetermination of that liability would be within the jurisdiction of the Tax Court.[112] That Court further held that the Commissioner could not levy or assess on property of the taxpayer in a "quick termination" case unless he first issued a notice of deficiency. The Court pointed out that otherwise the taxpayer is deprived of his right of prepayment judicial review by petition to the Tax Court, relegating him to payment, filing of refund claim and suit for refund. That Court also commented that this is an issue which had been the subject of extensive recent litigation with varying results, in the several circuits that

---

[105] Sec. 6861(e).

[106] Sec. 6861(b).

[107] Sec. 6861(c).

[108] Sec. 6861(c).

[109] *Erickson v. U.S.*, 309 F.2d 760, 10 AFTR 2d 5910 (Ct. Cl., 1962); *Papa*, 55 T.C. 1140 (1971).

[110] *Tyler Estate*, 9 B.T.A. 255 (1927).

[111] Sec. 6851.

[112] *Clark v. Campbell*, 501 F.2d 108, 34 AFTR 2d 74-5840 (5th Cir., 1974), *aff'g* 341 F. Supp. 171 (1972), 29 AFTR 2d 72-574.

had addressed the problem. The Second[113] and Seventh[114] Circuits have held to the contrary, that is, that an assessment made under Section 6851 and Section 6201 is not a "deficiency" within the purview of Section 6211 for which Section 6212(a) mandates that a notice be issued, contrasting to the views of the Fifth and Sixth Circuits. Certiorari was granted in *Laing*, the Second Circuit case, and on January 13, 1976, the Supreme Court reversed, sustaining the taxpayer's position.[115]

Section 2.10—Dissolved Corporations and Associations

One of the oft-litigated jurisdictional questions involves dissolved corporations. Under the rule that only the taxpayer may file a petition,[116] a notice of deficiency is valid even though the corporation to which it is issued has legally ended its existence. In such situations, who is qualified to appeal a deficiency determined against a "dissolved" corporation may present a knotty question. The cases involve two chief situations, that is, where a successor corporation appeals and where there is no successor corporation and an officer or stockholder of the dissolved corporation appeals in its behalf. In dissolved corporation cases, the law of the state of incorporation will establish the effect of the dissolution for Tax Court jurisdictional purposes.[117]

With respect to successor corporation cases, in general a true *successor* corporation cannot perfect a Tax Court appeal.[118] Cases arising under the laws of Delaware[119] and Missouri[120] support this rule. An early interesting case arose under the laws of the states of Washington and California with the Court holding that the merger of a Washington corporation into a California corporation made the California corporation

---

[113] *Laing v. U.S.*, 496 F.2d 853, 34 AFTR 2d 5033 (2nd Cir., 1974), *aff'g* 364 F. Supp. 469 (1973) 32 AFTR 2d 73-5789, *cert. granted*, Oct. 15, 1974.

[114] *Williamson v. U.S.* 31 AFTR 2d 73-800 (7th Cir., 1971), *aff'g* D.C. in unpublished opinion.

[115] *Rambo v. U.S.*, 492 F.2d 1060, 33 AFTR 2d 74-750 (6th Cir., 1974), *aff'g* unreported D.C. decision, 30 AFTR 2d 72-5630; *Laing*, United States Supreme Court, unofficially reported 37 AFTR 2d 76-530.

[116] Secs. 6212(b)(1); 6213(a).

[117] *Wheeler's Peachtree Pharmacy, Inc.*, 35 T.C. 177 (1960); *Jefferson Memorial Park*, T.C. Memo 1963-32, ¶63,032 P-H Memo T.C.

[118] *Bond Crown & Cork Co.*, 19 T.C. 73 (1952); *American Arch Co.*, 13 B.T.A. 552 (1928).

[119] *Carnation Milk Products Co.*, 20 B.T.A. 627 (1930).

[120] *Gideon-Anderson Co.*, 18 B.T.A. 329 (1929), *appeal dismissed*, 45 F.2d 1011 (8th Cir., 1930).

primarily liable for any deficiency of the Washington corporation and, therefore, a petition filed by the California corporation, based on a deficiency notice addressed to the Washington corporation, was within the jurisdiction of the Court.[121] This rule has also been applied under the laws of the states of New York, Illinois, Pennsylvania, Louisiana, Texas, Rhode Island and Delaware.[122]

What is the rule with respect to corporate consolidations? Where the state statute does not specifically provide, the general rule is to consider the constituents dissolved and a new corporation created, not identifiable with any of the consolidating companies.[123] One test to decide whether the constituents continue in existence is whether the state statute authorizing the consolidation contains words of grant of corporate powers to the consolidated corporation and, if so, the constituents are considered to be dissolved.[124] In certain cases, however, it has been held that the successor corporation may be estopped to deny liability for the dissolved corporation.[125] In another case jurisdiction attached on the same basis in the case of a corporation which had acquired the assets of its predecessor, continued the same business at the same location with the same officers of stockholders, and had had dealings with the Internal Revenue Service on behalf of its predecessor, holding itself out to the Service as the taxpayer.[126]

Where there is no successor corporation, state statutes provide the guidelines for the jurisdiction of the Court. For example, the statutes may provide that on the dissolution of a corporation it continues to act for the purpose of "closing up its business" (Delaware)[127] or not "bring about its total extinction." (Georgia).[128] State statutes vary as to the length of time a corporation may exist for the purpose of winding up its affairs. For example, two years has been held to be not an unreasonable time for that purpose.[129] Some states, such as Massachusetts, provide a period certain, as three years, for purposes of a suit, and an appeal taken

---

[121] *Alaska Salmon Co.*, 39 B.T.A. 455 (1939).

[122] Mertens, *op. cit.*, Sec. 50.29, n. 32-38 incl.

[123] *Grange National Bank*, 22 B.T.A. 1209 (1931).

[124] *Gideon-Anderson Co.*, 18 B.T.A. 329, *appeal dismissed without opinion*, 45 F.2d 1011 (8th Cir., 1930).

[125] *Comm'r v. Nichols & Cox Lumber Co.*, 65 F.2d 1009, 12 AFTR 910 (6th Cir., 1933). Mertens, *op. cit.*, Sec. 50.20, n. 41.

[126] *Union Bleachery v. Comm'r*, 97 F.2d 226, 21 AFTR 336 (4th Cir., 1938), *aff'g* B.T.A. Memo Op. Docket 34314 (1937).

[127] *Bahen & Wright, Inc.*, 176 F.2d 538, 38 AFTR 361 (4th Cir., 1949), *rev'g and rem'g* unreported T.C. order of dismissal.

[128] *Georgia Stevedoring Co.*, 40 B.T.A. 611 (1939).

[129] *George Wiedemann Brewing Co.*, 4 B.T.A. 664 (1926).

after that period would be improper.[130] In one interesting case under Illinois law, it was held that although actions might be brought *against* a corporation within two years after dissolution on any liability incurred prior thereto, the Court did not have jurisdiction with respect to a petition filed more than two years after dissolution.[131]

If the state statute lacks a provision by which the dissolved corporation is kept alive indefinitely for a term of years for purposes of suit, an officer does not have standing to prosecute an appeal, since he is not the taxpayer against whom the deficiency was determined.[132] The same rule applies to a corporate stockholder.[133]

Some states provide for the appointment of liquidators or trustees who may sue and be sued by or on behalf of the corporation; such liquidators or trustees would be the proper parties to prosecute an appeal.[134] A national bank which has been liquidated continues in existence to wind up its affairs and would be the proper party to appeal.[135] In short, the state statute in question should be examined carefully before filing a petition where there is any question as to the legal existence of the corporation.

Dissolved associations and trusts perhaps cause even trickier jurisdictional questions than dissolved corporations, although analogous. Since an association in the nature of a corporation is an even more amorphous entity than a legally constituted corporation, its existence and, therefore, whether it is a taxpayer for jurisdictional purposes, is dependent upon the law of the state where it operates. For example, it has been held that under Pennsylvania law, an individual who had some years prior surrendered his shares, was not a proper party to prosecute an appeal to the Court where state law provided that an association may sue or be sued in the association's name and that upon dissolution the members shall elect three liquidators.[136] Obviously, if the statute had been followed, such duly elected liquidators would have had standing to prosecute a Tax Court appeal.

It is clear that the Court retains jurisdiction if the taxpayer dies or is dissolved after a timely, proper petition has been filed.[137] In spite of

---

[130] *Union Plate & Wire Co.*, 17 B.T.A. 1229 (1929).

[131] *S. W. Pike Seedsman, Inc.*, 42 B.T.A. 751 (1940).

[132] *S. Hirsch Distilling Co.*, 14 B.T.A. 1073 (1929).

[133] *Consolidated Textile Corp.*, 16 B.T.A. 178 (1929), *appeal dismissed*, 48 F.2d 1078 (4th Cir., 1930).

[134] *Iberville Wholesale Grocery Co.*, 17 B.T.A. 235 (1929) (Louisiana)

[135] *Central National Bank*, 11 B.T.A. 1017 (1928).

[136] *McKean*, 15 B.T.A. 795 (1929). *Cf. National Bank of Commerce*, 34 B.T.A. 119 (1936).

[137] *Duggan*, 21 B.T.A. 740 (1930).

this rule, the Court has held that it does not have jurisdiction where a trust taxable as a corporation has distributed all its assets and ended its existence prior to the filing of a petition.[138] Likewise, the Court has held that it lacked jurisdiction where a taxpayer, an unincorporated association, had ceased to exist prior to the time its petition was filed by its former treasurer.[139]

In any case where a possible jurisdictional question exists, it is incumbent on the petitioner to plead specifically the necessary facts to show the Court that the person filing the petition is acting properly on behalf of the taxpayer, be it a dissolved corporation, a decedent, etc. For example, with respect to a dissolved corporation, the petition should set forth facts showing that the petitioner has lawful authority to act and should also set forth the statute by virtue of which he acts for the dissolved corporation. Failure to plead these essential facts is ground for dismissal of the proceeding on account of lack of jurisdiction, even on the court's own motion where the face of the petition shows defective pleading.[140]

Section 2.11–Estates and Fiduciaries

One of the most frequently litigated jurisdictional areas is that involving estates and their representatives. Since an appeal must be taken by the person to whom the deficiency notice is addressed, or the fiduciary legally entitled to initiate a case on behalf of such person, the address placed upon the notice may be a pivotal point,[141] especially in connection with estates.[142] As is well known, the death of a taxpayer and the settlement of his estate before discharging tax obligations do not avoid liability from tax on the ground that the Tax Court lacks jurisdiction.[143] It is now well established that an appeal should be taken in the case of

---

[138] *Main-Hammond Land Trust,* 17 T.C. 942 (1951), *aff'd on other grounds,* 200 F.2d 308, 42 AFTR 958 (6th Cir., 1952).

[139] *National Committee to Secure Justice in the Rosenberg Case,* 27 T.C. 837 (1957).

[140] Rules 13, 23(a)(1), 34(a) and (b); *Louisville Property Co.,* 41 B.T.A. 1249 (1940); *Georgia Stevedoring Co.,* 40 B.T.A. 611 (1939).

[141] The computation of the 90-day filing period may be vitally affected. *See* discussion *supra,* sections 2.02 and 2.06.

[142] *See U.S. v. Lyman,* 36 F. Supp. 53, 26 AFTR 310 (D.C., Mass., 1940), *modified and rem'd on other grounds,* 125 F.2d 67, 30 AFTR 1315 (1st Cir., 1942) *and Harrison v. Comm'r,* 107 F.2d 341, 23 AFTR 882 (6th Cir., 1939).

[143] *Farrell Estate,* 35 B.T.A. 265 (1937); *Whitehead,* 24 B.T.A. 1111 (1931), *aff'd,* 64 F.2d 118, 12 AFTR 382 (8th Cir., 1933), *cert. denied,* 290 U.S. 690 (1933).

estates by the duly appointed executor or administrator, even though the notice was addressed to the taxpayer.[144]

Examples of jurisdictional litigation concerning estates include a case where the Court denied jurisdiction over an appeal filed by a discharged executor based on a deficiency notice for income tax addressed to the estate.[145] The applicable state law provided that a decree discharging him as administrator relieved him of liability, but also deprived him of further authority to act for the estate.

In sustaining its jurisdiction, the Court held that a discharged executor was the proper person to file a petition where the notice of deficiency was mailed to him and he had not notified the Commissioner of the termination of his fiduciary capacity as required by the Code.[146]

Several cases have turned upon the very narrow point of whether a fiduciary was acting in his representative capacity or in an individual capacity. The Court has held that it lacks jurisdiction when a deficiency notice is sent to an administrator and he files a petition individually.[147] In other words, the petition must be an appeal by the petitioner in his fiduciary capacity, and not merely individually, for the Court to have jurisdiction in such a situation.[148] In another interesting case, the Court held that it lacked jurisdiction of a petition filed by trustees where the deficiency notice had been addressed to the executors, since trustees and executors of an estate are separate representatives.[149]

Perhaps much of the difficulty in many of these jurisdictional questions would be eliminated if the Court would follow the pronouncement of an appellate court that "the notice is only to advise the person who is to pay the deficiency that the Commissioner means to assess him; anything that does this unequivocally is good enough,"[150] In other words, adherence to its holding that the word "taxpayer" should not be given a "narrow or restricted meaning," would usually support jurisdic-

---

144 *Eisendrath,* 28 B.T.A. 744 (1933); *Nauts v. Clymer,* 36 F.2d 207, 8 AFTR 9836 (6th Cir., 1929); *Shay Estate,* B.T.A. Memo Op. Docket 93176 (1940).

145 *Rosenthal Estate,* B.T.A. Memo Op. Docket 97542 (1939), under Illinois law. *See also Dabney Estate,* 40 B.T.A. 276 (1939). *Cf. Lowrance,* 23 B.T.A. 1055 (1931).

146 *Borden Estate,* T.C. Memo Op. Docket 18887 (1950) ¶50,185 P-H Memo T.C.; *Eversole Estate,* 39 T.C. 1113 (1963).

147 *Melczer Estate,* 23 B.T.A. 124 (1931), *appeal dismissed,* 63 F.2d 1010, 12 AFTR 358 (9th Cir., 1933); *Hanify,* 21 B.T.A. 379 (1930).

148 *Eversole Estate,* 39 T.C. 1113 (1963); *Peterson Estate,* 45 T.C. 497 (1966).

149 *St. Louis Union Trust Co.,* 21 B.T.A. 76 (1930); *Fifth-Third Union Trust Co.,* 20 B.T.A. 88 (1930), *rev'd,* 56 F.2d 767, 10 AFTR 1415 (6th Cir., 1932).

150 *Olsen v. Helvering,* 88 F.2d 650, 19 AFTR 184 (2nd Cir., 1937).

tion.[151] Despite this language, however, the Court did not hesitate to deny jurisdiction of a proceeding brought by a life tenant in her individual capacity for the redetermination of a deficiency based upon a notice sent to her as trustee for the remaindermen.[152]

Once the Court has taken jurisdiction over the income tax deficiency of a decedent's estate by virtue of a timely petition by a duly appointed executor or administrator from a proper notice of deficiency, the Commissioner cannot place jurisdiction in any other court to redetermine such liability for the same taxable years so as to oust the jurisdiction of the Tax Court should a decision first be made by the other court.[153]

Section 2.12—Suspension of Assessment and Collection

Since the Tax Court was instituted as a litigate first-pay later tribunal, the filing of an appeal suspends collection of the tax, as well as the running of the statute of limitations on assessment and collection of the tax. There are, however, exceptions to this noncollection rule pending the appeal:[154]

1. The taxpayer may waive these restrictions by a writing filed with the Government;
2. Cases in which a mathematical error appears on the face of the return;
3. Bankruptcy and receivership cases;
4. Jeopardy assessments;
5. Cases on appeal to the circuit courts unless a bond, or letter of credit, is filed with the Court in a satisfactory amount; and
6. A tentative carryback adjustment in excess of the overassessment determined to be properly attributable to the carryback.

---

[151] See the excellent discussion of this welter of fiduciary-jurisdictional litigation at Sec. 50.33, Mertens, *op. cit.*, with copious notes, which contains many variations of this problem.

[152] *Shea*, 31 B.T.A. 513 (1934); *Sack*, 36 B.T.A. 595 (1937).

[153] *Lambert Estate*, 39 T.C. 954 (1963).

[154] Sec. 7421(a); *Bromberg v. Ingling*, 300 F.2d 859, 9 AFTR 2d 1008 (9th Cir., 1962), *rev'g* unreported D.C. decision.

Section 2.13—Seriousness of Filing Petition

A taxpayer's decision whether to appeal a deficiency notice to the Tax Court or seek other relief is a very serious one and should be made only after the most careful study, since a petition may be withdrawn only with the Commissioner's consent.[155]

The filing of a frivolous appeal, that is, not in good faith and for the purpose of delay, may give rise to an additional assessment for damages under Section 6673. Although seldom applied, this provision is a warning for taxpayers to consider seriously whether a petition should be filed, and such decision should be in the negative if the facts and law definitely fail to support the taxpayer.

Section 2.14—Private Foundation Tax Jurisdiction

Until 1969, the Court's jurisdiction was limited to income, estate and gift tax cases where a timely notice of deficiency or transferee liability had been issued. By the Tax Reform Act of 1969, however, its jurisdiction was extended to deficiencies in private foundation taxes under Code Sections 4940–4945, adding a new and different tax to the three previously authorized.[156]

Section 2.15—Declaratory Judgment Jurisdiction

By the Employee Retirement Income Security Act of 1974, again, its jurisdiction was drastically extended to include declaratory judgments relating to certain retirement plans for employees.[157] For the first time the Court has been given jurisdiction beyond the narrow limits of the tax deficiency concept. It is also the first time that any court in the federal judicial system has been given declaratory judgment jurisdiction in a tax controversy, which may serve to increase considerably the

---

[155] *Champion Rivet Co. v. U.S.*, 30 F. Supp. 234, 23 AFTR 1039 (Ct. Cl. 1939).

[156] Sec. 7454(b). *See also* Sec. 6214(c), as amended.

[157] Sec. 7476; Rules, Title XXI, effective Sept. 2, 1975: "Title XXI makes clear that, except as otherwise provided, the other Rules of Practice and Procedure of the Court, to the extent pertinent, are applicable to declaratory judgment litigation." Prefatory Note prepared by the Court's Rules Committee.

complexity and difficulty of cases coming before the Court, as well as to enhance its prestige.

In essence, Section 7476 of this new Act provides that in a case of actual controversy involving a determination by the Secretary of the Treasury, or his delegate, with respect to the initial qualification or continuing qualification of a retirement plan, or involving a failure to make a determination with respect to such issue, the Tax Court may make a declaration with respect to such initial qualification or continuing qualification upon the filing of an appropriate pleading.[158]

Such a pleading may be filed only by a petitioner who is the employer, the plan administrator or an employee who has qualified under appropriate future regulations as an interested party for purposes of pursuing administrative remedies within the Service.[159] The Court may hold any such pleading to be premature unless the petitioner can satisfy the Court that he has complied with the regulatory requirements with respect to notice to other interested parties that the proceeding is being initiated.[160] Further, the Court shall not issue a declaratory judgment or decree unless it determines that the petitioner has exhausted administrative remedies available to him within the Service.[161] This provision is, of course, identical with established requirements for a refund claim and subsequent suit. A petitioner shall not be deemed to have exhausted his administrative remedies before the expiration of 270 days after the request for such determination was made.[162]

No Tax Court proceeding may be maintained unless the plan or the amendment involved has been put into effect before the filing of the pleading.[163] There is a 90-day filing requirement as for tax deficiency petitions.[164] In view of the prospective enlargment of the retirement plan coverage and the creation of a new assistant commissionership by this Act

---

158Sec. 7476(a); Rules, Title XXI; especially Rules 210, 217: "To the extent pertinent, such practice and procedure ["in respect of declaratory judgment litigation of the United States District Courts"] may be used as guidelines for the application of the within Rules." Prefatory Note prepared by the Court's Rules Committee.

159Sec. 7476(b)(1); Rule 211.

160Sec. 7476(b)(2); Rule 211.

161Sec. 7476(b)(3); Rule 211: "Declaratory judgment cases will usually be decided on the basis of the administrative record made in the proceedings within the Internal Revenue Service in connection with a request for a determination on the qualification of a retirement plan or amendment thereto." Prefatory Note prepared by the Court's Rules Committee. Hence, it behooves a petitioner for a declaratory judgment to prepare his case most thoroughly in the administrative stage, contrary to frequent practice in many standard tax deficiency cases.

162Sec. 7476(b)(3); Rule 210.

163Sec. 7476(b)(4); Rules 210, 211.

164Sec. 7476(b)(5).

to administer this new law and other related provisions of the Code, future expansion of the volume of Tax Court cases is indicated. Certainly it is branching into an entirely new concept of tax law determination heretofore unknown to our judicial system. Thus, a real challenge for Tax Court administration and responsibility has been introduced after a half-century of tax deficiency jurisdiction.

Section 2.16—Pension Plan Excise Tax Jurisdiction

The 1974 Act also added new excise taxes for violation of statutory requirements respecting retirement plans.[165] These excise taxes generally follow the same procedures as the tax on self-dealing enacted in the 1969 Tax Reform Act with respect to private foundations.

The 1974 Act establishes procedure under which the Internal Revenue Service is to mail a notice of deficiency with respect to the first-level tax under Section 6212.[166] Thereafter, a prohibited transaction may be corrected to avoid a second-level tax at any time before the 90th day after the Service mails another such notice of deficiency with respect to the second-level tax.[167] However, the 90-day period may be extended by any period within which a deficiency cannot be assessed because of a timely petition filed with the Court, and may also be extended for a period which the Service determines is both reasonable and necessary to correct the prohibited transaction.[168]

---

[165] Sec. 4971-5.

[166] Sec. 4975(f)(6).

[167] Sec. 4975(f)(6).

[168] Sec. 4975(f)(6).

CHAPTER 3

The Commencement of a Case

Section 3.01—Filing the Petition

UPON RECEIPT OF A NOTICE OF DEFICIENCY or a notice of transferee or fiduciary liability, issued by the Commissioner, a case is commenced in the Court by filing a petition with the Court for redetermination of the determined deficiency, or the determined transferee or fiduciary liability.[1] A filing fee of $10.00 is due at the time of filing a petition, unless the petitioner establishes to the satisfaction of the Court that he is unable to make such payment, with the Court thereupon waiving payment of the fee.[2] The fee may be paid either in cash or by check, money order or other draft made payable to the order of "Clerk, United States Tax Court".[3]

Section 3.02—Service and Filing of Papers

With respect to service of papers, all pleadings, motions, orders, decisions, notices, demands, briefs, appearances or other similar documents or papers relating to a filed case, also referred to as "the papers in a case," shall be served on each of the parties to the case other than the party who filed the paper.[4] This of course is a familiar practice, similar to that in all other courts of record.

---

[1] Rule 20(a). *See also* Rules, Title XXI—Declaratory Judgments—Retirement Plans.

[2] Rule 20(b)

[3] Rule 11.

[4] Rule 21(a).

The new Rules, however, introduced a decided change in the manner of service of all papers except the petition, but subject to the election of a party. With respect to service of a petition, the prior practice has been retained so that all petitions are to be served by the Clerk.[5] With respect to all other papers, they are to be served on a party by the Clerk unless otherwise directed by the Court, or unless the filing party chooses to serve that paper directly on the party to be served or on his counsel, in which case the original paper when filed shall have a certificate by a party or his counsel that service has been so directly made. Such direct service by a party may be made by mail directed to the party or his counsel at his last known address.[6] Service by mail is complete upon mailing and the date of such mailing shall be the date of such service.[7] As an alternative to direct service by mail, service may be made by personal delivery to a party, or to his counsel or authorized representative.[8] In the case of a party other than an individual, such as a corporation or a corporate fiduciary, service should be on an authorized officer.[9]

Service shall be made on the Commissioner (the respondent) by service on, or directed to, his counsel at the office address shown in his answer filed in the case or, if no answer has been filed, on the Chief Counsel, Internal Revenue Service, Washington D.C. 20224.[10]

Service on a person other than a party shall be made in the same manner as service on a party, except as otherwise provided in the Rules or as directed by the Court.[11] If a party chooses to make direct service by mailing, it is strongly suggested that this be done by certified mail with return receipt requested in order to avoid later arguments as to whether, and on what day, its service was actually made. In view of recent uncertainty as to efficient deliveries of the United States mails, this advice is even more important than in former years when prompt delivery was usually assured.

Whether taxpayers and their counsel, or the Commissioner and his counsel, will avail themselves of this elective change in the manner of service will only be known by the passage of time and the result of accumulated experience. It is much less trouble to file with the Clerk and

---

[5]Rule 21(b)(1); Note.

[6]Rule 21(b)(1); Note.

[7]Rule 21(b)(1).

[8]Rule 21(b)(1).

[9]Rule 21(b)(1).

[10]Rule 21(b)(1).

[11]Rule 21(b)(1).

have him complete service than to do so directly and also there is an advantage in using this old method because it avoids any arguments on receipt of papers served by mailing. Further, after fifty years of experience in having the Clerk serve all papers, it is believed doubtful that many established attorneys will suddenly change their procedure and serve directly. Perhaps younger attorneys who have not been so accustomed to service by the Clerk will avail themselves of the direct mailing method, but even here, the line of least resistance would seem to be to file with the Clerk and have him complete service without any additional effort on the part of counsel for a petitioner.

It is unknown whether the Commissioner and his attorney, the Chief Counsel, have reached any policy decision on whether to avail themselves of the new provision for direct service, but at this time it is believed that the Commissioner and his counsel are continuing to follow Clerk filing and service procedure as in the past, rather than change over to direct mailing. It is believed that petitioners would receive much speedier service of papers if the Commissioner chose to mail directly from the branch offices of his attorneys throughout the land, rather than have them file their papers with the Clerk in Washington and then have the Clerk serve by mail as now occurs, and has, since the establishment of the Court. If this more expeditious receipt of service appeals to a sufficient number of the private tax bar, perhaps considerable pressure will be exerted on the Commissioner and his counsel to begin a policy of service by direct mail through the local branch offices, avoiding the mailing to the Clerk in Washington and the remailing by the Clerk to local private counsel which, using California as an example, requires several additional days before private counsel receives service. In the case of motions, briefs and similar deadline pleadings, the saving of several days in this service process could be most important for petitioner and his counsel. In any event, it is believed that this rule change thus far has been more often ignored than utilized. Only a mandatory mail service rule would be likely to cause a change in the time-honored method of service by the Clerk.

Whenever service is required or permitted to be made upon a party represented by counsel who has entered his appearance, service shall be made upon such counsel unless service upon the party himself is directed by the Court.[12] Where more than one counsel appears for a party, service will be made only on that counsel whose appearance was first entered of record, unless that counsel designates in writing filed with the Court other counsel of record to receive service.[13]

---

[12] Rule 21(b)(2).

[13] Rule 21(b)(2).

Section 3.03—The U.S. Marshal's Function

Another rule change is that service and execution of writs, process, or similar directives of the Court may be made by a United States Marshal, by his deputy, or by a person especially appointed by the Court for that purpose except that a subpoena may be served as provided in Rule 147(c).[14] The person making service shall make proof thereof to the Court promptly and in any event within the time in which the person served must respond.[15] Failure to make proof of service does not affect the validity of the service.[16]

The change effected by the new Rules for service by the United States Marshal's office is a result of the provisions of the Tax Reform Act of 1969 which created the Court as an Article I Court. Service by the Clerk may be inappropriate in such instances and, therefore, this new provision was required.

Section 3.04—Filing

Any pleadings or other papers to be filed with the Court must be filed with the Clerk in Washington, D.C., during business hours, except that the Judge presiding at any trial or hearing may permit or require documents pertaining thereto to be filed at that particular session of the Court, or except as otherwise directed by the Court.[17]

Section 3.05—Form and Style of Papers

As to the form and style of papers, the Court's Rules follow normal judicial procedural practice with respect to such things as caption, date and signature required. It should be noted that all prefixes and titles, such as "Mrs." or "Dr.", are to be omitted from the caption.[18] The full name and surname of each individual petitioner must be set forth in the petition.[19] When filing a petition for an estate or trust or other person for

---

[14] Rule 21(b)(3); Note.

[15] Rule 21(b)(3).

[16] Rule 21(b)(3).

[17] Rule 22.

[18] Rule 23(a)(1).

[19] Rule 23(a)(1).

whom a fiduciary acts, the name of the estate, etc., shall precede the fiduciary's name and title.[20]

Every paper filed with the Court shall be signed by either the party or his counsel, except as otherwise provided by the Rules.[21] The individual, either petitioner or counsel, shall sign in his own individual name, not the firm name.[22] As to a petitioner corporation or unincorporated association, the signature shall be the name of the corporation or association by one of its active and authorized officers or members.[23] The name, mailing address and telephone number of the party or his counsel shall be typed or printed immediately beneath the written signature.[24] The mailing address of a signatory, of course, shall include a firm name if it is an essential part of the accurate mailing address.[25] The signature date shall be shown on all papers filed with the Court.[26]

As to required number of copies of papers filed in the Court, the signed original, plus four conformed copies, must be filed for all papers except as otherwise provided in the Rules, such as for briefs.[27] Where filing is in more than one case (as a motion to consolidate, or in cases already consolidated), the number filed shall include one additional copy for each docket number in excess of one.[28]

The Court is very particular that all papers filed with the Court must be clear and legible.[29] Since the judges have to read voluminous documentary evidence in addition to pleadings and other papers filed with the Court, the reason for this concern is self-evident.

Rule 23(d) and (e) provides for the size and style of papers and also binding and covers, which latter the Court forbids except in the case of briefs. All citations shall be underscored when typewritten and in italics when printed.[30]

---

[20]Rule 23(a)(1).

[21]Rule 23(a)(3).

[22]Rule 23(a)(3).

[23]Rule 23(a)(3).

[24]Rule 23(a)(3).

[25]Rule 23(a)(3).

[26]Rule 23(a)(2).

[27]Rule 23(b).

[28]Rule 23(b).

[29]Rule 23(c).

[30]Rule 23(f).

Section 3.06–Appearance and Representation

As in all other courts, counsel may enter an appearance either by subscribing the petition or other initial pleading or document or subsequently by filing an entry of appearance, for which a form is provided by the Court.[31] If the petition or other paper initiating the participation of a party in a case is subscribed by counsel admitted to practice before the Court, that counsel will be recognized as representing that party and it will be unnecessary for him to enter a separate entry of appearance, provided that such initial pleading shall also contain the mailing address of counsel and other information required for entry of appearance.[32] Thereafter, counsel must notify the Clerk of any changes in applicable information to the same extent as if he had filed a subsequent separate entry of appearance.[33]

A separate entry of appearance, in duplicate, is required for each additional docket number in which counsel shall appear.[34] It is important to give the Clerk prompt written notice, filed in duplicate for each docket number, of any change in the required information.[35]

No entry of appearance by counsel not admitted to practice before the Court will be effective until he has been admitted, but he may be recognized as counsel in the pending case to the extent permitted by the Court with the understanding that he will be admitted promptly upon compliance with Rule 200.[36]

In the absence of appearance by counsel, a party will be deemed to appear for himself.[37] As in all other courts in civil matters, an individual party may represent himself.[38] A corporation or an unincorporated association may be represented by an authorized officer and an estate or trust may be represented by the fiduciary thereof.[39] Any such

---

[31] Rule 24(a)(1), (2), (3).

[32] Rule 24(a)(2).

[33] Rule 24(a)(2).

[34] Rule 24(a)(3).

[35] Rule 24(a)(3).

[36] Rule 24(a)(4).

[37] Rule 24(b); Note.

[38] Rule 24(b).

[39] Rule 24(b).

officer or fiduciary shall state, in the initial pleading or other paper filed by or for the party, his name, address, and telephone number and as with counsel, must promptly notify the Clerk in writing, in duplicate for each docket number involving that party, of any change in information.[40]

Withdrawal of counsel is strictly administered by the Court. Counsel of record desiring to withdraw his appearance, or any party desiring to withdraw the appearance of counsel of record for him, must file a motion with the Court requesting leave therefor and showing that prior notice of the motion has been given by him to his client, or his counsel, as the case may be. The Court may, in its discretion, deny such motion.[41] Certainly the Court will inquire into the specific circumstances giving rise to the withdrawal motion if there appears to be any question as to its propriety. Of course the Court will accept the withdrawal request of counsel, or of the client, unless there is some strong reason for denial.

If counsel of record dies, the Court shall be so notified and other counsel may enter an appearance thereafter.[42]

On rare occasions, a corporation, unincorporated association, estate or trust may file a petition through an officer or fiduciary and later decide to employ counsel therein. In such a situation and also where there is a change in the corporate officer or fiduciary, or a substitution of parties in a pending case, counsel subscribing the motion resulting in the Court's approval of the change or substitution shall thereafter be deemed first counsel of record for the new representative or party.[43] This is very important, because as previously pointed out, first counsel of record is recognized by the Court as "the" counsel of record to receive service of all papers and to be contacted with respect to any matter involving that pending case.

Section 3.07–Computation of Time

In all courts, the computation of time for performing any act under its rules may be critically important. Rule 25 is generally in accord with the computation of time by most other judicial tribunals. For example, the day of the act, event, or default from which a designated period of time begins to run shall not be included.[44] In the event of

---

[40] Rule 24(b).

[41] Rule 24(c).

[42] Rule 24(d); Note.

[43] Rule 24(e).

[44] Rule 25(a); Note.

service made by mail, the computation begins on the day after the date of mailing.[45] Saturdays, Sundays and all legal holidays are counted except when the allowed period is less than seven days. Also the last day of the period shall be included unless it is a Saturday, Sunday or a legal holiday in the District of Columbia, in which event the period runs until the end of the next day which is not a Saturday, Sunday or such a legal holiday. When such legal holiday falls on a Sunday, the next day shall be considered a holiday; and when such a legal holiday falls on a Saturday, the preceding day shall be considered a holiday.[46] Code Sections 6213 and 7502 govern the computation of the period within which to file a petition.[47]

Rule 25(b) lists the District of Columbia legal holidays which are in essence those recognized by the United States Government. Any other day appointed as a holiday by the President or the Congress shall also be recognized by the Court.

Rule 25(c) covers enlargement or reduction of time for filing papers which in general gives great flexibility to the Court in its discretion except for a period specified by statute. On the all-important subject of the dates for filing briefs, an extension of time for filing a brief granted to one party correspondingly extends a time for the other party and for filing succeeding briefs, unless the Court orders otherwise. As already highlighted, (and this cannot be over-emphasized), the Court cannot extend the statutory period within which to file a petition.

Throughout its years of existence, the Court has always been reasonable in granting extensions of time for filing all papers, including briefs, although it is necessary for the Court to make sure its work flow runs smoothly (it would be impaired if counsel abused its discretionary privilege). Accordingly, it behooves counsel to be as sparing as possible in requesting extensions of time for filing papers, including briefs, so as not to be considered by the Court as an habitual delaying offender. In other words, reserve extension requests for those urgent matters when further time is an absolute must and avoid making it a perennial habit.

---

[45] Rule 25(a); Note.

[46] Rule 25(a); Note.

[47] Rule 25(a).

CHAPTER 4

Pleadings

Section 4.01—General

ANYONE FAMILIAR WITH THE COURT'S RULES prior to January 1, 1974, or anyone familiar with the Federal Rules of Civil Procedure, will feel very much at home in drafting pleadings under the Court's present rules. The old rules were not dramatically changed and, where changes were made, they were generally derived from the Federal Rules. Under the notice rule of pleading, Rule 31 provides that "The purpose of the pleadings is to give the parties and the Court fair notice of the matters in controversy and the basis for their respective positions." If counsel always follows this precept, his pleadings should be adequate. Lifted from the Federal Rules, Rule 31 gives a general guide which should help in resolving conflicts about pleadings. Rule 31 goes on to make clear that pleadings shall be simple, concise and direct and no technical forms of pleadings are required. Again, this provision accords with good pleading practice in every court in the land. This should make transition from some other court to Tax Court practice smooth and easy for the practitioner.

Rule 31(c) also makes clear that a party may plead two or more statements of a claim or defense alternatively or hypothetically. The Rule also points out that if two or more statements are made in the alternative and one of them would be sufficient if made independently, the pleading is not made insufficient because one or more of the alternative statements is insufficient. In other words, one adequate statement will save the pleading. The Rule also provides that a party may plead multiple claims or defenses regardless of consistency or the grounds on which based, but there is the *caveat* in Rule 31(c) that all statements shall be made subject to the signature requirements of Rules 23 and 33. This "consistency" rule was not intended to represent a change in present Tax Court practice.[1]

Section 4.02–Form of Pleadings

Every pleading filed with the Court shall contain a caption setting forth the name of the court, the title of the case, the docket number after it becomes available and a designation to show the nature of the pleading.[2] In the initial pleading, the petition, the title of the case shall include the names of all parties, but in subsequent pleadings it is sufficient to state the name of the first party with an appropriate indication of other parties.[3] Although this Rule 32 represents a change from the prior rules, no change in present practice is involved, since these requirements have always been enforced by the Court.

Under Rule 32(b) all averments of a claim or defense, and all supporting statements, must be made in separately designated paragraphs, the contents of each of which shall be limited as far as practicable to a statement of a single item or a single set of circumstances.[4] Such paragraphs may be referred to by that designation in all succeeding pleadings. To clearly present the matters set forth for multiple claims and defenses, each claim and defense shall be stated separately.[5] This is simply common sense draftsmanship so that the Court and opposing counsel will be able to quickly identify separate claims or defenses and appropriately respond thereto.

Statements in a pleading may be adopted by reference in a different part of the same pleading or in another pleading or in a motion.[6] A copy of any written instrument which is an exhibit to a pleading is a part thereof for all purposes. Under this Rule, for example, the notice of deficiency attached to the petition is a part of that pleading, although representing only the deficiency notice issued by the Commissioner and the allegations made in that notice when it was issued.[7] If any facts are stated in the notice of deficiency attached to the petition, they are not

---

[1] Rule 31(a); Note.

[2] Rule 32(a); Note.

[3] Rule 32(a).

[4] Rule 32(b); Note. *See also* Rules, Title XXI.

[5] Rule 32(b).

[6] Rule 32(c).

[7] Rule 32(c); Note.

thus introduced and received in evidence and must be introduced in some other form in order to become a part of the findings of fact of the Court.

One of the most beneficial changes in former practice is found in Rule 33 which abolishes the requirement for verification of pleadings as a general rule although, of course, the Court can specifically direct verification.[8] In actual practice this will be a boon for counsel for taxpayers who frequently had to go to great lengths to locate the client, perhaps in a far removed portion of the country, with time running short for filing a petition. Now the signature of counsel is sufficient as set forth in Rules 23 and 33.

Section 4.03—Signing and Dating

Rule 33(b) should impress upon counsel or a *pro se* party the seriousness of his signature without verification. "Signature" means that the signer has read the pleading; to the best of his knowledge, information or belief, there is good ground to support it; that it is not frivolous; and that it is not interposed for delay.[9] The signature of counsel also constitutes his representation that he is authorized to represent the party or parties on whose behalf the pleading is filed. If a pleading is not signed, or signed with intent to defeat the purpose of Rule 33, it may be stricken and the action may proceed as though the pleading had not been filed. Similar action may be taken if scandalous or indecent matter is pleaded. For a willful violation of this Rule, counsel may be subjected to appropriate disciplinary action.[10]

It should again be noted that the date of signature must be placed on all papers filed with the Court under Rule 23(a)(2).

Section 4.04—The Petition

Trite but true that next to the stipulation of facts, nothing is more important in building a successful Tax Court case than the petition. Also trite but true, nothing will evoke more differences of opinion among able tax lawyers than the question: what constitutes a good petition? Immediately, one recalls the old chestnut of how long should a woman's skirt be (before mini-skirts and pants-suits)? Long enough to cover the subject but short enough to be interesting.

---

[8]Rule 33(b); Note.

[9]Rule 33(b).

[10]Rule 33(b).

The fact that a proceeding is initiated by the filing of a petition is the keynote of its critical nature. Its form is carefully regulated by the Rules, which have not been changed appreciably from prior Rules.[11] The petition must be typed or printed according to specifications; handwritten or telegraphic petitions will not be permitted or recognized.[12] The taxpayer is always "Petitioner" against the Commissioner as "Respondent." Upon receipt by the Clerk, a petition is docketed and assigned a number, of which parties are notified, and thereafter it must be placed upon all papers filed with the Court and referred to in all subsequent correspondence with the Court.

The petition should set forth appropriate allegations showing jurisdiction in the Court; a statement of the amount of the determined deficiency and the amount thereof in dispute; the nature of the tax and period for which it has been determined; clear and concise assignments of error (including those in which the burden of proof is by statute placed upon the Commissioner); clear and concise lettered statements of facts relied upon as supporting the assignments of error, except those assignments of error in respect of which the burden of proof is by statute placed upon the Commissioner; a prayer or prayers for relief; the signature of petitioner or his counsel (individually and not in the firm name of counsel), together with the address and phone number of petitioner or of counsel, which must be typed or printed immediately following the signature, and the date of signature.[13] A copy of the notice of deficiency (or liability) with so much of the accompanying statement, if any, as is "material to the issues raised by the assignments of error" should be attached to the petition.[14]

A suggested form for the petition is shown in the Appendix to the Rules and should be consulted if in doubt. Other suggested forms are in the Appendix to this book. Although the Court is as liberal in enforcing its pleadings Rules as other courts, such as the federal district courts, it is bad practice to begin a proceding with faulty draftmanship. Hence, careful preparation of the petition cannot be over-emphasized.

The general rule is that a separate petition must be filed with respect to each notice of deficiency or each notice of liability. A single petition may be filed, however, seeking redetermination with respect to multiple notices of deficiency or liability directed to one person alone, or

---

[11]Rule 34.

[12]Rule 34; *Rosenberg,* 32 B.T.A. 618 (1935); *Statler,* 27 B.T.A. 342 (1932) and *cf. Continental Petroleum Co.*, 87 F.2d 91, 18 AFTR 717 (10th Cir., 1936).

[13]Rule 34.

[14]Rule 34(b)(8).

to him and one or more other persons, with the proviso that the Court may require a severance and a separate case to be maintained with respect to one or more of such notices.[15] Where the notice of deficiency or liability is directed to more than one person, each such person desiring to contest it shall file a petition on his own behalf, either separately or jointly with any such other person, and each such person must satisfy all requirements of Rule 34 with respect to himself in order for the petition to be treated as filed by or for him.

Failure of the petition to satisfy the requirements of the Rules may be grounds for dismissal of the case, although not necessarily mandatory. The subject of joinder of petitioners is further treated in Rules 61 and 62. (Chapter 5, *infra*)

Undoubtedly, the pleading of the facts in Paragraph 5 is the most important part of the petition. It is comparable to the importance of the take-off of an airplane in comparison to the flight itself. Only facts may be pleaded, not legal conclusions or arguments. Frequently a taxpayer is disappointed when he reads the petition drafted by his attorney because it sounds rather objective instead of the advocate's exposition which he may be expecting. It should always be pointed out to the taxpayer-client that the petition is strictly limited as to its contents in that only assignments of error and pleadings of fact are permitted. Although motions to strike legal conclusions and arguments from a petition are rare, they will be disregarded by the Court even if not stricken.[16]

The Court will refuse to consider issues of fact not raised by the petition and argued for the first time in briefs after the trial.[17] Again it cannot be over-stressed that the facts should be carefully set forth in a logical step-by-step sequence. If possible, a chronological statement of facts will be best, but of course this depends upon the issues in the case.

As pointed out above, it is most important to the orderly handling of litigation that both the Court and the opposing party be adequately informed by the pleadings as to exactly what issues are presented for decision. This does not mean, however, that evidence should be pleaded but simply the basic facts and not minor details.

It is strongly suggested that a petition have short fact paragraphs and that they be lettered appropriately as sub-paragraphs which

---

[15]Rule 34(a).

[16]A Tax Court petition begins a *de novo* proceeding, so allegations as to past history of I.R.S. dealings are usually immaterial and argumentative and, therefore, should be avoided.

[17]*North American Coal Corp.*, 28 B.T.A. 807 (1933); *Jamieson Associates, Inc.*, 37 B.T.A. 92 (1938), *aff'd in part sub nom. Seaside Improvement Co.*, 105 F.2d 990, 23 AFTR 293 (2nd Cir., 1939); *cert. denied,* 308 U.S. 618 (1939); *Citizens National Trust & Savings Bank of Los Angeles,* 34 B.T.A. 140 (1936).

will facilitate admissions or denials in the Commissioner's answer. A recommended system of lettering is to use "(a)(i), (a)(ii), (a)(iii)," etc. It is believed that if each sub-paragraph is kept very short and is thus lettered, confusion in drafting the Commissioner's answer will be eliminated and the Court and the parties will be able to accurately describe the separate paragraphs and sub-paragraphs. This is necessary because each issue should bear a separate letter, as "(a), (b), (c), (d)," etc. Frequently, several pages will be required to plead the facts for one issue such as paragraph (a). That is why the (i), (ii), (iii) system is recommended to clarify the Government's response thereto in the answer.

One of the great difficulties in properly drafting a petition is that the petitioner's attorney is often employed not only after the receipt of the notice of deficiency, but frequently when a large portion of the 90-day period has expired. If the attorney is busily engaged in other matters, he frequently has only a few remaining days in which to prepare the petition, which also means assembling the necessary facts and deciding which of the Commissioner's adjustments in the notice of deficiency are to be assigned as error. If in doubt, of course, the attorney in this situation should plead every doubtful adjustment as an assignment of error. With respect to the facts, however, he is often severely handicapped by lack of time in assembling the facts in order to plead them properly so that he will not fall into any traps by pleading facts which turn out to be different or more extensive upon further investigation after the petition has been filed. An amended petition or an amendment to the petition often serves to overcome this time handicap in the appropriate case as will be more fully discussed hereinafter when amended pleadings are considered.

Section 4.05—The Answer

The Commissioner must file his answer within 60 days from the date of service of the petition or he must move with respect to the petition within 45 days from that date.[18] If an amended petition or amendments to the petition are filed, the Commissioner shall have like periods from the date of service of those papers within which to answer or move in response thereto, except as the Court may otherwise direct.[19]

---

[18] Rule 36(a), but if the Commissioner moves to dismiss for lack of jurisdiction before the answer date has expired, no answer is required until determination of the motion. *Jefferson Memorial Park,* T.C. Memo 1963-32, ¶63,032 P-H Memo T.C. Also the 60 day filing date will be strictly applied. *Quirk Estate,* 60 T.C. 520 (1973).

[19] Rule 36(a).

The answer shall be prepared so that it will fully advise the petitioner and the Court of the nature of the Commissioner's defense. It shall contain a specific admission or denial of each material allegation in the petition; however, if the Commissioner is without knowledge or information sufficient to form a belief as the truth of an allegation, he shall so state and such statement shall have the effect of a denial.[20] If the Commissioner intends to qualify or deny only a part of an allegation, he shall specify so much of it as is true and shall qualify or deny only the remainder.[21] In addition, the answer must contain a clear and concise statement of every ground, together with the facts in support thereof, on which the Commissioner relies and has the burden of proof.[22] Paragraphs of the answer shall be designated to correspond to those of the petition to which they relate. Every material allegation set forth in the petition and not expressly admitted or denied in the answer shall be deemed to be admitted.[23] An admission in the answer eliminates that issue from the necessity of proof by petitioner.[24]

Much criticism has been evoked from the practicing bar throughout the Court's history as to the inadequacy and uninformative nature of the Commissioner's typical answers. Some of this criticism is justified and some is not. Frequently, a petition is so poorly drawn that it would be impossible to prepare a meaningful answer thereto. On the other hand, many petitions are beautifully drafted to set forth in much detail the facts upon which the petitioner relies and yet the Commissioner will file an answer thereto which is nothing more or less than a general denial.

It is not uncommon for a multi-page petition of some 15 or 20 pages to be met with a one-page general denial answer. On the whole, however, the quality of the answer is usually commensurate with the quality of the petition, especially in more recent years when the Commissioner has made a greater effort to prepare more meaningful answers.

It should also be noted that frequently the Commissioner's counsel has very little information in his possession as to the veracity of the facts pleaded in the petition. Many examining agents fail to obtain sufficient evidence during their examination of the returns in question to provide a solid basis on which the Commissioner's counsel can admit very many pleaded facts. By the same token, the paucity of facts in the Commissioner's file also prevents his counsel from pleading affirmative facts, which otherwise might be done.

[20] Rule 36(b).

[21] Rule 36(b).

[22] Rule 36(b).

[23] Rule 36(c).

[24] *Weinstein,* 33 B.T.A. 105 (1935).

It is hoped that increasing vigilance by the Chief Counsel and his staff to exert greater effort in preparing adequate answers will bear fruit in due time. Where the petitioner's counsel participates in the examination of the returns which gave rise to the eventual Tax Court case, he can be helpful in furnishing facts to the examining agent which will then become a part of the administrative file in the hands of the Commissioner's counsel and enable him to admit facts more freely than otherwise would be the case. In other words, the shoe is frequently on the foot of petitioner's counsel for failure to supply basic facts when it could be done in such a way as to enable better pleadings to be prepared by Commissioner's counsel.

Section 4.06—The Reply

The petitioner has 45 days from the date of service of the answer within which to file a reply, or 30 days from that date within which to move with respect to the answer.[25] With respect to an amended answer or amendments to the answer, the petitioner has like periods from the date of service of those papers within which to reply or move in response thereto, except as the Court may otherwise direct.[26]

In response to each material allegation in the answer and the facts in support thereof on which the Commissioner has the burden of proof, the reply must contain a specific admission or denial; however, if the petitioner is without knowledge or information sufficient to form a belief as to the truth of an allegation, he shall so state, and such statement shall have the effect of a denial.[27] In addition, the reply must contain a clear and concise statement of every ground, together with the facts in support thereof, on which the petitioner relies affirmatively or in avoidance of any matter in the answer in which the Commissioner has the burden of proof.[28] In other respects, the requirements of pleading which apply to the answer also apply to the reply. The paragraphs of the reply shall be designated to correspond to those of the answer to which they relate.

Where a reply is filed, every affirmative allegation set forth in the answer and not expressly admitted or denied in the reply, shall be

---

[25]Rule 37(a).

[26]Rule 37(a).

[27]Rule 37(b); failure of petitioner to deny fact allegations could result in judgment on the pleadings. See *Weiss*, T.C. Memo Op. Docket 108212 (1943), ¶43,032 P-H Memo T.C., *but cf. Beringer*, 29 B.T.A. 250 (1933) *and McGlue*, B.T.A. Memo Op. Docket 100465 (1941), ¶41,041 P-H Memo B.T.A.

[28]Rule 37(b).

deemed to be admitted.[29] Where a reply is not filed, the affirmative allegations in the answer will be deemed denied unless the Commissioner, within 45 days after expiration of the time for filing the reply, files a motion for an order that specified allegations in the answer be deemed admitted.[30] That motion will be noticed for a hearing, at which the motion may be granted unless on or before the date thereof the required reply has been filed.[31] Any new material contained in the reply shall be deemed to be denied, since the Rules do not provide for a response by the Commissioner to a reply by the petitioner.[32]

A case shall be deemed at issue upon the filing of the answer, unless a reply is required under Rule 37, in which event it shall be deemed that issue is joined upon the filing of a reply or the entry of an order disposing of a motion under Rule 37(c) or the expiration of the period specified in Rule 37(c) in case the Commissioner fails to move.[33]

With respect to the fraud penalty, however, on which the respondent has the burden of proof, the Court may enter judgment for the penalty on the facts deemed admitted under Rule 37(c), but Rules 122 and 123 might be evoked, in addition to Rule 37(c). This attitude of the Court illustrates its abundance of precaution in considering the Commissioner's motion for a fraud penalty judgment on the pleadings even when there has been no appearance by the petitioner or his counsel. In other words, the Court tries to lean over backwards in such situations to make sure that the petitioner is being protected within the Rules and will only grant the Commissioner's motion for a fraud penalty order when the facts deemed admitted by his motion under Rule 37(c) definitely show fraudulent intent.

Section 4.07—Pleading Special Matters

A party must set forth in his pleading any matter constituting an avoidance or affirmative defense, including *res judicata,* collateral estoppel, waiver, duress, fraud and the statute of limitations. A mere denial in the responsive pleading will not be sufficient to raise any such issue.[34]

---

[29] Rule 37(c).

[30] Rule 37(c); but if the Commissioner fails to file such a motion, the allegations in the answer will be deemed to be denied. *Clark,* T.C. Memo 1955-252, ¶55,252 P-H Memo T.C.; *Sauer,* T.C. Memo 1964-174, ¶64,174 P-H Memo T.C.

[31] Rule 37(c).

[32] Rule 37(d); *Central National Bank,* 29 B.T.A. 530 (1933).

[33] Rule 38.

[34] Rule 39.

Section 4.08—Defenses and Objections Made by Pleading or by Motion

Every defense, in law or fact, to a claim for relief in any pleading must be asserted in the responsive pleading thereto if one is required, except that the following defenses may, at the option of the pleader be made by motion: (a) lack of jurisdiction; and (b) failure to state a claim upon which relief can be granted. If a pleading sets forth a claim for relief for which the adverse party is not required to serve a responsive pleading, he may assert at the trial any defense in law or fact to that claim for relief. If, on a motion asserting failure to state a claim upon which relief can be granted, matters outside the pleading are to be presented, the motion shall be treated as one for summary judgment and disposed of as provided in Rule 121, and the parties shall be given an opportunity to present all material made pertinent to a motion under Rule 121.[35]

Section 4.09—Amended and Supplemental Pleadings

As in practically all jurisdictions, a party may amend his pleading once as a matter of course at any time before a responsive pleading is served.[36] If the pleading is one to which no responsive pleading is permitted and the case has not been placed on a trial calendar, he may so amend it at any time within 30 days after it is served.[37] Otherwise, a party may amend his pleading only by leave of Court or by written consent of the adverse party; leave shall be given freely when justice so requires.[38] Remanded cases are governed by the same amendment rules as other cases.[39] As a matter of practice, the Court is very liberal in allowing amendments to pleadings so long as it can be shown that the other party is not harmed thereby. This is as it should be since liberal pleading rules have been invoked for many, many years in most courts.

---

[35] Rule 40.

[36] Rule 41(a).

[37] Rule 41(a).

[38] Rule 41(A); *Seaboard Oil Co.*, 1 B.T.A. 1259 (1925); *Neilson Estate*, T.C. Memo Op. Docket 14324 (1948) ¶48,185 P-H Memo T.C., but amendment granted over the Commissioner's objection in *Gilliam Mfg. Co.*, 2 B.T.A. 272 (1925); *American Smelting & Refining Co.*, 44 B.T.A. 131 (1941); *Buckeye Producing Co.*, 15 B.T.A. 435 (1929).

[39] *Chicago Railway Equipment Co.*, 13 B.T.A. 471 (1928), *aff'd in part and rev'd in part*, 39 F.2d 378, 8 AFTR 10511 (7th Cir., 1930), *rev'd*, 282 U.S. 295 (1931) 9 AFTR 590; *McDonald v. Commissioner*, 52 F.2d 920, 10 AFTR 511 (4th Cir., 1931), *rev'g and rem'g* 18 B.T.A. 800 (1930).

No amendments, however, should be allowed after expiration of the time for filing the petition which would involve conferring jurisdiction on the Court over a matter which otherwise would not come within the jurisdiction under the petition as then on file.[40] A motion for leave to amend a pleading must state the reasons for the amendment and should be accompanied by the proposed amendment.[41]

These provisions on amendments to pleadings do not represent a change in accustomed practice.

While normally pleadings are amended at the initiative of the parties, the Court may direct amendment on its own motion and Rule 41 is not intended to limit the latitude of the Court.[42]

A motion by the Commissioner to amend his answer to claim an increased deficiency must be timely made "at or before the hearing or a rehearing," under Section 6214(a).[43] As a party litigant, the Commissioner has no unqualified right to amend his answer, before or at the hearing, to claim an increased deficiency above that determined in the statutory notice, but must file an appropriate motion for leave to file similarly to a petitioner.[44] Obviously, the Court will treat the Commissioner as liberally as a petitioner in this regard. An amended answer, of course, may place the burden of proof upon the Commissioner, subject to the possible admission of the newly-pleaded facts under Rule 37(c).[45]

If the statutory notice specifies the details of the Commissioner's position, he should not be permitted to rely on a different, undisclosed ground without following the procedural Rules.[46] If the statutory notice is in broad, general terms, however, the Commissioner is given much greater latitude in advancing various contentions without

---

[40] Rule 41(a).

[41] Rule 41(a); better practice indicates the filing of a complete *new* petition, with all assignments of error and statement of facts which should be attached to the motion, although in particular cases amendments to the petition may suffice. *M. Morgenthau-Seixas, Inc.*, 25 B.T.A. 1235 (1932). Only pleadings will raise issues as to correct tax liability, not motions. *Mutual Lumber Co.*, 16 T.C. 370 (1951).

[42] Note to Rule 41(a); *Minnesota Tea Co.*, 296 U.S. 378 (1935), 16 AFTR 1258 and 302 U.S. 609 (1938), 19 AFTR 1258.

[43] *Rowan Drilling Co.*, 44 B.T.A. 189 (1941), *aff'd*, 130 F.2d 62, 29 AFTR 1050 (5th Cir., 1942); *Oster*, T.C. Memo 1964-335, ¶64,335 P-H Memo T.C.

[44] *Commissioner v. Erie Forge Co.*, 167 F.2d 71, 36 AFTR 896 (3rd Cir. 1948) (aff'g) T.C. Memo Op. Docket No. 2283 (1945) ¶45,384 P-H Memo T.C.; *Commissioner v. Long Estate*, 304 F.2d 136, 9 AFTR 2d 1755 (9th Cir. 1962), *aff'g* unreported T.C. order (1961).

[45] *Weaver* 32 T.C. 411 (1959), *aff'd*, 281 F.2d 238, 6 AFTR 2d 5191 (4th Cir. 1960); *Schneider Estate*, 29 T.C. 940 (1958); *Black*, 19 T.C. 474 (1952); *Corinblit*, T.C. Memo 1955-148, ¶55,148 P-H Memo T.C. (fraud penalties involved); *Accardi*, T.C. Memo 1957-73, ¶57,073 P-H Memo T.C. (transferee liability involved).

[46] *Swope* 51 T.C. 442 (1968); *Nash*, 31 T.C. 569 (1958); *Sorin*, 29 T.C. 959 (1958).

amending his answer.[47] The avoidance of surprise so as to unduly prejudice petitioner's trial position should be the Court's lodestone in issuing rulings on the Commissioner's motions to change positions or stake out new ground not entirely clear from the statutory notice.[48]

With respect to pleading amendments to conform to the evidence, when issues not raised by the pleadings are tried by express or implied consent of the parties, they will be treated in all respects as if they had been raised in the pleadings.[49] The Court, upon motion of any party at any time, may allow such amendment of the pleadings as may be necessary to cause them to conform to the evidence and to raise these issues, but failure to amend does not affect the result of the trial of these issues.[50]

If evidence is objected to at the trial on the ground that it is not within the issue as raised by a pleading, the Court may receive the evidence and at any time allow the pleadings to be amended to conform to the proof, and shall do so freely when justice so requires and the objecting party fails to satisfy the Court that the admission of such evidence would prejudice him in maintaining his position on the merits.[51] The amendment or amended pleadings permitted under Rule 41(d) shall be filed with the Court at the trial or with the Clerk in Washington within such time as the Court may fix.[52]

Upon motion of a party, the Court may, upon such terms as are just, permit him to file a supplemental pleading setting forth transactions or occurrences or events which have happened since the day of the pleading sought to be supplemented.[53] Permission may be granted even though the original pleading is defective in its statements of a claim for relief or defense. If the Court deems it advisable that the adverse party

---

[47] *Weaver,* 32 T.C. 411 (1959), *aff'd,* 281 F.2d 238, 6 AFTR 2d 5191 (4th Cir. 1960); *Payne,* 30 T.C. 1044 (1958); *Braunstein,* 36 T.C. 22 (1961), *aff'd,* 305 F.2d 949, 10 AFTR 2d 5125 (2nd Cir. 1962).

[48] *Lydon Estate,* T.C. Memo Op. Docket 25221 (1952) ¶52,331 P-H Memo T.C.

[49] Rule 41(b)(1); *A.B.C.D. Lands, Inc.,* 41 T.C. 840 (1964); *Decker v. Korth,* 219 F.2d 732, 47 AFTR 170 (10th C.A., 1955), *cert. denied,* 350 U.S. 830 (1955).

[50] Rule 41(b)(1). The Commissioner must amend his answer to conform to the proof or to raise a new issue, *Jahncke Service, Inc.,* 20 B.T.A. 837 (1930); otherwise, he may not claim an increased deficiency. *Burke,* T.C. Memo 1959-75, ¶59,075 P-H Memo T.C.

[51] Rule 41(b)(2); *Commissioner v. Finley,* 265 F.2d 885, 3 AFTR 2d 1328 (10th Cir. 1959), *aff'g* T.C. Memo (1957–16) ¶57,016 P-H Memo T.C., where amendment was filed several months after taking testimony. *But note* such cases as *Pierce Oil Corp.,* 30 B.T.A. 469 (1934) and *I. Frank Sons Co., Inc.,* 22 B.T.A. 40 (1931) holding the statute of limitations must be timely pleaded, not after trial and the filing of briefs. *But cf.* in a fraud case, *Weir v. Commissioner,* 283 F.2d 675, 6 AFTR 2d 5770 (6th Cir. 1960), T.C. Memo (1958-158) ¶58,158 P-H Memo T.C.

[52] Rule 41(b)(3).

[53] Rule 41(c).

plead to the supplemental pleading, it shall so direct, specifying the time therefor.[54] These provisions were adopted from FRCP 15(d) and represent an innovation in the Court's practice.

When an amendment of a pleading is permitted, it shall relate back to the time of the filing of that pleading unless the Court shall order otherwise, either on motion of a party or on its own initiative.[55]

It is too late to raise a new issue orally at a hearing, or in a brief, because the parties are entitled to have the opportunity to prepare for trial on factual issues.[56] If the Commissioner raises a new issue, which, of course, in this context means an issue not properly raised by the pleadings, "surprise" should be promptly claimed by the petitioner.[57] The courts have distinguished between the case where the Commissioner is trying to defend a statutory notice adjustment on grounds other than those originally set forth, and one where he is asserting an entirely new adjustment, which will not be treated as properly before the Court.[58]

These provisions of Rule 41 bring the Tax Court's amendatory practice into conformity with the other federal tax trial courts, thus representing some departure from prior practice.

Section 4.10—Motions Generally

Motion practice in the Tax Court now conforms generally with that under the Federal Rules of Civil Procedure. The Tax Court practice represents a gradual evolution over its 50 years of existence from a rather restrictive attitude to one of much more liberality, both in application of legal principles and also in flexibility in the locations of the hearings thereon and similar matters.

Except for motions made during trial, an application to the Court for an order shall be by motion in writing, which shall state with particularity the grounds therefor and shall also set forth the relief or

---

[54] Rule 41(c).

[55] Rule 41(d).

[56] *Rogers,* 31 B.T.A. 994 (1955), *aff'g, rev'g and rem'g* 107 F.2d 394, 23 AFTR 895 (2nd Cir. 1939); *H.D. Crosswell, Inc.,* 6 B.T.A. 1315 (1927). *Cf. Jamieson Associates, Inc.,* 37 B.T.A. 92 (1938); *Ruge,* 26 T.C. 138 (1956).

[57] *Moore v. Commissioner,* 202 F.2d 45, 43 AFTR 253 (5th Cir. 1953), *aff'g* 17 T.C. 1030 (1951); *Timanus,* 32 T.C. 631 (1959), *aff'd,* 278 F.2d 297, 5 AFTR 2d 1447 (4th Cir. 1960); likewise, where one party contends the other has abandoned an issue. *Boe v. Commissioner,* 307 F.2d 339, 342, 10AFTR2d 5458 (9th Cir. 1962), *aff'd* 35 T.C. 720 (1961).

[58] *Bair,* 16 T.C. 90, 98 (1951), *aff'd,* 199 F.2d 589, 42 AFTR 732 (2nd Cir. 1952); *J.T. Slocomb Co. v. Commissioner,* 334 F.2d 269, 14 AFTR 2d 5086 (2nd Cir. 1964), *aff'g* 38 T.C. 752 (1962), contrasted with *Carter,* T.C. Memo 1957-65, ¶57,065 P-H Memo T.C., *aff'd on this ground but rev'd and remanded on other grounds,* 257 F.2d 595, 2 AFTR 2d 5160 (5th Cir. 1958).

order sought.[59] If there is no objection to a motion in whole or in part, the absence of such objection shall be stated on the motion, preferably over the signature of the other party or his counsel.[60] As a matter of actual practice, the office of Regional Counsel representing respondent in a particular case is most cooperative in either joining in motions or endorsing motions as not being subject to objection. This cooperative attitude greatly reduces the necessity for written responses or oral arguments on most motions. Of course, there still remain many types of motions, such as a motion for more definite statement, which cannot be the subject of endorsement without objection.

In the discretion of the Court, a motion may be disposed of in one or more of three ways. First, the Court may take action after directing that a written response be filed. In that event, the motion is served upon the opposing party who must file a response within such period as the Court may direct.[61] Written response to a motion shall conform, of course, to the same requirements of form and style as applied to motions.[62] Second, the Court may take action after directing a hearing which normally is held in Washington but which, on the Court's own motion or upon the written request of any party to the motion, may be heard in any other location which serves the convenience of the parties and the Court.[63] Third, the Court may take such action as it deems appropriate, on such prior notice, if any, which the Court may consider reasonable. The action of the Court may be taken with or without written response, hearing or attendance of a party to the motion at the hearing.[64]

These three methods of disposing of a motion illustrate the flexibility of the Court, which is also typical of a federal district court in dealing with motions. For example, the Court may dispose of a motion without a written response and without a hearing, but frequently the Court prefers both a written response and a hearing. The liberalized evolution of the Court's motion practice is indicated most strongly by its willingness to hear motions wherever one or more of the parties may prefer. Ordinarily a taxpayer will prefer to have a motion heard elsewhere than in Washington to save travel expense, and now the Court is quite willing to assign a judge to hear such a motion when he is in that vicinity, typically when he is enroute to or from a trial calendar that would take him near the desired location, and, of course, when a reporter and courtroom are available.

---

[59] Rule 50(a).

[60] Rule 50(b).

[61] Rule 50(b)(1).

[62] Rule 50(b)(1).

[63] Rule 50(b)(2).

[64] Rule 50(b)(3).

As to attendance at a motion hearing, if a motion is noticed for hearing, a party to the motion may, prior to or at the time for such hearing, submit a written statement of his position together with any supporting documents. This statement may be submitted in lieu of, or in addition to, attendance at the hearing.[65] Again in actual practice most parties do not need to travel to Washington to present a response to a motion of a simple nature and usually a written response thereto will suffice. It should be noted, however, that respondent can most conveniently have his Washington counsel appear at a hearing on a motion there, which means that respondent is always represented by counsel at a Washington motion hearing. Hence, a taxpayer's counsel refrains from appearing at a Washington motion hearing at his peril since he knows that respondent's counsel will be there arguing in person. If the motion is of any importance or difficulty, it well behooves petitioner's counsel to be there in order to meet any arguments of respondent's counsel which might not be in writing. Again, this is a matter of judgment on the part of counsel because if he feels his written response is adequate, he can save the time and expense of a trip to Washington to appear at the hearing. The best solution would seem to be for taxpayer's counsel to request the motion hearing to take place at his preferred location rather than in Washington in order that he may appear and make his oral presentation. There is no substitute for person-to-person confrontation before the Court if the motion is important or difficult.

If there are defects in a pleading to which a motion or order is directed, filing of a proper pleading correcting the defects may eliminate the necessity of a hearing on such a motion.[66] Again in actual practice this is the preferred solution: take action swiftly with a properly amended pleading and avoid lengthy motion disagreements which frequently have little bearing on the merits of the case. Usually, the local attorney for the respondent will call or otherwise contact petitioner's counsel and point out the defects in the pleadings to which a motion might otherwise be required, and thus give counsel an opportunity to cure the defect without even a motion being filed. The same course of action also applies with respect to many other situations which otherwise would require motions by respondent. Throughout the years, a high degree of cooperation has existed between counsel for respondent and counsel for petitioners in this regard, thus substantially reducing the motion load of the Court.

The variety of possible motions is as varied in the Tax Court as in a federal district court or the Court of Claims. Motions might include,

---

[65] Rule 50(c).

[66] Rule 50(d).

but are not limited to: for judgment on the pleadings;[67] to vacate dismissal;[68] to reopen the record, following the filing by the judge of Findings and Opinion, to receive additional evidence;[69] to correct a rendered opinion;[70] for reconsideration of a case;[71] for an adjournment or an extension of time in a myriad of circumstances; to withhold judgment pending decisions in other cases;[72] for change in designation of the place of hearing; to sever for preliminary determination the issue of jurisdiction or some other legal question before proceeding with a trial on the facts; for substitution of parties or counsel; for subpoena; to withdraw a settlement stipulation;[73] to amend the pleadings to conform to the evidence; and to correct the Court's findings of fact and opinion.[74] This is not meant to be an all-inclusive list but simply illustrative. Motions are as variegated as imaginative counsel create.

Considerable sophisticated motion practice has arisen with respect to motions to shift the burden of proof to respondent under Section 534 involving unreasonable accumulation of earnings and profits. (Rule 142(e), which will be discussed in Chapter 9 *infra.*)

Section 4.11—Motion for More Definite Statement

Rule 51 provides for a motion for more definite statement or, as frequently called, a motion for a bill of particulars. This motion lies in the case of a pleading to which a responsive pleading is permitted or required which is so vague or ambiguous that a party cannot reasonably be required to frame a responsive pleading.[75] The motion, of course, must point out the defects complained of and the details desired. Rule 51 refers to Rules 70 and 90 for other procedures available to narrow the issues or to elicit further information as to the facts involved or the positions of the parties.

---

[67] *Lewis,* T.C. Memo 1958-69, ¶58,069 P-H Memo T.C.; *United Motor Coach Co.,* 22 T.C. 578 (1954).

[68] *Saigh,* 26 T.C. 171 (1956).

[69] *Willett,* T.C. Memo 1958-20, ¶58,020 P-H Memo T.C., *aff'd,* 277 F.2d 586 5 AFTR 2d 1223 (6th Cir. 1960); *Farber,* 44 T.C. 408 (1965).

[70] *Baldwin Estate,* T.C. Memo 1961-89, ¶61,089 P-H Memo T.C.

[71] *Richardson,* T.C. Memo 1958-59, ¶58,059 P-H Memo T.C., *aff'd in part and rev'd in part on other grounds,* 264 F.2d 400, 3 AFTR 2d 833 (9th Cir. 1959).

[72] *Sneed,* 33 B.T.A. 478 (1935); *Vose Estate,* 20 T.C. 597 (1953).

[73] *Spector,* 42 T.C. 110 (1964).

[74] *Rolle Estate,* T.C. Memo 1965-92, ¶65,092 P-H Memo T.C.

[75] Rule 51(a); *Gutterman Strauss Co.,* 1 B.T.A. 243 (1924); *Biggs,* T.C. Memo 1968-240, ¶68,240 P-H Memo T.C.

Whether there will be an order to make the pleading more definite is a matter within the discretion of the Court, and in actual practice the Court is more likely to deny than to grant such a motion. For example, if the respondent can study his administrative record, such as the revenue agent's report, and accompanying exhibits, the protest, if any, and the statutory notice of deficiency, he may well be able to ascertain the theory of the taxpayer's case, even though the petition itself may be rather unenlightening. In such a situation, counsel for the respondent seldom files a motion for more definite statement but proceeds to file his responsive answer based on his overall knowledge of the controversy.

There are situations where a pleading may be sufficiently definite or represent a sufficient statement, and yet the adverse party may be entitled to further information for other reasons, such as to frame an affirmative defense. In that event, other procedures, such as those provided by Rules 70 and 90, might be viewed as preferable to a motion for a more definite statement.[76] This philosophy illustrates the attitude of the Court to discourage motions for more definite statement if at all possible.

If the required response is not made within such period as the Court may direct, the Court may strike the pleading to which the motion is directed or may make such other order as it deems just.[77]

This Rule is intended to compel litigants to set forth their positions in sufficient detail to inform the opposing party of the nature of the claim or defense being made. Naturally, the purpose of this Rule is to limit the proof and the scope of examination at the trial and prevent surprise. The Court has denied the respondent's motion for a more definite statement where its only purpose seemed to be to secure evidence to offset the evidence which might be presented by the petitioner.[78]

Although it is recognized that most answers filed by the respondent are uninformative and consist primarily of general denials of the petition, even though available proof in the Commissioner's files might permit a more responsive answer, a motion for a more definite statement in the answer generally is not looked upon with favor by the Court unless the petitioner can show that the desired information will simplify the preparation and presentation of the case. Rather than filing such a motion

---

[76] Note to Rule 51(a).

[77] Rule 51(b).

[78] *Gutterman Strauss Co.*, 1 B.T.A. 243 (1924); *Schlossberg,* 2 B.T.A. 683 (1925).

in seeking an amended answer, proceeding by way of Rules 70 and 90 may be the wiser course of action.[79]

The Court has held that where the Commissioner is ordered to make a further and better statement of his defense he cannot refuse to do so on the ground that the Government's disclosure of its evidence before the Tax Court prior to a pending criminal trial might impair prosecution by affording the petitioner an opportunity to develop defenses and by minimizing the possible effectiveness of cross-examination if he should take the stand.[80] Thus, the Court has held that the trial of the civil case is independent of the criminal action.[81] Hence, the failure or refusal of the Commissioner to comply with the Court's order to file an amended answer making a more complete statement of his defense under such circumstances may result in the answer being stricken and such action will be sustained on appeal if it is not an abuse of discretion.[82] This position of the Court has very recently been re-enunciated in a case involving the allegation of "tainted evidence" in a criminal fraud examination.[83]

Section 4.12–Motion to Strike

Upon motion made by a party before responding to a pleading or, if no responsive pleading is permitted by the Rules, upon motion made by a party within 30 days after the service of the pleading, or upon the Court's own initiative at any time, the Court may order stricken from any pleading any insufficient claim or defense or any redundant, immaterial, impertinent, frivolous or scandalous matter. Likewise, the Court may order stricken any such objectionable matter from briefs, documents or any other papers on responses filed with the Court.[84]

---

[79] Failure to move for a "better statement" in the answer under Rule 51 will not jeopardize petitioner's challenge of the Commissioner's determination during the hearing.. *Clark v. Commissioner,* 266 F.2d 698, 3 AFTR 2d 1333 (9th Cir. 1959), *aff'g and rem'g* T.C. Memo 1957-129, ¶57,129 P-H Memo T.C. *See also X-Ray, Inc.* T.C. Memo 1959-118, ¶59,118 P-H Memo T.C.

[80] *Commissioner v. Licavoli,* 252 F.2d 268, 1 AFTR 2d 881 (6th Cir. 1958), *aff'g* T.C. order and accompanying memorandum entered June 14, 1956, ¶56,187 P-H Memo T.C.

[81] See the enlightening orders of the Court in fraud cases, including net worth cases, in *Lassoff,* T.C. Memo Op. Docket 46030 (1953); *Fay,* T.C. Memo Op. Docket 8730 (1953) ¶53,012 P-H Memo T.C.; *Coleman,* T.C. Memo Op. Docket 45787 (1953). The Note at 10 Tax L. Rev. 267, 272 (1955) contains a copy of the order which the Court has developed in net worth fraud cases.

[82] *Commissioner v. Licavoli,* 252 F.2d 268, 1 AFTR 2d 881 (6th Cir. 1958), *aff'g* T.C. order and accompanying memorandum entered June 14, 1956, ¶56,187 P-H Memo T.C.

[83] *Suarez,* 58 T.C. 792 (1972); final decision 61 T.C. 841 (1974), Government's appeal to 5th Cir. *dismissed nolle pros.* December 4, 1974.

[84] Rule 52.

Section 4.13—Motion to Dismiss

A case may be dismissed for cause upon motion of a party or upon the Court's initiative. The chief ground for granting a motion to dismiss is the failure to file a timely petition. Failure to properly prosecute a petition is also a ground for dismissal.[85]

Section 4.14—Timely Filing and Joinder of Motions

Motions must be made timely, unless the Court shall permit otherwise. Generally, motions shall be separately stated and not joined together except that motions under Rule 51 (motions for more definite statement) and Rule 52 (motion to strike) directed to the same pleading or other paper may be joined.[86]

Section 4.15—Motion to Withdraw Petition

A motion to withdraw a petition rarely comes before the Court and usually it receives a negative response. In a recent case, the Court denied such a motion and in its opinion extensively reviewed the applicable legal principles.[87] The Court assumed that the motion was seeking to withdraw the petition so that the petitioner could pay the deficiency and sue for refund. After discussing the applicable cases, the Court concluded that the respondent had been prejudiced by the filing of the petition in that he had been precluded from assessing and collecting the deficiency he claimed to be owing. Under these circumstances the Court held that the petitioner could not be permitted to withdraw his petition without prejudice.

Section 4.16—Motion for Leave to Intervene

The Court has discretionary power to permit intervention when in its discretion such action is necessary to administer justice under the facts of a particular case.[88] For example, intervention has been permitted

---

[85]Rule 53. A decision dismissing the proceeding shall be considered as the Court's decision "that the deficiency is the amount determined by the Secretary or his delegate." Code Section 7459(d).

[86]Rule 54.

[87]*Ming Estate*, 62 T.C. 519 (1974).

[88]*Levy Trust v. Commissioner*, 341 F.2d 93, 15 AFTR 2d 1304 (5th Cir. 1965), *aff'g* unreported T.C. order. Rule 216.

where the executors of an estate filed a petition contesting a deficiency in estate tax on the ground that the value of a claim against a certain individual had been erroneously determined, the individual having agreed to pay any estate tax resulting from the inclusion of the claim in the decedent's gross estate.[89] The individual was permitted to intervene upon his showing that he had an interest in the estate, had agreed to pay the tax and was under the necessity of showing, contrary to the interest of the executors, that the claim had no value. The Court has also allowed intervention in a case where, at the time the original petition, purporting to be that of the petitioner, was filed by its president, the corporation had been dissolved and the liquidator was the only person authorized to act on behalf of the corporation.[90]

It should be noted, however, that intervention is an unusual remedy and that it must be an exceptional case to cause the Court to grant a motion for intervention by a third party.

Section 4.17–Postponement of Trial

The filing of a motion of any nature does not constitute cause for postponement of a trial.[91] If a petitioner desires to postpone a trial, he should file a motion under Rule 134 governing continuances of cases which have been placed on a trial calendar. The provisions of that rule will, of course, govern the granting or denial of such a motion.

Section 4.18–Service of Motions

The rules applicable to service of pleadings generally apply to service of motions.[92]

---

89 *Central Union Trust Co.*, 18 B.T.A. 300 (1929).

90 *Louisiana Naval Store, Inc.*, 18 B.T.A. 533 (1929).

91 Rule 50(e).

92 Rule 50(f).

CHAPTER 5

Parties

Section 5.01—Proper Parties: Capacity

A CASE SHALL BE BROUGHT by and in the name of the person against whom the Commissioner determined the deficiency (in the case of a notice of deficiency) or liability (in the case of a notice of liability), or by and with the full descriptive name of the fiduciary entitled to institute a case on behalf of such person.[1] A case timely brought is not subject to dismissal on the ground that it is not properly brought on behalf of a party until a reasonable time has been allowed after objection for ratification by such party of the bringing of the case; and such ratification shall have the same effect as if the case had been properly brought by such party.[2] Where the deficiency or liability is determined against more than one person in the notice by the Commissioner, only such of those persons who shall duly act to bring a case shall be deemed a party or parties.[3]

This rule should serve as ample protection against the harsh effect of a dismissal where a technical defect has occurred in the institution of a case on behalf of the proper party. As the rule makes clear, where the intention is to file a petition on behalf of a party, the spirit and intent of this provision permit correction of errors as to the proper party or his identity in a petition otherwise timely and correct. This liberality of treatment with respect to a possible defective party petitioner is repeated throughout the Rules in order to evidence the

---

[1] Rule 60(a) and Rule 23(a)(1). *See also* Rules, Title XXI.

[2] Rule 60(a); Note.

[3] Rule 60(a); Note.

Court's pervasive desire to prevent in all possible cases the dismissal of a petition and the consequent result of the taxpayer having to pay the tax immediately and then sue for refund, rather than to have his day in court on a petition where he has shown his intent to file a petition but has erred in a technical manner.

With respect to every petition, the Commissioner shall be named the respondent.[4] Since this is the case, Tax Court decisions need only be cited in the name of the petitioner as there is the same adversary, or respondent, in every case filed in the Court.

The capacity of an individual, other than one acting in a fiduciary or other representative capacity, to engage in litigation in the Court shall be determined by the law of his domicile.[5] The capacity of a corporation to engage in such litigation shall be determined by the law of the state under which it was organized.[6] The capacity of a fiduciary or other representative to litigate in the Court shall be determined in accordance with the law of the jurisdiction from which he derives his authority.[7]

Whenever an infant or incompetent person has a representative, such as a general guardian, committee, conservator, or other like fiduciary, the representative may bring a case or defend in the Court on behalf of the infant or incompetent person.[8] If an infant or incompetent person does not have a duly appointed representative, he may act by his next friend or by a guardian *ad litem.*[9] Where a party attempts to represent himself and, in the opinion of the Court, there is a serious question as to his competence to do so, the Court, if it deems justice so requires, may continue the case until appropriate steps have been taken to adjudicate the question by a court having jurisdiction so to do, or may take such other action as it deems proper.[10]

Section 5.02—Permissive Joinder of Parties

This is one of the most important innovations in the new Rules which should be a great benefit to many petitioners. Any per-

---

[4]Rule 60(b).
[5]Rule 60(c); Note.
[6]Rule 60(c).
[7]Rule 60(c).
[8]Rule 60(d); Note.
[9]Rule 60(d).
[10]Rule 60(d).

son to whom a notice of deficiency or notice of liability has been issued may join with any other such person in filing a petition in the Court which is timely with respect to the notice issued to each joining party.[11] Even after a petition has been filed, any such person may join therein with the consent of all the petitioners and the permission of the Court.[12]

Joinder is permitted only where all or part of each participating party's tax liability arises out of the same transaction, occurrence, or series of transactions and occurrences and, in addition, there is a common question of law or fact relating to those parties.[13] It is believed that if there is a common question of law or fact relating to those parties who are filing a joint petition, the presence of other questions of law or fact involved in the case of one or the other of such joining petitioners will not prevent the filing of a joint petition. In other words, the presence of one common question of law or fact arising out of the same transaction, occurrence, or series of transactions and occurrences, should be sufficient to warrant the filing of a joint petition.

Under past practice, frequently multiple petitioners to the number of one hundred, or even more, were required to file separate petitions and each had to pay a separate filing fee. The paper work attendant upon this proliferation of petition filing was enormous in such situations. Even when only four or five petitioners were required to file separate petitions, the paper work was burdensome. The Court has now adopted this modernizing rule which meets the test of good practice and common sense and which should prove a boon to the practicing bar.

Since January 1, 1974, the reported cases indicate many joint petitions involving ten or more separate petitioners in one petition. The situation arises frequently, for example, with respect to partners and also shareholders who share a common question of law or fact. The provision allowing petitioners who file a later petition to join in a prior petition also should be very helpful.

As a corollary to Rule 61(a) permitting joinder of parties in one petition, Rule 61(b) provides for severance of parties under appropriate conditions. The Court may make such orders as will prevent a party from being embarrassed, delayed, or put to expense by the inclusion of a party; or may order separate trials or make other orders to prevent delay or prejudice; or may limit the trial to the claims of one or more parties, either dropping other parties from the case on such terms as are just or

[11]Rule 61(a); Note. *See also* Rule 215.

[12]Rule 61(a).

[13]Rule 61(a) and Rule 34.

holding in abeyance the proceedings with respect to them.[14] Any claim by or against a party may be severed and proceeded with separately.[15]

The approach of this Rule is to give very broad scope to joinder within the terms of the Rule, but at the same time to make clear that the Court has retained ultimate, very broad discretion to sever the parties or their claims to the extent it considers appropriate. Such severance or separation may be made by the Court in its discretion, with or without a motion. In short, the Court has stated in no uncertain terms that it will retain control of the pleadings affecting joinder of parties in order to accomplish substantial justice.

Section 5.03—Misjoinder of Parties

Misjoinder of parties is not ground for dismissal of a case.[16] The Court may order a severance on such terms as are just.[17]

Section 5.04—Substitution of Parties; Change or Correction in Name

If a petitioner dies, the Court, on motion of a party or the decedent's successor or representative or on its own initiative, may order substitution of the proper parties.[18] If a party becomes incompetent, the Court, on motion of a party or the incompetent's representative or on its own initiative, may order his representative to proceed with the case.[19]

On motion made where a fiduciary or representative is changed, the Court may order substitution of the proper successors.[20] The Court, on motion of a party or on its own initiative, may order the substitution of proper parties for other cause.[21] On motion of a party or on its own initiative, the Court may order a change of, or correction in, the name or title of a party.[22]

---

[14]Rule 61(b); Note.
[15]Rule 61(b)
[16]Rule 62; Note.
[17]Rule 62.
[18]Rule 63(a).
[19]Rule 63(b); Note.
[20]Rule 63(c); Note.
[21]Rule 63(d).
[22]Rule 63(e).

CHAPTER 6

Pretrial Practice, Including Settlement Aspects

Section 6.01–General

UP TO THIS POINT in the Court's procedure, all has been prologue. You have chosen the Tax Court as the forum to resist the Commissioner's determination of a tax deficiency, and perhaps an addition to tax as well; you have prepared and timely filed an adequate petition for the proper party; the Court has jurisdiction of your case; no interlocutory motions are pending; the Commissioner has timely filed his answer; you have timely filed a reply, if one is necessary; you breathe a sigh of relief (or do you?), and the case is at last at issue before the Court on the merits, a process which may have taken several years from the beginning of the examining officer's investigation, depending on your choice of administrative procedure. Now what? To explain "now what?" will be the purpose of this chapter.

A preliminary suggestion at this point is to tuck away the case file for a few days (or a few weeks) before you open it again on your desk for further intensive work. This interim rest period will enable you the better to see the forest from the trees, as you have been engrossed in the minute details of the case, especially the preparation of the petition. Now you need to get a broad perspective of your entire case, so that you can plan strategy and tactics with a sharper focus on the overall picture.

Also at this point "now what?" will depend greatly on when you entered the case and, thus, the extent of your knowledge of the facts and the applicable law. If you were employed very early, ideally when the return examinations started, you should already have an intensive knowledge of both the facts and law. You may have conferred with the client or other knowledgeable persons a few, or many times; you may have conferred with the examiner's Group Manager; you may have represented your client in a district conference and an Appellate Division conference; and you may have consulted with possible expert witnesses, if appropriate.

Unfortunately, in too many cases for the taxpayer's good, you may not have been employed until a late procedural stage, perhaps after receipt of the 30-day letter from the District Director transmitting the report of examination, or even after receipt of the notice of deficiency.

In rare cases you might have prepared, or assisted in preparing, the return, or returns, in question. If so, you should have superior knowledge of the facts and law.

As the two most critical aspects of an air flight are the take-off and the landing, so the two most critical aspects of a Tax Court case are the pretrial phase (the take-off) and the actual trial (the landing.) Failure of smooth functioning in either aspect usually spells trouble. Of the two, the first is believed to be the most critical, involving as it does both settlement negotiations and trial preparation. The first phase sets the stage for all that follows. Mistakes here are difficult to correct whthout leaving at least a trace of an adverse impression. So, you should really bear down at this stage and give the case your best thinking. Try to devise the most persuasive presentation of the facts; put yourself in your opponent's shoes and imagine what would most impress you; let your creative talents work as you build your case step by step, logically, and you hope, convincingly.

When you are still in this soul-searching, overview stage of the case, remember that most of the facts are within your possession, or at least readily accessible. This is the aspect of a federal civil tax case which is perhaps the most unlike other civil litigation, where facts are ordinarily in the hands of both parties. What facts respondent has were largely obtained by the examining officer, or during administrative conferences. If you can envision the flow of the facts as coming from a hose, you have the nozzle in your hands and thus can play them about almost at will, as you would play the water from a real hose. Here is where the advocate's true skill, ability and resourcefulness become most evident: in his thorough gathering of the relevant facts, followed by his adroit, timely and persuasive presentation to the Government representatives. For it can never be overemphasized—the initiative rests with the petitioner, a tactical advantage which should be fully exploited. If you lag in seizing and holding the initiative, an aggressive Government representative will likely do so, because tax cases abhor a vacuum, just as Nature does.

Along this same line of thought, remember what is at stake in every Tax Court case—an item that either appears in a tax return, or should have appeared there, according to the Commissioner. Again this truism reflects your advantage in what should be your initial superior knowledge of the case. For example, the Commissioner has typically said in an income tax deficiency notice that an item of income was not properly reported or that an item was improperly deducted. Who should know the facts for either income or deductions better than the taxpayer or his representatives? But too often, through carelessness, lethargy, ineptitude, or a dozen other reasons, plaintiff's counsel allows his initial tactical advantage to deteriorate and soon finds himself on the defensive. The origin of the well-worn football truism—"the best defense is a good offense"—may be shrouded in antiquity, but its teaching applies to tax cases as well. If you fail to exploit your initial offensive advantage as plaintiff's counsel with potential possession of most, if not all, relevant facts, you may soon find yourself on the defensive.

Section 6.02—Preliminary Preparatory Steps

But you may properly ask—how do I seize and hold the offensive at this stage? One obvious answer is to stop and prepare a skeleton trial brief *now,* not after the case has progressed closer to the actual trial stage. This first draft need not be exhaustive, but rather a checklist of the most salient factors, pro and con, for your guidance as you begin the settlement and trial consideration on parallel tracks. For here you must realize that the vast majority of Tax Court cases—between 80 percent and 90 percent—are settled without trial, and that many issues are settled even in cases requiring the trial of one or more issues. Settlement is the name of the game in tax cases, as in all civil litigation, and trial is the exception, not the rule.

Note that typically tax cases involve multiple issues, or adjustments by the Commissioner. Such cases peculiarly lend themselves to settlement because of the obvious opportunity of trading off issues as compared to single-issue cases. It is often a practical misnomer to refer to a Tax Court *case,* when in reality it should be thought of as *cases,* even though it bears only one docket number.

Your skeleton trial brief should alert you to gaps in your evidentiary material and strengths and weaknesses in your legal position on each issue. Some issues, such as deduction for officers' compensation, may be entirely factual, with little or no legal research required. Other issues, such as the correct basis of assets acquired by a corporation from another corporation, may be entirely legal, thus requiring extensive research, if not undertaken at an earlier stage. Whichever the situation as to required factual development or legal research, now, now, now is the time to get busy, to bear down, to know your case inside out and outside in. In the words of General Nathan Bedford Forrest, who led cavalry units for the late Confederacy: "Get there fustest with the mostest." Time spent right here will pay large dividends when you first go to the conference table with the Government representatives. Their first impression of you and your mastery of the case will be most important, although not crucial. Certainly you can later overcome a poor initial showing, but why not put your best foot forward, when it's just as easy that way?

You may believe that you have adequately gathered the facts at an earlier stage, typically when you were preparing the petition. In most cases, however, additional facts, or refinements thereof, will be discovered upon further study.

In addition, you must now flesh out the facts with the actual evidence. Most tax cases are proved chiefly by documentary evidence. To the extent still necessary at this stage, you should obtain legible copies of all pertinent documents and accounting records. You must try to find out exactly what documentary evidence was obtained by the examining officer or was furnished the Government after the examination. Obviously, all documentary evidence will be necessary for both settlement and trial, so this work cannot be wasted effort.

As your assembly of facts and legal research continues, your overall knowledge of the case should grow, which in turn should lead to wisdom in strategical handling. Your evaluation of each issue for possible settlement should be broadened and sharpened as you do this work. Except in the rarest of issues, such as tax-exempt questions, recurring issues or legal issues where you feel the law is overwhelmingly with you, always think first in terms of settlement, not trial. It will usually serve your client best. It is also what the Government representatives are first considering, despite rumors to the contrary. The Commissioner is not spoiling for a fight, as the saying goes, in most cases. Exceptions exist, of course, as in prime issue cases, but even there you can often achieve settlement if you skillfully strive.

Section 6.03–Settlement Negotiations Begin

In the cry of "Arnie's Army" (Arnold Palmer, of course), "the game is on." You have mastered the facts and law and now feel you are ready to more than hold your own in verbal combat–what now?

As counsel of record, you will receive a form letter, or a phone call, from the assigned conferee in the Branch Office of the Appellate Division having jurisdiction of your case, inviting a conference to explore the possibility of settlement. The suggested conference date has been previously cleared with the trial attorney in the appropriate Branch Office, your counterpart. If the suggested conference date is inconvenient, another will be chosen and you are now ready to go to the conference table.

As pointed out in Chapter 1, soon after the enactment of the 16th Amendment it became apparent to the administrative officers charged with the responsibilities thereunder that adequate settlement machinery and procedure must be created to deal with the increasing volume of taxpayer complaints about proposed assessments of additional liability. Originally the pay first–file refund claim – and then refund suit was the only method for redressing a tax wrong. With the creation of the United States Board of Tax Appeals in 1924, an independent tribunal in the Executive Branch was created to act as the final forum for redressing such wrongs on a litigate first–pay later basis. But there had also to be created at the same time an administrative process for screening such disputes before reaching the Board or it would have been swamped by the incoming volume of cases.

Hence, there was created in the Internal Revenue Service a predecessor organization to the present Appellate Division, which by various names functioned on a national basis in Washington, D.C., but also traveled to different cities throughout the country on occasion as the Board would hold hearings in such cities. Efforts would be made at that time to reach settlements in as many cases as possible, but it was soon realized that this procedure was cumbersome and unwieldy. In the late 1930's, therefore, the Service began to decentralize this appellate settlement procedure with the designated title of Technical Staff, having offices located in major cities throughout the country. Trial attorneys in the office of the Chief Counsel of the Service were likewise decentralized throughout the country to serve as legal counsel to the Appellate Division. Decentralization gradually proceeded until completion just prior to World War II. All such field offices, known as Division offices and sub-offices thereunder, were then functioning officially.

In more recent times, the name was changed from Technical Staff to Appellate Division, and the "Divisions" were first changed to "Districts" and then to "Regions", their present name, with seven regions, each having one or more branch offices in major cities throughout the country. In most cities, there are both Appellate Division and Regional

Counsel offices, although in some smaller cities there is only an Appellate Division office served by Regional Counsel attorneys from some other larger city in the region.

Not only are the two offices usually housed in the same location, but of course they work very closely together in all respects. Their relationship essentially is that of attorney-client. The Appellate Division, as the client, has the primary settlement jurisdiction and the Regional Counsel's office has the concurring settlement jurisdiction. If a case is not settled, the Appellate Division loses all settlement jurisdiction at the time of the call of the Tax Court calendar on which a case is set for trial and Regional Counsel assumes sole settlement jurisdiction.

If your office is in a major city, you will likely have an Appellate Division and Regional Counsel's office there, which means that it is most convenient for you to participate in conferences with those offices. All settlement conferences are, of course, joint with both the Appellate Division conferee and the Regional Counsel attorney assigned to your case. If you do not live in a major city, your travel will likely be short because there is at least one Appellate Division and Regional Counsel's office in almost every populous state and in some states there are two, as in California with Los Angeles and San Francisco. This can be quite important if two or more conferences are required in your case in order to minimize time and expense. Naturally you should try to accomplish as much in one conference as possible in order to minimize the number of conferences. Although the appellate conferee and the trial attorney are cooperative in arranging multiple conferences, they also prefer to limit the number of conferences so as to conserve their time and permit it to be spent on other cases.

You will find the appellate conferee and the trial attorney to be courteous and eager to learn all the facts and to hear your points of law. They will always meet you halfway in your presentation.

At the regional level there are an Assistant Regional Commissioner, Appellate, and a Regional Counsel, who are responsible for the operations of their entire region, which may include several offices. There is an Appellate Branch Chief in charge of the appellate conferees in each branch office, and his counterpart is the Assistant Regional Counsel in charge of the trial attorneys.

Who are the appellate conferees? They are career Internal Revenue Service officials, most of whom began as examining officers and were promoted to their present positions. Some have served previously as District conferees, but many were promoted directly from the position of examining officer. Some tend to specialize in estate and gift tax matters, but all are versed in the income tax cases. They are a cross-section of career Government tax specialists, just as the practitioners who confer with them are a cross-section of the federal tax bar. They have one function and one only, namely, to settle cases and they strive to that end. They are resourceful in devising settlement techniques and they try to have an open and impartial mind in weighing the respective strengths and weaknesses of the parties.

The Appellate Division is the only Internal Revenue Service agency permitted to settle cases on the basis of litigating hazards regardless of the amount involved. This authority applies to non-Tax Court cases on protest, as well as Tax Court cases. Regional counsel attorneys rarely participate in non-Tax Court cases, and then only at the special request of the Appellate Division. Many conferees are expert accountants or law school graduates and members of the Bar, although it must be understood that they are not trial attorneys. They are skilled in analyzing and interpreting the facts and the law; the trial of the case before the Tax Court is the sole province of the Regional Counsel's office.

Like any other tax specialist, they will be most impressed with your full knowledge of the facts and the law and your clear exposition thereof at the conference table. One of the great beauties of the conference table is its informality, permitting facts to be presented in an easy, even "folksy" way, as contrasted with the much more formal manner required in the Court. Likewise, arguments on the fact and on the law can be much more quickly presented at the conference table than in the more legalistic surroundings of the court room.

All in all, it was a happy day for the American taxpayer when the Service early devised the Appellate Division technique at the inception of the United States Board of Tax Appeals. The two offices have gone hand in hand for a bit more than 50 successful years. Since between 8,000 and 10,000 new cases are filed with the Court each year, it could not handle this tremendous volume without a settlement-minded agency, in the form of the Appellate Division, working for the Commissioner. It should not be overlooked, of course, that many tax controversies are settled at lower levels in the administrative process, but the larger and tougher cases usually rise to the top in the form of Tax Court cases and there the Appellate Division must crack those tough nuts, along with the close cooperation of the Regional Counsel trial attorney, as well as the attorney for the petitioner, if the Court is to avoid drowning in this flood of potential litigation.

And now you have received your invitation to confer with the Appellate Division and Regional Counsel's attorney either by letter or phone. What now? You should appear at the first conference ready and willing to discuss all facts and law questions with dispatch and good humor. The Government representatives are people, just like you, and they will appreciate a sense of humor at the proper time to remove the tension from the controversy when it might seem oppressive. Bear in mind that all tax controversies are potential litigation and litigation usually means friction. A little timely oil in the process will do wonders to accomplish pleasant results.

You should have analyzed your case by this time so as to be able to indicate at the first conference which issues you are willing to concede and which issues you think the Government should concede, and then concentrate on the issues with the most difficult questions, some of which may be settled and some of which may have to be tried. This is not to say that you hope to arrive at an overall settlement in the first conference in most cases, but you should be able to clear out the dead wood and identify the issues to be further considered to the extent possible. There will be a natural sparring between you and the Government representatives just as in any lawsuit, but in a tax case the areas of sparring are frequently narrowed by virtue of the particular nature of the issues involved. Don't waste time on trivialities and don't try to argue points which lack merit. You will simply lose face and take up valuable time.

After this first conference, you should return to your office and prepare a memorandum summarizing the conference developments, additional questions raised by the Government representatives, additional assembling of facts required and possible indicated additional legal research. You should also indicate your feelings as to possible settlement of the various issues, or if it is a one-issue case, whether settlement thereof appears likely or whether trial appears more probable at this time. You should, of course, inform your client appropriately of the highlights of the conference, either by telephone or preferably by confirming letter so that there will be a record of your actions which will also come in very handy at the time of billing.

Section 6.04—Settlement Negotiations Progress

In most cases, now will be a good time to start the preparation of a stipulation of facts, using your skeleton trial brief as the backbone and then fleshing it out with other facts more recently developed and also with points and facts discussed at the first conference. Without exception, it is advisable for petitioner to prepare the first draft of the stipulation of facts. He has most of the facts in his possession, he has the burden of proof, and it usually gives a psychological advantage. This suggestion should be made near the end of the first settlement conference with respect to any issues which appear to be seriously in dispute. Other issues which appear to be very weak, as well as those more susceptible of settlement, can wait fact stipulation preparation until a later time and may not be necessary to prepare at all.

The first conference will also indicate whether subsequent conferences are necessary, which is likely in most cases, especially difficult or complex ones. It is apparent that these settlement conferences are tantamount to a substitute for a pre-trial conference practice in other courts. It is in essence "voluntary" discovery, a process which starts with the examining agent, perhaps involuntarily as far as the taxpayer is concerned, but becomes voluntary as the taxpayer endeavors to persuade the Government representatives of the merits of his case. Many practitioners are coy in presenting facts to the Government representatives at various stages of this procedure, feeling that they should hold back a few aces for later use. There are situations, of course, where this may be wise, but in most cases if a taxpayer desires a settlement, the sooner he discloses his strong facts and law arguments, the better. The longer he withholds his ace cards, the more apt the Government is to believe he has none.

If these conferences are properly prepared for, full factual and legal development should result, leading to a more accurate evaluation of litigating strength by both parties well in advance of the trial date. Since the vast majority of Tax Court cases result in settlement, it is obvious that most practitioners, as well as the Government representatives, have done their homework throughout the Court's existence.

As you go forward in preparing your case for a second or third conference with the appellate conferee and trial attorney, bear in mind that each may take a diverse view of the strength or weakness of your case, which you may be able to exploit to your advantage. If you can perceive such a difference in viewpoint between the two Government representatives, you can press your strong points appropriately and this often results in arriving at a settlement that is better than one representative might have recommended by himself. This is, of course, one reason many practitioners choose to file Tax Court petitions rather than protests in cases which are apparently headed to the Appellate Division by one route or the other, that is, to insure that there will be two representatives at the table, rather than one, on the Government's side.

Despite the beneficial settlement possibilities of this divide-and-conquer approach, it can also be borne in mind that, if it is at all possible, the two Government representatives will present a common settlement front.

The best time to settle any case is now, whenever that may be, but it should be noted that settlement is possible at any time—during or after trial, or even after decision and during the appeal. The reason for these later dates of settlement is that in certain cases one party or the other will not "bite the bullet" as the saying goes, until all of the evidence has actually been introduced in Court, the demeanor of witnesses can be observed, or many other things can happen to cause one or the other party to re-evaluate his litigating position.

If your case has one or more solely fact issues, as most cases do, concentrate on settling them if at all possible, because the Court abhors trying them. Foremost in this category are valuation issues, typically closely-held stock and real estate. If each side has expert opinions, exchange them. Let the experts confront each other at the negotiating table. The respective representatives, plus the experts, know infinitely more about the issue than the Court ever will, which you will be told in chambers, if not before in a joint pretrial telephone conversation. Hence, you should strive to the utmost to try your case at the conference table rather than in open court and thereby achieve a settlement.

Travel and entertainment expense deductions, bad debt deductions, reasonable compensation—all and many more such fact issues are usually advisable to be settled, rather than tried. Of course, there are exceptions, but they are rare.

Multiple-issue cases naturally lend themselves to settlement more readily than single-issue cases or legal-issue cases. Even so, almost *every* case is susceptible of settlement if the representatives of both parties are so minded.

If your case is settled, the Appellate Division will make the computation of the agreed deficiency and transmit copies thereof to you and to Regional Counsel, after which Regional Counsel will prepare the necessary stipulation of settlement for filing with the Court with the request that an order be entered in accordance therewith, which the Court does as a matter of course after Regional Counsel files the stipulation with the Clerk. If one or more issues are settled, yet one or more issues remain to be tried before the Court, the settled issues will be embodied as paragraphs in the stipulation of facts to be filed with the Court at the time of the trial.

Bear in mind again that on the morning of the call of the calendar of the Tax Court trial session on which your case is set, Regional Counsel obtains sole settlement jurisdiction. If you have a strong stomach and feel that the trial attorney has a much more sympathetic ear for your case than the appellate conferee, you can hold out until that hour with the hope that settlement will then be agreed to by the Regional Counsel's office. This is a very rare situation and one not to be counted upon in most cases.

Section 6.05—The Stipulation of Facts Process

In the meantime, assuming the entire case has not been settled, you have continued to be busy correcting, refining and adding to the first draft of the stipulation of facts. Even though you are still negotiating settlement, it is wise to transmit a draft of the fact stipulation to the trial attorney at the earliest feasible and appropriate date for his consideration. If nothing else, speed in furnishing the stipulation shows clearly that you are deadly serious about the case, have deep knowledge of the relevant facts and have devoted considerable effort to preparing the case for trial.

In addition to these benefits, preparing a draft of the stipulation of facts will begin to tell you what discovery proceedings may be appropriate and necessary. It will also indicate to you whether there is a shorter method for disposing of the case without settlement other than an actual trial, such as by way of motion for judgment on the pleadings or motion for summary judgment.

It is very important that you move expeditiously in arranging your settlement conferences and in preparing your first draft of the stipulation of facts, because the discovery rules in Title VII have severe time limitations which could present real difficulties in your preparation for trial if you do not allow sufficient lead time as you go forward with your proceedings.[1]

As you progress in stipulating facts, never overlook the great benefit to you, as counsel for taxpayer, that it affords, because since the burden of proof is on the petitioner, except in specified cases, every stipulated fact means one less fact to be proved in court. It is well known that it is more easy to stipulate a fact than to prove it in court in most situations. Even though you may have to spend considerable time in preparing the stipulation and in obtaining agreement on its language from the Government trial attorney, it is usually much less time-consuming and costly to do this than to wait and prove the fact in open court, to say nothing of meeting the requirements of Rule 91 with its stringent provisions for full stipulations.

From its origin in 1924, the Tax Court has insisted on full fact stipulation more than any other tribunal and has been successful to an unparalleled degree in achieving this objective. For that reason the

---

[1] Rules 70-73, 90.

stipulation of facts process is the hallmark of the Tax Court, its *sine qua non*. In truth, the Tax Court must stipulate or perish under its avalanche of new cases.

Another strong reason for the Court's emphasis on the stipulation of facts process is the nature of a tax controversy itself. Most facts in a tax controversy are susceptible of stipulation, quite unlike many other types of civil court cases. Documentary evidence usually predominates in a Tax Court trial record. Oral testimony in many cases is the exception, rather than the rule. Oral testimony frequently is necessary only to flesh out the stipulated fact skeleton. In the future, requests for admissions under Rule 90, when coupled with a comprehensive stipulation of facts under Rule 91, should increasingly minimize oral testimony.

The very nature of a tax controversy accounts for the ease with which facts are normally stipulated. If introduced in open court, such evidence would require many hours of unproductive time. When stipulated, the Court's time is saved, the parties' time and expense are saved and petitioner, who has the burden of proof, can be sure that he has meticulously set forth the facts of record without any concern that there will be a slip-up in introduction of such facts so that the record might later be defective. In other words, the stipulation of facts should give petitioner's counsel peace of mind with the knowledge that in one document he has carried his burden of proof on all of the basic facts set forth therein, while if he had to introduce such facts piecemeal in evidence, he might very well slip up and fail to meet the same meticulous standard that would be embodied in a stipulation. In short, this makes assurance doubly sure. In view of the many benefits to petitioner in stipulating all possible facts, plus the stringent requirements of Rule 91, it always behooves petitioner's counsel to get started quickly in drafting a fact stipulation and submitting it to counsel for respondent at the earliest possible date.

Section 6.06—Trial Status Orders and Revenue Procedure 60-18

The close relationship between Tax Court trial proceedings and the Internal Revenue Service settlement system is nowhere more evident than in the interplay of the Court's Trial Status Order (T.S.O.) procedure and Revenue Procedure 60-18 governing the course and timing of settlement negotiations.

Revenue Procedure 60-18, promulgated by the Commissioner early in 1960, revolutionized the existing settlement procedures in Tax Court cases, which might be charitably described as *laissez-faire*. The Chief

Counsel, of course, was its leading proponent for obvious reasons. Theretofore, since the Court's creation, there had been no established cutoff date for settlement negotiations with the Appellate Division and Regional Counsel. The result for Regional Counsel was often chaos, since many pre-1960 Tax Court case settlements were "courthouse steps" settlements. True to other litigation settlements, that is just when Regional Counsel frequently received the case for trial preparation—almost on the courthouse steps. Some private practitioners were even accused of dilatory settlement negotiations, prolonged to the last minute, unsuccessfully, with the known intention of not settling. The strategy was said to be to keep Government counsel dangling as close to trial as possible so that he would be hopeful of settlement and would thus not undertake serious trial preparation until the eleventh hour, theoretically, at least, to the petitioner's trial advantage. Also remember that the Government attorney usually has several assigned cases and thus must concentrate on those which appear to be probable trials.

In view of these and perhaps other circumstances, Revenue Procedure 60-18 was issued to require that all settlement negotiations be concluded not later than 90 days prior to the beginning date of the Trial Session on which a case is calendared. At that time, the Appellate Division must transmit the case file to Regional Counsel for trial preparation, absent a settlement agreement, at least in principle, if not in complete detail. In general, this procedure has been strictly enforced, albeit much weeping and gnashing of teeth from veteran practitioners at its adoption because of the radical change in their career-long practice.

In recent years, it has become more accepted and followed without much grumbling, especially by more recent practitioners who have never known any other settlement procedure. Its hardship lies in causing premature preparation in some cases, but on balance it tends to serve a useful purpose. There is a strong view that the period should be shorter, perhaps 60, rather than 90, days, which would provide ample trial preparation time in most cases, especially considering that Regional Counsel is participating in settlement negotiation conferences, fact stipulation meetings and can normally arrange to borrow portions of the file from Appellate Division as needed. Nevertheless, Revenue Procedure 60-18 appears to be here to stay, at least for the foreseeable future, and practitioners must learn to live with it.

Be assured that Revenue Procedure 60-18 does not prevent settlements from occurring at any time after the cutoff date; just the formal conference negotiations are prohibited thereafter. Telephone calls are permitted to make settlement proposals (and perhaps subtly comment on settlement aspects). At meetings to consider the stipulation of facts, a settlement proposal, plus appropriate persuasive remarks, is not forbidden. Suffice to say, there are as many ways to achieve settlement within the 90-day period as there are ingenious practitioners.

Soon after Revenue Procedure 60-18 was issued, the Tax Court paralleled its settlement-trial procedures to conform. Its Trial Status Reports are mailed to counsel for all parties in each case approximately six months prior to the proposed Trial Calendar, requesting return thereof approximately 100 days prior to such Calendar Date, which is designated in the T.S.O. The questions in the T.S.O. are designed to inform the Court as to the probability of settlement or trial and the estimated trial time of probable trials, which enables the Court to plan more efficiently the frequency and length of trial sessions. These Reports sometimes result in the cancellation, or postponement, of a proposed Trial Session. They also alert practitioners to the imminence of a Trial Session with its triggering of the application of Revenue Procedure 60-18. Thus, T.S.O.'s and Revenue Procedure 60-18 are closely interrelated.

Many practitioners regularly coordinate their T.S.O. response with Regional Counsel so as the better to inform the Court of settlement-trial probabilities. This cooperative practice also benefits a petitioner by eliminating premature trial preparation, for example, in a case which should be reported to the Court as not ready to be set for trial. All in all, Revenue Procedure 60-18 and the Court's T.S.O. system have generally improved settlement and trial procedure.

Section 6.07—The Trial Date Nears

By this time the Notice for Hearing has been received noting the beginning date of the Court's trial session at the designated place of hearing. It is here assumed that all issues raised by the petition have not been resolved by settlement agreement and at least one such issue must be submitted to the Court for trial. At least a partial stipulation of facts has been prepared and portions thereof agreed to by the parties. Since petitioner has the burden of proof in most cases, his counsel must now decide exactly which proceedings to follow under the Court's Rules.

If counsel feels that there are additional facts which should be stipulated but which have not been agreed to at this time, he should carefully study Rule 91 with its stringent stipulating provisions in order to decide whether to file a motion to compel stipulation under Rule 91(f)(1) seeking a "show cause" order with respect thereto. He should also consider whether to file a request for admission under Rule 90 if he has not already done so. Bear in mind that the use of these rules in aid of stipulation, as well as use of the discovery rules, is a matter of judgment for petitioner's counsel. The timing of the use of any of these rules is, of course, very important and varies from case to case. For example, in some cases it may be wise to file a request for admission under Rule 90 prior to the receipt of the notice for trial, if it has already been ascertained that opposing counsel will not stipulate a fact which the other party believes should be stipulated. It is recommended that Rule 90 never be used hastily, because it might be considered abrasive and might cause opposing counsel to stiffen his opposition to the stipulation of a particular fact. Persuasion toward stipulation at the conference table is believed preferable to formal action under Rule 90 in all possible cases. Obviously, if counsel is met by a stonewall negative position on the part of his opposing counsel, he may have no recourse but to follow Rule 90 or Rule 91(f)(1), but these are the exeptional cases.

The Court has placed very sharp teeth in Rule 91 to make sure that the stipulation process continues to be the mainstay of practice in the Court. In the hands of counsel who is making every good-faith effort to stipulate facts, Rule 91 gives him full support from the Court. A summary of its provisions will illustrate its strong impact. Former Rule 31 was considered quite strong in itself, but Rule 91 is even tougher and can be ignored only at the extreme peril of counsel for either party.

Under Rule 91, the parties are required to stipulate, to the fullest extent to which complete or qualified agreement can ordinarily be reached, all matters not privileged which are relevant to the pending case, regardless of whether such matters involve fact or opinion or the application of law to fact. Included in matters required to be stipulated are all facts, all documents and papers or contents or aspects thereof, and all evidence which fairly should not be in dispute. Objection on the ground of materiality or relevance is not to be regarded as just cause for refusal to stipulate, although it should be noted either in the stipulation or appropriately at the trial of the case. The incidence of the burden of proof has no bearing on the requirement for complete stipulation. Documents or papers or other exhibits attached to and found with the stipulation are considered to be a part thereof.

All facts should be included in the stipulation, regardless of whether they may have been obtained through discovery or requests for admission or through any other authorized procedure which are regarded as aids to stipulation but not separate documents. In short, the stipulation should be as complete as possible within its four corners without having to refer to other, separate documents.

The published note to Rule 91 contains the following excellent explanation:

> Requests to admit, as provided in Rule 90, and the stipulation procedure in this Rule, may overlap to some extent. The stipulation procedure is more comprehensive, supported by affirmative action of the Court, and mandatory in all cases. The request for admissions is elective, dependent on the action of a requesting party, and is relatively rigid. The stipulation process is more flexible, based on conference and negotiation between parties, adaptable to statements on matters in varying degrees of dispute, susceptible of defining and narrowing areas of dispute, and offering an active medium for settlement. The request for admissions, typically used before the stipulation stage occurs, should reinforce the stipulation process.

As to the form of stipulations, they must be in writing, signed by the parties thereto or by their counsel, and must conform to the requirements of Rule 23 as to form and style of papers, except that the stipulation need only be filed in duplicate and only one set of exhibits is required. Naturally, the stipulation should be as clear and concise as possible with separate items stated in separate paragraphs, appropriately lettered or numbered. Petitioner's exhibits are numbered; respondent's exhibits are lettered and joint exhibits are jointly numbered and lettered, as 1-A, 2-B, etc.

Good practice requires that any objection to all or any part of the stipulation should be noted in the stipulation, but the Court will also consider any objection to a stipulated matter made at the commencement of the trial or for good cause shown made during the trial.

Although a stipulation shall be treated as a conclusive admission, the stipulation and the admissions therein shall be binding and have effect only in the pending case and not for any other purpose, and cannot be used against any of the parties thereto in any other case or proceeding.

What about the recalcitrant party who arbitrarily or unreasonably refuses to stipulate? The Court has provided very sharp teeth for enforcement purposes in Rule 91(f). Since the Rules are set forth in their entirety in the appendix, the detailed provisions of these requirements will not be repeated herein, but suffice to say the Court will take a very stern view of unreasonable refusal to stipulate facts which are susceptible of stipulation and, unless a party can show that a genuine fact dispute exists, or that in the interest of justice a matter ought not to be deemed stipulated, the Court will enforce its "show cause" order which will be issued *ex parte* subject to response by the nonstipulating party.[2]

Section 6.08–Discovery in General

Until the advent of the new Rules, the stipulation of facts process, intertwined as it is with the settlement negotiation process, constituted a voluntary discovery system which worked most successfully throughout the first 50 years of the Court's existence. A solid body of practitioner opinion felt that any tampering with this voluntariness might lead to considerable stonewalling by counsel in possession of most, if not all, the facts and frequently reluctant to yield them without a struggle, especially if the Rules seemed to countenance such resistance to voluntary disclosure. Whether this fear is well-founded can only be discerned after a reasonable test period under the new Rules. But first, an examination of the scope of the discovery provisions of the new Rules is appropriate. Despite some popular thought to the contrary, the Court did not adopt the Federal Rules of Civil Procedure for discovery, although many portions were lifted in their entirety.

Section 6.09–Discovery–Requests for Admission

Although Rule 90 covering requests for admission is described as an aid to stipulation in the Notes to the Rules, in many respects it is really a discovery process.[3] If such a request should be filed prior to an honest effort to stipulate a fact which should be admitted, it might irritate opposing counsel and cause more trouble than it is worth. Rule 90 provides that a party may serve upon any other party a written request for the admission of the truth of any matters which are not privileged and are relevant to the subject matter involved in the pending action, provided such matters are set forth in the request and relate to statements or opinions of fact or of the application of law to fact, including the genuineness of any documents described in the request. The same time frame covers requests for admission as governs general discovery procedures under Rule 70(a)(2), indicating again the close connection between Rule 90 and the discovery procedures under Rule 70(a)(2), under Title VII.

It is noteworthy that requests for admission, as well as stipulations of fact, include opinions of fact and the application of law to fact,

---

[2]Rule 91(f) and Note thereto.

[3]*Pearsall,* 62 T.C. 94 (1974).

two areas that might well be considered beyond the scope of a stipulation of facts or of admitted facts. How far the Court will go in these two areas is uncertain, but it is believed that it will take a restrictive position in enforcing either Rule 90 or Rule 91 unless the moving party can show clearly that justice will be done by requiring the admission or stipulation of an opinion of fact or application of law to fact.

Section 6.10–Other Discovery Methods

In addition to the requests for admission under Rule 90, what else has the Court done to initiate discovery proceedings which were unknown under the old Rules? Perhaps the negative should be asked: what other discovery methods did the Court omit? No discovery depositions are permitted under the new rules, either *ex parte* or by Court order. As the Note to Rule 70 well states this decision of the Court:

> Whatever additional benefits might be obtained by the use of discovery depositions would appear to be outweighed by the problems and burdens they entail for the parties as well as the Court. Provision for discovery depositions in conformity with the Federal Rules at this time would represent too drastic a departure from present Tax Court practice, with uncertain effect in view of the context of Tax Court litigation.

In short, the Court was plowing new ground by adopting any discovery rules and it decided not to plow too deep a furrow by adopting a discovery deposition rule. Whether any discovery rules should be adopted is, of course, a matter of sharp disagreement by knowledgeable persons, but at least the Court has eliminated the major source of discovery friction, that is, oral depositions at the will of a party.

The rules permit a party to obtain discovery by written interrogatories (Rule 71), by production of documents or things (Rules 72 and 73) and by requests for admission (Rule 90). Rule 70(a)(1) makes clear that "the Court expects the parties to attempt to attain the objectives of discovery through informal consultation or communication before utilizing the discovery procedures provided in these Rules."

Section 6.11–Timing of Discovery

The timing of discovery is, of course, strictly limited. Discovery shall not be commenced, without leave of Court, before the expiration of thirty (30) days after joinder of issue and shall be completed, unless otherwise authorized by the Court, no later than seventy-five (75) days prior to the date set for call of the case from a trial calendar.[4]

Section 6.12–Scope of Discovery

As to the scope of discovery, the information or response sought through discovery may concern any relevant matter not privileged. If the information or response appears reasonably calculated to lead to discovery of admissible evidence, it is not grounds for objection that the information or response will be inadmissible at the trial. Also, consistent with Rules 90 and 91, if the information or response sought is otherwise proper, it is not objectionable merely because it involves an opinion or contention that relates to fact or to the application of law to fact. The Court may order that the information or response sought need not be furnished or made until some designated time or a particular stage has been reached in the case or until a specified step has been taken by a party.[5]

The Note to Rule 70 points out that "With certain exceptions and subject to the limitations of these Rules, the scope of allowable discovery is intended to parallel the scope of allowable discovery under the Federal Rules." The Note goes on to say that "the 'work product' of counsel and material prepared in anticipation of litigation or for trial, are generally intended to be outside the scope of allowable discovery under these Rules, . . ."

Under Rule 70(c), upon request of the other party and without any showing except the assertion that he lacks and has no convenient means of obtaining a copy of a statement made by him, a party shall be entitled to obtain a copy of any such statement which has a bearing on the subject matter of the case and is in the possession or control of another party to the case. This provision may well be applied by petitioner's counsel as much, or more, than any discovery rule, because frequently a taxpayer has made a statement to an examining officer or a special agent, for example, without being given a copy at that time.[6] There may well be few occasions when the shoe is on the other foot, because it is difficult to envision many situations where a government representative has given a statement to a taxpayer or his counsel.

---

[4]Rule 70(a)(2), *see Kabbaby*, 64 T.C. 393 (1975).

[5]Rule 70(b); the burden of proof has no bearing on the discoverability of facts, *Piscatelli*, 64 T.C. 424 (1975).

[6]*See Phelps*, 62 T.C. 513 (1974) (Memoranda prepared by IRS agents of interview statements by petitioners). To a certain extent, Rules 70(c) and 72 may afford overlapping relief. *See P. T. & L. Construction Co.*, 63 T.C. 404 (1974).

As to the use of material obtained by discovery, it may be used at trial or in any proceeding in the case prior or subsequent to trial, to the extent permitted by the Rules of Evidence. Such answers or information or responses will not be considered as evidence until offered and received as evidence. Objections to discovered material should be made as with respect to any other proffered evidence.[7]

To avoid harassment of a party, the Court has included very stringent protective rules and sanctions in Title X beginning with Rule 100 which will be treated hereinafter.

The most searching discovery innovation is Rule 71 governing interrogatories. Thereunder, any party may, without leave of Court, serve upon any other party written interrogatories to be answered by the party served or, if the party served is a public or private corporation or a partnership or association or governmental agency, by an officer or agent who shall furnish such information as is available to the party.[8] Written answers must be filed in response to these written interrogatories.

It should be carefully noted that this provision is limited to discovery by one party from another party, and that interrogatories cannot be served on third persons. Further, this provision may be initiated without involvement of the Court, with the Court becoming involved only if objections are filed by the responding party or there is some other source of complaint as the procedure develops.[9] Practitioners familiar with the Federal Rules will recognize these safeguard provisions.

Under Rule 71(b) all answers shall be made in good faith and as completely as the answering party's information shall permit. The answering party, however, is required to make reasonable inquiry and ascertain readily obtainable information. An answering party may not give lack of information or knowledge as an answer or as a reason for failure to answer, unless he states that he has made reasonable inquiry and that information known or readily obtainable by him is insufficient to enable him to answer the substance of the interrogatory.[10] In other words, the Court will not require a party to go to unreasonable lengths to obtain information required to answer an interrogatory, but only require him to make a reasonable inquiry.

As to procedure, under Rule 71(c) each interrogatory shall be answered separately and fully under oath, unless it is objected to, in which event the reasons for the objection shall be stated in lieu of the answer.

---

[7] Rule 70(d).

[8] Rule 71(a).

[9] Rule 71(a); Note thereto.

[10] Rule 71(b). Health is no ground for refusing to answer interrogatories. *Piscatelli,* 64 T.C. 424 (1975).

The answers are to be signed by the person making them, and the objection shall be signed by the party or his counsel. The party, on whom the interrogatories have been served, shall serve a copy of its answers, and objections if any, upon the propounding party within 45 days after service of the interrogatories upon him, but the Court may allow a shorter or longer time. The burden is on the propounding party to move for an order with respect to any objection or other failure to answer an interrogatory.[11]

With respect to prospective expert testimony, under Rule 71(d), a party may require any other party by written interrogatories (i) to identify each person whom the other party expects to call as an expert witness at the trial of the case, giving his name, address, vocation or occupation, and a statement of his qualifications, and (ii) to state the subject matter and the substance of the facts and opinion to which the expert is expected to testify, and give a summary of the grounds for each such opinion.

There are many situations where it would be a great burden on the responding party to search and extract information from available materials in order to respond properly to interrogatories. In conformity with the Federal Rules, Rule 71(e) permits the responding party to make available to the propounding party the proper records from which the answers may be derived or ascertained so that he can have a reasonable opportunity to examine such records and in effect obtain such information for himself.

Section 6.13—The Court Looks at Discovery

In keeping with its announced policy of continuing its reliance primarily on the stipulation of facts process for obtaining and presenting the relevant facts to the Court, it has frowned on premature discovery actions, such as filing interrogatories before exhausting the fact stipulation possibilities. The Court has sustained the respondent's motion for a protective order under Rule 103 to written interrogatories under Rules 70 and 71, with the matter held in abeyance for a reasonable period of time and with the parties directed to engage in informal discovery before resorting to Rule 71.[12] These cases make clear that the Court will pursue a "go slow" approach to all discovery efforts.[13]

---

[11]Rule 71(c).

[12]*The Branerton Corporation,* 61 T.C. 691 (1974); *Hoeme,* Docket No. 110-74, Order entered May 31, 1974.

[13]*Ross,* Docket No. 5197-73, Order entered May 29, 1974.

In another case, the Court required the respondent to produce a depreciation study by a national certified public accounting firm for *in camera* inspection, taking the request for interrogatories under advisement.[14] In a later order, the Court refused to require respondent to produce this accounting study because it was "privileged as an intra-agency study and opinion."[15] The request for certain other interrogatories was granted in part and denied in part with sharp criticism of both parties for proceeding in this fashion and with the admonition that they should try to develop the facts without requiring the Court to police their efforts.[16]

The production of documents and things is covered by Rule 72, which requires that the request must set forth the items to be inspected, either by individual item or by category, with each item and category being described with reasonable particularity. The request shall specify a reasonable time, place and manner of making the inspection and performing the related acts. The party upon whom the request is served must serve a written response within 30 days after service of the request, but the Court may allow a shorter or longer time. The response shall state, with respect to each item or category, that inspection and related activities will be permitted as requested, unless the request is objected to in whole or in part, in which event the reasons for objection shall be stated. If objection is made to part of an item or category, that part shall be specified. To obtain a ruling on an objection by the responding party, the requesting party shall file an appropriate motion with the Court.[17]

Rule 72, of course, operates without participation of the Court, as does Rule 71, and only if a requesting party feels aggrieved is the Court drawn into the matter.

Because of the very nature of tax litigation, involving as it usually does documentary evidence, this rule may prove to be more useful to both parties than any other discovery provision. In the earliest reported case under this rule, petitioner requested respondent to produce several documents, most of which were in the hands of other government agencies.[18] As to those documents, the procedural rules of these agencies permitted petitioner to obtain them upon a designation with reasonable specificity of the records and documents sought. Respondent resisted furnishing the documents on this ground and his position was sustained by

---

[14]*Morgan,* Docket No. 1251-74, Order entered September 19, 1974.

[15]*Morgan,* Docket No. 1251-74, Order entered March 4, 1975.

[16]*Shapiro,* Docket No. 178-74, Memorandum Sur Order entered November 12, 1974.

[17]Rule 72(a), (b).

[18]*Marsh,* 62 T.C. 256 (1974). *See also Teichgraeber,* 64 T.C. (453) (1975).

the Court. The Court pointed out, however, that "if the petitioner, after such a good faith effort, is not able to obtain these documents which she deems vital to her case, then the Court is not without the ability to see that her interests are adequately protected."[19]

In another interesting case disposed of by a Memorandum Sur Order, the Court granted petitioner's request that respondent produce statements by a decedent to a Special Agent of the Federal Bureau of Investigation, which apparently were already in the possession of respondent.[20] Petitioner's counsel, however, was directed not to divulge their contents to certain named persons, or their counsel.

The Court denied respondent's request for petitioner to produce documents by another Memorandum Sur Order on the ground that the requested documents were unnecessary for respondent to establish the desired facts.[21] The Court also pointed out that if petitioner made certain proof, the fact question would be rendered moot by virtue of a specific statutory provision.

In a significant decision under Rule 72, the Court denied petitioner's effort to obtain a copy of a national technical advice ruling which the Court held was a work product prepared in anticipation of trial, even though prepared in the national office of the Service and not by the Regional Counsel attorney assigned to try the case.[22] The Court pointed out, however, that petitioner could still use written interrogatories to ascertain the respondent's litigating position.

In what may well be a landmark decision construing the scope of Rule 72,[23] the Court had to consider petitioner's request for production of a report of a Special Agent, the report of an Appellate Division conferee and the statement of a witness made to a Special Agent. After carefully considering all of the pertinent facts and points involved, the Court granted in part and denied in part petitioner's request. The Court first held that the requested documents were not prepared in anticipation of litigation and were thus not protected by the "work product" doctrine. The Court further held that portions of the Special Agent's report were protected by a qualified privilege and were not relevant and need not be produced. The remainder of the Special Agent's

---

[19] *Marsh*, 62 T.C. 256 (1974).

[20] *Skopp Estate*, Docket No. 4016-71, Memorandum Sur Order entered June 10, 1974.

[21] *Burton*, Docket No. 8382, Memorandum Sur Order entered September 27, 1974.

[22] *Ataka America, Inc.*, Docket No. 7154-70, Memorandum Sur Order entered November 6, 1974, *and Teichgraeber*, 64 T.C. 453 (1975), which extends to private letter rulings.

[23] *P. T. & L. Construction Co.*, 63 T.C. 404 (1974). *See also Murphy*, T.C. Memo 1975-88, ¶75,088 P-H Memo T.C. *and House of Tobacco*, Docket No. 738-7, Order entered April 2, 1975 (Special Agent's Report).

report was required to be produced. The Court also held that the entire Appellate Division conferee's report was subject to a qualified privilege and was irrelevant to the development of factual information and would thus not be subject to production. Lastly, the Court held that the question-and-answer statement of the third party witness to the Special Agent should be produced.

The discovery rules will be useful as a club over the head of a recalcitrant possessor of discoverable facts. At first such a party may resist the discovery procedure, but later may change his position and agree to furnish the requested information. In such a case, petitioners had moved the Court to compel respondent to produce Appellate Division papers which would explain depreciation deductions allowed for prior years so that the current year could be properly disposed of.[24] Originally, respondent resisted this motion, but when petitioners' motion was called for hearing, respondent's counsel stated that under the particular circumstances, he would produce the requested documents within 30 days.

To assure that a transferee will not be stifled in his search for necessary evidence to present his position, the Court adopted Rule 73 covering examination of records of other persons by transferees. As the Note points out: "It is intended to be cumulative rather than exclusive of other pretrial procedures." Under the Rule, it will be enforced so as not to result in undue hardship to a taxpayer or preceding transferee, but in the opinion of the Court to do only what is necessary to enable the transferee to ascertain the taxpayer's liability or that of a preceding transferee.

Section 6.14—Enforcement and Protective Discovery Provisions

After 50 years of discovery voluntariness in the Court, Title X covering enforcement and protective provisions for the Court's new discovery procedures under Rules 100 to 104, inclusive, represents a sharp departure from prior practice. True, the Federal Rules have been largely followed here, but veteran practitioners may be pardoned for a note of sadness to realize that the Court has concluded that its Rules must contain these mandatory provisions.

The sequence, timing and frequency of discovery steps are governed by Rule 101 which provides, unless the Court orders otherwise for the convenience of the parties and witnesses and in the interests of justice, that the discovery procedures may be used in any sequence, and

---

[24]*Matson Navigation Company,* Docket No. 1625-74, Order entered February 27, 1975.

the fact that a party is engaged in any such method or procedure shall not operate to delay the use of any such method of procedure by another party. The Rule also makes clear that no discovery procedure shall be used in such a way as to delay the progress of a case toward trial status or the trial of a case on the date for which it is noticed, unless in the interests of justice the Court shall order otherwise. Unless the Court orders otherwise under Rule 103, the frequency of use of the discovery procedures is not limited.

Rule 102 requires a party to make sure that his response to a request for discovery, including a request for admission, is as currently accurate as he can make it.

If the Court is to have discovery procedures, it must also provide protection against annoyance and harassment and undue burden and expense, which is done by Rule 103.[25] Again, the Federal Rules have been followed for this purpose.

The enforcement teeth are contained in Rule 104 which provides several broad actions which may be taken by the Court where there has been no response or inadequate response, to discovery requests, even to the extent of punishment for contempt of court.[26] Rule 104 is derived from the Federal Rules.

If the parties continue their voluntary discovery system as the Court requires under Rule 91, in accord with the long-established philosophy of the Court, seldom will Title X need to be invoked. Perhaps it is there like a policeman to be called upon should there be a murder in the house. Normal practice should not require its application.

Section 6.15–Pretrial Conferences

Although the Court's Rules have provided for pretrial conferences since 1963, they are rarely held in Tax Court cases compared to district court and Court of Claims cases, the other companion federal trial courts. The separation in distance between both trial attorneys on the one hand and the Court on the other hand in Washington partially accounts for their rarity. Further, the settlement conferences which might begin with the district conference and would certainly include the Appellate Division conferences, in effect provide informal pretrial conferences conducted by the parties themselves rather than by the Court.

---

[25] See *Greenberg's Express, Inc.*, 62 T.C. 327 (1974), holding that Rule 103(a)(10) may not be used to obtain access to documents which might be obtained by other available procedures. *See also Piscatelli,* 64 T.C. 424 (1975) *and Woodard Estate,* 64 T.C. 457 (1975).

[26] *Burton,* Docket No. 8382-72, Memorandum Sur Order entered September 27, 1974.

The Court, however, is willing to afford the parties a pretrial conference if requested, especially in difficult or complex cases, in order to narrow the issues, assist in stipulating facts, simplify the presentation of evidence or otherwise assist in trial preparation or possible disposition by way of settlement.[27] Usually, pretrial conferences are held in Washington well in advance of the trial session, but they may be held at the place of hearing of the session, ordinarily on the first Monday or Tuesday of the trial calendar.[28] If pressed by the parties, the Court might hold such a conference in the trial city at an earlier date than the date of the trial session, or by a conference telephone call with advance notice on specified questions.[29]

The Court has continually evidenced a trend toward flexibility in holding pretrial conferences at the convenience of the parties, just as this trend has been evidenced in many other procedural ways in recent years. Even though the Court's headquarters are in Washington, D.C., it is entirely possible for a judge or special trial judge who is sitting in or near a city where a party desires a pretrial conference, to accommodate that party on the spot without a great deal of waiting. On the other hand, many practitioners prefer that the judge who will preside at the actual trial also be the judge who conducts the pretrial conference. A proper motion to this effect would be looked upon with favor by the Chief Judge, who has the power to decide such questions. In other words, the Court has shown a fine disposition to work with the parties to their mutual advantage in holding convenient pretrial conferences and in all other ways which will serve the interests of justice, lead to more settled cases and shorten trial time if settlement is impossible.

If a petitioner moves for a pretrial conference in advance of the hearing date, the judge to be assigned to the particular trial session is normally assigned to conduct the conference if at all possible. When such a motion for a pretrial conference is filed, exclusive settlement jurisdiction is thereupon lodged in the Office of Regional Counsel, thus eliminating the joint settlement jurisdiction of the Appellate Division at that point. This development ordinarily must await the call of the calendar at the particular trial session as previously mentioned. Thus, the filing of a preliminary pretrial conference motion also produces what may be a desirable side effect in a particular case in conferring upon Regional Counsel sole settlement jurisdiction at that early stage in the proceeding.

Rule 110(c) expressly provides that if a case is not yet listed on a trial calendar, the Chief Judge, in his discretion, upon motion of either

---

[27]Rule 110(a).

[28]Rule 110(b).

[29]Rule 110(c).

party or upon his own motion, may list the case for a pretrial conference upon a calendar in the place designated for trial, or may assign the case for a pretrial conference either in Washington, D.C. or in any other convenient place. For example, it may be just as convenient for the parties to have a pretrial conference speedily in a city perhaps only 100 miles or so from the location of the parties and they may decide to have the pretrial conference in that city rather than have the judge travel to their city.

A request or motion for a pretrial conference must include a statement of the reason therefor and the Court must be satisfied that the conference is not requested for purposes of delay.[30]

Section 6.16—Depositions—General

Although Title VIII, entitled "Depositions", consists of six rather lengthy Rules 80 to 85, inclusive, the Note to Rule 80 effectively summarizes that "Depositions are adopted in these Rules only for the purpose of perpetuating or preserving evidence." Further, in addition to the above restrictive language, this note also says that "The use of depositions under these Rules generally is not favored, unless it can be shown that the required objective exists." In short, Title VIII is to be used very sparingly and then only when evidence cannot be perpetuated or preserved in any other way.

A noteworthy provision of Rule 80 is that such depositions for this limited purpose may be taken either by the filing of an application with the Court or by agreement of the parties. Of these two methods, agreement of the parties is certainly preferable if at all possible.[31] In most cases there should be no difficulty in obtaining such an agreement. Rule 81 covers the taking of depositions in a pending case before trial; Rule 82 covers taking depositions in anticipation of commencing a case in the Court; and Rule 83 covers taking depositions in connection with an ongoing trial. Rule 84 provides for taking these depositions upon written questions, which may be necessary in certain unusual cases but the normal, oral deposition method is much to be preferred if possible. Rule 85 covers objections, errors and irregularities in connection with depositions.

Section 6.17—Depositions in Pending Case

If a party to a pending case desires to perpetuate his own testimony or that of any other person or to preserve any relevant docu-

---

[30] Rule 110(d).

[31] Rule 81(d).

ment or thing, he may file an application for an order of the Court authorizing him to take a deposition for such purpose. Such depositions may be taken only where there is a substantial risk that the person, document or thing involved will not be available at the trial of the case, and shall relate only to testimony or documents or things which are not privileged and are relevant.[32]

The application to take such a deposition must be signed by the party seeking the deposition or by his counsel, and shall show the following:

(i) the names and addresses of the persons to be examined;

(ii) the reasons for deposing those persons rather than waiting to call them as witnesses at the trial;

(iii) the substance of the testimony which the party expects to elicit from each of those persons;

(iv) a statement showing how the proposed testimony or document or thing is material to a matter in controversy;

(v) a statement describing any books, papers, documents, or tangible things to be produced at the deposition by the persons to be examined;

(vi) the time and place proposed for the deposition;

(vii) the officer before whom the deposition is to be taken;

(viii) the date on which the petition was filed with the Court, and whether the pleadings have been closed and the case placed on a trial calendar; and

(ix) any provision desired with respect to payment of expenses, fees, and charges relating to the deposition.[33]

The application may be filed with the Court at any time after the case is docketed in the Court, but must be filed at least 45 days prior to the trial date. The deposition must be completed and filed with the Court at least ten days prior to the trial date. The application and a conformed copy thereof, together with an additional conformed copy for each additional docket number involved and an additional conformed copy for each person to be served, shall be filed with the Clerk, who shall serve a copy on each of the other parties to the case as well as on such other persons who are to be examined pursuant to the application. Such other parties or persons shall file their own objections or other response,

---

[32]Rule 81(a).

[33]Rule 81(b)(1).

with the same number of copies, within 15 days after such service of the application. A hearing on the application will be held only if directed by the Court. Unless the Court shall determine otherwise for good cause shown, an application to take a deposition will not be regarded as sufficient ground for granting a continuance from a date or place of trial theretofore set. If the Court approves the taking of a deposition, it will issue an order which will include in its terms the name of the person to be examined, the time and place of the deposition, and the officer before whom it is to be taken.[34]

The party seeking to take a deposition may name, as the deponent in his application, a public or private corporation or a partnership or association or governmental agency, and shall designate with reasonable particularity the matters on which examination is requested. The organization so named shall designate one or more officers, directors, or managing agents, or other persons who consent to testify on its behalf, and may set forth, for each person designated, the matters on which he will testify. The persons so designated shall testify as to matters known or reasonably available to the organization.[35]

With respect to domestic depositions, that is, within the United States or a territory or insular possession subject to the dominion of the United States, depositions shall be taken before an officer authorized to administer oaths by the laws of the United States or of the place where the examination is held, or before a person appointed by the Court. A person so appointed has the power to administer oaths and to take such testimony.[36]

In a foreign country, depositions may be taken on notice (i) before a person authorized to administer oaths or affirmations in the place in which the examination is held, either by the law thereof or by the law of the United States, or (ii) before a person commissioned by the Court; and a person so commissioned shall have the power, by virtue of his commission, to administer any necessary oath and take testimony, or (iii) pursuant to a letter rogatory. A commission or a letter rogatory shall be issued on application and notice and on terms that are just and appropriate. It is not requisite to the issuance of a commission or a letter rogatory that the taking of the deposition in any other manner is impracticable or inconvenient; and both a commission and a letter rogatory may be issued in proper cases. A notice or commission may designate the person before whom the deposition is to be taken either by name or

---

[34]Rule 81(b)(2).

[35]Rule 81(c).

[36]Rule 81(e)(1).

descriptive title. A letter rogatory may be addressed "To The Appropriate Authority in (here name the country)." Evidence obtained by deposition or in response to a letter rogatory need not be excluded merely for reason that it is not a verbatim transcript or that the testimony was not taken under oath or for any similar departure from the requirements for depositions taken within the United States under the Rules.[37]

No deposition shall be taken before a person who is a relative or employee or counsel of any party, or is a relative or employee or associate of such counsel, or is financially interested in the action. These requirements may be waived in the certificate of return to the Court.[38]

As for the taking of the deposition, all necessary arrangements must be made by the party filing the application or, in the case of a stipulation, by such other persons as may be agreed upon by the parties.[39] Attendance by the persons to be examined may be compelled by the issuance of a subpoena, and production likewise may be compelled of exhibits required in connection with the testimony being taken. The officer before whom the deposition is taken shall first put the witness on oath (or affirmation) and shall personally, or by someone acting under his direction and in his presence, record accurately and verbatim the questions asked, the answers given, the objections made, and all matters transpiring at the taking of the deposition which bear on the testimony involved. Examination and cross-examination of witnesses, and the marking of exhibits, shall proceed as permitted at trial. All objections made at the time of examination shall be noted by the officer upon the deposition. Evidence objected to, unless privileged, shall be taken subject to the objections made.[40]

If an answer is improperly refused and as a result a further deposition is taken by the interrogating party, the objecting party or deponent may be required to pay all costs, charges, and expenses of that deposition to the same extent as is provided generally in Rule 81(g) where a party seeking to take a deposition fails to appear at the taking of the deposition. At the request of either party, a prospective witness of the deposition, other than a person acting in an expert or advisory capacity for a party, shall be excluded from the room in which, and during the time that, the testimony of another witness is being taken; and if such person remains in the room or within hearing of the examination after such request has been made, he shall not thereafter be permitted to testify, except by the

[37]Rule 81(e)(2).

[38]Rule 81(e)(3).

[39]Rule 81(f)(1).

[40]Rule 81(f)(2).

consent of the party who requested his exclusion or by permission of the Court.[41]

With respect to the expense of taking depositions, the party taking the deposition shall pay all the expenses, fees, and charges of the witness whose deposition is taken by him, any charges of the officer presiding at or recording the deposition other than for copies of the deposition, and any expenses involved in providing a place for the deposition. The party taking the deposition shall pay for the Court's copy; and, upon payment of reasonable charges therefor, the officer shall also furnish a copy of the deposition to any party or the deponent. By stipulation between the parties or on order of the Court, provision may be made for any costs, charges, or expenses relating to the deposition.[42]

Failure to attend or to serve a subpoena is a serious matter. If the party authorized to take a deposition fails to attend and proceed therewith and another party attends in person or by attorney pursuant to the arrangements made, the Court may order the former party to pay to such other party the reasonable expenses incurred by him and his attorney in attending, including reasonable attorney's fees. If the party authorized to take a deposition of a witness fails to serve a subpoena upon him and the witness, because of such failure, does not attend, and if another party attends in person or by attorney because he expects the deposition of that witness to be taken, the Court may order the former party to pay to such other party the reasonable expenses incurred by him and his attorney attending, including reasonable attorney's fees.[43]

Rule 81 also contains meticulous requirements for execution and return of the deposition.[44] When the testimony is fully transcribed, the deposition shall be submitted to the witness for examination and shall be read to or by him, unless such examination and reading are waived by the witness and by the parties. Any changes in form or substance, which the witness desires to make, shall be entered upon the deposition by the officer with a statement of the reason given by the witness for making them. The deposition shall then be signed by the witness, unless the parties by stipulation waive the signing or the witness is ill or cannot be found or refuses to sign. If the deposition is not signed by the witness within 30 days of its submission to him, the officer shall sign it and state on the record the fact of the waiver or of the illness or absence of the witness, or the fact of the refusal to sign together with the reason, if any,

---

[41]Rule 81(f)(2).

[42]Rule 81(g)(1).

[43]Rule 81(g)(2).

[44]Rule 81(h).

given therefor; and the deposition may then be used as fully as though signed unless the Court determines that the reasons given for the refusal to sign require rejection of the deposition in whole or in part.

As to form, the deposition shall show the docket number and caption of the case as they appear in the Court's record, the place and date of taking the deposition, the name of the witness, the party by whom called, the names of counsel present and whom they represent. The pages of the deposition shall be securely fastened. Exhibits shall be carefully marked, and when practicable annexed to, and in any event returned with, the deposition, unless, upon motion to the Court, a copy shall be permitted as a substitute after an opportunity is given to all interested parties to examine and compare the original and the copy. The officer shall execute and attach to the deposition the required certificate.

Unless otherwise authorized or directed by the Court, the officer shall enclose the original deposition and exhibits, together with such other copies for the parties and deponent as to which provision for payment therefor shall have been made, in a sealed packet with registered or certified postage or other transportation charges prepaid, and shall deliver the same to the Clerk or shall direct and forward the same to the Court at its mailing address. Upon written request of the party or his counsel, the officer may deliver a copy to him or his representative in lieu of sending it to the Court, in which event the officer shall attach to his return to the Court that written request and shall so state it in the certificate.[45]

At the trial or in any other proceeding in the case, any part or all of the deposition, so far as admissible under the rules of evidence applied as though the witness were then present and testifying, may be used against any party who was present or represented at the taking of the deposition or who had reasonable notice thereof, in accordance with any of the following provisions:

(1) The deposition may be used by any party for the purpose of contradicting or impeaching the testimony of deponent as a witness.

(2) The deposition of a party may be used by an adverse party for any purpose.

(3) The deposition may be used for any purpose if the Court finds: (A) that the witness is dead; or (B) that the witness is at such distance from the place of trial that it is not practicable for him to attend unless it appears that the absence of the witness was

---

[45]Rule 81(h).

procured by the party seeking to use the deposition; or (C) that the witness is unable to attend or testify because of age, illness, infirmity, or imprisonment; or (D) that the party offering the deposition has been unable to obtain attendance of the witness at the trial, as to make it desirable in the interests of justice, to allow the deposition to be used; or (E) that such exceptional circumstances exist, in regard to the absence of the witness at the trial, as to make it desirable in the interests of justice, to allow the deposition to be used.

(4) If only part of a deposition is offered in evidence by a party, an adverse party may require him to introduce any other part which ought in fairness to be considered with the part introduced, and any party may introduce any other parts.[46]

Section 6.18–Depositions Before Commencement of Case

A person who desires to perpetuate his own testimony or that of another person or to preserve any document or thing regarding any matter that may be cognizable in the Court, may file an application to take a deposition for such purpose.[47] In addition to the standard matters required in an application to take the deposition under the Rules, such application shall show:

1. The facts showing that the applicant expects to be a party to a case cognizable in the Court but is at present unable to bring it or cause it to be brought;
2. The subject matter of the expected action and his interest therein. Such an application will be entered upon a special docket, and service thereof and pleading with respect thereto will proceed subject to the requirements otherwise applicable to a motion. The hearing on such an application may be required by the Court. If the Court is satisfied that the perpetuation of the testimony or the preservation of the document or thing may prevent a failure or delay of justice, it will make an order authorizing the deposition and including such other terms and conditions as it may deem appropriate consistently with the Rules. If the deposition is taken, and if thereafter the expected case is commenced, the deposition may be used in that case subject to the Rules which would apply if the deposition had been taken after commencement of the case.[48]

---

[46]Rule 81(i).

[47]Rule 82; *Hall,* Re: Perpetuation of Pike Testimony, Docket No. 4-74-D, Memorandum Sur Order entered June 18, 1974.

[48]Rule 82.

Section 6.19–Depositions After Commencement of Trial

Likewise, a deposition may be taken under the Rules after trial has commenced, upon approval or direction of the Court. If so, the Court may impose such conditions to the taking of the deposition as it may find appropriate.[49]

Section 6.20–Depositions upon Written Questions

A party may make an application to the Court to take a deposition, otherwise authorized under Rules 81, 82 or 83, upon written questions rather than oral examination.[50] The oral examination provisions apply in all respects to such a deposition except to the extent clearly inapplicable or otherwise provided in Rule 84. Unless there is special reason for taking the deposition on written questions rather than oral examination, the Court will deny the application, without prejudice to seeking approval of the deposition upon oral examination. The taking of depositions upon written questions is not favored, except when the deposition is to be taken in a foreign country, in which event the deposition must be taken on written questions unless otherwise directed by the Court for good cause shown.[51]

An application to take written depositions shall have the written questions annexed thereto. With respect to such application, the 15-day period for filing objections prescribed by paragraph (b)(2) of Rule 81 is extended to 20 days, and within that 20-day period the objecting or responding party shall also file with the Court any cross-questions which he may desire to be asked at the taking of the deposition. The applicant shall then file any objections to the cross-questions, as well as any redirect questions, within 15 days after service on him of the cross-questions. Within 15 days after service of the redirect questions on the other party, he shall file with the Court any objections to the redirect questions, as well as any recross questions which he may desire to be asked. No objection to a written question will be considered unless it is filed with the Court within such applicable time. An original and five copies of all questions and objections shall be filed with the Clerk, who will make service thereof on the opposite party. The Court for good cause shown may enlarge or shorten the time in any respect.[52]

---

[49]Rule 83.

[50]Rule 84(a).

[51]Rule 84(a).

[52]Rule 84(b).

The officer taking the deposition shall propound all questions to the witness in their proper order. The parties and their counsel may attend the taking of the deposition but shall not participate in the deposition proceeding in any manner.[53]

The execution and filing of the deposition upon written questions must conform to the requirements for oral depositions.[54]

Section 6.21—Objections, Errors and Irregularities in Taking Depositions

All errors and irregularities in the procedure for obtaining approval for the taking of a deposition are waived, unless made in writing within the time for making objections or promptly where no time is prescribed. Objection to taking a deposition because of disqualification of the officer before whom it is to be taken is waived, unless made before the taking of the deposition begins or as soon thereafter as the disqualification becomes known or could be discovered with reasonable diligence.[55]

As to the use of a deposition in trial, in general an objection may be made at the trial or hearing to the use of a deposition, in whole or in part as evidence, for any reason which would require the exclusion of the testimony as evidence if the witness were then present and testifying. However, objections to the competency of a witness or to the competency, or relevancy of testimony are waived by failure to make them before or during the taking of the deposition, if the ground of the objection is one which might have been removed if presented at that time.[56]

As to manner and form, errors and irregularities occurring at the oral examination and the manner of taking deposition, in the form of the questions or answers, in the oath or affirmation, or in the conduct of the parties, and errors of any kind which might have been cured if promptly presented, are waived unless reasonable objection thereto is made at the taking of the deposition.[57]

As to errors by the officer, errors in the manner in which testimony is transcribed or the deposition is prepared, signed, certified, sealed, endorsed, transmitted, filed or otherwise dealt with by the pre-

---

[53]Rule 84(c).

[54]Rule 84(d).

[55]Rule 85(a), (b).

[56]Rule 85(c).

[57]Rule 85(d).

siding officer, are waived unless a motion to correct or suppress the deposition or some part thereof is made with reasonable promptness after such defect is, or with due diligence might have been, ascertained.[58]

Section 6.22–The Court Looks at Title VIII

Despite the absolute prohibition for discovery depositions in the Rules, the Court has already been required to rule on several such applications. In each such case, the Court has made it crystal clear that it does not intend to expand discovery procedures to include oral depositions and that Titles VII and VIII mean what they say.[59]

---

[58]Rule 85(e).

[59]*Gauthier,* 62 T.C. 245 (1974); *Hoch,* Docket No. 6262-73, Memorandum Sur Order entered April 9, 1974; *Hall,* Re: Perpetuation of Pike Testimony, Docket No. 4-74-D, Memorandum Sur Order entered June 18, 1974.

CHAPTER **7**

Decision Without Trial on Submitted Cases

Section 7.01–General

THIS IS AN IMPORTANT PROCEDURAL AREA where the new Rules significantly expand opportunities for the parties to dispose of unsettled cases without trial where there is no genuine issue of fact. The new procedures permitted in Title XII, especially in Rules 120 and 121, should mark a real advance by the Court in deciding cases where there is no genuine issue of fact and without the necessity of even placing the case on a trial calendar.

Section 7.02–Judgment on the Pleadings

Judgment on the pleadings under Rule 120 serves much the same purpose as the archaic demurrer under common-law practice. After the pleadings are closed but within such time as not to delay the trial, any party may move for a judgment on the pleadings. Such motion shall be disposed of before trial unless the Court determines otherwise.[1]

Such a motion is obviously appropriate only where the pleadings do not raise a genuine issue of material fact, but rather involve only issues of law.

If, on a motion for judgment on the pleadings, matters outside the pleadings are presented to, and not excluded by, the Court, the motion shall be treated as one for summary judgment and shall be

---

[1] Rule 120(a).

disposed of as provided in Rule 121. If this is done, all parties shall be given reasonable opportunity to present all material made pertinent to such a motion by Rule 121.[2]

An interesting case under Rule 120 involved the question of whether fraud of guardians could be imputed to the infants. The Court denied petitioner's motion under Rule 120.[3]

The Court granted respondent's motion under Rule 120 where petitioner's only contention was constitutional exemption from tax because of his nationality.[4] The respondent's Rule 120 motion was sustained where a mother's nonqualification as a dependent, prevented her son's qualification as "head of a household."[5]

The Court granted another Rule 120 motion by the respondent where the petitioner pleaded that a member of the Quaker faith was not subject to income tax.[6] In yet another respondent victory, the Court held that a district court judgment was *res judicata* of petitioner's tax liability for the taxable years in question.[7]

The decided cases indicate that the Commissioner will use Rule 120 to good advantage to dispose of many cases expeditiously, rather than leave them for later disposition under lengthier proceedings.

Section 7.03–Summary Judgment

The adoption of a summary judgment rule certainly represents one of the most helpful additions to the Court's former practice. Basically, Rule 121 stems from the Federal Rules of Civil Procedure; those familiar with such Rules will be at home with Rule 121. Such a motion is available only if there is no genuine issue of a material fact. Such motion may be made at any time commencing 30 days after the pleadings are closed, but within such time as not to delay the trial.[8]

Regardless of the state of the pleadings, through materials outside the pleadings a party may be able to show that there is no genuine issue of material fact. Such outside materials may consist of affidavits, interrogatories, admissions, documents or other materials which demonstrate the absence of a fact dispute.

---

[2]Rule 120(b).

[3]*Prudden,* Docket No. 7032-73, Order and Memorandum Sur Order entered 4/15/74.

[4]*Gaines,* T.C. Memo 1975-54, ¶75,054 P-H Memo T.C.

[5]*O'Donovan,* Docket No. 9144-73 S, Memorandum Sur Order Entered 4/17/74.

[6]*Kent,* T.C. Memo 1974-304, ¶74,304 P-H Memo T.C.

[7]*Shaheen, Jr.,* 62 T.C. 359 (1974).

[8]Rule 121(a).

One of the most helpful provisions is that "A partial summary adjudication may be made which does not dispose of all the issues in the case."[9] This provision will enable many petitioners to have one or more issues of law decided in advance of the trial of one or more issues of fact. Prior to the new Rules, it was necessary to file a motion to sever the issues and try a law issue first, but this was cumbersome and was often opposed by respondent.

The Court has responded to this new provision with alacrity. One interesting case involved respondent's motion for summary judgment in two parts, one of which was denied as having a genuine issue of fact but the other granted which involved the allocation of alimony payments between child support and alimony, as to which there was no genuine issue of fact.[10] The Court found that the clear and unambiguous language of the controlling agreement specified the allocation of these payments.

In another case, the Court granted respondent's motion for a partial summary judgment as to an item of additional income which was clearly taxable as commissions with no genuine issue of material fact.[11]

In a motion for partial summary judgment by a petitioner under Rule 121 involving Section 482, the Court denied the motion because of its conclusion that there were genuine issues of material facts.[12] As a useful tool to dispose of law questions, however, Rule 121(b) should prove noteworthy.

Respondent's motion for summary judgment on the ground that petitioners were collaterally estopped from litigating respondent's determination of deficiencies for prior taxable years was sustained by the Court.[13] There was a prior judgment of a district court with respect to the identical liability involved in the Tax Court case.[14]

Petitioner's summary judgment motion was denied in another case involving alimony or property settlement where it was clear that a genuine material fact issue existed.[15]

Respondent prevailed in a summary judgment motion involving the disallowance of a deduction for contribution to a profit-sharing trust with no genuine issue of fact remaining.[16] On the other hand, a petitioner

---

[9] Rule 121(b).

[10] *Giordano,* 63 T.C. 462 (1975), on appeal 5th Cir.

[11] *Henry,* 62 T.C. 605 (1974). *See also Reese,* 64 T.C. 395 (1975).

[12] *J. Ray McDermott & Co., Inc.,* Docket No. 5301-73, Memorandum Sur Order Entered 7/9/74.

[13] *Gammill,* 62 T.C. 607 (1974).

[14] *Cf. Shaheen,* 62 T.C. 359 (1974), where the identical result was reached under Rule 120.

[15] *Hoeme,* 63 T.C. 18 (1974).

[16] *Allied Investment Credit Corporation,* T.C. Memo 1975-2, ¶75,002 P-H Memo T.C.

failed to sustain his motion under Rule 121 involving exemptions for minor children, which is obviously not the kind of case lending itself to such a motion.[17]

Another helpful provision of Rule 121 covers a case not fully adjudicated on such a motion, but where facts have been developed which will be helpful upon the trial of the case. In this situation, the facts so specified by the Court shall be deemed established, which means that a party will not have to introduce them in evidence again, and the trial shall be conducted accordingly.[18] In other words, even though a motion for summary judgment may be denied in whole or in part, it may save time by establishing facts at that point which will avoid their reintroduction in evidence at the hearing.

Under Rule 121(d) supporting and opposing affidavits must be made on personal knowledge, must set forth facts that would be admissible in evidence, and must show affirmatively that the affiant is competent to testify to the matters stated in the affidavit. The Court may permit affidavits to be supplemented or opposed by answers to interrogatories, depositions, further affidavits, or other acceptable materials, so long as the other applicable provisions of the Rules are followed. A very important provision is that when a motion for summary judgment is made and supported as provided in Rule 121, an adverse party may not rest upon the mere allegations or denials of his pleading, but his response, by affidavits or as otherwise provided in the Rule, must set forth specific facts showing that there is a genuine issue for trial. If he does not so respond, a decision, if appropriate, may be entered against him.[19]

The Court will see that the interests of justice are served by this Rule. Should it appear from the affidavits of a party opposing the motion that he cannot for reasons stated present by affidavit facts essential to justify his opposition, the Court may deny the motion or may order a continuance to permit affidavits to be obtained or other steps to be taken or may make such other order as is just. Where it appears from the affidavits of a party opposing the motion that his only legally available method of controverting the facts set forth in the supporting affidavits of the moving party is through cross-examination of such affiants or the testimony of third parties from whom affidavits cannot be secured, such a showing may be deemed sufficient to establish that the facts set forth in such supporting affidavits are genuinely disputed.[20]

---

[17]*Carlson,* T.C. Memo 1974-299, ¶74,299 P-H Memo T.C.

[18]Rule 121(c).

[19]Rule 121(d).

[20]Rule 121(e).

Bad faith affidavits will invoke the penalties set forth in Rule 121(f), which include the contempt of court citation.

Section 7.04—Submission Without Trial

In addition to disposition by judgment on the pleadings or by summary judgment, the Court's practice includes disposition by submission without trial and without waiting for a case to be calendared for trial.[21] Usually this Rule will be invoked for fully stipulated facts,[22] but where sufficient facts have been admitted, established by deposition or included in the records in some other way, as well as by stipulation, a case may be submitted at any time by notice of the parties filed with the Court. The Chief Judge will assign such a case to a hearing judge, who will fix a time for filing briefs or for oral argument.[23]

Rule 122(b) makes clear that a petitioner normally having the burden of proof, submits a case to the Court under this Rule at his peril, since it does not alter the burden of proof, or the requirements otherwise applicable with respect to adducing proof, or the effect or failure of proof.

Section 7.05—Default and Dismissal

There must be, of course, a default and dismissal rule, which is covered by Rule 123. As to default, if a party fails to plead or otherwise proceed as provided by the Rules, or as required by the Court, he may be held in default by the Court either on motion of another party or on the Court's initiative, and thereafter the Court may enter a decision against the defaulting party, upon such terms and conditions as the Court may deem proper, or it may impose such sanctions under Rule 104 as the Court may deem appropriate. The Court may, in its discretion, conduct hearings to ascertain whether a default has been committed, to determine the decision to be entered or the sanctions to be imposed, or to ascertain the truth of any matter.[24] Obviously, the Court will apply this rule sparingly and only in the face of the most outrageous facts.

The Court may dismiss a case at any time and enter a decision against the petitioner for failure properly to prosecute or to comply with

---

[21] Rule 122(a).

[22] *Medco Products Co., Inc.*, 62 T.C. 509 (1974); *Draper Estate*, 64 T.C. 23 (1975).

[23] Rule 122(a).

[24] Rule 123(a); *Cox, Transferee*, Docket No. 9216-72, Order and Decision Entered 6/17/74.

the Rules or any order of the Court or for any cause which the Court deems sufficient.[25]

To temper justice with mercy, Rule 123(c) provides that for reasons deemed sufficient by the Court and upon motion expeditiously made, the Court may set aside a default or dismissal or the decision rendered thereon. But lest a petitioner relax unduly under the merciful provisions of Rule 123(c), Rule 123(d) provides that a decision rendered upon a default or in consequence of a dismissal, other than a dismissal for lack of jurisdiction, shall operate as an adjudication on the merits.

The Court has always functioned in an equitable fashion, even though it has no equity jurisdiction. Consequently, it is safe to say that Rule 123 will be administered fairly and equitably so that no taxpayer who deserves a better fate will be harmed.

All in all, Title XII should result in more expeditious disposition of cases involving solely legal issues. Past practice has seemed to inhibit such dispositions, but in view of the numerous tax cases where no genuine fact questions exist, increasing dispositive motion practice should result as practitioners become more familiar with these opportunities. Certainly the respondent has made good use of the summary judgment technique.

---

[25] Rule 123(b).

CHAPTER 8

Trial Calendars and Continuances

Section 8.01—Motions

BASIC MOTION PRACTICE IN THE COURT has been described in Chapter 4. Although motions are ordinarily heard in Washington, D. C. on a regular Wednesday motion calendar throughout the year, the Court, on its own motion or on a motion of a party, may direct otherwise.[1] In recent years, there has been an increasing trend on the part of the Court to accommodate parties, especially petitioners, by setting hearings on motions in the city designated as the place of trial. This is not to say that the Court has been showing favoritism to petitioners in this regard, but simply to point up the fact that respondent has counsel residing in all major cities and, if not residing there, residing at a place quite close to the hearing city. On the other hand, since petitioners are scattered throughout the land, it is much more difficult for a California petitioner than for respondent to have a motion argued in Washington.

Certainly, should respondent desire a motion to be heard in a city other than Washington, which would be equally convenient for petitioner, it is clear that the Court would be happy to accommodate respondent. The point is that the Court is striving diligently to be available and accessible to parties throughout the country on short notice on motions which must be ruled on quickly if the results are to be most valuable to the parties.

---

[1] Rule 130(a).

The Court may hear a motion *ex parte* where a party fails to appear at such a hearing.[2] Under established motion practice a written response also will be considered by the Court if a party does not choose to have counsel present at the hearing.

Section 8.02—Report Calendars

On a calendar specifically set for the purpose or on a trial calendar, and after notice to the parties of the time and place, any case at issue may be listed and called, first, for report as to whether the case is to be tried or otherwise disposed of, and if the latter, for a report as to its status.[3] Second, if it is to be tried, there will be a report on the status of preparation for trial, with particular reference to the stipulation requirements of Rule 91.[4] With respect to any case on such a calendar, the Court may consider other matters and take such action as it deems appropriate.[5]

Report calendars are especially helpful in connection with complex cases where the trial time is estimated to be at least several days and where the Court is interested in the progress of the parties toward settlement of some, or all, of the disputed issues and is also interested in the trial time if all issues are not settled. Often one or both of the parties will request that a case, or a group of cases, be set on a report calendar in order to ensure that there is orderly progress in the case and to keep the Court advised of such progress or lack thereof.

Section 8.03—Trial Calendars

The setting of a trial calendar in any hearing city is intermeshed with the operation of the Court system of Trial Status Orders as explained in Chapter 6. Not less than 90 days in advance, unless otherwise authorized by the Chief Judge, the Clerk will notify the parties of the place and time for which the calendar is set.[6] Normally, calendars begin on a Monday at ten o'clock A.M. Occasionally, a calendar will begin on a Tuesday, especially when Monday is a legal holiday, or on some later day in the week if a courtroom is not available for use by the Court on Monday.

---

[2] Rule 130(b).

[3] Rule 131.

[4] Rule 131.

[5] Rule 131.

[6] Rule 132(a).

This is a subject which has vexed the Court throughout the years, namely, the obtaining of a suitable courtroom in cities in which it does not have its own courtroom, where the Court must obtain use of a courtroom and judge's chambers from either a district court or some federal tribunal. In many cities, including New York, Chicago, Los Angeles and others, the Court has its own courtroom and chambers, which in some instances it shares with other federal tribunals and agencies who require a hearing room only intermittently.

In years past, the Court was forced to use courtrooms occupied by state courts in some cities, but this practice was unsatisfactory at best, and in recent times has been avoided if at all possible. The Court has been able to obtain its own room in an increasingly large number of cities; for example, when a new federal office building is constructed, additional space in the older building is released which is converted into a courtroom for the Tax Court and other traveling federal judicial tribunals, such as the trial judges of the United States Court of Claims. Obviously, where the Court sits in a city only once or twice a year, there is no pressing need for its own courtroom, but it makes a very awkward situation, nevertheless, when federal courtroom space is scarce in such a city. Sometimes the lack of a courtroom in a designated hearing city will require the Court to sit in the nearest adjacent smaller city that has an available room. For example, Louisville trial calendars have been held either in Frankfort, Kentucky or New Albany, Indiana, when no Louisville courtroom is available.

Each case appearing on a trial calendar will be called at the time and place scheduled. At the call, counsel or the parties must indicate their estimate of the time required for trial. The cases for trial will thereupon be tried in due course, but not necessarily in the order listed.[7] For example, the Court normally accommodates *pro se* petitioners and other cases requiring a very short time for submission on the first day or days of the trial calendar, such as Monday and Tuesday, and then sets the longer trials on later days in the session. Over the period of its existence, there has been a high degree of cooperation between counsel for respondent and petitioner in trying to agree on a day certain, such as Wednesday or Thursday, for the trial of a particular case, and then requesting the Court to honor that agreement if at all possible, which the Court always endeavors to do. There are rare cases, of course, where the parties cannot be accommodated on the day which they select, but this represents the exception rather than the rule.

In recent years, there has been a growing trend for the Court to hold informal pretrial conferences in chambers during the first or second

---

[7] Rule 132(b).

day of a trial calendar in order to assist in facilitating settlement of some or all issues and also in narrowing and simplifying issues to be tried. Likewise, there has been a growing trend on the part of several judges to require pretrial memoranda, exchanging of expert opinions, and even trial briefs prior to the call of the calendar. All these steps are to the good since they facilitate progress at the trial calendar.

Most trial calendars are set for a projected period of five trial days from Monday to Friday, which means that the parties must be ready to go forward at any time in the day when their case is reached and not wait until the beginning of the following court day. For example, many cases start in mid-morning or mid-afternoon rather than at the opening of court on the following day. If this practice were not followed, the Court could not dispose of its heavy work load efficiently as it has always done. The Court normally sits about six or seven hours each day, from 9 or 9:30 to 4:30 or 5 with several interim recesses and the usual luncheon recess.

As in other federal courts, the Tax Court works very harmoniously with counsel in an effort to handle its trial calendars with convenience and dispatch. This means that counsel for both parties should always get together, cooperate and talk over trial matters in advance for their mutual benefit and also for the benefit of the Court. If they fail so to cooperate, the Court may cause them to on its own motion, but voluntary cooperation is much the best policy.

Where a case has been estimated for trial time of several days or even longer than a week, it will normally be placed on a special calendar at a designated time and place,[8] which might not be the original hearing city if the parties agree on another city for that purpose so as to speed up the disposition of the case. This is necessary because most trial calendars are scheduled for only one week, and a longer trial will obviously disrupt the shorter cases set on a regular trial calendar.

Section 8.04—Continuances

A case or matters scheduled on a calendar may be continued by the Court upon motion or on its own initiative.[9] Court action, on cases or matters set for hearing or trial or other consideration, will not be delayed by a motion for continuance unless it is timely, sets forth good and sufficient cause and complies with all applicable rules.[10] Conflicting

[8] Rule 133.
[9] Rule 134.
[10] Rule 134.

engagements of counsel or employment of new counsel will not be regarded as grounds for continuance unless the motion for continuance, in addition to otherwise satisfying Rule 134, is filed promptly after notice is given of the hearing or trial or other scheduled matter, or unless extenuating circumstances for later filing are shown which the Court deems adequate. A motion for continuance, filed 30 days or less prior to the date to which it is directed, may be set for hearing on that date.[11] In practice the Court is reasonable in granting continuances for good cause shown, but certainly will not be imposed upon by the parties if it feels that there has been any dereliction in duty. In short, the Court must be convinced that the requested continuance will serve the interests of justice before it will be granted. Again, as a matter of practice, the Court will ordinarily grant the first requested continuance for cause shown without much more than perhaps mild criticism of the requesting attorney, but any future continuances will have to be very strongly presented to receive favorable consideration by the Court.

The best policy is to be ready for trial on the scheduled date if at all possible and save requests for continuances for such emergencies as illness or unavoidable absence of a key witness.

---

[11]Rule 134.

CHAPTER 9

Trials

Section 9.01—Place of Trial

SINCE THIS IS A CIRCUIT-RIDING COURT, most trials are held elsewhere than in Washington, D.C., the headquarters city. This is not to say that many trials are not held in Washington, since cases arising in the District of Columbia, of course, and in adjacent areas, such as Maryland and Virginia, are often held in Washington. In addition, for a multitude of reasons, many petitioners prefer that cases be held in Washington, especially petitioners on the eastern seaboard.

The request for place of trial represents the first initiative accorded a petitioner, since he should file a request for the place at which he would prefer the trial to be held at the time of filing the petition.[1] Except in extraordinary cases, such request will be automatically granted by the Court. If the petitioner does not file such a request, the respondent, at the time he files his answer, shall file a request showing the place of trial preferred by him. Appendix IV (in Rules) lists cities where the Court's regular trial sessions are held. They are ordinarily the only cities at which the Court will hold trial sessions, but as pointed out heretofore, if a court room is not available in one of these cities, then the Court will hold trials at an adjacent city where a courtroom is available. In any event, it is wiser to request that the trial be held in one of the listed cities rather than in a different city, because the Court is not likely to depart from its accustomed places of trial. For example, since Indianapolis is the only city in which the Court ordinarily sits in Indiana, assuming the courtroom is available, it would be unwise to request the hearing in Fort Wayne, South

---

[1] Rule 140(a).

Bend or Evansville, the three next largest cities in the state. If a petitioner should do so, the Court would most likely fix Indianapolis as the place of trial or might await the request of the respondent for place of trial before entering its order to this effect.

The request for place of trial should be filed separately from the petition or answer and is subject to the general requirements applicable to filing motions.[2] The Court will designate a place of trial which involves as little inconvenience and expense to taxpayers as is practicable.[3] The parties will be promptly notified of the place at which the trial will be held,[4] normally by return mail where the petitioner requests a place of hearing which is on the list shown in the appendix.

If either party desires a change in the designation of the place of trial, he must file a motion to that effect, stating fully his reasons therefor.[5] This is frequently required where a petitioner moves from one part of the country to another prior to the issuance of the notice of the time of trial. It is good practice to file a motion for change of place of trial very promptly, since such motions, made after the notice of the time of trial has been issued, will not be deemed to have been timely filed.[6]

Section 9.02–Consolidation; Separate Trials

When cases involving a common question of law or fact are pending before the Court, it may order a joint hearing or trial of any or all of the matters in issue; it may order all the cases consolidated; and it may make such orders concerning proceedings therein as may tend to avoid unnecessary costs or delay or duplication. Similar action may be taken where cases involve different tax liabilities of the same parties, notwithstanding the absence of a common issue.[7]

Ordinarily, there is no need to consolidate cases until the time of trial, since if cases are settled in advance of trial, separate stipulations must be filed in any event. It is only at trial time that consolidation becomes necessary for practical purposes.

By the same token, the Court, in furtherance of convenience or to avoid prejudice, or when separate trials will be conducive to expedition or economy, may order a separate trial of any one or more claims or

[2]Rule 140(b).

[3]Rule 140(c).

[4]Rule 140(c).

[5]Rule 140(d).

[6]Rule 140(d).

[7]Rule 141(a).

defenses or issues, or of the tax liability of any party or parties. The Court may enter appropriate orders or decisions with respect to any such claims, defenses, issues or parties that are tried separately.[8]

Section 9.03–Burden of Proof

The burden of proof shall be upon the petitioner in all cases, except as otherwise provided by statute or determined by the Court; and except that, in respect of any new matter, increases in deficiency and affirmative defenses, pleaded in his answer, it shall be upon the respondent.[9] Familiar examples of statutory burden of proof upon respondent are with respect to fraud, transferee liability and assertion that more than 25 percent of gross income was unreported to extend the statute of limitations to six, instead of three, years.[10]

A recent addition to the statutory burden of proof on respondent cases is that in any case involving the issue of the knowing conduct of a foundation manager as set forth in Sections 4941, 4944 or 4945, the burden of proof is on the respondent, which must be carried by clear and convincing evidence.[11]

The distinction between (a) burden of proof and (b) burden of producing and going forward with proof is most important, but frequently misunderstood. The burden of proof is fixed by statute and can never be shifted. The burden of producing and going forward with proof, however, may be shifted by the making of a *prima facie* case by the bearer of the burden of proof. When this occurs, the other party must go forward with proof or risk a Court decision that the burden of proof bearer has also successfully carried his burden of proof.[12]

Illustrative of these basic principles is an interesting decision holding that where the burden of producing and going forward with proof has been shifted from petitioner to the respondent and he has been ordered to present independent, constitutionally untainted evidence to sustain determined deficiences, the respondent's determination cannot be sustained after he refuses to present any evidence and declines to go forward with the proof.[13]

---

[8]Rule 141(b).

[9]Rule 142(a).

[10]Rule 142(b), (d).

[11]Rule 142(c).

[12]*Byrum,* 58 T.C. 731 (1972).

[13]*Suarez,* 58 T.C. 792 (1972) *and* 61 T.C. 841 (1974).

Every tax attorney soon learns that the burden of proof is a powerful weapon in the Commissioner's hands in most Tax Court cases. Often the presence of this burden will determine the course of settlement negotiations; if it cannot be overcome, a modest settlement might be considered preferable to a gallant trial defeat. In those rare cases where the burden of proof rests on the Commissioner, the shoe is, of course, on the other foot with reverse implications.

In the final analysis, counsel for petitioner must usually wrestle with the soul-searching decision of whether he has met his double trial burdens—(1) going forward with the proof and (2) ultimately overcoming the presumption of correctness attaching to the Commissioner's deficiency determination.

Section 9.04—Burden of Proof in Unreasonable Accumulation of Earnings Cases

One of the several new provisions of the Rules which should be helpful to petitioners is Rule 142(e) involving the accumulated earnings tax under Section 531. Where the notice of deficiency is based in whole or in part on an allegation of accumulation of corporate earnings and profits beyond the reasonable needs of the business, the burden of proof with respect to such allegation is determined in accordance with Section 534. If the petitioner has submitted to the respondent a statement which is claimed to satisfy the requirements of Section 534(c), the Court will ordinarily on timely motion filed after the case has been calendared for trial, rule prior to the trial on whether such statement is sufficient to shift the burden of proof to the limited extent set forth in Section 534(a)(2).[14]

Prior to the decision of the Court in *Chatham Corporation*[15] in 1967, the Court had adopted the opposite view, that is, it would not rule prior to the trial on whether petitioner's statement was sufficient to shift the burden of proof. This position was exemplified in *The Shaw-Walker Company*[16] and similar cases. There are still no sharp teeth in Rule 142(e) because of the restrictive limitation of the word "ordinarily" governing the ruling by the Court. In actual practice, it is predicted that this Rule will mean what the presiding trial judge deems it to mean, that is, if he deems it to indicate that the Court should rule in advance of trial on the burden of proof, he will likely do so, but if he is of the opposite

[14]Rule 142(e).

[15]48 T.C. 145 (1967).

[16]39 T.C. 293 (1962).

persuasion and favors the *Shaw-Walker Company* approach, he can still rely on the word "ordinarily" and refuse to so rule in advance of trial.

Why is this advance ruling so important to a petitioner? If a petitioner has filed a complete and detailed statement of his grounds for retaining earnings under Section 534(c) and is able to obtain a ruling from the Court several weeks or months prior to trial that the burden of proof is on the respondent to overcome such grounds, there is a very strong probability that the respondent will accede to petitioner's position and drop the accumulated earnings case in its entirety. Most accumulated earnings cases turn on the necessities for the retention of earnings and this is why the burden of proof is such a pivotal point. If a petitioner must wait until actual trial to go forward with the evidence and prove affirmatively its grounds for retention of earnings which it has already set forth in its Section 534(c) statement, a settlement without hearing is much less likely, even though the respondent may concede the issue after trial and without submission to the Court for final decision.

A constant difficulty on this issue are the disparate views of the 16 judges as to the application of Section 534(c) and the burden of proof rule. Some judges take an extreme view that the Congress really did not change the meaning of the basic statute by this provision, whereas at the other extreme several judges give full effect to Section 534(c) and rule well in advance, upon proper motion, and with respect to each ground set forth in the statement. This points up the necessity of filing a most complete and adequate statement under Section 534(c) in order to be prepared for a thorough oral argument and ruling by the Court on each particular ground set forth in the statement.

Another advantage of an adequate Section 534(c) statement is that it may also persuade either the Audit Division or the Appellate Division to yield on the issue even prior to the issuance of a statutory notice of deficiency. In other words, the examining agent has assumed the responsibility for asserting the application of the accumulated earnings tax in his report, but frequently the facts for the taxpayer have not been fully assembled or presented to the examining officer. This may be done most effectively in a complete Section 534(c) statement, which will be very important as the case goes forward, either administratively or judicially.

As the Rule indicates, a motion to shift the burden of proof under Section 534(c) should be filed after the case has been calendared for trial, which means within approximately 90 days of the trial date.[17] Good practice normally indicates that a hearing on the motion be requested in Washington at the earliest convenient date prior to the trial

---

[17] Rule 142(e).

date, and also that the motion set forth a request that the hearing judge for the particular trial calendar be assigned to hear this motion. This is most important because it is wise to begin to inform the hearing judge at the earliest possible date of the grounds for retention of earnings so that he will be well advised thereon even if the motion should not be granted and the case remain on the trial calendar. In many cases, the judge will sustain petitioner on one or more grounds in the statement and reject one or more grounds therein.

Section 9.05–Evidence

In general, trials are conducted in accordance with the rules of evidence applicable in trials without a jury in the United States District Court for the District of Columbia. To the extent applicable to such trials, those rules include the rules of evidence in the Federal Rules of Civil Procedure and any rules of evidence generally applicable in the federal courts (including the United States District Court of the District of Columbia.)[18] With the adoption of the new Federal Rules of Evidence, effective July 1, 1975, this rule is made more definite and certain.

Throughout its history, the Court has applied quite liberal rules of receiving evidence, which is normal and natural in view of the fact that the court is an expert tribunal sitting without a jury. If otherwise inadmissible evidence is received at the trial, along with properly admissible evidence, the Court can well winnow the wheat from the chaff before rendering its decision. Appellate courts are much more likely to reverse on the court's refusal to admit evidence than on its admission of doubtful evidence. Hence, the Court follows the appellate court trend in this regard and is seldom reversed because of its admission or refusal to admit evidence.

It is most important to present completely all available evidence at the trial. The Court seldom gives a second bite at the apple.

"It is the policy of this Court to try all the issues raised in a case in one proceeding to avoid piecemeal and protracted litigation."[19]

"Reconsideration of proceedings already concluded is generally denied in the absence of substantial error or unusual circumstances."[20]

---

[18]Rule 143(a).

[19]*Robin Haft Trust,* 62 T.C. 145 (1974); *Second Carey Trust,* 41 B.T.A. 800 (1940), *aff'd,* 126 F. 2d 526, 28 AFTR 1371 (D.C. Cir. 1942), *cert. denied,* 317 U.S. 642 (1942).

[20]*Robin Haft Trust,* 62 T.C. 145 (1974); *Selwyn Operating Corporation,* 11 B.T.A. 593 (1928).

"In the interest of efficient performance of the judicial work, a second trial is not ordinarily granted to consider a new theory which could have been presented in the first trial."[21]

The Court denied the respondent's request to reopen the trial record to receive substitute evidence in the light of the Court's ruling that proferred evidence was inadmissible.[22]

Strict enforcement of the stipulation of facts rule usually results in a minumum of oral evidence to be offered at the trial of most cases. Of course, there are many exceptions to this situation, as in fraud cases where the evidence may consist almost entirely of oral evidence. But in the vast majority of cases before the Court, the evidence is primarily documentary in nature, which means that very little oral testimony is required to flesh out the documentary fact skeleton.

Ex parte affidavits, statements in briefs and unadmitted allegations in pleadings do not constitute evidence.[23]

As to depositions, testimony taken by deposition shall not be treated as evidence until offered and received in evidence by the Court. Error in the transcript of a deposition may be corrected by agreement of the parties, or by the Court on proof if deemed satisfactory to show an error exists and the correction to be made.[24]

The Court is very strict as to the legibility of documentary evidence. A *clearly legible* copy of any book, record, paper or document may be offered directly in evidence in lieu of the original, where there is no objection or where the original is available but admission of a copy is authorized by the Court; however, unless impractical, the Court may require the submission of the original. Where the original is admitted in evidence, a *clearly legible* copy may be substituted later for the original or such part thereof as may be relevant, upon leave granted at the discretion of the Court.[25] In actual practice, since clear and distinct photocopies are now readily available, seldom is an original document left in the files of the Court after the hearing. As a matter of fact, seldom is the original document even introduced in evidence at the outset, since the parties are now able to agree on the use of photocopies without difficulty in most cases and thus avoid having to place the original document in evidence and withdraw it later upon substitution by a photocopy.

---

[21] *Robin Haft Trust,* 62 T.C. 145 (1974); *Pierce Oil Corporation,* 30 B.T.A. 469 (1934).

[22] *Patz,* Memorandum and Order entered 7/23/74.

[23] Rule 143(b).

[24] Rule 143(c).

[25] Rule 143(d)(1).

Exhibits received in evidence may be disposed of as the Court deems advisable. A party desiring the return at his expense of any exhibit belonging to him, shall, after decision of the case by the Court has become final, make written application to the Clerk, suggesting a practical manner of delivery.[26] In practice, the Clerk has now adopted a policy of returning all exhibits to petitioner, assuming he offered them in evidence, at a reasonable time after the decision of the case has become final. This is an automatic process and does not require the petitioner to affirmatively request the return of exhibits. In many cases, however, the petitioner desires the return of a document as soon as possible and, therefore, he should follow Rule 143(d)(2) in such cases. The prevalent use of photocopies, however, has made this situation much less important than in the past.

As to interpreters, the Court may appoint an interpreter of its own selection and fix his reasonable compensation, which shall be paid by one or more of the parties or otherwise as the Court may direct.[27]

Section 9.06—Exceptions Unnecessary

Formal exceptions to rulings or orders of the Court are unnecessary. It is sufficient that a party, at the time of the ruling or order of the Court is made or sought, makes known to the Court the action which he desires the court to take or his objection to the action of the Court and his grounds therefor; and, if a party has no opportunity to object to a ruling or order at the time it is made, the absence of an objection does not thereafter prejudice him.[28]

This Rule is quite liberal to protect both parties in their possible appeal of a decision. In short, the Court has made clear that it will not allow a technical defect to prevent proper appeal with respect to its rulings or orders.

Section 9.07—Exclusion of Proposed Witnesses

This new rule simply formalizes the long-standing practice of the Court which has been in accord with general trial court practice. On its own motion or on motion of a party, the Court may exclude from the

---

[26] Rule 143(d)(2).

[27] Rule 143(e).

[28] Rule 144.

courtroom any or all persons, other than parties whom the parties expect or intend to call as witnesses in the case. In connection with any such exclusion, the Court may issue to witnesses (actual or potential), counsel and parties, such instructions as it may deem appropriate in the circumstances. In the discretion of the Court, it may refuse to apply this provision to a person acting in an advisory capacity to counsel for either party. A certified public accountant, for example, who is assisting counsel might come within this exception, as might an Appellate Conferee in the same capacity. Undue delay in moving for such exclusion of a person may be treated by the Court as sufficient grounds for denying the motion, pointing up the necessity of planning in advance and acting promptly at the outset of the trial to move for exclusion under this rule.[29]

Among other measures which the Court may take in the circumstances, it may punish as for a contempt (i) any witness who remains within hearing of the proceedings after such exclusion has been directed, that fact being noted in the record; and (ii) any person (witness, counsel or party) who willfully violates instructions issued by the Court with respect to such exclusion.[30]

Section 9.08—Determination of Foreign Law

A party who intends to raise an issue concerning the law of a foreign country must give notice in his pleadings or other reasonable written notice. The Court, in determining foreign law, may consider any relevant material or source, including testimony, whether or not submitted by a party or otherwise admissible. The Court's determination shall be treated as a ruling on a question of law.[31]

Section 9.09—Subpoenas

Every subpoena shall be issued under the seal of the Court, shall state the name of the Court and the caption of the case and shall command each person to whom it is directed to attend and give testimony at a time and place therein specified. A subpoena, including a subpoena for the production of documentary evidence, signed and sealed but otherwise in blank, shall be issued to a party requesting it, who shall fill it

---

[29]Rule 145(a).

[30]Rule 145(b).

[31]Rule 146. *See Reese,* 64 T.C. 395 (1975).

in before service. Subpoenas may be obtained from the clerk in Washington or from a deputy clerk at a trial session.[32]

A subpoena may also command the person to whom it is directed to produce the books, papers, documents, or other tangible things designated therein; but the Court, upon motion made promptly and in any event at or before the time specified in the subpoena for compliance therewith, may (i) quash or modify the subpoena if it is unreasonable and oppressive, or (ii) condition denial of the motion upon the advancement by the person in whose behalf the subpoena is issued of the reasonable cost of producing the books, papers, documents or tangible things.[33]

A subpoena may be served by a United States Marshal, or by his deputy, or by any other person who is not a party and is not less than 18 years of age. Service of a subpoena upon a person named therein shall be made by delivering a copy thereof to such person and by tendering to him fees for one day's attendance and the mileage allowed by law. When the subpoena is issued on behalf of the Commissioner, fees and mileage need not be tendered. The person making service of a subpoena shall make his return thereon in accordance with the form appearing in the subpoena.[34]

The detailed rules for issuance and response to a subpoena for taking depositions are set forth in Rule 147(d) and should be carefully followed in the limited applicable situations. In most cases involving the taking of a deposition, which of course is only to preserve and perpetuate testimony, a subpoena should be unnecessary because usually the deposition will be taken by stipulation of the parties. If not, where the deposition is taken on application of a party instead of by stipulation, good practice will indicate that prior arrangements should be made with the person who will be deposed for the production of the necessary documents or things in connection with the deposition. This practice is much to be preferred to the use of a subpoena for taking depositions.

As in most other trial courts, failure by any person without adequate excuse to obey a subpoena so served upon him may be deemed a contempt of the Court.[35]

Section 9.10—Fees and Mileage

Any witness summoned to a hearing or trial, or whose deposition is taken, shall receive the same fees and mileage as witnesses in the

---

[32] Rule 147(a).

[33] Rule 147(b).

[34] Rule 147(c).

[35] Rule 147(e).

United States district courts. No witness, other than one for the Commissioner, shall be required to testify until he shall have been tendered the fees and mileage to which he is entitled according to law. The party at whose instance a witness appears shall be responsible for the payment of the fees and mileage to which that witness is entitled.[36]

Section 9.11–Failure to Appear or to Adduce Evidence

The unexcused absence of a party or his counsel when a case is called to trial will not be grounds for a delay. The case may be dismissed for failure properly to prosecute, or the trial may proceed and the case be regarded as submitted on the part of the absent party or parties.[37] The stringency of this rule clearly indicates that if petitioner or his counsel cannot be present when a case is to be called for trial, prior arrangements should be made with counsel for respondent for delay in moving for failure properly to prosecute or in making appropriate arrangements to cover the situation. Normally, counsel for respondent will cooperate if counsel for the petitioner acts reasonably under the particular facts governing the situation.

Failure to produce evidence, in support of an issue of fact as to which a party has the burden of proof and which has not been conceded by his adversary, may be grounds for dismissal or for determination of the affected issue against that party. The mere filing of a stipulation of facts does not relieve the party upon whom rests the burden of proof of the necessity of properly producing other evidence in support of facts not adequately established by the stipulation of facts.[38] In short, even though the parties have diligently labored to bring forth a stipulation of facts as complete as possible, this does not relieve petitioner, or respondent, as the case may be, of adducing other evidence in court to sustain his burden of proof if there is any doubt as to whether the stipulation of facts itself contains all necessary relevant evidence.

Section 9.12–Record of Proceedings

Hearings and trials before the Court are stenographically reported or otherwise recorded, and a transcript thereof is made if, in the opinion of the Court or the judge presiding at a hearing or trial, a permanent record is deemed appropriate. Transcripts are supplied to the

---

[36] Rule 148.

[37] Rule 149(a).

[38] Rule 149(b).

parties and other persons at such charges as are fixed and approved by the Court.[39] In practice, all regular trial sessions are stenographically recorded from the opening of court to the close of the last case set for trial at that session. Likewise, all hearings in Washington on motions and related matters are similarly recorded. Either party may order a copy of the transcript of record, and the Court always orders a copy. In recent times, most hearings are tape recorded which indicates the passing of the availability of the shorthand reporter or even the stenotype reporter.

Whenever the testimony of a witness at a trial or hearing which was stenographically reported or otherwise recorded is admissible in evidence at a later trial or hearing, it may be proved by the transcript thereof duly certified by the person who reported the testimony.[40]

Section 9.13–Briefs

This is truly a court of written argument, not oral argument, although oral argument may be permitted by the presiding judge upon proper motion by a party or upon his own motion.[41] Oral argument is, however, the extremely rare exception rather than the rule, being used chiefly in simple cases where the parties are able to sum up the facts and the law immediately after the hearing and receive a bench decision. For every one such simple case, there are literally thousands of more complex cases which involve multiple issues and which simply do not lend themselves to meaningful oral argument at the conclusion of a hearing. In such cases, it is possible for a party to request an oral argument at some later date upon receipt of the transcript and perhaps after filing written briefs, but granting such a request is entirely within the discretion of the Court. It would be opposed in many cases by counsel for respondent since he would presumably have to travel to Washington for such an argument, although an oral argument could be set in the hearing city on an occasion when the trial judge was in or near that city for other trial calendars.

In recent years, there has been an increasing trend by the judges to the use of pretrial briefs, or summaries of the facts and law, and it is believed that this trend will continue to the advantage of all concerned. The mainstay of argument before the Court, however, continues to be the post-trial briefs which may be either simultaneous or seriatim. Again the

---

[39] Rule 150(a).

[40] Rule 150(b).

[41] Rule 151(a).

increasing trend has been the use of simultaneous briefs with reply briefs thereafter. Rule 151 sets forth in detail the timing, service, number of copies and form and contents of these post-trial briefs.

As to the contents, certainly the briefs are critical documents in every case because they usually afford the parties their only argumentative opportunity. Consequently, the most careful attention should be lavished upon their preparation. Unfortunately, the quality of briefs filed with the Court is depressingly low in spite of their importance.

The findings of fact should be scrupulously detailed and reflect every fact that the party feels is relevant to the decision in the case and also to provide the Court with sufficient background to properly write his opinion. These requested findings of fact should be carefully buttressed by appropriate references to the pages of the transcript or the exhibits or other sources relied upon to support the requested fact.

Many parties fail to include a concise statement of points on which the party relies. This again is a vital part of the brief, because the trial judge may well look to this page first in order to have a clear knowledge of which points seem most important to the party. If these points are haphazardly prepared, or even omitted, the party starts off at a disadvantage in his brief.

The argument portion of the brief cannot be overemphasized. How long should it be? Again, as with respect to the drafting of a good petition, it should thoroughly cover the subject, leave no stone unturned in presenting the case, but not bore the judge. Redundancy and repetition should be avoided, but at the same time the best points should be hammered home more than once in many situations so that the Court will not misapprehend their force and effect.

All relevant citations should support the fact arguments. Adverse decisions should be distinguished in the opening brief if the party knows that the other party will cite them in his brief. If not, it is best to wait until the reply brief before distinguishing cases which may or may not be included in the other party's opening brief.

There are as many ways to write a good brief as there are good brief writers, but all share certain common denominators. Clarity of expression, completeness of fact statement, careful analysis of the legal points involved, a felicity of expression—these attributes, at least, will be found in all good briefs. The main thing is to work, work, work until your brief is as near perfect as you can make it. You should begin with an opening draft and then edit and polish and embellish until it shines like a rare jewel. Only then should you feel that you have done everything possible to achieve success.

Section 9.14—the Anatomy of a Tax Court Trial

Trial lawyers differ somewhat in their techniques. Nevertheless, there are many fundamental qualities which are common to all good trial lawyers, including those trying Tax Court cases. The difference is primarily in emphasis because of the nature of the issues before the Court.

To begin at the outset of a trial, differences of opinion exist as to an appropriate opening statement. My personal preference is for a complete statement which will fully inform the Court of the issues and facts relied upon by petitioner. Bearing in mind that petitioner always has the burden of proof in Tax Court cases except for the rare statutory exceptions, a good opening statement gives petitioner the first opportunity to put his best foot forward. Many attorneys look on the opening statement as a perfunctory evil which they should dispose of as quickly as possible. The Court is anxious to learn as much about the case as possible and up to that point it has only the pleadings for information purposes, unless the judge has requested a pretrial memorandum brief. Since the notice of deficiency is frequently rather sparse, and since the petition may likewise be less than informative, he is awaiting word from petitioner's attorney as to what he should know about the case and if the attorney lets him down, he may enter the trial proceedings in a state of perplexity, if not confusion.

A detailed opening by petitioner's counsel will usually contrast sharply with the opening statement by respondent's counsel, since the latter does not have in his possession many of the pertinent facts and is not in a position to explain to the Court how the evidence will unfold. This, of course, is especially important if the case requires considerable oral testimony.

Since the evidence in most tax cases consists chiefly of the stipulation of facts and attached exhibits, the opening statement should contain a full explanation of the most significant portions of the stipulation and the exhibits. This will enable the Court to strike through many of the superfluous passages and get to the heart of the case for which the Court should be appreciative to counsel.

After the opening statements, petitioner, of course, must begin the presentation of his case. His first decision and a vital one, will be the order of his witnesses. My recommendation is to lead with an ace if at all possible.[42] In other words, begin with a very strong witness, usually the

---

[42]*Delaware Trucking Co., Inc.*, T.C. Memo 1973-29, ¶73,029 P-H Memo T.C.; *Atkinson*, 31 T.C. 1241 (1959).

chief witness, which will enlighten the Court and also should give the Court a good first impression of petitioner's evidence. Sometimes chronological fact development requires the use of minor witnesses in advance of primary witnesses, but if at all possible, save the minor witnesses for the tail end of the trial.

Another trial axiom is never use two or more witnesses where one ace is available.[43] This will avoid a witness being tripped up by the testimony of another witness, especially if the rule of excluding witnesses is in effect.

Since petitioner has the burden of proof, which is the burden of final persuasion, omission of relevant evidence will be fatal. This causes some attorneys to introduce excessive evidence on the theory that it is better to include everything possible than to leave anything out. It is my recommendation that this temptation should be resisted to the utmost. I believe that a "tight" record is preferable to a lengthy, unwieldy record in most cases. A good trial brief will point up the critical items of evidence which must be introduced and, after they are in the record, try to avoid introducing other evidence simply to be on the safe side. Of course, if there is any real doubt, it is better to flood the record than to choke it. My philosophy is to stipulate the maximum facts, making sure that every possible relevant fact is included therein, and then limit the oral testimony to the remaining minimum.[44]

You should prepare your witnesses for cross-examination, since respondent has to rely primarily on cross-examination to elicit his evidence. Always try to anticipate respondent's approach and arguments by putting yourself in his place and thinking what you would do if your roles were reversed. By doing so, you can better prepare your witnesses for cross-examination so that it will not be an ordeal for them.

As to cross-examination, under the new Federal Rules of Evidence, it will be restricted to the scope of the direct examination under most situations. Obviously, the Court will allow wider scope of cross-examination hearing the case without a jury than would otherwise be true. It is believed that under the new Rules of Evidence, however, the Court will tighten up the scope of cross-examination as compared to its prior practice.

Because of the pervasive nature of the stipulation of fact process, most Tax Court trials are short, dull and uninteresting to the spectator. The nuts and bolts of the case should be in the stipulation of

[43] *Geiger & Peters, Inc.*, 27 T.C. 911 (1957); *Ball*, 54 T.C. 1200 (1970).

[44] *Weaver Popcorn Co., Inc.*, T.C. Memo 1971-281, ¶71,281 P-H Memo T.C.; *Lewis*, 47 T.C. 129 (1966).

facts.[45] The oral testimony is usually the "frosting on the cake." Not so, of course, in cases involving essentially fact questions, such as reasonable compensation, valuation, intent and fraud. But in the typical Tax Court case, involving technical issues, oral testimony is relatively unimportant.[46]

In the trial of a case, in essence, try to put your mind in the place of the judge's mind—what will persuade him? Different approaches may be indicated from judge to judge. Try to learn the characteristics of each judge to the extent possible, which is, of course, difficult because of the infrequency of your appearance before a particular Tax Court judge. It is possible, however, by keen observation, inquiring of other lawyers and by careful reading of opinions of each judge as they are issued, especially on issues similar to your case, to arrive at an analysis of a judge's philosophy and approach to many of the questions and issues that will arise in the course of your trial.

In every case conduct yourself as a gentleman or gentlewoman. Be courteous and pleasant at all times regardless of what may transpire in the courtroom. Admittedly, this is an admonition which may be difficult to follow at times, but it is remarkable how good conduct on your part will inspire good conduct on the part of all others with whom you may be having dealings in the courtroom, including the judge, opposing counsel and hostile witnesses. Although it would be impossible to prove, undoubtedly some cases are even won or lost because of the good or bad conduct of counsel for one of the parties.

My philosophy is to look upon a trial as an adversary proceeding in which points are scored for action, inaction, conduct and misconduct. The scoring of these points begins from the time you start to prepare a case for trial, as you proceed through the settlement negotiating and stipulation of fact processes and then as you actually enter the courtroom and begin the trial. Even the way you conduct yourself at the counsel table will be carefully observed by most judges. Clothing, demeanor, attitude, even the expression on your face, can begin to set the tone for the trial. A scowling counsel normally will not score as many points as a pleasant counsel. This is not to say that you should go about constantly in a mirthful manner, but that you should exude pleasant self-confidence. Only as you are well prepared inwardly will you outwardly reflect the aura of the successful advocate. When all is said and done, even the advocate is on trial to a certain extent and you should make sure that your conduct is an advantage, not a disadvantage, to your client.

---

[45] *Ball,* 54 T.C. 1200 (1970); *Austin State Bank,* 57 T.C. 180 (1971).

[46] *Austin State Bank,* 57 T.C. 180 (1971).

As the master of the courtroom, the hearing judge has an all-important role in the outcome of every case. He will not be swayed by courtroom appearance or conduct, but he should notice it, favorably or unfavorably. It is true that judges are people and that as all people vary, so all judges vary in the treatment of parties litigant and their counsel. Some are much more pleasant and courteous than others, but when your trial judge seems to be a bit difficult in manner, remember that he is more likely to have a favorable reaction to your own good conduct. A judge who is difficult to deal with at the beginning of a trial may in the end turn out to be most satisfactory provided you present your case thoroughly and well in a spirit of good will.

CHAPTER **10**

Post-Trial Proceedings, Including Appeals

Section 10.01—Decision

IF A CASE IS DECIDED FOR ONE PARTY or the other party, no computation for entry of decision is necessary since the statutory notice of deficiency will be the determinant if the decision is for respondent and, of course, there will be no deficiency in the ordinary case where decision is for petitioner.[1] In most Tax Court cases, however, more than one issue is before the Court, which means that a computation of tax liability for entry of decision to that effect is necessary unless all issues are decided entirely for one party or the other. Further, even in one-issue cases, such as valuation or compensation issues, the decision of the Court may not be entirely for one party or the other.

In all cases, therefore, where the Court's decision is not entirely for one party or the other, it is necessary for a computation of the correct tax liability under the decision of the Court to be prepared and filed with the Court in order for it to enter its final decision and order.[2] Where the Court has filed its opinion determining the issues in the case, it withholds entry of its decision for the purpose of permitting the parties to submit computations pursuant to the Court's determination of the issues, showing the correct amount of the deficiency, liability, or overpayment to be entered as its decision.[3] In practice, the respondent (through the Appel-

---

[1] Rule 155(a).

[2] Rule 155.

[3] Rule 155.

late Division) prepares the first computation of liability under the Court's opinion and submits it to counsel for the petitioner for verification or for suggested change. Should the petitioner disagree with the respondent's computation thus submitted, normally counsel for the petitioner and counsel for the respondent and the Appellate Division conferee meet for the purpose of discussing the reasons for the petitioner's disagreement with this computation. Generally, any disagreements can be resolved by such a meeting.

When the parties do reach agreement as to the amount of the deficiency or overpayment to be entered as the decision pursuant to the findings and conclusions of the Court, they promptly file with the Court an original and two copies of such computation, stipulating therein their agreement that the figures shown are in accordance with the findings and conclusions of the Court.[4] Shortly thereafter the Court will then enter its decision reflecting the figures shown in the computation.

If, however, the parties cannot agree as to the amount of the deficiency, liability, or overpayment to be entered as the decision in accordance with the findings and conclusions of the Court, either party may file with the Court a computation of the tax liability believed by him to be in accordance with the Court's findings and conclusions.[5] The Clerk thereupon serves a copy thereof upon the opposite party, places the matter upon a motion calendar for argument in due course before the judge who heard the case, and serves notice of the argument upon both parties.[6] If the opposite party fails to file objection, accompanied or preceded by an alternative computation, at least five days prior to the date of such argument or any continuance thereof, the Court may enter its decision in accordance with the computation already submitted. If computations are submitted by both parties which differ as to the amount to be entered as the decision of the Court, the parties will be afforded an opportunity to be heard in argument thereon on the fixed date, and after hearing such arguments and considering the details of the two computations submitted by the parties, the Court will thereupon determine the correct deficiency, liability, or overpayment and will enter its decision accordingly.[7]

Rarely do the parties fail to agree on the computation of the correct liability, because good practice dictates that they should sit down at the table together and try to iron out any differences. This is quite preferable to submitting different computations to the Court prematurely

---

[4]Rule 155(a).

[5]Rule 155(b).

[6]Rule 155(b).

[7]Rule 155(b).

and then having these computations set for oral argument, normally in Washington, before the judge who heard the case. This is time-consuming and much more expensive than conferring with opposing counsel and endeavoring to resolve any computation differences.

There are rare cases, of course, where even counsel of goodwill cannot arrive at an agreed computation and these must be submitted to the Court and argued just as any other disputed point of fact or law.

Any argument under this Rule 155 will be confined strictly to consideration of the correct computation of deficiency, liability or overpayment resulting from the findings and conclusions made by the Court, and no argument will be heard upon or consideration given to the issues or matters disposed of by the Court's findings and conclusions or to any new issues. This Rule is not to be interpreted as affording an opportunity for retrial or reconsideration.[8]

All pre-1974 practitioners will recognize this Rule 155 as the successor to Rule 50 of the prior Rules.

Section 10.02–Estate Tax Deduction Developing at or After Trial

If the parties in an estate tax case are unable to agree under Rule 155, or under a remand, upon a deduction involving expenses incurred at or after the trial, any party may move to reopen the case for further trial on that issue.[9] It is noted that it is unnecessary for the petition or an amendment thereto to raise the issue for this Rule to apply.

Section 10.03–Harmless Error

No error in either the admission or exclusion of evidence, and no error or defect in any ruling or order or in anything done or omitted by the Court or by any of the parties is ground for granting a new trial or for vacating, modifying, or otherwise disturbing a decision or order, unless refusal to take such action appears to the Court inconsistent with substantial justice.[10] At every stage of a case the Court will disregard any error or defect which does not affect the substantial rights of the parties.[11]

---

[8] Rule 155(c).
[9] Rule 156.
[10] Rule 160.
[11] Rule 160.

Section 10.04—Motion for Reconsideration of Findings or Opinion

Any motion for reconsideration of an opinion or findings of fact, with or without a new or further trial, must be filed within 30 days after the opinion has been served, unless the Court shall otherwise permit.[12]

Section 10.05—Motion to Vacate or Revise Decision

Any motion to vacate or revise a decision, with or without a new or further trial, must be filed within 30 days after the decision has been entered, unless the Court shall otherwise permit.[13]

Section 10.06—No Joinder of Motions Under Rules 161 and 162

Motions under Rules 161 and 162 must be made separately from each other and not joined to or made part of any other motion.[14]

Section 10.07—Appeals—How an Appeal Is Taken

Review of a decision of the Court by a United States Court of Appeals is obtained by filing a notice of appeal with the Clerk of the Tax Court within 90 days after the decision is entered.[15] If a timely notice of appeal is filed by one party, any other party may take an appeal by filing a notice of appeal within 120 days after the Court's decision is entered.[16] For other requirements governing such an appeal, Rules 13 and 14 of the Federal Rules of Appellate Procedure govern. (A suggested form of the notice of appeal is contained in Rules Appendix I, P.69.) Code Section 7482(b) provides the governing rules for the determination of the venue, that is the Circuit Court of Appeals to which the appeal is to be taken. Generally, the appeal is taken in the circuit in which the return or returns in question were filed, but the parties may stipulate by agreement another circuit to have venue with respect to that appeal.

---

[12] Rule 161.

[13] Rule 162.

[14] Rule 163.

[15] Rule 190(a).

[16] Rule 190(a).

Section 10.08–Preparation of the Record on Appeal

The Clerk will prepare the record on appeal and forward it to the Clerk of the Court of Appeals pursuant to the notice of appeal filed with the Court, in accordance with Rules 10 and 11 of the Federal Rules of Appellate Procedure.[17] In addition, at the time the Clerk forwards the record on appeal to the Clerk of the Court of Appeals he shall forward to each of the parties a copy of the index on appeals.[18]

Section 10.09–Bond to Stay Assessment and Collection

The filing of a notice of appeal does not stay assessment or collection of a deficiency determined by the Court unless on or before the filing of the notice of appeal, a bond is filed with the Court in accordance with Section 7485(a)(1).[19] In an important decision which may be helpful to many taxpayers, the Court has held that a bond with surety consisting of an Irrevocable Letter of Credit substantially in excess of the decided deficiency, from a bank of great resources, will satisfy the statutory requirements.[20] The Court bottomed its decision on the adequacy of the surety "because there is an unconditional promise to pay any liability finally determined and the bank has sufficient financial resources." The Court distinguished the *Coors* case from its decisions involving the amount of the bond or a deposit of collateral in lieu of surety.[21]

---

[17] Rule 191.

[18] Rule 191.

[19] Rule 192.

[20] *Adolph Coors Company*, 62 T.C. 300 (1974).

[21] *Barnes Theatre Ticket Service, Inc.*, 50 T.C. 28 (1968)–the amount of the bond; *Kahn Estate*, 60 T.C. 964 (1973)–deposit of collateral in lieu of a surety on the bond.

CHAPTER 11

Practice Before the Court and Special Trial Judges

Section 11.01—Admission to Practice

IN ORDER TO PRACTICE BEFORE THE COURT, an applicant for admission must establish to the satisfaction of the Court that he is a citizen of the United States, of good moral character and repute, and is possessed of the requisite qualifications to represent others in the preparation and trial of cases.[1] An attorney at law may be admitted to practice upon filing with the Admissions Clerk a completed application accompanied by a fee of $10.00 and a court certificate from the Clerk of the appropriate court showing that the applicant has been admitted to practice before, and is a member in good standing of, the Bar of the Supreme Court of the United States, or of the highest or appropriate court of any State, or Territory, or of the District of Columbia.[2] A current court certificate is one executed within 60 calendar days preceding the date of the filing of the application.[3]

An applicant, not an attorney at law, must file with the Admissions Clerk a completed application accompanied by a fee of $10.00.[4] In addition, such an applicant, as a condition of being admitted to practice, must give evidence of his qualifications satisfactory to the

---

[1] Rule 200(a)(1).
[2] Rule 200(a)(2).
[3] Rule 200(a)(2).
[4] Rule 200(a)(3).

Court by means of a written examination given by the Court, and the Court may require such person, in addition, to give similar evidence by means of an oral examination.[5] Any person who has thrice failed to give such evidence by means of such written examination shall not thereafter be eligible to take another examination for admission.[6]

An application for admission to practice before the Court must be on the form provided by the Court. Application forms and other necessary information will be furnished upon request addressed to the Admissions Clerk, United States Tax Court, Box 70, Washington, D.C. 20044.[7] An applicant for admission by examination must be sponsored by at least three persons heretofore admitted to practice before the Court, and each sponsor must send a letter of recommendation directly to the Admissions Clerk of the Court, where it will be treated as a confidential communication.[8] The sponsor must send his letter promptly, stating therein fully and frankly the extent of his acquaintance with the applicant, his opinion of the moral character and repute of the applicant, and his opinion of the qualifications of the applicant to practice before the Court.[9] The Court may in its discretion accept such an applicant with less than three such sponsors.[10]

For applicants other than attorneys at law, the required written examinations are held in Washington, D.C. on the last Wednesday of October of each year, and at such other times and places as the Court may designate.[11] The Court will notify each applicant whose application is in order of the time and place at which he is to present himself for examination, and the applicant must present that notice to the examiner as his authority for taking an examination.[12]

In practice, very few non-lawyers have been admitted to Court practice under this examination requirement. Since the Court is now an Article I Court, within the foreseeable future it is predicted that only lawyers will be practicing before it.

Where the application fee is paid by check or money order, it should be made payable to the order of the "Treasurer of the United States".[13] Upon approval of an application for admission and satisfaction of the other applicable requirements, an applicant will be admitted to

---

[5]Rule 200(a)(3).

[6]Rule 200(a)(3).

[7]Rule 200(b).

[8]Rule 200(c).

[9]Rule 200(c).

[10]Rule 200(c).

[11]Rule 200(d).

[12]Rule 200(d).

[13]Rule 200(e).

practice before the Court upon taking and subscribing the oath or affirmation prescribed by the Court and shall receive a certificate of admission.[14] Each person admitted to practice before the Court must promptly notify the Admissions Clerk of any change in office address for mailing purposes.[15]

Corporations and firms will not be admitted to practice or be recognized before the Court.[16]

Section 11.02–Conduct of Practice Before the Court

Practitioners before the Court shall carry on their practice in accordance with the letter and spirit of the Code of Professional Responsibility of the American Bar Association.[17] The Court may require any practitioner before it to furnish a statement, under oath, of the terms and circumstances of his employment in the case.[18]

Section 11.03–Disqualification, Suspension or Disbarment.

The Court may deny admission to, suspend, or disbar any person who, in its judgment, does not possess the requisite qualifications to represent others, or who is lacking in character, integrity, or proper professional conduct.[19] Upon the conviction of any practitioner admitted to practice before the Court for a criminal violation of any provision of the Internal Revenue Code or for any crime involving moral turpitude, or where any practitioner has been suspended or disbarred from the practice of his profession in any state or the District of Columbia, the Court may, in the exercise of its discretion, forthwith suspend such practitioner from the Bar of the Court until its further order.[20] Otherwise, no person shall be suspended for more than 60 days or disbarred until he has been afforded an opportunity to be heard.[21] A judge of the Court may immediately suspend any person for not more than 60 days for contempt or misconduct during the course of any trial or hearing.[22]

---

[14]Rule 200(f).
[15]Rule 200(g).
[16]Rule 200(h).
[17]Rule 201(a).
[18]Rule 201(b).
[19]Rule 202.
[20]Rule 202.
[21]Rule 202.
[22]Rule 202.

Section 11.04—Special Trial Judges (Formerly Commissioners of the Court)

The Chief Judge may from time to time designate a special trial judge (formerly a commissioner) appointed under Section 7456(c) of the Code, to deal with any matter pending before the Court in accordance with its rules and such directions as may be prescribed by the Chief Judge.[23] In the past the Court has sparingly used special trial judges except in Small Tax Cases.

Subject to the specifications and limitations in the order designating a special trial judge and in accordance with the applicable provisions of the Rules, the special trial judge has and shall exercise the power to regulate all proceedings in any matter before him, including the conduct of trials, pretrials, conferences, and hearings on motions, and to do all acts and take all measures necessary or proper for the efficient performance of his duties.[24] He may require the production before him of evidence upon all matters embraced within his assignment, including the production of all books, statements, vouchers, documents, and writings applicable thereto, and he has the authority to put witnesses on oath and examine them.[25] He may rule upon the admissibility of evidence, in accordance with provisions of Sections 7453 and 7463, and may exercise such further and incidental authority, including ordering the issuance of subpoenas, as may be necessary for the conduct of trial or other proceedings.[26]

Section 11.05—Special Trial Judge's Post-Trial Procedure

Except in Small Tax Cases (see Rule 183) or as otherwise provided, the following procedure is prescribed in cases tried before a special trial judge:

> (a) *Proposed Findings and Briefs.*[27] Each party shall file his initial brief, including his proposed finding of fact and legal argument, within 60 days after the date on which the trial is concluded,

---

[23]Rule 23(c) and Rule 180, as modified by United States Tax Court General Order No. 4, October 4, 1975, effective January 1, 1976, changing the title of "Commissioner" to "Special Trial Judge," except as the statutory designation of "commissioner" may be required.

[24]Rule 181.

[25]Rule 181.

[26]Rule 181.

[27]Rule 182(a).

unless otherwise directed. The party thereafter desiring to file a responsive brief shall do so, including any objections to any proposed findings of fact, within 30 days after the expiration of the period for filing the initial brief, unless otherwise directed. Rule 151 governs the content, form, number of copies, and other applicable requirements, for the proposed findings of fact and briefs.

(b) *Special trial judge's report.*[28] After all the briefs have been filed by all the parties, or the time for doing so has expired, the special trial judge shall file his report, including his findings of fact and opinion. A copy of the report shall forthwith be served on each party.

(c) *Exceptions.*[29] Within 45 days after service of the special trial judge's report, a party may file with the Court a brief setting forth any exceptions of law or of fact to that report. Within 30 days of service upon him of such brief, any other party may file a brief in response thereto. In any brief filed pursuant to this paragraph, a party may rely in whole or in part upon the briefs previously submitted by him to the special trial judge under paragraph (a) above. Unless a party shall have proposed a particular finding of fact, or unless he shall have objected to another party's proposed finding of fact, the Court may refuse to consider his exception to the special trial judge's report for failure to make such a finding desired by him or for inclusion of such finding proposed by the other party, as the case may be.

(d) *Oral Argument and Decision.*[30] The Division to which the case is assigned may, upon motion of any party or on its own motion, direct oral argument. The Division *inter alia* may adopt the special trial judge's report or may modify it or may reject it in whole or in part, or may receive further evidence or may recommit it with instructions. The Division shall give due regard to the circumstance that the special trial judge had the opportunity to evaluate the credibility of witnesses; and the findings of fact recommended by the special trial judge shall be presumed to be correct.

These provisions of the Rules make clear that the decision on the case is to be made by a judge, but Rule 182 expands the alternatives available in reviewing the determinations of the special trial judge as embodied in his report. The judge to whom the case is assigned, may take any action he deems appropriate for a proper disposition of the case, even with respect to the special trial judge's findings of fact, although they are accorded special weight insofar as those findings are determined by the

---

[28]Rule 182(b).

[29]Rule 182(c).

[30]Rule 182(d).

opportunity to hear and observe the witness. This expanded Rule 182 accords substantially to Court of Claims Rule 147(b), so practitioners who are familiar with Court of Claims practice will find the new practice before a Tax Court special trial judge quite similar. It is obvious that this Rule 182 is intended to make the use of special trial judges more effective and to broaden its scope to the extent required by the anticipated increasing volume of Tax Court cases. Especially in the light of the expanded jurisdiction of the Court under the Tax Reform Act of 1969 and the Pension Reform Act of 1974, it may well be that the special trial judge's practice in the Tax Court will become as extensive in the future as in the Court of Claims presently, although this would appear to be some years away.

Rule 183 makes clear that Rule 182 does not apply to Small Tax Cases under Rule 171. A special trial judge who conducts the trial of such Small Tax Case shall, as soon after such trial as shall be practicable, prepare a summary of the facts and reasons for his proposed disposition of the case, which then shall be submitted promptly to the Chief Judge, or to a Judge or Division of the Court, if the Chief Judge shall so direct.[31]

---

[31] Rule 183.

CHAPTER 12

Small Tax Cases

Section 12.01—Introduction

FOR MANY YEARS the Court had experienced difficulty in procedurally resolving problems arising in cases involving small amounts of deficiency, yet meaning as much to each aggrieved taxpayer as the larger cases to those taxpayers. Typically, these small cases were handled *pro se,* which usually resulted in the taxpayer-petitioner being at a trial disadvantage with respondent's legal counsel. At the same time, many of these taxpayers in small cases complained to their congressional representatives that it was cumbersome and expensive for them to receive a fair Court hearing at minimum expense.

The Court strove diligently to solve this problem under existing statutes in several ways, perhaps the chief of which was to assist in settlement negotiations informally by means of pretrial conferences in chambers at the time of calendar call. If settlement was unavailing, the Court often tried to assist the *pro se* taxpayer in presenting his evidence in all proper respects and respondent's counsel cooperated to the extent possible.

The Court also solicited the assistance of the Section of Taxation, American Bar Association, in calling the attention of *pro se* petitioners to the availability of Lawyers' Referral Services established by bar associations in most principal cities. This effort, however, proved fruitless despite intensive joint effort by the Court and the Taxation Section.

Hence, effective December 30, 1970, the Congress enacted Code section 7463 to govern the Court's conduct of cases involving \$1,500 or less (effective January 1, 1974, as increased from \$1,000 in the original statute.) The statutory intent is to simplify court procedure in these cases and thereby to enable a *pro se* petitioner to prepare and file his own petition and conduct his own trial if he so desires.

Section 12.02—General

Except as otherwise provided in Title XVII, the other rules of practice of the Court are applicable to a "Small Tax Case."[1]

Section 12.03—Definition

The term "Small Tax Case" means a case in which:

(a) neither the amount of the deficiency, nor the amount of any claimed overpayment, placed in dispute (including any additions to tax, additional amounts, and penalties) exceeds

(1) $1,500.00 for any one taxable year in the case of income or gift taxes, or

(2) $1,500.00 in the case of estate taxes;

(b) the petitioner has made a request in accordance with Rule 172 to have the proceedings conducted under Section 7463; and

(c) the Court has not entered an order in accordance with Rule 172(d) or Rule 173, discontinuing the proceedings in the case under Section 7463.[2]

Section 12.04—Election of Small Tax Case Procedure

With respect to classification of a case as a Small Tax Case under Section 7463, the following shall apply:

(a) a petitioner who wishes to have the proceedings in his case conducted under Section 7463 may so request at the time he files his petition;

(b) if the Commissioner opposes the petitioner's request to have the proceedings conducted under Section 7463, he shall at the

[1] Rule 170.

[2] Rule 171.

time he files his answer submit an accompanying motion in which he shall set forth the reasons for his opposition;

(c) a petitioner may, at any time after the petition is filed and before trial, request that the proceedings be conducted under Section 7463. Upon filing of such request, the Commissioner will be given due time in which to indicate whether he is opposed to it, and he shall state his reasons therefor in the event of such opposition;

(d) if such request is made in accordance with the provisions of Rule 172, the case will be docketed as a Small Tax Case. The Court, on its own motion or on the motion of a party to the case, may, at any time before the trial commences, enter an order directing that the Small Tax Case designation shall be removed and that the proceedings shall not be conducted under the Small Tax Case Rules. If no such order is entered, the petitioner will be considered to have exercised his option and the Court shall be deemed to have concurred therein, in accordance with Section 7463, at the commencement of the trial.[3]

Section 12.05—Discontinuance of Proceedings

After the commencement of a trial of a Small Tax Case, but before the decision in the case becomes final, the Court may order that the proceedings be discontinued under Section 7463, and that the case be tried under the rules of practice other than the Small Tax Case Rules, but such order will be issued only if (1) there are reasonable grounds for believing that the amount of the deficiency, or the claimed overpayment, in dispute will exceed $1,500 and (2) the Court finds that justice requires the discontinuance of the proceedings under Section 7463, taking into consideration the convenience and expenses for both parties that would result from the order.[4]

Section 12.06—Representation

A petitioner in a Small Tax Case may appear for himself without representation or may be represented by any person admitted to practice before the Court.[5]

---

[3]Rule 172.

[4]Rule 173.

[5]Rule 174.

Section 12.07–Pleadings

With respect to the form and content of the petition in a Small Tax Case, it shall be substantially in accordance with Form 2 shown in the Appendix to the Court's Rules or shall, in the alternative, comply with the requirements for a petition not in a Small Tax Case. It must also contain in addition (A) the office of the Internal Revenue Service which issued the deficiency notice, (B) the taxpayer identification number (for example, the Social Security number) of each petitioner, and (C) a request that the proceedings be conducted under Section 7463.[6] The usual filing fee of $10 payable at the time of filing is required for a Small Tax Case, but the Court may waive payment of this fee if the petitioner establishes to its satisfaction that he is unable to make such payment.[7] No verification is required unless the Court directs otherwise.[8] The answer of the Commissioner must be in accord with answers generally under Rule 36.[9] No reply is necessary unless the Court shall otherwise direct, but if so, the reply must conform to Rule 37(b). In the absence of a requirement of a reply, the provisions of the second sentence of Rule 37(c) shall not apply and the affirmative allegations of the answer will be deemed denied.[10]

Section 12.08–Preliminary Hearings

If, in a Small Tax Case, it becomes necessary to hold a hearing on a motion or other preliminary matter, the parties may submit their views in writing and may, but shall not ordinarily be required to, appear personally at such hearing. However, if the Court deems it advisable for the petitioner or his counsel to appear personally, the Court will so notify the petitioner or his counsel and will make every effort to schedule such hearing at a place convenient to them.[11] This provision illustrates the lengths to which the Court will try to go to accommodate the parties in a Small Tax Case in order to carry out the Congressional mandate to provide a ready hearing for taxpayers in Small Tax Cases at a minimum of expense. The Court has continued to administer these provisions always with this cardinal precept in mind and holds hearings in many small cities, for example, to accommodate taxpayers in Small Tax Cases.

---

[6] Rule 175(a)(1).

[7] Rule 175(a)(2).

[8] Rule 175(a)(3).

[9] Rule 175(b).

[10] Rule 175(c).

[11] Rule 176.

Section 12.09—Trial

As to the place of trial at the time of filing the petition, the petitioner may request the place where he would prefer the trial to be held. If the petitioner has not filed such a request, the respondent, at the time he files his answer, shall file a request showing the place of trial preferred by him, which, of course, is the standard procedure in all other Tax Court cases. The Court will make every effort to designate the place of trial at the location most convenient to that requested where suitable facilities are available, but the Court does likewise in all other cases.[12]

As to the conduct of the trial and the rules of evidence, these cases will be conducted as informally as possible consistent with orderly procedure, and any evidence deemed by the Court to have probative value shall be admissible.[13] In actual practice the Court will lean over backward to admit any evidence proffered by a petitioner in a Small Tax Case in order to make sure that justice is done and that he does not lose his case on any technicality or evidentiary difficulty.

Neither briefs nor oral arguments will be required in Small Tax Cases, but the Court on its own motion or upon request of either party may permit the filing of briefs or memorandum briefs.[14]

Section 12.10—Transcripts of Proceedings

The hearing in, or trial of, a Small Tax Case shall be stenographically reported or otherwise recorded but a transcript thereof need not be made unless the Court otherwise directs.[15]

Section 12.11—Number of Copies of Papers

Only an original and two conformed copies of *any* paper need be filed in a Small Tax Case. An additional copy shall be filed for each additional docketed case which has been, or is requested to be, consolidated.[16]

---

[12]Rule 177(a).

[13]Rule 177(b).

[14]Rule 177(c).

[15]Rule 178.

[16]Rule 179.

APPENDIX—
Specimen Forms

PREFATORY NOTE FROM THE AUTHOR

IN AN EFFORT TO BE OF GREATEST ASSISTANCE to the tax bar, this appendix contains several petitions which were filed in docketed Court cases. In addition, other selected forms—hopefully those most frequently encountered in actual practice—have also been included. Not all of these were filed in actual cases. To have included a form for every conceivable motion would have been unwise because of limited usefulness. In any event, these forms represent an effort to do "as I do," not just "as I say," since most were filed in the author's cases.

Where the particular case was tried and decided by the Court, the pleadings appear without deletion or change. Where the case was settled before trial, identifying names and terms have been deleted. Where the form was not a pleading in a docketed case, fictitious names are used.

An effort has been made to include a representative cross-section of petitions in a variety of cases, since petitions form the backbone of the pleadings in every case.

Not every possible form of motion has been included, as many are virtually self-explanatory, such as a continuance motion. Therefore, only the principal motions, especially those new under the present Rules, have been included.

It is hoped that these forms will prove useful in preparing your own pleadings. Always remember that each petition, however, must be tailor-made to suit its own facts, and that painstaking attention to detail in preparation of petitions, and other pleadings, is well worth the extra effort in subsequent settlement negotiations and eventual trial, if not settled.

Form A

HAMMOND LEAD PRODUCTS, INC.–T.C. Memo. 1969-14 (1969), *aff'd* (7th Cir. 1970) 425 F.2d 31

PETITION

This petition exemplifies one of the most familiar factual cases, the deduction of reasonable officers' compensation. Note the particularity with which the relevant supporting facts are pleaded. This petition represents an effort to fully inform the Court of the basic facts so it may easily follow the evidence to be adduced at the trial.

TAX COURT OF THE UNITED STATES

HAMMOND LEAD PRODUCTS, INC., Petitioner, v. COMMISSIONER OF INTERNAL REVENUE, Respondent.	Docket No. 913-67

PETITION

The above-named petitioner hereby petitions for a redetermination of the deficiency set forth by the Commissioner of Internal Revenue in his notice of deficiency (correspondence symbols Form L-21 Code 430 RES:0c) dated November 29, 1966, and as a basis of its proceeding alleges as follows:

1. The petitioner is a corporation organized and existing under the laws of the State of Indiana, with its principal office and place of business at 5231 Hohman Avenue, Hammond, Indiana 46320. The returns for the period here involved were filed with the District Director of Internal Revenue for the District of Indiana, Indianapolis Division.

2. The notice of deficiency (a copy of which is attached and marked "Exhibit A"*) was mailed to the petitioner on November 29, 1966.

3. The deficiency as determined by the Commissioner is in income tax for the taxable years ended July 31, 1963, 1964 and 1965 in the respective amounts of $22,016.48, $34,043.96 and $43,738.93, substantially all of which is in controversy.

4. The determination of tax set forth in the said notice of deficiency is based upon the following errors:

(a) In determining the taxable income for the taxable years 1963, 1964 and 1965, the Commissioner erroneously disallowed the deduction for compensation of officers in the respective amounts of $39,320.98, $61,936.51 and $83,979.25.

(b) In determining the taxable income for the taxable years 1963, 1964 and 1965, the Commissioner erroneously disallowed the deductions for travel and entertainment expense in the respective amounts of $2,028.78, $2,976.66 and $3,978.94.

(c) In determining the taxable income for the taxable years 1963, 1964 and 1965, the Commissioner erroneously disallowed the deductions for convention expense in the respective amounts of $65.91, $109.31 and $157.63.

(d) In determining the taxable income for the taxable years 1963, 1964 and 1965, the Commissioner erroneously disallowed the deduction for automobile expense for each such year in the amount of $600.00.

5. The facts upon which the petitioner relies as the basis of this proceeding are as follows:

(a)(i) In determining the taxable income for the taxable years 1963, 1964 and 1965, the Commissioner has disallowed the claimed deductions for compensation of officers in the respective amounts of $39,320.98, $61,936.51 and $83,979.25. Such disallowances were arrived at by reducing the claimed deductions for compensation of William Wilke, Jr., and William Wilke, III, for the taxable year 1963 in the respective amounts of $28,205.19 and $11,115.79; for the taxable year 1964 in the respective amounts of $40,329.40 and $21,607.11; and for the taxable year 1965 in the respective amounts of $51,478.83 and $32,500.42. The claimed compensation deductions for such years for Willard F. Haas, John S. Nordyke and Ruth C. Sliger, three other officers, were not changed by the Commissioner.

(a)(ii) William Wilke, Jr., was petitioner's president from its founding in 1930 until January 29, 1965, when he was elected chairman of its board of directors. He graduated with a degree in Mechanical Engineering from Cornell University, Ithaca, New York, in 1909. He has been active in the lead business since 1915. He was president of Metal Refining Company, Hammond, Indiana, from 1919 to 1929. He and his brother, Erwin L. Wilke, were the co-founders of petitioner. Erwin L. Wilke was active in its executive management until his death in 1954.

(a)(iii) As president until 1965 and now chairman of the board, William Wilke, Jr., holds responsibilities for major decisions of company policy. He is at

*Not reproduced.

petitioner's executive offices daily and has close and intimate knowledge of the day-to-day progress and developments of the course of the business. In conjunction with William P. Wilke, III, he makes all major decisions as to purchases of pig lead and basic sales policies. Because of his wide, extensive and broad knowledge of the industry, he is uniquely qualified for expert determination of policy. Mr. Wilke, Jr., continues to be the inspirational leader of the business, so that the growth, success and good reputation of petitioner are closely linked and depend largely on his judgment and knowledge of the business. He has been the guiding genius of petitioner's growth from scratch in the depression year of 1930 to pre-eminence in its industry.

(a)(iv) William P. Wilke, III, graduated from Cornell University with a degree in Mechanical Engineering in 1934. His first employment was with Bethlehem Steel Company in its Loop training program. He was a cold strip mill foreman with that company from 1938 to 1941. From 1942 to 1944 he was a project engineer with the Chicago Ordnance District. He became an employee of petitioner in 1944 and has continued in an executive capacity with petitioner to the present time. He was elected as vice president on January 15, 1951, as a director on January 18, 1954, secretary-treasurer by appointment of the board of directors on March 15, 1954 and by election on January 17, 1955, and was elected president on January 29, 1965. He is also vice president of Southeastern Lead Company, Tampa, Florida. He was a director of the Lead Industries Association from 1960 to 1964 and was its vice president from 1962 to 1964. He holds patents in the field of cold rolling of steel and in the manufacturing of corrosion-inhibitive pigments and polyvinyl chloride stabilizers. He was chosen to represent the domestic lead chemical industry in hearings before the United States Tariff Commission in 1963, 1965 and 1966. He is also active in community affairs.

(a)(v) During the taxable period and for many prior years, Mr. Wilke, III, has expended tremendous time and effort in the development of petitioner's business. His imaginative and creative contributions to the business, together with those of his father, William Wilke, Jr., have accounted for most of petitioner's great increase in sales and profits. Mr. Wilke, Jr., and Mr. Wilke, III, work as a top executive team in formulating all matters of major policy and program and then placing their decisions into profitable production. Petitioner's technical and production personnel are extremely intelligent and capable, thus requiring corporate leadership of a challenging and highly sophisticated nature. Together they also determine petitioner's financial policies. During the last two years petitioner spent over $250,000.00 on improving, modernizing and expanding plant facilities without the need of outside financing because of the prudent financial policies of these two dedicated chief executives.

(a)(vi) The lead chemical business is one of low margins, demanding technical skill and high capital investment. Errors in market judgment can be fatal. The price of lead today is 14.00 cents per pound. To battery companies petitioner's selling price for lead oxide is 15.10 cents per pound. The raw material price is 90% of the sales price of petitioner's product, which is comprised of 95% lead metal and 5% oxygen. A one cent per pound miscalculation in the market price of lead could prove ruinous. Petitioner is the sixth or seventh largest purchaser of primary pig lead in the United States. Some of these companies have key men whose primary function is the purchasing of lead, whereas this is only one of the many duties of Mr. Wilke, Jr., and Mr. Wilke, III. Lead is an international commodity (as are lead pigments and chemicals). The price of lead is a sensitive mechanism reflecting from day to day the changing expectations of the trade and world market conditions. Experience and judgment in lead market analysis, as supplied by these two officers, are primary keys to petitioner's success. Experience is gained through a long period of intelligent insight, observation and ability to act and perform before the market moves, not after. Judgment is a quality of incalculable value. The measure of their judgment is best illustrated by the results of petitioner's policies and confidence of its customers.

(a)(vii) William Wilke, Jr., and Erwin L. Wilke had the courage, technical knowledge, business reputation and foresight to conceive and organize petitioner in the depression year of 1930 on August 22. Operation commenced in December, 1930. The original line of products manufactured was lead oxides, which consist of red lead and litharge. Red lead and litharge are oxides of lead having the definite chemical compositions:

Pb_3O_4 – red lead

PbO – litharge

(a)(viii) The process of manufacturing these chemicals involves the procurement of extremely pure pig lead of 99.99+% purity. The lead is melted in a kettle and carefully metered into a reaction vessel in which the molten lead is agitated in the presence of air at a closely controlled temperature and pressure. As the surface of the agitated lead combines with oxygen, some of the lead oxide produced is air-swept from the reaction vessel into a settling chamber. The product collected in the settling chamber consists of approximately 30% free lead (Pb) and 70% lead oxide (Pb0, litharge).

(a)(ix) The 70% lead oxide and 30% free lead product is the starting crude oxide material for the production of pure litharge and pure red lead. The crude oxide is calcined in precision furnaces, designed by petitioner's officers, under carefully controlled conditions of temperature and air flow to convert the crude oxide material to 100% Pb0, litharge. Additional calcining at another precisely determined temperature causes the reaction $6Pb + O_2 \longrightarrow 2Pb_3O_4$ to take place, thus producing red lead.

(a)(x) These processes were unique at the outset of petitioner's operation and remain so today. The design and development by William Wilke, Jr., Erwin L. Wilke and William P. Wilke, III, produce materials of extremely uniform particle size, and to date no other manufacturer can produce lead oxides by similar processes.

(a)(xi) The lead oxide industry is an extremely competitive one which has long been dominated by two giants, National Lead Company and Eagle-Picher Company. Nevertheless, petitioner has been able to compete and actually enhance its relative position by imaginative, progressive and aggressive policies in all phases of operation. Illustrative of the difficulties and problems of petitioner's type of business is the experience of The Glidden Company, which was engaged in manufacturing exactly the same line of products as petitioner, yet in 1951 it found the competition so keen and profits so lean that it decided to abandon the manufacture of lead oxides and related products. William P. Wilke, III, and William Wilke, Jr., arranged to buy the Glidden plant equipment in July, 1951, for $8,500.00, for which replacement cost would have been well over $150,000.00.

(a)(xii) Petitioner's products are in the nature of raw materials to the industries which it serves. Petitioner's customer industries are principally engaged in the manufacture of glass, ceramic ware, batteries, paint products and electronic products, as well as plastics. Reliability and continuity of supply are extremely important, and the diligence and reputation of William Wilke, Jr., in administering the company, especially in its earlier years, played the crucial role in meriting the confidence of petitioner's customers.

(a)(xiii) In the 1950's it became apparent that the range of products petitioner manufactured had to be expanded to meet more demanding current technological requirements. Specifically, the newer fields were those of electronic glasses and ceramics, including lead-zirconate titanates for ultrasonics and sonar applications. To meet these requirements, as well as those for special optical glasses, a long-term program was developed and carried out under the leadership of William Wilke, Jr., and William P. Wilke, III, which culminated in the introduction of a continuing line of new products.

(a)(xiv) Petitioner commenced manufacture of lead silicate in the early 1950's. This product was already being made by National Lead Company and Eagle-Picher Company, as well as manufacturers in England. William P. Wilke, III, with encouragement and assistance from William Wilke, Jr., designed an entirely new type of glass furnace to produce lead silicates. This processing furnace has proved to be so successful that petitioner has attained a dominant position in the lead silicate field. Petitioner preferred to maintain trade secrecy rather than patent this design. Both Owens-Illinois and Harshaw Chemical, two of petitioner's major customers with large research organizations, have signed disclosure agreements when petitioner showed them how to melt lead glass. Harshaw built a furnace of petitioner's designed in France, and Owens-Illinois is building a plant using petitioner's design. The pilot plant which Owens-Illinois built from petitioner's ideas is walled off and marked "No Admittance" except by special pass.

(a)(xv) A quick process, basic carbonate, white lead plant was established in the late 1950's.

(a)(xvi) Petitioner introduced granular litharge as the most economical PbO addition for electrical lead glass. The savings to Corning Glass, Owens-Illinois and Westinghouse, three of petitioner's major customers, amount to nearly $750,000.00 annually.

(a)(xvii) Petitioner is the only manufacturer of UHP lead chemicals, which bring premium prices and help achieve technical and physical properties unattainable with ordinary products. Although the chemicals produced by petitioner are in a sense raw materials, they are a very special type of raw materials with closely controlled physical and chemical properties. Petitioner deals in impurity levels in the range of ten-thousandths of one percent or in parts per million. The introduction of petitioner's "Ultra High Purity" lead chemicals (UHP) played an important role in the growth of its business, as well as being technically important to the over-all economy.

(a)(xviii) A new family of pigments is already being established in oleoresinous paint formulations under U.S. Patent 3,080,248 (granted March 5, 1963 to William P. Wilke, III). It has shown exceptional promise in electrophoresis and is currently receiving very serious attention as an anti-corrosive pigment for automotive primers.

(a)(xix) Petitioner's sales are made throughout the United States with less than 10 percent being made in Indiana. Petitioner's competitors boast of multi-plant operations and claim to have superior technical staffs. Petitioner has overcome these competitive advantages by continuous reliable service and actually giving superior technical advice and assistance to its customers.

(a)(xx) The course chosen for the development of petitioner has been conceived and directed by William Wilke, Jr., and William P. Wilke, III, for the past twelve years. Prior to the death of Erwin L. Wilke, William P. Wilke, III, was primarily responsible for production functions, and since that time, March 1, 1954, major executive functions have been carried out jointly by William P. Wilke, III, and William Wilke, Jr.

(a)(xxi) During the taxable period, as well as since February 9, 1931, the compensation of William Wilke, Jr., was based on $1.00 per ton of sales and 5 percent of the net profits of the company. E.L. Wilke's compensation had been based on the same formula. William P. Wilke, III, was appointed to succeed E.L. Wilke, deceased, on March 15, 1954, and since that date the compensation of William P. Wilke, III, has been based on the same formula which applied to E.L. Wilke.

(a)(xxii) Petitioner has enjoyed a steady growth under the chief executive management of Mr. Wilke, Jr., E.L. Wilke, and Mr. Wilke, III. Its sales have increased from $188,036.98 in 1931 to $4,493,462.13 in 1963, $6,036,977.42 in 1964, and $7,716,645.96 in 1965. Its profits have increased from $40.90 in 1931 to $139,719.77, $136,373.24 and $189,206.53 in 1963, 1964, and 1965, respectively. Petitioner has paid substantial dividends each year since 1937, with the exception of the years 1941 and 1947, when special conditions prevented payment. During each of the years 1949 to 1962, inclusive, petitioner paid dividends in the amount of $53,750.00. During the taxable years 1963 and 1964, petitioner paid dividends in the amount of $107,500.00, and in the taxable year 1965 in the amount of $110,000.00.

(a)(xxiii) The compensation of William Wilke, Jr., and William P. Wilke, III, was reasonable for services actually rendered to petitioner for the taxable years 1963, 1964 and 1965. Such compensation was comparable to that of officers employed by like companies. Petitioner is entitled to the claimed deductions for such compensation paid to Mr. Wilke, Jr., and Mr. Wilke, III, and the Commissioner has erroneously disallowed the portions of such compensation in the amounts of $39,320.98, $61,936.51 and $83,979.25 for the taxable years 1963, 1964 and 1965, respectively.

(b) The Commissioner has disallowed portions of petitioner's claimed deductions for travel and entertainment expense for each of the taxable years 1963, 1964 and 1965 in the respective amounts of $2,028.78, $2,976.66 and $3,978.94

which were incurred by William Wilke, Jr., on behalf of petitioner. For the taxable year 1963, petitioner reimbursed Mr. Wilke, Jr., $1,790.00 and paid Hilton Credit Corporation $238.78. For the taxable year 1964, petitioner reimbursed Mr. Wilke, Jr., $2,500.00 and paid $88.68 to Golden Door Restaurant, $105.63 to South Shore Country Club, and $282.35 to Hilton Credit Corporation. For the taxable year 1965, petitioner reimbursed Mr. Wilke, Jr., $2,379.87 and paid $224.46 to Golden Door Restaurant, $1,149.42 to South Shore Country Club, and $225.19 to Hilton Credit Corporation. All of such amounts were incurred by William Wilke, Jr., for entertainment of petitioner's customers and associates, which are deductible as ordinary and necessary business expenses of petitioner under Section 162(a) of the Internal Revenue Code.

(c) During each of the taxable years 1963, 1964 and 1965, William P. Wilke, III, attended industry conventions on behalf of petitioner, accompanied by his wife. Her presence was essential to assist her husband in discharging his official and business entertainment responsibilities at the conventions. She would not have attended these conventions except to assist her husband in properly performing his business duties. The respective amounts of $65.91, $109.31 and $157.63 were incurred by petitioner as expense of Mrs. Wilke's attendance at such conventions. Such amounts constitute ordinary and necessary business expenses of petitioner and are allowable as deductions under Section 162(a).

(d) The Commissioner has disallowed petitioner's claimed deductions for automobile expense of William Wilke, Jr., for the taxable years 1963, 1964 and 1965 in the amount of $600.00 for each such year. Such amounts were expended for necessary business travel of Mr. Wilke, Jr., and, therefore, such amounts constitute ordinary and necessary expenses of petitioner which are deductible under Section 162(a).

WHEREFORE, petitioner prays that the Court may hear the case, redetermine the deficiencies herein in accordance with the assignments of error contained in paragraph 4 hereinabove, and for all other appropriate relief in the premises.

COUNSEL FOR PETITIONER

Form B

WEAVER POPCORN COMPANY, INC.–T.C. Memo 1971-281

PETITION

This petition illustrates another classic ultimate fact question, namely, whether shareholders' advances constitute debt or equity. Petitioner has also been able to put its best foot forward at the outset in the petition and lay the groundwork for an extensive stipulation of facts, which is also reproduced hereinafter.

TAX COURT OF THE UNITED STATES

WEAVER POPCORN COMPANY, INC., Petitioner, v. COMMISSIONER OF INTERNAL REVENUE, Respondent.	Docket No. 2178-69

P E T I T I O N

The above-named petitioner hereby petitions for a redetermination of the deficiency set forth by the Commissioner of Internal Revenue in his notice of deficiency (correspondence symbols L21 Code 430-BMW-jeb) dated March 3, 1969, and as a basis of its proceeding alleges as follows:

1. The petitioner is a corporation organized and existing under the laws of the State of Indiana, with its principal office and place of business at Van Buren, Indiana. The returns for the period here involved were filed with the District Director of Internal Revenue for the District of Indiana, Indianapolis, Indiana.

2. The notice of deficiency (a copy of which is attached and marked "Exhibit A"*) was mailed to the petitioner on March 3, 1969.

*Not reproduced.

3. The deficiency as determined by the Commissioner is in income tax for the taxable years ended December 31, 1964, 1965 and 1966 in the respective amounts of $10,224.93, $8,953.07 and $7,819.17, substantially all of which is in controversy.

4. The determination of tax set forth in the said notice of deficiency is based upon the following error:

(a) In determining the taxable income for the taxable years 1964, 1965 and 1966, the Commissioner erroneously disallowed deductions for interest in the respective amounts of $19,924.00, $16,205.95 and $15,386.75.

5. The facts upon which the petitioner relies as the basis of this proceeding are as follows:

(a) (i) Petitioner was organized as a corporation under the laws of the state of Indiana on or about June 1, 1955, at which time the assets, liabilities and operations of a partnership known as "Weaver Popcorn Company" were transferred to the newly-organized corporation in exchange for one class of common voting stock and debentures under Section 351 of the Internal Revenue Code. The partnership consisted of four partners, I. E. Weaver, Paul L. Weaver, W. I. Weaver and D. M. Repp, all possessing equal distributive shares.

(ii) Because of his advanced age of 72 years in 1955, I. E. Weaver had curtailed his management responsibilities and, therefore, concluded that he should not continue to place such a substantial portion of his personal estate at risk in the newly-incorporated business. Accordingly, it was decided that he should receive most of his corporate interest as debt securities, rather than higher-risk equity securities. Hence, he received debentures in the amount of $74,644.69 and common stock in the amount of $1,000.00 in exchange for his partnership interest. P. L. Weaver, W. I. Weaver and D. M. Repp, the remaining partners, all of whom continued to be responsible for management of the business, each received debentures in the amount of $23,544.69 and common stock in the amount of $42,600.00 in exchange for their respective partnership interests.

(iii) The debentures were issued for a term of ten years with fixed interest to be paid thereon at the rate of five percent per annum. Such interest has always been paid each year within the year for which it was payable, starting with the taxable year 1955 and continuing to and including the taxable year 1966, the last taxable year involved in the instant proceeding.

(iv) The principal reason for organizing the corporation to acquire the partnership business and continue to operate it in corporate form was to limit the personal liability of the individual partners for debts and claims against the business. Further, the partners concluded, upon counsel of legal and accounting advisers, that upon the death, or withdrawal, of any of the partners, it would be more feasible to continue the business in corporate, rather than in unincorporated, form. Another reason leading to the decision to incorporate was that by 1955 the popcorn business had become quite hazardous and risky, since it was necessary to contract at least a year in advance for much of the popcorn and pay the agreed price therefor, even though later the price of the finished product might drop and the business suffer thereby. Further, there was no futures market in popcorn by means of which a processing company, such as petitioner, could hedge its risk.

(v) In 1955, the four individuals named in subparagraph (a)(i) formed a new partnership, known as "Weco Farms," for the operation of two farms, one of which consisted of considerable acreage. The cash subsequently accumulated by this partnership was used to repay petitioner's bank loans to the maximum extent possible. By the end of 1959, such loans from Weco Farms to petitioner aggregated approximately $131,500.00.

(vi) In 1959, petitioner's corporate structure had been recapitalized pursuant to Section 368(a)(1)(E) of the Internal Revenue Code, under which the original common stock was exchanged for Class A common stock, Class B common stock and preferred stock, with the Class A common stock the only class of voting stock. This recapitalization was decided upon in order that those shareholders active in the management of petitioner might be able to retain voting control.

(vii) Late in 1959, the partners of Weco Farms, who were also the shareholders of petitioner, concluded that it would be advisable for petitioner to acquire the assets and liabilities of the farming partnership, and, accordingly, as of the first business day in 1960, petitioner acquired such assets and liabilities in exchange for Class A common stock, preferred stock and debentures.

(viii) About 1963, P. L. Weaver and W.I. Weaver began to have serious disagreements as to the operating policies of petitioner. In order to resolve these disagreements, late in 1964 the shareholders agreed that petitioner's farm division should be incorporated as a separate corporation and that all of its shares should be distributed to P. L. Weaver under Section 355 of the Internal Revenue Code. On June 11, 1965, the Commissioner of Internal Revenue issued a ruling that such proposed transaction came within the provisions of Section 355, and, accordingly, such transaction was thereafter carried out according to its terms.

(ix) In view of the foregoing facts, it was the intention of all parties involved that the debentures issued by petitioner, as set forth hereinabove, constitute indebtedness of petitioner. The debentures had a definite maturity date of ten years from date of issuance, and repayment was expressly provided for. The payment of these debentures was not subordinated to petitioner's general creditors. The interest rate provided on these debentures was reasonable, and the certainty of payment of interest was provided for and was not based on petitioner's earnings. The holders of these debentures had unrestricted right to enforce payment of principal and interest. Certain of these debentures are now held by outsiders, not the sole shareholders of petitioner. The holders of these debentures have no right to share in petitioner's profits, and no voting rights with petitioner's management. At all times from 1955, the date of incorporation, to and including 1966, the final tax year involved in this proceeding, the amount of equity capital held by petitioner has been substantial in relation to its indebtedness.

(x) Petitioner paid the respective amounts of $19,924.00, $16,205.95 and $15,386.75 as interest on its debentures which were issued, and which had the provisions, as set forth hereinabove, and, accordingly, such amounts are deductible as interest expense under Section 163 of the Internal Revenue Code.

WHEREFORE, petitioner prays that the Court may hear the case, redetermine the deficiency herein in accordance with the assignment of error contained in paragraph 4, hereinabove, and for all other appropriate relief in the premises.

COUNSEL FOR PETITIONER

Form C

EDMUND F. BALL AND VIRGINIA B. BALL–54 T.C. 1200 (1970)

PETITION

This petition illustrates a multiple-issue case, where the facts are pleaded with brevity. Frequently this is advisable, especially in multiple-issue cases, where the petition might become very lengthy if the facts should be pleaded in detail. Also, a shorter petition is advisable if counsel for petitioner has had insufficient time for thoroughly assembling the facts.

TAX COURT OF THE UNITED STATES

EDMUND F. BALL and VIRGINIA B. BALL, Husband and Wife, Petitioners, v. COMMISSIONER OF INTERNAL REVENUE, Respondent.	Docket No. 4151-68

PETITION

The above-named petitioners hereby petition for a redetermination of the deficiency set forth by the Commissioner of Internal Revenue in his notice of deficiency (correspondence symbols L21 Code 430:RES:cph) dated June 28, 1968, and as a basis of their proceeding allege as follows:

1. The petitioners are individuals, husband and wife, residing at 1707 Riverside Avenue, Muncie, Indiana 47303. Their joint income tax returns for the period here involved were filed with the District Director of Internal Revenue for the District of Indiana, Indianapolis, Indiana.

2. The notice of deficiency (a copy of which is attached and marked "Exhibit A"*) was mailed to the petitioners on June 28, 1968.

3. The deficiency as determined by the Commissioner is in income tax for the taxable years 1962, 1963, and 1964 in the respective amounts of $34,141.11, $20,008.18, and $19,362.28, substantially all of which is in controversy.

4. The determination of tax set forth in the said notice of deficiency is based upon the following errors:

(a) In determining the taxable income for the taxable years 1962, 1963, and 1964, the Commissioner erroneously disallowed the deductions for contributions in the respective amounts of $657.16, $67.50, and $173.33.

(b) In determining the taxable income for the taxable years 1962, 1963, and 1964, the Commissioner erroneously disallowed the deductions for interest paid on indebtedness in the respective amounts of $3,159.38, $3,402.87, and $7,085.46.

(c) In determining the taxable income for the taxable years 1962, 1963, and 1964, the Commissioner erroneously disallowed the deductions for intangible drilling expense in the respective amounts of $22,003.13, $9,108.18, and $7,598.53.

(d) In determining the taxable income for the taxable year 1962, the Commissioner erroneously disallowed the deduction for casualty loss in the amount of $2,934.10 and erroneously held that such deduction was a capital loss.

(e) In determining the taxable income for the taxable years 1962, 1963, and 1964, the Commissioner erroneously increased interest income in the respective amounts of $9,994.75, $8,561.55, and $8,576.00.

(f) In determining the taxable income for the taxable years 1963 and 1964, the Commissioner erroneously increased taxable income in the respective amounts of $550.00 and $150.00 received as travel reimbursement from Ball Brothers Company.

(g) In determining the taxable income for the taxable year 1964, the Commissioner erroneously disallowed the deduction for casualty loss in the amount of $200.00.

(h) In determining the taxable income for the taxable year 1964, the Commissioner erroneously increased taxable income in the amount of $1,200.00 in connection with acquisition of a beach lot.

5. The facts upon which the petitioners rely as the basis of this proceeding are as follows:

(a) (i) Petitioners deducted the amount of $1,632.16 as their share of a contribution of books and prints to Wabash College by the E. B. Ball Heirs Trust during the taxable year 1962. The Commissioner has disallowed the amount of $632.16 of such claimed deduction. The fair market value of the books and prints

*Not reproduced.

given to Wabash College in 1962 was $4,896.50, and, therefore, petitioners are entitled to the claimed deduction of $1,632.16.

(ii) For the taxable year 1963, the Commissioner has disallowed the claimed deduction for contributions in the amount of $1,567.50, of which $45.00 was given to Leland Taxpayers Association and $22.50 to Leland Civic League, or a total of $67.50. Such total amount of $67.50 constitutes an allowable deduction for contributions under Section 170 of the Internal Revenue Code, and the Commissioner has erroneously disallowed this portion of petitioners' claimed deduction for contributions in 1963.

(iii) For the taxable year 1964, the Commissioner has disallowed the amount of $173.33 of the claimed deduction for contributions under Section 170 of the Internal Revenue Code. Petitioners gave a second set of sails for a boat to the Y.M.C.A. in 1964, the fair market value of which was $90.00, and, accordingly, such amount constitutes an allowable deduction for contributions for such year. The Commissioner also disallowed the amount of $83.33, which was petitioners' distributive share of a gift from E. B. Ball Heirs Trust to the Frank Hanighan Memorial Fund. Such amount constitutes an allowable deduction for contributions under Section 170 of the Internal Revenue Code, and the Commissioner's disallowance thereof is erroneous.

(b) During the taxable years 1962, 1963, and 1964, petitioners paid interest on indebtedness to four banks in the respective total amounts of $3,159.38, $3,402.87, and $7,085.46. Petitioners' bank indebtedness on which such interest was paid was not incurred or continued to purchase or carry obligations the interest on which is wholly exempt from income tax. Accordingly, such interest payments constitute allowable deductions for the taxable years 1962, 1963, and 1964 under Section 163 of the Internal Revenue Code, and the Commissioner's disallowance thereof is erroneous.

(c) During the taxable years 1962, 1963, and 1964 petitioner Edmund F. Ball participated as a co-owner in an enterprise which was engaged in oil and gas exploration and development known as Mid-America Minerals, Inc. (in 1964 known as Calvert Mid-America, Inc.). This organization filed timely partnership returns (Form 1065) with the District Director of Internal Revenue for the District of Oklahoma, Oklahoma City, Oklahoma, for each of such taxable years. On each of such returns, elections were made as follows:

> "This organization qualifies under Subdivisions (i) and (iii) of Section 1.761-1(a) (2) of regulations promulgated under the Internal Revenue Code of 1954; and all members of the organization elect that it be excluded from all of Subchapter K (Sec. 761 IRC). A copy of the agreement (or provisions of the oral agreement) is available at the office of the operator.
>
> "If for any reason this organization is considered to be a partnership, all co-owners elect to deduct currently as expenses all expenditures for intangible drilling and development costs of oil and gas wells as provided in Section 263 (c) of the 1954 Internal Revenue Code."

Accordingly, petitioner Edmund F. Ball is entitled to the claimed deductions for his share of the intangible drilling costs of this enterprise for the taxable years 1962, 1963, and 1964 in the respective amounts of $22,003.13, $9,108.18, and $7,598.53, and the Commissioner's disallowance thereof is erroneous.

(d) Petitioners claimed a deduction for casualty loss in the amount of $2,934.10 for the taxable year 1962. A storm damaged several buildings which were used for business purposes and which cost $3,904.54 to repair. Petitioners received $970.44 as insurance proceeds on account of such damage and deducted the remainder, or $2,934.10, as a casualty loss. There was no involuntary conversion of a capital asset. Accordingly, petitioners are entitled to the claimed deduction.

(e) During the taxable years 1962, 1963, and 1964, petitioner Edmund F. Ball made loans to a corporation known as B. B. and S. Properties, Inc., without any interest being due and payable thereon. Petitioner Edmund F. Ball received no interest income on such indebtedness to him of B. B. and S. Properties, Inc. during the taxable years 1962, 1963, and 1964. The Commissioner has held that petitioner Edmund F. Ball had imputed interest income in the respective amounts of $9,994.75, $8,561.55, and $8,576.00 for the taxable years 1962, 1963, and 1964 under Section 482 of the Internal Revenue Code by reason of such outstanding indebtedness to him without interest being paid thereon. Petitioner's loans to this corporation are not within the purview of Section 482. The Commissioner's action is erroneous, and petitioner Edmund F. Ball realized and received no interest income on account of such outstanding indebtedness from B. B. and S. Properties, Inc. during the taxable years 1962, 1963, and 1964.

(f) Petitioner Edmund F. Ball received travel reimbursement from Ball Brothers Company, of which he was an executive, in the respective amounts of $550.00 and $150.00 for the taxable years 1963 and 1964. The Commissioner has increased petitioner Edmund F. Ball's taxable income by such amounts. Such amounts were expended by petitioner Edmund F. Ball as ordinary and necessary expenses on behalf of Ball Brothers Company during the taxable years 1963 and 1964, and, accordingly, such amounts do not constitute taxable income to petitioner Edmund F. Ball for such years.

(g) Petitioners claimed a casualty loss in the amount of $375.53 because of destruction of a tree during the taxable year 1964. Such amount constitutes an allowable deduction for casualty loss, and the Commissioner's disallowance of $200.00 of such claimed deduction is erroneous.

(h) During the taxable year 1964, a lot in the area of Galveston, Texas, was conveyed to petitioner Virginia B. Ball because of damage caused to land in which she held a life estate. The Commissioner has determined that petitioner Virginia B. Ball realized taxable income of $1,200.00 by virtue of her acquisition of this lot. Petitioner Virginia B. Ball did not realize taxable income of $1,200.00, or any other amount, on account of the acquisition of this lot, since its value would constitute either reimbursement of a loss, or an adjustment to basis. Further, if any ordinary income was realized on the acquisition of this lot, the amount of $1,200.00 is erroneous, as the fair market value of the lot was less than such amount.

WHEREFORE, petitioners pray that the Court may hear the case, redetermine the deficiency herein in accordance with the assignments of error contained in paragraph 4 hereinabove, and for all other appropriate relief in the premises.

COUNSEL FOR PETITIONERS

Form D

DELAWARE TRUCKING CO., INC.–T.C. Memo 1974-34

PETITION

This is a Section 531 petition, preceded by a Section 534 statement, also included herein, *presenting five grounds for retention of earnings.* In addition, other extenuating circumstances for nonapplication of this penalty tax are set forth. Facts to rebut tax motivation, should it be held that excessive earnings were accumulated, are also pleaded.

June 28, 1971

District Director of Internal Revenue
U. S. Treasury Department
Audit Division
500 Century Building
36 South Pennsylvania Street
Indianapolis, Indiana 46204

In re: Delaware Trucking Company, Inc.
301 W. Seymour
Muncie, Indiana 47305

Your Reference: L113 Code 430:LJS:rn

Dear Sir:

Pursuant to your letter dated June 3, 1971, in which it was stated that you propose issuance of statutory notices of deficiency for the taxable years ended December 31, 1967, December 31, 1968, and December 31, 1969, setting forth amounts with respect to Section 531 of the Internal Revenue Code relating to the accumulated earnings tax, there is submitted herewith, under the provisions of Section 534(c), a statement of the grounds on which the taxpayer relies to establish that all or any part of the earnings and profits have not been permitted to accumulate beyond the reasonable needs of the business, together with facts sufficient to show the basis thereof.

The portion of its earnings and profits which was retained by Delaware Trucking Company, Inc. (hereinafter "the taxpayer") as of December 31, 1967, December 31, 1968, and December 31, 1969, was retained:

(1) to meet the needs of the taxpayer for working capital with which to conduct the normal operations of its business;

(2) to provide funds necessary for the replacement of, and additions to, its fixed assets;

(3) to provide funds for additional insurance premiums;

(4) to provide funds for future income tax resulting from use of an accelerated depreciation method;

(5) to provide funds to offset probable future loss on disposition of a subsidiary; and

(6) to provide funds for the acquisition of a building for its principal office and place of business.

GROUNDS FOR RETENTION OF EARNINGS AND FACTS SUFFICIENT TO SHOW THE BASIS THEREOF

1. Earnings were Retained to Meet the Needs of the Taxpayer for Working Capital with which to Conduct the Normal Operations of Its Business.

NATURE OF THE BUSINESS OPERATION

The taxpayer is actively engaged in the trucking business. It reports its income on the basis of a fiscal year ending December 31, and by the use of the accrual method of accounting.

A. WORKING CAPITAL REQUIREMENTS

The taxpayer needs working capital to conduct its current business operations, including labor expense, administrative expense, the extension of credit to customers, and miscellaneous operating expenses. The term "working capital" is employed herein in the sense in which it is customarily employed in the business community, that is, it is a net amount composed of all those assets customarily classified as "current", less all liabilities due and payable within twelve months.

The taxpayer must enter into a new labor contract every three years with the Teamsters' Union. It executed a new three-year contract with the Teamsters' Union in February, 1967. This contract provided for substantial graduated wage increases during the taxable years 1967, 1968 and 1969.

Taxpayer's expenses steadily increased prior to 1967 because of the effects of inflation. As of December 31, 1967, December 31, 1968, and December 31, 1969, the taxpayer reasonably anticipated that inflation would cause continued expense increases for future years.

Based upon the terms of its 1967 contract with the Teamsters' Union, together with estimated inflationary expense increases based upon prior experience, taxpayer reasonably anticipated that it needed to retain earnings as of December 31, 1967, December 31, 1968, and December 31, 1969, for future working capital requirements in an additional amount approximating 75% of the annual working capital requirements computed under the formula used in *Bardahl International Corporation,* 25 TCM 935 (1966).

It has been the taxpayer's policy to finance its working capital needs out of its retained earnings and to avoid borrowing for this purpose.

There is attached hereto as "Exhibit 1"* and incorporated herein by this reference, a schedule reflecting the computation of taxpayer's working capital needs under the *Bardahl* formula, plus the addition covering future higher labor costs and other expenses.

Accordingly, as of December 31, 1967, taxpayer needed not less than the amount of $90,486; as of December 31, 1968, not less than the amount of $97,197; and as of December 31, 1969, not less than the amount of $129,665 as working capital to conduct its normal business operations.

2. Earnings were Retained to Provide Funds Necessary for the Replacement of and Additions to Its Fixed Assets.

Taxpayer has maintained a program of replacement of fixed assets, including trucks and equipment, plus additions thereto, in an effort to be competitive. Taxpayer anticipates and plans this program at least two years in advance of actual acquisition. During the taxable years 1968, 1969 and 1970 (hereinafter "the taxable period") net expenditures for such purposes were in the respective amounts of $102,675.32, $57,807.42 and $31,770.30. For the taxable year 1971, anticipated expenditures for such purposes were in the amount of $90,000. There is attached hereto "Exhibit 2,"* which sets forth the specific items of fixed assets acquired during the taxable period and anticipated to be acquired in the taxable year 1971. Such exhibit is incorporated herein by this reference.

As of December 31, 1967, the reasonably anticipated needs of taxpayer for replacement of, and additions to, its fixed assets consisted of acquisitions in the total amount of $160,482.74 during the taxable years 1968 and 1969, the detail of which is set forth in "Exhibit 2."

As of December 31, 1968, the reasonably anticipated needs of taxpayer for replacement of, and additions to, its fixed assets consisted of acquisitions in the total amount of $89,577.72 during the taxable years 1969 and 1970, the detail of which is set forth in "Exhibit 2."

As of December 31, 1969, the reasonably anticipated needs of taxpayer for replacements of, and additions to, its fixed assets consisted of acquisitions in the

*Not reproduced.

amount of $31,770.30 during the taxable year 1970 and planned acquisitions in the amount of $90,000 during the taxable year 1971, or a total of $121,770.30.

Taxpayer had specific and definite plans for the above-stated acquisitions of fixed assets as of December 31, 1967, December 31, 1968, and December 31, 1969, as set forth in "Exhibit 2." Accordingly, as of December 31, 1967, taxpayer needed to retain earnings of not less than $160,482.74; as of December 31, 1968, taxpayer needed to retain earnings of not less than $89,577.72; and as of December 31, 1969, taxpayer needed to retain earnings of not less than $121,770.30, for acquisition of fixed assets.

3. Earnings were Retained to Provide Funds for Additional Insurance Premiums.

Taxpayer's trucking fleet was insured during the taxable period, and had been prior thereto, by Continental Casualty Company under a retrospective rating plan by which the premium charge during the policy period is predicated on its loss experience.

In taxpayer's industry, serious accidents are a continuous hazard. Taxpayer has been advised by its insurer that even a single fatal accident could increase its insurance premium for a three-year policy period by as much as $30,000.

Accordingly, taxpayer needed to retain earnings of at least $30,000 as of December 31, 1967, December 31, 1968, and December 31, 1969, for the payment of contingent additional insurance premiums under its retrospective coverage.

4. Earnings were Retained to Provide Funds for Future Income Tax Resulting from Use of an Accelerated Depreciation Method.

During the taxable period, taxpayer deducted depreciation on its trucks and trailers under the double declining balance method, one of the accelerated methods permitted by Section 167 of the Internal Revenue Code. The use of an accelerated depreciation method results in lower income tax in the early years and increased income tax in the later years of the taxable period covered by the deductions.

Accordingly, taxpayer needed to retain earnings to pay increased income tax in later years by reason of deducting depreciation under an accelerated method during the taxable period in the amount of $11,535 as of December 31, 1967, $11,078 as of December 31, 1968, and $13,853 as of December 31, 1969.

5. Earnings were Retained to Provide Funds to Offset Probable Loss on Future Disposition of a Subsidiary.

During the taxable period, Cox Motor Transport, Inc. was taxpayer's wholly-owned subsidiary, which had sustained net operating losses in each year of the taxable period, and for five years prior thereto. Throughout the taxable period, and for five years prior thereto, taxpayer was liable to the seller in the amount of $10,200 on account of the acquisition cost of the subsidiary.

During the taxable period, taxpayer entertained very little hope that the subsidiary could ever operate profitably and, therefore, anticipated that within the foreseeable future the subsidiary would have to be liquidated or otherwise disposed of at a substantial loss.

Accordingly, taxpayer needed to retain earnings of not less than $50,000 as of December 31, 1967, December 31, 1968, and December 31, 1969, to offset the probable loss on the future disposition of its subsidiary.

6. Earnings were Retained to Provide Funds to Acquire a Building for Taxpayer's Principal Office and Place of Business.

For several years prior to 1967, as well as during the taxable period, taxpayer leased its principal office and place of business at 301 West Seymour Street, Muncie, Indiana. Prior to 1967 taxpayer decided that it would be advantageous and desirable to acquire comparable property rather than to lease it.

Based upon discussions with owners and investigation of sales prices of comparable properties, taxpayer concluded that it could purchase comparable property for approximately $80,000.

Accordingly, as of December 31, 1967, December 31, 1968, and December 31, 1969, taxpayer needed to retain earnings of not less than $80,000 for the purchase of comparable property it then occupied as its principal office and place of business.

The foregoing statement has been prepared in accordance with Section 534(c) of the Internal Revenue Code and Section 1.534-2(d) of the Treasury Regulations pertaining to the Code.

Respectfully submitted,

DELAWARE TRUCKING CO., INC.

By ______________________

Evelyn S. Snyder
Its President

UNITED STATES TAX COURT

DELAWARE TRUCKING COMPANY, INC. Petitioner, v. COMMISSIONER OF INTERNAL REVENUE Respondent.	}	Docket No. 8211-71

PETITION

The above-named petitioner hereby petitions for a redetermination of the deficiency set forth by the Commissioner of Internal Revenue in his notice of deficiency (Correspondence Symbols L113 Code 430:LJS:rn) dated September 16, 1971, and as a basis of its proceeding alleges as follows:

1. The petitioner is a corporation organized and existing under the laws of the state of Indiana with its principal office at 301 West Seymour, Muncie, Indiana 47305. The returns for the period here involved were filed with the District Director of Internal Revenue for the District of Indiana, Indianapolis, Indiana.

2. The notice of deficiency was mailed to petitioner on September 16, 1971. A copy of the notice of deficiency is attached hereto and marked "Exhibit A."*

3. The deficiency as determined by the Commissioner is in income tax for the taxable years ended December 31, 1967, December 31, 1968, and December 31, 1969, in the respective amounts of $16,372.28, $29,558.47 and $16,841.64, all of which is in controversy.

4. The determination of tax set forth in the said notice of deficiency is based upon the following error:

(a) In determining the liability for the taxable years ended December 31, 1967, December 31, 1968, and December 31, 1969, the Commissioner erroneously held that the petitioner was subject to the accumulated earnings tax under Section 531 of the Internal Revenue Code.

5. The facts upon which petitioner relies as the basis of this proceeding are as follows:

(a)(i)(A) Petitioner is engaged in the trucking business. It reports its income on the basis of a fiscal year ending December 31, and by the use of the accrual method of accounting.

*Not reproduced.

(a)(i)(B) During the taxable years ended December 31, 1967, December 31, 1968, and December 31, 1969, (hereinafter usually "the taxable period") petitioner needed working capital to conduct its current business operations, including labor expense, administrative expense, the extension of credit to customers and miscellaneous operating expenses. Petitioner's "working capital" is a net amount composed of all those assets generally classified as "current", less all liabilities due and payable within twelve months.

(a)(i)(C) Petitioner must enter into a new labor contract every three years with the Teamsters' Union. It executed a new three-year contract with the Teamsters' Union in February, 1967, which provided for substantial graduated wage increases during the taxable period. Further, petitioner's other business expenses steadily increased prior to the taxable period because of the effects of inflation. As of December 31, 1967, December 31, 1968, and December 31, 1969, petitioner reasonably anticipated that inflation would cause continued expense increases for future years.

(a)(i)(D) Based upon the terms of its 1967 contract with the Teamsters' Union, together with other estimated inflationary expense increases based upon prior experience, petitioner reasonably anticipated that it needed to retain additional amounts for working capital above the amounts computed for working capital needs in fiscal years prior to the taxable period.

(a)(i)(E) It has been petitioner's policy to finance its working capital needs out of its retained earnings, and to avoid borrowing for this purpose, for many years prior to the taxable period and petitioner intended to continue that policy during the taxable period.

(a)(i)(F) Taking into account its increasing expenses caused by inflation, the ordinary working capital requirements of petitioner for one business cycle were $90,486.00, $97,197.00 and $129,665.00 for the taxable years ended December 31, 1967, December 31, 1968, and December 31, 1969, respectively.

(a)(ii)(A) Petitioner has maintained a program of replacement of fixed assets, including trucks and equipment, plus additions thereto, in an effort to be competitive. Petitioner anticipates and plans this program at least two years in advance of actual acquisition. During the taxable years 1968, 1969 and 1970, petitioner's net expenditures for such purposes were in the respective amounts of $102,675.32, $57,807.42 and $31,770.30. For the taxable year 1971, anticipated expenditures for such purposes were in the amount of $90,000.00

(a)(ii)(B) As of December 31, 1967, the reasonably anticipated needs of petitioner for replacement of, and additions to, its fixed assets were not less than $160,482.74, the total of its expenditures for this purpose during the taxable years 1968 and 1969.

(a)(ii)(C) As of December 31, 1968, the reasonably anticipated needs of petitioner for replacement of, and additions to, its fixed assets were not less than $89,577.72, the total of its expenditures for this purpose during the taxable years 1969 and 1970.

(a)(ii)(D) As of December 31, 1969, the reasonably anticipated needs of petitioner for replacement of, and additions to, its fixed assets consisted of expenditures in the amount of $31,770.30 during the taxable year 1970 and planned expenditures in the amount of $90,000.00 during the taxable year 1971, or a total of $121,770.30.

(a)(ii)(E) Petitioner had specific and definite plans for the above-stated acquisitions of fixed assets as of December 31, 1967, December 31, 1968, December 31, 1969. Accordingly, as of December 31, 1967, petitioner needed to retain earnings of not less than $160,482.74; as of December 31, 1968, petitioner needed to retain earnings of not less than $89,577.72; and as of December 31, 1969, petitioner needed to retain earnings of not less than $121,770.30, for acquisition of fixed assets.

(a)(iii) Petitioner's trucking fleet was insured during the taxable period, and had been prior thereto, by Continental Casualty Company under a retrospective rating plan by which the premium charge during the policy period is predicated on its loss experience. In petitioner's industry, serious accidents are a continuous hazard. Petitioner has been advised by its insurer that even a single fatal accident could increase its insurance premium for a three-year policy period by as much as $30,000.00. Accordingly, petitioner needed to retain earnings of at least $30,000.00 as of December 31, 1967, December 31, 1968, and December 31, 1969, for the payment of contingent additional indurance premiums under its retrospective coverage.

(a)(iv) During the taxable period, petitioner deducted depreciation on its trucks and trailers under the double declining balance method, one of the accelerated methods permitted by Section 167 of the Internal Revenue Code. The use of an accelerated depreciation method results in lower income tax in the early years and increased income tax in the later years of the taxable period covered by the deductions. Accordingly, petitioner needed to retain earnings to pay increased income tax in later years by reason of deducting depreciation under an accelerated method during the taxable period in the amount of $11,535.00 as of December 31, 1967, $11,078.00 as of December 31, 1968, and $13,853.00 as of December 31, 1969.

(a)(v) During the taxable period, Cox Motor Transport, Inc. was petitioner's wholly-owned subsidiary, which had sustained net operating losses in each year of the taxable period, and for five years prior thereto. Throughout the taxable period, and for five years prior thereto, petitioner was liable to the seller in the amount of $10,200.00 on account of the acquisition cost of the subsidiary. During the taxable period petitioner entertained very little hope that the subsidiary could ever operate profitably and, therefore, anticipated that within the foreseeable future the subsidiary would have to be liquidated or otherwise disposed of at a substantial loss. Accordingly, petitioner needed to retain earnings of not less than $50,000.00 as of December 31, 1967, December 31, 1968, and December 31, 1969, to offset the probable loss on the future disposition of its subsidiary.

(a)(vi) For several years prior to 1967, as well as throughout the taxable period, petitioner leased its principal office and place of business at 301 West Seymour Street, Muncie, Indiana. Prior to 1967 petitioner decided that it would be advantageous and desirable to acquire comparable property rather than to lease it. Based upon discussions with owners and investigation of sales prices of comparable properties prior to, and during the taxable period, petitioner concluded that it could purchase comparable property for approximately $80,000.00. Accordingly, as of December 31, 1967, December 31, 1968, and December 31, 1969, petitioner needed to retain earnings of not less than $80,000.00 for the purchase of comparable property for its principal office and place of business.

(a)(vii) Petitioner's earnings and profits were not permitted to accumulate beyond the reasonable needs of the business during the taxable years ended December 31, 1967, December 31, 1968, and December 31, 1969. Compelling reasons have required petitioner to retain earnings and profits to meet its vital business necessities.

(a)(viii) During the taxable period, and for many years prior thereto, petitioner's income was received primarily from one customer, The Chrysler Corporation, a major automobile manufacturer. "Piggyback" hauling of automobiles by railroad was providing a new form of competition, which petitioner's management feared would reduce its hauling volume during the taxable period and in subsequent years. Railroad rates applicable to carload lots also constituted a threat to petitioner's revenue volume during the taxable period, since railroad rates were lower than trucking rates. Hence, petitioner's profits during the taxable period, and for subsequent years, were dependent upon its retaining Chrysler's business, as well as upon the continued success of the automobile industry. Since most of its financial eggs were in this one basket, petitioner's management concluded during the taxable period, and prior thereto, that it must follow a conservative financial approach with respect to the accumulation of earnings to guard against the loss of its primary customer, the increased competition from railroads, and the possible decline in volume of the automobile industry, beset with many problems during the taxable period, especially increased foreign competition.

(a)(ix) No loans or advances have been made to shareholders or to officers. No payments have been made for the benefit of, or on behalf of, shareholders or officers.

(a)(x) There have been no investments in unrelated businesses, or for purposes not related to the business of petitioner.

(a)(xi) During the taxable period, petitioner's common stock was owned as follows:

	Shares
Marguerite M. Oliver	95
Evelyn S. Snyder (Granddaughter of Mrs. Oliver)	25
Osa Sisk (unrelated to Mrs. Oliver or Mrs. Snyder)	10
Trustee under the Will of Hortance L. Oliver (husband of Mrs. Oliver)	255
Treasury	15
Total	400

(a)(xii) Under the provisions of the Will of Hortance L. Oliver, the governing instrument, annual income to the extent of $5,000.00 is distributable to each of Marguerite M. Oliver and his daughter, Florence O. Sowers, during their lifetimes, and any income above $10,000.00 is to be accumulated for the benefit of a remainderman. The Trust is to terminate, and the principal and accumulated income is to be distributed to the remainderman, upon the death of the survivor of the two income beneficiaries. Hence, during the lifetimes of the two income beneficiaries, any income in excess of $10,000.00 income annually is taxable to the Trustee. Both Mrs. Oliver and Mrs. Sowers were living throughout the taxable period.

(a)(xiii) Of petitioner's stockholders, only Evelyn S. Snyder had substantial taxable income during the taxable period and she owned only 25 shares, or 6 2/3% of the total outstanding stock. Had petitioner paid dividends during the taxable period, the additional income tax thereon to its stockholders would have been very small. Most of the dividends would have been paid to the Trustee under the Will of Hortance L. Oliver, which had no other taxable income during the taxable period, and which, under the Will, would have distributed $10,000.00 thereof to Mrs. Oliver and Mrs. Sowers, taxable at very low rates, and which would have been taxable on any dividend received above $10,000.00 at a very low rate.

(a)(xiv) Petitioner was not availed of during the taxable years ended December 31, 1967, December 31, 1968, and December 31, 1969, for the purpose of avoiding the income tax with respect to its shareholders through the medium of permitting its earnings and profits to accumulate instead of being distributed and is, therefore, not subject to the accumulated earnings tax imposed by Section 531 of the Internal Revenue Code.

(a)(xv) On June 3, 1971, pursuant to section 534(b) of the Internal Revenue Code, the Commissioner of Internal Revenue advised petitioner by letter that he proposed the issuance of a statutory notice of deficiency for the taxable years 1967, 1968 and 1969 under Section 531, relating to the tax on accumulated earnings. On July 20, 1971, petitioner filed with the Commissioner of Internal Revenue a statement of the grounds, together with sufficient facts to show the basis thereof, on which petitioner relies to establish the reasonableness of its accumulation of earnings under Section 534 of the Internal Revenue Code. A copy of such statement is attached hereto, marked "Exhibit B" and incorporated herein by this reference. The burden of proof is on the Commissioner of Internal Revenue with respect to the grounds set forth in such statement filed July 20, 1971, on which petitioner relies to establish that all, or any part of, its earnings and profits have not been permitted to accumulate beyond the reasonable needs of the business.

WHEREFORE, petitioner prays that the Court may hear the case, determine that the burden of proof is upon the respondent with respect to the grounds set forth in Exhibit B, determine that petitioner has no liability for accumulated earnings tax provided by Section 531 of the Internal Revenue Code for the taxable years 1967, 1968 and 1969, and for such other relief as may be appropriate in the premises.

COUNSEL FOR PETITIONER

Form E

AUSTIN STATE BANK–57 T.C. 180 (1971)

PETITION

This petition illustrates pleading an unusual issue, namely, whether a long-existing state bank qualifies as a "bank" under Section 581 of the Internal Revenue Code of 1954. *(It also contains the reasonableness of officers' compensation issue.)*

Note again the brevity of the pleading caused by lack of knowledge of the Commissioner's position. Hence, it was wiser to plead only the bank statutory fundamentals and then develop rebuttal arguments later after reaching the negotiating table.

TAX COURT OF THE UNITED STATES

AUSTIN STATE BANK,
Petitioner,
v. — Docket No. 755-69
COMMISSIONER OF INTERNAL REVENUE,
Respondent,

PETITION

The above-named petitioner hereby petitions for a redetermination of the deficiency set forth by the Commissioner of Internal Revenue in his notice of deficiency (correspondence symbols Form L21 Code 430-LED-jeb) dated December 17, 1968, and as a basis of its proceeding alleges as follows:

1. The petitioner is a corporation organized and existing under the laws of the State of Indiana, with its principal office and place of business at Austin, Indiana. The return for the period here involved was filed with the District Director of Internal Revenue for the District of Indiana, Indianapolis, Indiana.

2. The notice of deficiency (a copy of which is attached and marked "Exhibit A"*) was mailed to the petitioner on December 17, 1968.

3. The deficiency as determined by the Commissioner is in income tax for the taxable year ended December 31, 1964 in the amount of $27,951.30, all of which is in controversy.

4. The determination of tax set forth in the said notice of deficiency is based upon the following errors:

(a) In determining the taxable income for the taxable year 1964, the Commissioner erroneously held that petitioner was a personal holding company under Section 542 of the Internal Revenue Code.

(b) In determining the taxable income for the taxable year 1964, the Commissioner erroneously disallowed the deduction for officers' compensation in the amount of $15,200.00.

(c) In determining the taxable income for the taxable year 1964, the Commissioner erroneously disallowed the deduction for pension plan contribution in the amount of $5,266.81.

(d) The Commissioner erred in determining any deficiency for the taxable year 1964 because of the expiration of the period of limitations on assessment and collection of additional tax for such year under Section 6501(a) of the Internal Revenue Code prior to the issuance of the instant statutory notice of deficiency.

5. The facts upon which the petitioner relies as the basis of this proceeding are as follows:

(a) (i) Petitioner obtained its charter as a state bank under the state banking laws of Indiana in October, 1909, with authorized capital stock of 250 shares, all of which were subscribed for and issued. There has been no change in the number of shares outstanding from that date to and including December 31, 1964, the end of the taxable period involved herein.

(ii) Under the effective Indiana banking laws, it was necessary for petitioner to renew its charter each twenty years, and, therefore, the petitioner bank was rechartered under Indiana banking laws in 1929. Prior to 1949, the end of the next twenty-year period, the Indiana banking statutes were amended to eliminate the twenty-year rechartering provision, and, hence, in 1949 petitioner's charter was amended to make it perpetual.

(iii) During the taxable year 1964, and for all years prior thereto since its organization, petitioner was a "bank" incorporated and doing business under the laws of the state of Indiana, a substantial part of the business of which consists of receiving deposits and making loans and discounts, and which is subject by law to supervision and examination by the state of Indiana, which has supervision over banking institutions incorporated and doing business under its laws. Petitioner was a "bank" within the meaning of Section 581 of the Internal Revenue Code during the taxable year 1964, and for all years prior thereto since its organization, and is subject to all

*Not reproduced.

provisions of the internal revenue laws applying to "banks" as defined in section 581. Petitioner was not a personal holding company within the meaning of Section 542 of the Internal Revenue Code during the taxable year 1964 and was not, therefore, subject to the personal holding company tax imposed by Section 541 as determined by the Commissioner.

(b) Petitioner paid the chairman of its board of directors, Ivan H. Morgan, a salary in the amount of $10,000.00, and its president, Elsinore Morgan, a salary in the amount of $5,200.00, during the taxable year 1964. Such amounts constitute reasonable compensation for services actually rendered by Ivan H. Morgan and Elsinore Morgan in their respective corporate offices during such year. They were the sole executives of petitioner and made all decisions required of management with respect to policy matters and also day-to-day operations of petitioner. Such amounts are, therefore, deductible as ordinary and necessary business expenses under Section 162 of the Internal Revenue Code, and the Commissioner's disallowance of such salary payments is erroneous.

(c) During the taxable year 1964, petitioner paid or accrued the amount of $23,752.19 as total nondeferred compensation to all covered employees under its qualified pension plan under Section 401 of the Internal Revenue Code, and claimed the amount of $6,295.66 as a deduction on account of its contribution to such pension plan. By virtue of his disallowance of the claimed deductions for officers' compensation paid to its two officers, as set forth in paragraph (b), hereinabove, the Commissioner has disallowed the amount of $5,266.81 of the total claimed deduction for contribution to pension plan of $6,295.66. Since the amount of officers' compensation paid to its two officers was reasonable and deductible, as set forth in paragraph (b), hereinabove, the Commissioner's disallowance of the pension plan contribution deduction in the amount of $5,266.81 is erroneous.

(d) The period for assessment and collection of additional income tax for the taxable year ended December 31, 1964 expired March 15, 1968, under Section 6501(a) of the Internal Revenue Code. The instant notice of deficiency was mailed to petitioner on December 17, 1968, after the expiration of the period of limitations for assessment and collection of additional income tax for the taxable year 1964. Accordingly, the Commissioner is barred from assessing and collecting additional income tax from petitioner for the taxable year 1964.

WHEREFORE, petitioner prays that the Court may hear the case, determine that there is no deficiency in income tax due from petitioner for the taxable year ended December 31, 1964, and for all other appropriate relief in the premises.

COUNSEL FOR PETITIONER

Form F

ESTATE OF RUDOLPH G. LEEDS—54 T.C. 781 (1970)

PETITION

This petition is included to illustrate the pleading of an estate tax case, with unusual charitable trust deduction and marital deduction issues. Note the paraphrasing of the pertinent portions of the Will and a summarization of the relevant state court proceeding.

Since the contemplation of death issue is obviously very strong for petitioner, its pleading is understated.

TAX COURT OF THE UNITED STATES

ESTATE OF RUDOLPH G. LEEDS, Edward H. Harris, Jr., Executor, Petitioner, v. COMMISSIONER OF INTERNAL REVENUE, Respondent.	Docket No. 396-69

PETITION

The above-named petitioner hereby petitions for a redetermination of the deficiency in estate tax set forth by the Commissioner of Internal Revenue in his notice of deficiency (correspondence symbols L-50 Code 430:RES:cph) dated November 5, 1968, and as a basis of its proceeding alleges as follows:

1. The petitioner is the Estate of Rudolph G. Leeds, who died November 21, 1964, a resident of Richmond, Wayne County, Indiana. Edward H. Harris, Jr. was duly appointed and duly qualified as the executor of such estate, and letters of administration were grante; to him as executor of such estate by the Wayne Circuit Court, Richmond, Wayne County, Indiana. The estate tax return for the Estate of Rudolph

G. Leeds was filed with the Director of Internal Revenue for the District of Indiana, Indianapolis, Indiana.

2. The notice of deficiency (a copy of which is attached hereto and marked "Exhibit A"*) was mailed to the petitioner on November 5, 1968.

3. The deficiency as determined by the Commissioner is in estate tax in the amount of $112,858.70, all of which is in controversy, and, in addition, petitioner claims a refund of a portion of the estate tax paid.

4. The determination of tax set forth in the said notice of deficiency is based upon the following errors:

(a) In determining the amount of the taxable estate, the Commissioner erroneously included transfers during decedent's life in the amount of $15,000.00.

(b) In determining the amount of the taxable estate, the Commissioner erroneously disallowed administration expenses in the amount of $10,500.00.

(c) In determining the amount of the taxable estate, the Commissioner erroneously disallowed the deduction for a charitable bequest to Palladium Fund in the amount of $29,492.47.

(d) In determining the amount of the taxable estate, the Commissioner erroneously increased the marital deduction in the amount of $22,231.41 and erroneously failed to allow an additional marital deduction in the amount of $128,934.64.

(e) In determining the amount of the taxable estate, the Commissioner erroneously failed to allow any amount as additional deductions for attorney fees and administration expenses which have been, and will be, incurred in representation of the executor in the administrative and judicial determination of the correct amount of the estate tax liability.

(f) In determining the deficiency herein, the Commissioner erroneously failed to correctly reflect all estate tax payments by the executor.

5. The facts upon which the petitioner relies as the basis of this proceeding are as follows:

(a) (i) In December of each of the years 1952 to 1963, inclusive, decedent transferred to Edward H. Harris, Jr., by gift four shares of common stock of Palladium Publishing Corporation. The Commissioner has held that the gifts of four shares of such stock in each of the years 1961, 1962 and 1963 were made in contemplation of death and included the amount of $5,000.00 as the determined fair market value of each such gift, or a total of $15,000.00, in the gross estate under Section 2035 of the Internal Revenue Code.

(ii) Mr. Harris, the donee, was the co-publisher with the decedent of *The Palladium-Item* newspaper, which was owned by said Palladium Publishing Corporation. His father had been closely associated with decedent in the publication of this

*Not reproduced.

newspaper, and, therefore, close and warm ties of admiration and affection existed between decedent and Mr. Harris.

(iii) Although the decedent was 78 years of age at the time of his death, he was actively engaged in supervising the publication of *The Palladium-Item* newspaper and in attending to his other wide and varied business and personal affairs at the time of his death. His death came very suddenly, following an evening spent with his wife and married friends of long standing, with whom it had been their custom to meet each week. Decedent was in vigorous good health and was not concerned by any forebodings of impending death, either at the time of death or during the three-year period prior thereto.

(iv) These gifts were a part of a long-standing pattern of gifts to Mr. Harris and others and were associated with thoughts of life, not death. Such gifts were not transfers made in contemplation of death under Section 2035.

(b) Petitioner has paid a total of $63,000.00 in executor and attorney's fees, of which $52,500.00 has been claimed as deductions in the fiduciary income tax returns. The remaining balance thereof, $3,500.00 in executor fees and $7,000.00 in attorney fees, is an allowable deduction in computing the net estate tax under Section 2053(a) of the Internal Revenue Code.

(c) (i) Under Items VI and VII of decedent's will, property of the fair market value of $43,100.00 was transferred to trustees for the benefit of Elizabeth Kolp Popp during her lifetime, and at her death the remainder to the trustees of Palladium Fund, a charitable trust. Elizabeth Kolp Popp, whose name has been changed to Elizabeth Kolp, was 70 years of age at decedent's death. Her life estate in such property had a value for estate tax purposes of $13,507.53. The remainder in said trust, which will pass to the trustees of said Palladium Fund at her death, had a value for estate tax purposes of $29,492.47.

(ii) Palladium Fund is a trust created under decedent's will exclusively for charitable purposes, with all contributions or gifts to such trust to be used by the trustees exclusively for charitable purposes, no part of the activities of such trustees being the carrying on of propaganda, or otherwise attempting to influence legislation, and no part of its net earnings inuring to the benefit of an individual. Under Item VII-2(a) of decedent's will, all of the trust property, and all income accrued thereon, shall be held, administered and disposed of by the trustees of the Fund primarily as a pension, unemployment and insurance fund for the employees of Palladium Publishing Corporation, which is engaged in the publication of a daily newspaper known as the *Palladium-Item,* and the wives and minor children of said employees. The purpose of this trust is to secure regular employees of the *Palladium-Item* and their dependents against the hazards of unemployment, over which they have no control, due principally to sickness, accident, disability, death and old age. In view of the foregoing facts, Palladium Fund is a charitable trust to which bequests, legacies, devises or transfers are deductible in computing the estate tax under Section 2055(a)(3) of the Internal Revenue Code, and, accordingly, petitioner is entitled to deduct the amount of $29,492.47, the value of the remainder interest of the trust for the benefit of Elizabeth Kolp, under section 2055(a)(3).

(iii) Item VII of decedent's will devised and bequeathed the residue to Palladium Fund after a joint life estate to Florence S. Leeds, Edward H. Harris and Luther M. Feeger, which terminates upon Mrs. Leeds' death. She died June 4, 1966. Petitioner hereby claims any additional charitable deduction which might arise upon the recomputation of the estate tax liability herein.

(d) (i) The amount of $680,000.46 was claimed as the marital deduction on the estate tax return under Section 2056 of the Internal Revenue Code. By virtue of determined and uncontested adjustments in the notice of deficiency, the value of decedent's adjusted gross estate has been increased to the amount of $1,689,608.59, thereby entitling petitioner to a marital deduction in the amount of $844,804.29, in lieu of the amount of $680,000.46 deducted on the return.

(ii) The Commissioner has allowed the amount of $702,231.87 as the marital deduction in computing the determined deficiency herein, thereby increasing the claimed marital deduction in the amount of $22,231.41. The Commissioner's holding is based upon his erroneous finding that the marital deduction should bear its ratable portion of the federal estate tax, Indiana inheritance tax, claims and administration expenses. Under Items I and VII of decedent's will, fifty percent of decedent's adjusted gross estate passed directly to the surviving spouse, Florence Smith Leeds, without diminution for federal estate tax, Indiana inheritance tax, claims or administration expenses.

(iii) In November, 1966, the executor filed a petition in the Wayne Circuit Court at Richmond, Indiana, requesting a construction of the decedent's will, a determination as to the order in which the shares of distributees in the estate should abate, and an order designating the persons and the beneficiaries in said will to whom distribution is to be made and the proportions, parts and amounts to which each of such distributees was entitled. All interested persons and beneficiaries under the will were made parties to this suit, which was a true adversary proceeding. The court appointed an impartial, qualified attorney to appear as guardian ad litem for Palladium Fund and the employees and all persons interested in this Fund. The employees of the Palladium Publishing Corporation, beneficiaries under Palladium Fund, were also represented in court by their own independent attorney. After the completion of the pleadings and trial in open court, the Wayne Circuit Court entered its order on May 1, 1967, which, among other things, found that by Item I of the will the decedent directed his executor to pay all lawful claims and liabilities in the estate and expenses of administration and that the federal estate tax and Indiana inheritance tax were to be paid from the residue remaining in the estate, the same being property described in Item VII of the will, and from all income received by the executor during the administration of the estate. The court further found that the decedent had made bequests to his surviving spouse, Florence Smith Leeds, which, when added to life insurance paid to her, would equal an amount in value of fifty percent of decedent's adjusted gross estate, as finally determined for federal estate tax, and that the same would be the marital deduction in the estate, under Section 2056 of the Internal Revenue Code, and that the executor should pay from the residue of the estate all federal estate tax and Indiana inheritance tax and that none of such taxes were to be paid from property devised and bequeathed to the surviving spouse or from life insurance received by her.

(iv) By virtue of the provisions of decedent's will, and in accordance with its construction by a court of competent jurisdiction in an adversary proceeding, a marital deduction in the amount of $831,166.51 is allowable in computing the net estate under Section 2056 of the Internal Revenue Code, instead of the amount of $702,231.87 determined by the Commissioner.

(e) Additional legal fees and administration expenses have been incurred in representing the executor in resisting the asserted estate tax deficiency before the Internal Revenue Service. Additional legal fees and administration expenses will be incurred in representing the executor in resisting the asserted estate tax deficiency in this Court. The total amount of such additional legal fees and administration expenses is unascertained at this time. The total amount of such fees and expenses as finally determined will constitute an additional deduction from the gross estate in computing the taxable estate.

(f) In computing the asserted deficiency herein, the Commissioner has reflected only the amount of $152,920.06 as tax paid by the executor on page 4 of the statement attached to the statutory notice of deficiency. In addition to such amount of $152,920.06, the executor also paid the additional amounts of $19,530.00 and $48,676.92, making a total estate tax paid by the executor prior to the issuance of the statutory notice of deficiency in the amount of $221,126.98. Under assignments of error (a) to (d) hereinabove, the correct estate tax liability is $207,405.56, resulting in an overpayment in the amount of $13,721.42, without taking into account the additional deductions set forth in assignments of error (c) (iii) and (e) hereinabove. Petitioner makes claim to the refund thus resulting in the amount of $13,721.42, plus any additional refund which may be due under subparagraphs (c)(iii) and (e) hereinabove.

WHEREFORE, petitioner prays that this Court may hear this proceeding, determine that there is no deficiency in estate tax due herein, determine that there is a refund due the petitioner in accordance with the assignments of error contained herein, and for such other relief as may be appropriate in the premises.

COUNSEL FOR PETITIONER

Form G

PERRY S. LEWIS AND ESTHER LEWIS–47 T.C. 129 (1966)

PETITION

This petition is included to illustrate pleading (1) the oft-encountered redemption of stock issue; (2) the medical expense deduction and (3) the delinquency penalty issue.

Again, note the paraphrasing of the controlling agreement, rather than its quotation, which is believed to be more effective and easier for the Court to read and quickly understand.

TAX COURT OF THE UNITED STATES

PERRY S. LEWIS and
ESTHER LEWIS,
Husband and Wife,

Petitioners,

v.

COMMISSIONER OF INTERNAL REVENUE,

Respondent.

Docket No. ____________

PETITION

The above-named petitioners hereby petition for a redetermination of the deficiency set forth by the Commissioner of Internal Revenue in his notice of deficiency (correspondence symbols Form L-21 Code 430:LJS:va) dated November 14, 1963, and as a basis of their proceeding allege as follows:

1. Petitioners are individuals, husband and wife, whose address is C.M.R. 9, Crawfordsville, Indiana. Their joint returns for the period here involved were filed with the District Director of Internal Revenue, Indianapolis, Indiana.

2. The notice of deficiency (a copy of which is attached and marked "Exhibit A"*) was mailed to the petitioners on November 14, 1963.

3. The deficiencies as determined by the Commissioner are in income taxes and addition to tax for the years and in the amounts as set forth hereinbelow, all of which is in controversy:

Year	Deficiency	Addition to Tax Section 6651 (a) 1954 Code
December 31, 1959	$1,596.87	
December 31, 1960	1,701.45	
December 31, 1961	1,703.52	$329.52

4. The determination of tax and addition to tax set forth in the said notice of deficiency is based upon the following errors:

(a) In determining taxable income for the taxable years 1959, 1960, and 1961, the Commissioner erroneously held that the amount of $10,000.00 received by petitioner Perry S. Lewis in each of the years 1959, 1960, and 1961 from Perry Lewis Company, Inc. in redemption of stock was essentially equivalent to a dividend and, therefore includible as ordinary income for such years.

(b) In determining taxable income for the taxable years 1959, 1960, and 1961, the Commissioner erroneously reduced capital gains by the respective amounts of $1,940.00 for each of such years.

(c) In determining taxable income for the taxable years 1959, 1960, and 1961, the Commissioner erroneously decreased the deduction for medical expense for such years in the respective amounts of $138.00, $42.00, and $60.00.

(d) The Commissioner erroneously determined that petitioners are liable for the addition to tax under Section 6651(a) for the taxable year 1961.

5. The facts upon which petitioners rely as the basis of this proceeding are as follows:

(a)(i) Prior to July 1, 1956, Perry S. Lewis (hereinafter referred to as the "petitioner") was the owner of 495 shares of the common stock of Perry Lewis Co., Inc. (hereinafter referred to as the "Corporation"), an Indiana corporation with its principal office and place of business at Crawfordsville, Indiana, where it was engaged in business as a regularly authorized dealer for Ford Motor Company. On July 1, 1956, petitioner and the Corporation entered into a written agreement under which the Corporation agreed to buy, and petitioner agreed to sell, all of his 495 shares of common stock of the Corporation at a price of $100.00 per share. The agreement further provided that the Corporation would pay petitioner $500.00 per month on the purchase price until the total amount, $49,500.00, together with interest thereon as provided in the contract, had been paid in full.

*Not reproduced.

(ii) The agreement of July 1, 1956, also provided that the Corporation was not obligated to pay more than $6,000.00 in any one calendar year, although it had the right to pay more than such amount if it chose to do so. The contract provided that the Corporation must pay interest on the unpaid balance of the purchase price at the rate of 5 percent per annum and that the agreed monthly payment of $500.00 should include interest on the unpaid balance of the purchase price.

(iii) The agreement also provided that the parties should determine the amount of principal paid on the purchase price at the end of each calendar year and at that time petitioner would deliver to the Corporation the number of shares paid for at the rate of $100.00 per share in the preceeding calendar year. The agreement contained usual provisions for termination and release should the Corporation default in making the required payments, and also provided that the petitioner could demand payment in full for the remaining unpaid balance on the contract should controlling interest in the Corporation change.

(iv) The agreement also provided that each certificate making up the total of 495 shares owned by petitioner on July 1, 1956, should bear the statement thereon that the stock was subject to the agreement of July 1, 1956 between petitioner and the Corporation.

(v) The parties carried out the agreement of July 1, 1956 in accordance with its terms. Petitioner received the amount of $10,000.00 from the Corporation in each of the years 1959, 1960, and 1961 pursuant to such agreement and reported such amounts as capital gain in the joint returns he and his wife filed for each such year. The amounts of $10,000.00 received in each of the years 1959, 1960, and 1961 by petitioner in redemption of stock of the Corporation were not amounts essentially equivalent to a dividend distribution of the Corporation. The Corporation agreed to purchase all of petitioner's stock under the agreement of July 1, 1956, and the amounts received by petitioner under such agreement are entitled to capital gain treatment under Section 302(b)(1), (2), and (3) of the Internal Revenue Code of 1954.

(b) Petitioner correctly reported capital gain on his receipt of $10,000.00 from the Corporation in each of the years 1959, 1960, and 1961 in the joint returns he and his wife filed for such years, and the Commissioner's action in decreasing such capital gain is erroneous.

(c) During each of the years 1959, 1960, and 1961, petitioner was required to travel between Crawfordsville, Indiana, and Indianapolis, Indiana, for medical treatments by an Indianapolis physician. He claimed the amount of 10 cents per mile for such travel in computing the medical expense deduction on the joint returns he and his wife filed for such years. The Commissioner has determined that only the amount of 4 cents per mile should be allowed for this purpose. The amount of 10 cents per mile is reasonable for such travel. It is not in excess of the amount allowed by the United States Government for automobile travel of its employees during such years. Petitioner is entitled to the claimed deductions for such travel in computing his medical expense deduction for such years in the total amounts of $230.00, $70.00, and $100.00, each of these amounts being based on actual mileage traveled.

(d) The Commissioner has determined that petitioners are liable for the addition to tax under Section 6651(a) of the Internal Revenue Code of 1954 on the ground that the return for the taxable year 1961 was not filed within the time prescribed by Section 6072(a) of the Code. If such return was not timely filed, petitioners are not liable for such addition to tax because their failure to file such return timely was due to reasonable cause and not due to willful neglect. Any delay in filing this return was due to the severe illness of both petitioners. Since a joint return requires the signature of both spouses, their signatures could not be affixed to the return on or before the due date and before the date of actual filing. Accordingly, any delay in filing this return was due to reasonable cause and not due to willful neglect, and the petitioners are not liable for the asserted addition to tax.

WHEREFORE, the petitioners pray that the Court may hear this case, determine that no deficiency is due from the petitioners for the taxable years 1959, 1960, and 1961, determine that no addition to tax is due from petitioners for the taxable year 1961, and for all other appropriate relief in the premises.

COUNSEL FOR PETITIONERS

Form H

PETITION

This petition illustrates a case presenting mixed questions of law and fact, namely, an investment credit issue. Many of the facts are susceptible of stipulation, but other facts must be presented by oral testimony. It is intended to give the Court a clear picture of the question presented, so that the presiding judge can easily follow the testimony.

UNITED STATES TAX COURT

Petitioner, v. COMMISSIONER OF INTERNAL REVENUE, Respondent.	Docket No. __________

PETITION

The above-named petitioner hereby petitions for a redetermination of the deficiency set forth by the Commissioner of Internal Revenue in his notice of deficiency (Correspondence Symbols L-50 Code 430:BMW:pm) ________, and as a basis of its case alleges as follows:

1. The petitioner is a corporation with principal office at __________, Indianapolis, Indiana 46204. The return for the period here involved was filed with the Office of the Internal Revenue Service at Covington, Kentucky.

2. The notice of deficiency (a copy of which is attached and marked "Exhibit A"*) was mailed to petitioner on __________, and was issued by the Office of The Internal Revenue Service at Indianapolis, Indiana.

3. The deficiency as determined by the Commissioner is in income tax for the calandar year _____ in the amount of ________, all of which is in dispute. Further, petitioner claims the overpayment resulting from the assignments of error herein.

*Not reproduced.

4. The determination of tax set forth in the said notice of deficiency is based upon the following errors:

(a) In determining the deficiency for the calandar year 1969, the Commissioner erroneously disallowed the amount of ________ of the claimed investment credit.

(b) In determining the taxable income for the calendar year 1969, the Commissioner erroneously failed to allow a deduction for the net operating loss carryback from the calendar year 1972.

(c) In determining the taxable income for the calendar year 1969, the Commissioner erroneously failed to allow the investment credit carryback from the calendar year 1972.

5. The facts upon which the petitioner relies, as the basis of this case, are as follows:

(a)(i) On April 8, 1969, President ___________ decided that ___________ Railroad Company would purchase _____ locomotives of 2000 h.p. for $29,825,000 under its 1969 capital equipment program. This decision was reached by ___________ at a meeting in New York City attended by nine key rail executives of ___________ and an outside consultant. _______________, Chairman of the ___________ Board, was informed of this decision by letter from ___________ on April 9, 1969.

(a)(ii) The figures upon which ________ based his decision were derived from a presentation prepared for him by his staff for such meeting of April 8, which showed that ___________ had a shortage of switch-locomotives that would become crucial by October, 1969. The presentation also listed the various horsepower switching units that were marketed by the only two reliable and responsible domestic manufacturers of diesel-electric locomotives:

____________________________ Corporation and ____________________________

It also clearly showed that the locomotive that would provide the most versatile service at the lowest cost was the 2000 h.p. _____ road-switcher. It had the horsepower and high-speed trucks that permitted it to be used as a road locomotive, together with the relatively low price that made its use as a switching unit economical. The prices used in the presentation were determined from bids received within the previous six months for similar locomotives purchased by ___________ and _________________, in both of which ___________ was the largest shareholder. The presentation also had available _____ and _____ current price lists.

(a)(iii) The determinative feature in favor was the October, 1969, deadline. The production of so large a number of locomotives in such a short period of time obviously would require adjustment of schedules by the manufacturer. Since approximately 1100 locomotives were installed by all American railroads in 1969, such a large order would materially affect the capacity of the manufacturer. For that reason, ____________ had made oral inquiries of ___________ as to delivery times prior to the April 8th meeting.

(a)(iv) Prior to the meeting of April 8, ___________ advised that it could not deliver any 2000 h.p. units before November 1969, although it had 24 units of

3300 h.p. that would be available in August and September if __________ would be willing to reconsider its requirements. Prior to the meeting of April 8, ____ promised __________ that it would be able to deliver 150 locomotives of 2000 h.p. by September 30, 1969.

(a)(v) As a result of __________ decision on April 8, 1969, a __________ executive telephoned the manager of the ______________, on the same day and orally promised him that, since __________ had promised delivery by October, it had the order. Both parties understood that this oral agreement was subject to the condition that no third party would enter a more favorable Clayton Act bid. Both parties understood that, because of the time factor, this could not happen. After this telephone call of April 8 and before April 19, __________ placed orders with outside suppliers for additional steel and other materials and components which would be needed to produce the promised locomotives. __________ also made plans to reserve production space and increase its daily production from four to five locomotives. It also made plans to add necessary personnel and actually added 178 employees in April, ____________ also ordered radios for installation in 150 locomotives and took steps to secure ratification of the order from its Board of Directors.

(a)(vi) ____________ promulgated Clayton Act Solicitation No. ____________ on April 11, 1969, which stated that proposals to supply 150 locomotives of 2000 to 2300 h.p. would be opened on April 25, 1969. __________ had to follow that procedure, which embodied a two-week delay, because one of its directors was also a member of the board of __________ Corporation. On April 25, 1969, all bids were opened and ________ bid for 150 units of 2000 h.p. was accepted and the contracts were signed the same day.

(a)(vii) __________ price was exactly in the amounts used in the presentation to __________ based on the earlier bids and the delivery date was the same as promised orally. ________ bid was $2,500 higher per unit than ________ price and for delivery starting in November. Further, it was unresponsive, since it also proposed to sell 24 units of 3300 h.p. as part of the total of 150 units.

(a)(viii) Petitioner claimed investment credit under section 38 pursuant to the binding contract rule of section 49 of the Internal Revenue Code of 1954 in the amount of __________ on account of the purchase of sixty of the locomotives from as set forth in (a)(i) to (a)(vii), hereinabove. Petitioner is treated as their owner for investment credit purposes within Sections 38 and 49 of the Internal Revenue Code of 1954 under a trust agreement and an equipment lease. These locomotives were constructed and acquired pursuant to a contract which was binding on April 18, 1969, and at all times thereafter. The Commissioner has erroneously disallowed the claimed investment credit on the ground that "The binding contract to purchase did not exist on April 18, 1969, and all times thereafter." Since the requisite binding contract did exist on April 18, 1969, and at all times thereafter, petitioner is entitled to the claimed investment credit.

(b) Petitioner sustained a net operating loss for the calendar year 1972, the exact amount of which is unascertained at the time of filing this petition. Petitioner is, therefore, entitled to a carryback net operating loss deduction for the calendar year 1969.

(c) Petitioner has a carryback investment credit from the calendar year 1972 to the calendar year 1969, which is unascertained at the time of filing this petition.

WHEREFORE, petitioner prays that the Court may hear this case, determine that there is no deficiency for the calendar year 1969, determine that petitioner is entitled to an overpayment for the calendar year 1969 in accordance with the assignments of error herein, and for all other relief in the premises.

COUNSEL FOR PETITIONER

Form I

PETITION

This petition illustrates pleading two issues which are entirely legal and thus presumably all facts are susceptible of stipulation. Under present rules, *motion for summary judgment might be appropriate.*

TAX COURT OF THE UNITED STATES

Petitioner, v. COMMISSIONER OF INTERNAL REVENUE, Respondent.	Docket No. ____________

PETITION

The above-named petitioner hereby petitions for a redetermination of the deficiency set forth by the Commissioner of Internal Revenue in his notice of deficiency (correspondence symbols 430-LJS-jeb) dated February 10, 1969, and as a basis of its proceeding alleges as follows:

1. The petitioner is a corporation organized and existing under the laws of the state of Delaware, with its principal office and place of business at ________ , Indiana. The returns for the period here involved were filed with the District Director of Internal Revenue for the District of Indiana, Indianapolis, Indiana, by ______________ an Indiana corporation, the transferor. Petitioner is a transferee of the assets of said ______________ an Indiana corporation, within the meaning of the internal revenue laws, and is liable for any deficiency in income tax due from the transferor for the taxable period involved herein.

2. The notice of transferee liability (a copy of which is attached and marked "Exhibit A")* was mailed to the petitioner on February 10, 1969.

3. The deficiency as determined by the Commissioner is in income tax for the taxable year ended August 31, 1964, and for the final year of the transferor, which the

*Not reproduced.

Commissioner has determined to end November 30, 1964, but which petitioner alleges to end August 31, 1965, in the respective amounts of $2,260.14 and $601,608.47. The determined deficiency in the amount of $2,260.14 for the taxable year ended August 31, 1964 is not in controversy. Of the determined deficiency for the final taxable year of the transferor, ending either November 30, 1964 or August 31, 1965, in the amount of $601,608.47, only the amount of $599,538.99 is in controversy.

4. The determination of tax set forth in the said notice of transferee liability is based upon the following errors:

(a) In determining the taxable income for the final taxable year of the transferor, the Commissioner has erroneously determined that such final taxable year ended November 30, 1964, instead of August 31, 1965.

(b) In determining the taxable income for the final taxable year of the transferor, the Commissioner erroneously included as ordinary income the amount of $1,178,098.00 determined to be the portion of the sales proceeds allocated to tools and dies which had been claimed and allowed as deductions in prior years.

5. The facts upon which the petitioner relies as the basis of this proceeding are as follows:

(a) The final taxable year of the transferor, ______________ , an Indiana corporation (hereinafter "the transferor"), did not end prior to August 31, 1965. Although the transferor had made distribution of the major portion of its assets to its shareholders in liquidation during the calendar year 1964, it was necessary to retain assets for the purpose of settling certain of its outstanding obligations, including Indiana state income tax liabilities. The settlement and final disposition of such potential claims required continuation of the transferor and precluded the required statutory dissolution proceedings from being undertaken until after August 31, 1965. Accordingly, the Commissioner has erroneously determined that the final taxable year of the transferor terminated on or about November 30, 1964, when in truth and in fact such taxable year did not terminate until on or about August 31, 1965. Hence, petitioner's tax liability for its final taxable year must be computed under the statutory provisions governing a corporate taxable year ending August 31, 1965.

(b)(i) The Commissioner has "determined that $1,178,098.00 is the portion of the sales proceeds allocated to tools and dies from which full tax benefits have been derived through deductions in prior years. That portion of the proceeds representing a recovery of the amounts of such previously deducted items is treated as ordinary income under Section 61 of the Internal Revenue Code of 1954 and not as nonrecognized gain under section 337(a) of the Code."

(ii) The transferor entered into a purchase agreement dated as of September 4, 1964, as amended by an agreement dated as of September 25, 1964, for the sale of all of its assets, other than cash, government securities, and trade accounts receivable as of August 31, 1964, to ______________ (now ______________ , petitioner herein), a wholly-owned subsidiary of ______________ Company, which guaranteed the obligations of ____________ under the purchase agreements. The agreements also provided that ____________ would have the right to the use of the name "______________" upon the closing of these transactions.

(iii) On or about October 28, 1964, the transferor adopted a plan of complete liquidation in conformity with Section 337 of the Internal Revenue Code and, pursuant thereto, the purchase agreements dated as of September 4 and September 25, 1964 were carried out according to their terms and the transferror sold all of its assets, except those expressly excluded, to ________ (now ______________, petitioner herein) and distributed all of its assets, except those retained to meet claims, to its shareholders within the twelve months' period beginning on the date of the adoption of the plan.

(iv) The determined amount of additional income of $1,178,098.00 represents claimed and allowed deductions for tools and dies by the transferor in taxable years prior to the taxable year beginning September 1, 1964 and ending August 31, 1965 as alleged by petitioner, but ending November 30, 1964 as determined by the Commissioner. Such deductions for tools and dies were correctly reported and claimed in the returns of the transferor for such prior taxable years. The inclusion of such amount of $1,178,098.00, representing such deductions in such prior years, in taxable income for the final taxable year of the transferor is not within the provisions of Section 61 of the Internal Revenue Code and, further, is clearly contrary to the provisions of section 337. The transferor did not realize taxable income in the amount of $1,178,098.00, or any other amount, by reason of its prior deductions for tools and dies, and its subsequent complete liquidation and distribution of assets to its shareholders under section 337 of the Code. Accordingly, such determined additional income of $1,178,098.00 is not includible in the transferor's taxable income for its final taxable year beginning September 1, 1964, whether such taxable year ends November 30, 1964 or August 31, 1965.

WHEREFORE, petitioner prays that the Court may hear the case, determine that there is a deficiency in income tax due from the transferor for the taxable year ended August 31, 1964 in the amount of $2,260.14, determine that the final taxable year of the transferor began September 1, 1964 and ended August 31, 1965, determine that there is a deficiency in income tax from the transferor for its final taxable year beginning September 1, 1964 and ending August 31, 1965 in the amount of $2,069.48, determine that petitioner is liable as transferee for such deficiencies for the taxable years ended August 31, 1964 and August 31, 1965 set forth hereinabove, and for all other appropriate relief in the premises.

COUNSEL FOR PETITIONER

Form J

PETITION

This petition is included primarily to illustrate the joining of multiple petitioners who were partners in one petition, now permitted for the first time under Rule 61, and to illustrate the pleading of alternative positions which would result in refunds if sustained. Another reason for its inclusion is to illustrate the importance of careful factual development in the petition which tends to put petitioner's best foot forward at the outset. Such detailed factual pleading is possible only when petitioner's counsel has been employed sufficiently in advance of the petition due date to permit careful fact investigation.

UNITED STATES TAX COURT

JOHN AND MARY DOE
Husband and Wife,

ROBERT AND SUE ROE
Husband and Wife,

THOMAS AND RUTH POE
Husband and Wife

Petitioners,

v.

COMMISSIONER OF INTERNAL REVENUE

Respondent.

Docket No. 68-501

PETITION

The above-named petitioners hereby petition for a redetermination of the deficiencies set forth by the Commissioner of Internal Revenue in his notices of deficiency (Correspondence symbols L-21 Code 430:RLW:wa, L-21 Code

430:RLW:jb, L-21 Code 430-RLW:np), dated January 2, 1971, and as a basis for their case allege as follows:

1. Petitioners are individuals, husband and wife, with legal residence at the following addresses:

> John and Mary Doe, 101 Main Street,
> Robert and Sue Roe, 201 Second Street,
> Thomas and Ruth Poe, 301 Third Street,
> all of Indianapolis, Indiana.

All of these individuals filed joint income tax returns for the calendar year 1968 with the Internal Revenue Service Center, Covington, Kentucky.

2. The notices of deficiency (copies of which are attached and marked "Exhibit A, Exhibit B and Exhibit C", inclusive*) were mailed to the petitioners on January 2, 1971. Five copies of Exhibit A (John and Mary Doe) and two copies of Exhibits B and C (the other two joint petitioners) are attached.

3. The deficiencies as determined by the Commissioner are in income tax for the calendar year 1968 as follows, all of which are in dispute:

> John and Mary Doe–$2,000
> Robert and Sue Roe–$1,800
> Thomas and Ruth Poe–$1,700

4. The determination of tax set forth in the said notices of deficiency is based upon the following errors:

(a) In determining the tax liability for the calendar year 1968, the Commissioner has erroneously increased taxable income of each husband petitioner in the amount of $5,000 as additional partnership income from The Company.

(b) In determining the tax liability for the calendar year 1968, the Commissioner has erroneously decreased the reported capital gain of The Company of each husband petitioner in the amount of $2,500.

5. The facts upon which petitioners rely as the basis of this proceeding are as follows:

(a)(i) Mary Doe, Sue Roe and Ruth Poe are petitioners herein solely because they are the wives of John Doe, Robert Roe and Thomas Poe, respectively, and as such executed joint returns for 1968 with their husbands. Hence, John Doe, Robert Roe and Thomas Poe will be referred to as "petitioners" hereinafter.

(a)(ii) The Commissioner has determined that each distributive share of partnership income from The Imperial Company ("Imperial") for the calendar year 1968 was in the amount of $30,000 instead of a loss in the amount of $25,000, thereby increasing 1968 partnership income for each petitioner in the amount of

*Not reproduced.

$5,000. Partnership income for the calendar year 1968 was correctly reported and, accordingly, the Commissioner's determination that Imperial's correct ordinary income for such year was $90,000 is erroneous.

(iii) In 1968, petitioners, who had been associated in prior real estate investment ventures, were contacted by Widget Corporation ("Widget,") to develop an industrial center in which Widget would be the principal tenant. Later in 1968, the specific site on the south side of Indianapolis was selected and options to purchase the various parcels (the "subject land") were secured by an agent. The options were exercised and the subject land purchased in 1969.

(iv) At the time the options were exercised and the land purchased, petitioners planned and intended to own and retain the industrial center as a personal investment. To carry out this intent petitioners sought to obtain financing in an amount sufficient to cover the entire project development costs. The manager of the Indianapolis office of a mortgage banking company was contacted with regard to the desired financing of the project.

(v) During this time period, a "tight" money market prevailed and financing of sizable real estate projects was very difficult. Despite their best efforts, petitioners were unable to secure the desired conventional first-mortgage financing for this center and, therefore, had to utilize another financing technique for the purchase and leaseback of the subject land and the remainder obtained in the form of a leasehold mortgage loan. This was the largest amount of long-term financing which petitioners could obtain at that time on terms which would permit its repayment from the projected industrial center rental schedule.

(vi) The financing agreement was entered into with Acme Company ("Acme") only after petitioners had exhausted all efforts to obtain conventional first-mortgage financing. Petitioners had not previously considered a sale of the subject land and later agreed to sell the land only as a last resort financing technique when it became apparent that they would not be able to obtain conventional first-mortgage financing in the desired amount.

(vii) Petitioners formed Imperial, a general partnership, on March 15, 1969, which acquired all rights and assumed all obligations of petitioners with respect to the subject land and the improvements thereon. Thus, Imperial became owner of the subject land. Construction began on the improvements located on the subject land in 1969 and was completed in 1970.

(viii) In 1970, petitioners became aware of decided changes in the mortgage money market with much "easier" conditions prevailing than in late 1969 when it entered into its financing commitment. At that time, they attempted to cancel their commitment with Acme and obtain through other mortgage companies more favorable conventional first-mortgage financing sufficient to cover the entire project cost, so that Imperial could retain ownership of the land and not be required to enter into a sale and leaseback of the land, in accord with petitioners' original intent. Acme refused to permit Imperial to cancel the commitment and required it to complete the sale and leaseback of the subject land as provided in the commitment.

(ix) On June 30, 1970, all of the final documents were executed by Imperial and Acme to conclude the commitment, including the conveyance of the subject land by Imperial to Acme and the concurrent leaseback.

(x) The subject land was not sold in the ordinary course of Imperial's trade or business, nor of any of its partners. The subject land was purchased for investment purposes by petitioners and was sold only because Imperial could not obtain conventional first-mortgage total financing for the entire project.

(xi) $500,000 of the land sale-leaseback proceeds, together with the mortgage loan proceeds, was used by Imperial to pay for the total shopping center project development costs.

(xii) The financing technique used by Imperial to obtain sufficient funds for this entire project, which included the sale and leaseback of the subject land as an integral part of the technique, did not produce economic gain for petitioners on the sale aspect of the entire transaction with Acme. The sale and leaseback of land was, and still is, a commonly-used technique for the financing of the acquisition and development of commercial real estate in a "tight" money market. It was the functional equivalent of an extension of credit by Acme to Imperial. Accordingly, petitioners realized no gain on this sale and leaseback of the subject land to Acme and they have erroneously reported capital gain on such sale and leaseback. Petitioners are entitled to refund of the tax paid upon such capital gain.

(xiii) If this Court should not sustain petitioners' position set forth in paragraph (a)(xii) hereinabove, the sale of the subject land was not in the ordinary course of Imperial's trade or business, or of that of its partners, and, accordingly, the gain thereon was not ordinary income.

WHEREFORE, petitioners pray that the Court may hear this proceeding, decide and order that no deficiency in income tax for the calendar year 1968 is due and owing from petitioners, decide and order that petitioners are entitled to refunds of income tax for 1968 of $2,000 for John and Mary Doe, $2,500 for Robert and Sue Roe, and $2,750 for Thomas and Ruth Poe, and for all other appropriate relief in the premises.

COUNSEL FOR PETITIONERS

Form K

WEAVER POPCORN COMPANY, INC.–T.C. Memo. 1971-281

"STIPULATION OF FACTS"

This stipulation of facts is included to illustrate the successful use of a stipulation of facts in a winning case. The importance of a full stipulation of facts cannot be over-emphasized. With this stipulation of facts, very little oral testimony was required to complete the record and carry the petitioner's burden of proof on this ultimate fact issue of whether notes constituted debt capital or equity capital. (See petition hereinabove.)

IN THE UNITED STATES TAX COURT

WEAVER POPCORN COMPANY, INC.,

Petitioner,

v. Docket No. 2178-69

COMMISSIONER OF INTERNAL REVENUE,

Respondent.

STIPULATION OF FACTS

It is hereby stipulated and agreed between the Commissioner of Internal Revenue and the above-entitled taxpayer, by their respective undersigned attorneys, that the following facts shall be taken as true, *provided,* however, that this stipulation does not waive the right of either party to introduce other evidence not at variance with the facts herein stipulated, or to object to the introduction in evidence of any such facts on the grounds of immateriality or irrelevancy.

1. Weaver Popcorn Company, Inc. (hereinafter "petitioner") is a corporation organized under the laws of the state of Indiana on June 1, 1955, with its principal office and place of business at Van Buren, Indiana. Petitioner is engaged in the business of growing and processing popcorn. Petitioner keeps its books and records

and prepares its income tax returns on the accrual method of accounting and on the basis of the calendar year ending December 31. True copies of its income tax returns for the taxable years ended December 31, 1964, 1965 and 1966 (hereinafter usually "the taxable period"), which were filed with the District Director of Internal Revenue for the District of Indiana, Indianapolis, Indiana, are attached hereto as "Exhibits 1-A, 2-B and 3-C."*

2. Use of the terms "debenture" or "interest" or other terms connoting indebtedness in any stipulation herein or any document attached hereto shall be taken as descriptive of the securities at issue in the view of the petitioner but shall not be taken as an admission of the nature of such securities by the respondent. Respondent contends that the "debentures" constitute equity and not debt.

3. Petitioner was the successor to a partnership composed of I.E. Weaver; his sons, P.L. Weaver and W.I. Weaver; and his son-in-law, D.M. Repp. Schedules reflecting condensed balance sheets for this partnership for the taxable years 1950 to and including May 31, 1955, and condensed earnings statements for the same taxable period as reflected on the books and records of the partnership, are attached hereto as "Exhibits 4 and 5."*

4. On June 1, 1955, the assets and liabilities of this partnership were transferred to petitioner, which had been organized on that date for the purpose of receiving such assets and liabilities and continuing to operate the partnership business. There is attached hereto as "Exhibit 6"* a schedule reflecting the assets and liabilities of the partnership on June 1, 1955 immediately prior to the transfer thereof to petitioner and the assets and liabilities as received by petitioner on June 1, 1955, together with a schedule of the partners' capital as of June 1, 1955 immediately prior to this transfer, and a schedule of the common stock and debentures received by the partners in exchange for the partnership assets immediately after the transfer on June 1, 1955, all as reflected on the books and records of the partnership and of petitioner.

5. By action of its board of directors at a meeting held December 30, 1959, petitioner caused its articles of incorporation to be amended to provide for two classes of common stock, A and B, and a class of preferred stock, in lieu of the one class of common capital stock theretofore existing. A true copy of the minutes of such meeting of petitioner's directors, setting forth such amendment of its articles of incorporation, is attached hereto as "Exhibit 7."*

6. On January 4, 1960, the first regular business day in 1960, petitioner acquired the assets and liabilities of Weco Farms, a partnership, theretofore owned and operated in equal shares by I.E. Weaver, P.L. Weaver, W.I. Weaver and D.M. Repp. The acquisition of Weco Farms was accomplished by the issuance of debentures, preferred stock and Class A common stock. There is attached hereto as "Exhibit 8"* a true copy of petitioner's journal entries reflecting the transactions involved in petitioner's recapitalization and in its acquisition of Weco Farms. There is attached as "Exhibit 9"* a balance sheet prepared from petitioner's books and records reflecting petitioner's recapitalization and its acquisition of Weco Farms.

*Not reproduced.

7. On June 11, 1965, the Commissioner of Internal Revenue issued a ruling to petitioner in response to its request therefor, a true copy of which is attached hereto as "Exhibit 10."*

8. There is attached hereto as "Exhibit 11"* a schedule setting forth condensed balance sheets of petitioner as of the end of each taxable year from its date of organization to and including the taxable year ended December 31, 1966, as reflected on its books and records.

9. There is attached hereto as "Exhibit 12"* a schedule setting forth earnings statements of petitioner as of the end of each taxable year from its date of organization to and including the taxable year ended December 31, 1966, as reflected on its books and records.

10. There is attached hereto as "Exhibit 13"* a schedule setting forth the amounts of petitioner's bank balances and the amounts of United States Treasury Bills held by petitioner as of the end of each calendar month during the taxable period as reflected on petitioner's books of account.

11. The stock of B & L Popcorn Company was owned 75 percent by petitioner and 25 percent by Gerald Lee during the taxable period.

12. Petitioner has declared no dividends since it was organized.

13. I.E. Weaver is the husband of Della Weaver and the father of Paul L. Weaver, Welcome I. Weaver and Mabelle Weaver Repp, and the father-in-law of D.M. Repp. Adah Weaver is the wife of Welcome I. Weaver; and Pat S. Weaver, M.E. Weaver and Barbara Weaver are their children.

14. The respondent has not disallowed petitioner's claimed deductions for each of the taxable years 1964, 1965 and 1966 for interest paid in the amount of $600.00 on its debentures in the face amount of $12,000.00 held by Methodist Memorial Home of Warren, Indiana. Such debentures were received by the Home from Paul L. Weaver, Welcome I. Weaver and Mabelle Repp in the face amount of $4,000.00 from each.

15. There is attached hereto as "Exhibit 14"* a schedule designated "Detail of 1964-1966 Debenture Interest" setting forth the interest paid and dates of payment to all debenture holders during the taxable period.

16. There is attached hereto as "Exhibit 15"* a schedule designated "Reconciliation of Debentures By Holder as of December 31, 1964."

17. There is attached hereto as "Exhibit 16"* a schedule designated "Analysis of Notes Payable by Lender 1964-1966."

18. During the year 1964 and until August, 1965, petitioner had a line of credit with American Fletcher National Bank & Trust Company of Indianapolis, Indiana, in

*Not reproduced.

the amount of $740,000.00 and with The First National Bank in Huntington of $60,000.00. In order to obtain this line of credit, it was necessary for the principal shareholders of petitioner to guarantee such indebtedness. There is attached hereto as "Exhibit 17"* a true copy of the "Continuing Guaranty" to American Fletcher National Bank & Trust Company dated September 1, 1961 executed by petitioner's principal shareholders. There is attached hereto as "Exhibit 18"* a true copy of the "Continuing Guaranty" to The First National Bank in Huntington dated September 1, 1961 executed by petitioner's principal shareholders. Each such "Continuing Guaranty" was in effect from such date to August, 1965.

19. From August, 1965, to and including December 31, 1966, petitioner had a line of credit with American Fletcher National Bank & Trust Company and The First National Bank in Huntington in the aggregate amount of $880,000.00. There is attached hereto as "Exhibit 19"* a true copy of the "Continuing Guaranty" to American Fletcher National Bank & Trust Company dated August, 1965, executed by petitioner's principal shareholders. Such "Continuing Guaranty" was in effect to and including December 31, 1966. It was necessary for petitioner's principal shareholders to guarantee such indebtedness in order for petitioner to obtain this line of credit. In connection with the line of credit extended in 1965, the banks also required Welcome I. Weaver and Mabelle W. Repp, two of petitioner's principal shareholders, to execute a "Negative Pledge Agreement," a true copy of which, dated August 30, 1965, is attached hereto as "Exhibit 20."* There are attached hereto as "Exhibits 21 and 22,"* respectively, true copies of a letter dated January 7, 1965 from Don A. Wirick, Vice President, American Fletcher National Bank & Trust Company, to D.R. Wygant, President, The First National Bank in Huntington, and a letter dated February 3, 1965 from petitioner, by Welcome I. Weaver, to Mr. Wygant.

20. Petitioner paid Paul L. Weaver the total amount of $90,745.09 in March, 1965. Such amount was the total face amount of all the debentures held by Mr. Weaver on that date as shown on "Exhibit 14."

21. There are attached hereto as "Exhibits 23 and 24,"* respectively, true copies of a debenture issued by petitioner June 1, 1955 and of a debenture issued January 4, 1960, which are representative and identical with all other debentures issued on such dates except for the differing holders and amounts.

22. Except for the debentures described hereinbelow, petitioner's debentures issued June 1, 1955 which were outstanding on June 1, 1965, the maturity date set forth therein, were returned to petitioner and the words, "Paid by renewal debenture date June 1, 1975" were written thereon. New debentures were thereupon issued, dated June 1, 1965, payable June 1, 1975, and a true copy of such a debenture issued June 1, 1965, representative and identical with all other debentures issued thus June 1, 1965 except for the differing holders and amounts, is attached hereto as "Exhibit 25."*

*Not reproduced.

The exceptions to the above-stated facts were as follows:

(1) On or about January 22, 1963, Paul L. Weaver, Welcome I. Weaver and Mabelle Repp each delivered to petitioner debentures in the amount of $5,000.00 issued June 1, 1955 aggregating $15,000.00. In lieu thereof, petitioner thereupon issued Debenture #30-A to The Methodist Memorial Home for the Aged, Warren, Indiana, in the face amount of $12,000.00, with due date of January 22, 1973, and Debentures #31-A, 32-A and 33-A, each in the face amount of $1,000.00, with maturity date of January 22, 1973, to Paul L. Weaver, Welcome I. Weaver and Mabelle Repp.

(2) On or about May 31, 1965, I.E. Weaver delivered to petitioner debentures issued June 1, 1955 aggregating $17,100.00. In lieu thereof, petitioner thereupon issued to I.E. Weaver Debenture #39-A in the face amount of $2,100.00 and Debentures #40-A, 41-A and 42-A, each in the face amount of $5,000.00, aggregating $17,100.00, all with maturity date of January 1, 1969.

(3) On or about December 1, 1959, I.E. Weaver delivered to petitioner debentures issued June 1, 1955 aggregating $15,000.00. In lieu thereof, petitioner thereupon issued Debentures #37, 38 and 39, each in the face amount of $5,000.00, with maturity date of December 1, 1969, to Paul L. Weaver, Mabelle Repp and Welcome I. Weaver, respectively.

(4) On or about January 2, 1961, I.E. Weaver delivered to petitioner Debenture #15 issued June 1, 1955 in the face amount of $644.69. In lieu thereof, petitioner issued Debenture #41 to Mabelle Repp in the face amount of $3,700.00, with maturity date of January 2, 1971, and Debenture #42 to I.E. Weaver in the face amount of $944.69, with maturity date of January 2, 1971.

23. During the taxable period, the outstanding stock of Weaver Farms, Inc. was owned as follows:

Name	No. of Shares
I.E. Weaver	10
Mrs. I.E. Weaver	18
Paul L. Weaver	228
Welcome I. Weaver	234
Mrs. D. Meredith Repp	234
Children of Paul L. Weaver (12 shares each)	96
Children of Welcome I. Weaver (30 shares each)	90
Children of Mrs. D. Meredith Repp (30 shares each)	90
	1,000

24. There is attached hereto as "Exhibit 26"* a schedule designated "Balances Due Banks" by petitioner during the taxable period.

*Not reproduced.

25. There is attached hereto as "Exhibit 27"* a true copy of a portion of the minutes of a meeting of petitioner's board of directors held April 20, 1965. No action was taken by petitioner's board of directors with respect to the exceptions set forth in subparagraphs (1), (3) and (4) of paragraph 22 hereinabove.

____
Counsel for Petitioner

____
Chief Counsel
Internal Revenue Service

*Not reproduced.

Form L

AUSTIN STATE BANK–57 T.C. 180 (1971)

"STIPULATION OF FACTS"

This stipulation exemplifies maximum utilization of the stipulating process, thus minimizing the need for oral testimony. Note how the fact skeleton in the petition hereinabove has been fleshed out in this stipulation of facts, once the Court's theory of the case was learned at the negotiating table. (See petition hereinabove.)

IN THE UNITED STATES TAX COURT

AUSTIN STATE BANK,
Petitioner,
v.
COMMISSIONER OF INTERNAL REVENUE
Respondent.

Docket Nos. 755-69
2387-69

STIPULATION OF FACTS

It is hereby stipulated and agreed between the Commissioner of Internal Revenue and the above-entitled taxpayer, by their respective undersigned attorneys, that the following facts shall be taken as true, *provided,* however, that this stipulation does not waive the right of either party to introduce other evidence not at variance with the facts herein stipulated, or to object to the introduction in evidence of any such facts on the grounds of immateriality or irrelevancy.

1. Petitioner was organized as a corporation under the laws of the state of Indiana on April 30, 1909, under the provisions of an Indiana "Act for the Incorporation of Banks of Discount and Deposit," approved February 7, 1873, and the amendments thereto. Such original charter was renewed in 1929 under the laws of the state of Indiana for a period of twenty years; a true copy of such amended articles

of incorporation dated April 17, 1929 is attached hereto as "Exhibit 1."* Such charter was made perpetual April 18, 1949 under a 1933 amendment to the Banking Laws of Indiana, and a true copy of the Petition for Approval of Proposed Amendment to Articles of Incorporation and of the Articles of Amendment of the Articles of Incorporation reflecting such action is attached hereto as "Exhibit 2."*

2. Petitioner's principal place of business since organization to, and including, the taxable period was Austin, Indiana.

3. Petitioner's Articles of Amendment of the Articles of Incorporation were approved July 20, 1950 to provide for five directors, and a true copy of the Petition for Approval of Proposed Amendment to Articles of Incorporation and such Articles of Amendment are attached hereto as "Exhibit 3."*

4. Petitioner has kept its books of account, and filed its income tax returns, on the cash receipts and disbursements basis since organization to, and including, the taxable period. Petitioner filed its income tax returns for the taxable years 1964, 1965 and 1966 (hereinafter sometimes the "taxable period") with the District Director of Internal Revenue at Indianapolis, Indiana. True copies of such returns are attached hereto as "Exhibits 4, 5 and 6,"* respectively.

5. There is attached hereto as "Exhibit 7"* a schedule setting forth the amounts of the deposit balances held by petitioner as of December 31 of each year of the taxable period, as reflected on petitioner's books of account, with respect to (a) commercial accounts, (b) nonprofit organization and political subdivision accounts, (c) Ivan H. and Elsinore Morgan and their immediate family and related accounts, and (d) petitioner's officers' and employees' accounts. The differences between the total deposits and the total of the deposits in "Exhibit 7"* for each year consist of individual accounts and the account of the State of Indiana.

6. There is attached hereto as "Exhibit 8"* a true copy of petitioner's Register of Discounted Bills covering the years 1964, 1965 and 1966.

7. There are attached hereto as "Collective Exhibit 9"* true copies of the following notes held by petitioner during the taxable period, dated October 14, 1964, 1965 and 1966:

R. E. Perrin
Carl Morton
Culver Field
P. H. Paulson
Roland M. Weir
Harold W. Fields
Garland Langdon
J. L. Bubul

All of the loans evidenced by such notes were originally made in 1958 and subsequently renewed annually.

*Not reproduced.

8. There is attached hereto and marked "Exhibit 10"* a schedule setting forth petitioner's loans outstanding during the taxable period.

9. Petitioner is required to make at least two statements of condition annually under §18-1501 of Burns' Indiana Statutes, and such statements are subject to publication under §18-1502 of such Statutes. True copies of such reports of condition of petitioner as of June 30 and December 31 for each year during the taxable period are attached hereto as "Exhibits 11, 12, 13, 14, 15 and 16,"* respectively.

10. Petitioner's board of directors employed Ernst & Ernst, Certified Public Accountants, to make annual examinations of petitioner's books and records. True copies of the reports of such examinations by Ernst & Ernst dated July 28, 1964, July 7, 1965, and August 31, 1966 are attached hereto as "Exhibits 17, 18 and 19,"* respectively.

11. In order to receive public funds as deposits, petitioner must make a proposal to receive such public funds to the political subdivision or public agency involved, and such political subdivision or public agency must execute an agreement with petitioner for it to hold such funds on deposit.

True copies of such proposals by petitioner to receive public funds on deposit for the periods recited therein and agreements between petitioner and the following political subdivisions or public agencies involving the taxable period, together with the corporate resolution and Board of Finance Resolution, are attached hereto as "Exhibits 20, 21, 22, 23, 24 and 25,"* respectively:

State of Indiana, approved 3/19/63		Exhibit 20
State of Indiana, approved 2/15/65		Exhibit 21
Jennings Township Trustee–Scott County Jennings Township Justice of Peace	approved 2/18/63	Exhibit 22
Jennings Township Trustee–Scott County Jennings Township Justice of Peace	approved 2/15/65	Exhibit 23
Scott County School Corporation, District #1, approved 8/18/64		Exhibit 24
Scott County School Corporation, District #1, approved 2/15/65		Exhibit 25

12. There are attached hereto as "Exhibits 26, 27, 28, 29 and 30,"* respectively, true copies of the following deposit slips of petitioner reflecting deposits by the State of Indiana:

March 16, 1961	$2,000,000.00
March 12, 1963	15,000.00
April 3, 1965 (Certificate of Deposit)	62,800.00
May 31, 1966 (Certificate of Deposit)	32,000.00
December 29, 1966 (Certificate of Deposit)	50,000.00

*Not reproduced.

13. There is attached hereto as "Exhibit 31"* a true copy of petitioner's Deposit Ledger reflecting deposits by the State of Indiana on the dates shown.

14. No interest was payable on deposits of public agencies except where such deposits were in the form of certificates of deposit.

15. As a bank chartered under the laws of the State of Indiana, petitioner is subject to supervision and examination by the Department of Financial Institutions of the State of Indiana under §18-225, Burns' Indiana Statutes. During the taxable period, petitioner was examined as of the close of business on August 22, 1964, December 29, 1965, and December 17, 1966, by an examiner of the Division of Banks and Trust Companies, Department of Financial Institutions, State of Indiana, and formal reports thereon were filed.

16. Petitioner exercised no fiduciary powers during the taxable period.

17. Petitioner has not declared or paid any dividends since at least 1957.

18. As of January 1, 1964, the stock of petitioner was owned as follows:

Name	Address	No. of Shares
Lloyd Jones	Scottsburg, Ind.	5
Ivan E. Morgan	Austin, Ind.	29
Marion Lyons	Austin, Ind.	8
T.N. Lyons	Austin, Ind.	20
Diann Morgan	Austin, Ind.	2
Elsinore Morgan	Austin, Ind.	45
Fern Morgan	Austin, Ind.	37
Ivan H. Morgan	Austin, Ind.	12
John Scott Morgan	Austin, Ind.	64
Margaret E. Morgan	Indianapolis, Ind.	8
Michele Morgan	Austin, Ind.	10
Lena Weir	Austin, Ind.	5
John L. Bubul	Scottsburg, Ind.	5
	Total	250

As of January 1, 1965, to and including December 31, 1966, the stock of petitioner was owned as follows:

Name	Address	No. of Shares
Lloyd Jones	Scottsburg, Ind.	5
Estate of Ivan E. Morgan, Deceased		29
Marion Lyons	Austin, Ind.	27
Diann Morgan	Austin, Ind.	2
Elsinore Morgan	Austin, Ind.	45
Ivan H. Morgan	Austin, Ind.	12
John Scott Morgan	Austin, Ind.	64

*Not reproduced.

Name	Address	No. of Shares
Margaret E. Morgan	Indianapolis, Ind.	26
Michele Morgan	Austin, Ind.	10
Lena Weir	Austin, Ind.	5
John L. Bubul	Scottsburg, Ind.	5
John E. Nichols	Terre Haute, Ind.	6
William R. Nichols	Terre Haute, Ind.	6
Steven S. Nichols	Terre Haute, Ind.	6
George O. Nichols	Terre Haute, Ind.	2
	Total	250

19. The family of Ivan H. Morgan controls the Morgan Packing Company, Inc.

20. Each director receives a fee in the amount of $20.00 for attending each directors' meeting.

21. Petitioner is not a member of the Federal Reserve System or insured by the Federal Deposit Insurance Corporation.

22. Citizens Fidelity Bank & Trust Company, Louisville, Kentucky, acts as agent for petitioner in purchasing United States government securities for petitioner's account.

23. Petitioner made pension plan contributions for Ivan H. Morgan and Elsinore Morgan during the taxable period as follows:

	Ivan H. Morgan	Elsinore Morgan
1964	$3,736.29	$1,530.52
1965	3,828.11	1,996.66
1966	3,920.19	2,090.26

24. There is attached hereto as "Exhibit 32"* a schedule setting forth petitioner's deposits in other banks as of December 31, 1964, December 31, 1965, and December 31, 1966.

25. There is attached hereto as "Exhibit 33"* a schedule setting forth petitioner's depository liabilities as of December 31 of each of the years 1957 to 1968, inclusive.

26. Petitioner's directors during the taxable period were Ivan H. Morgan, Elsinore Morgan, Lena Weir, Lloyd Jones and John L. Bubul.

27. There are attached hereto as "Exhibits A, B, C, D, E, F and G,"* respectively, true copies of petitioner's income tax returns for the taxable years 1957 to 1963, inclusive.

28. There are attached hereto as "Exhibits H and I,"* respectively, true copies of petitioner's income tax returns for the taxable years 1967 and 1968.

29. The statutory period for assessment of income tax against petitioner for the taxable year 1964 had not expired prior to the issuance of the statutory notice on

*Not reproduced.

December 17, 1968, and, accordingly, the respondent is not barred from assessing additional income tax for such taxable year.

30. There are attached hereto as "Collective Exhibit 34"* true copies of the minutes of all meetings of petitioner's board of directors during the taxable period.

31. There are attached hereto as "Exhibits 35, 36 and 37"* true copies of the minutes of the meetings of petitioner's shareholders held January 13, 1964, January 11, 1965 and January 11, 1966, respectively, the only meeting of petitioner's shareholders held during the taxable period.

32. There are attached hereto as "Exhibits 38, 39, 40 and 41"* true copies of minutes of meetings of petitioner's board of directors held December 15, 1960, January 8, 1962, December 10, 1962 and December 13, 1963.

33. There is attached hereto as "Exhibit 42"* a true copy of by-laws adopted by petitioner's board of directors at its regular meeting August 9, 1950.

34. Petitioner's book of original entry designated "Register of Discounted Bills," from which "Exhibit 8" was taken, is the authentic book of account reflecting petitioner's loans for the years listed therein.

____
Counsel for Petitioner

____
Chief Counsel
Internal Revenue Service

*Not reproduced.

Form M

DELAWARE TRUCKING CO., INC.–T.C. Memo 1974-34

"MOTION FOR ORDER THAT BURDEN OF PROOF IS ON THE RESPONDENT UNDER SECTION 534 OF THE INTERNAL REVENUE CODE"

This motion illustrates the wisdom of pleading sufficient detail as to oral argument request so that the Court may intelligently rule without having to ascertain additional facts.

UNITED STATES TAX COURT

DELAWARE TRUCKING CO., INC. Petitioner, v. COMMISSIONER OF INTERNAL REVENUE Respondent.	Docket No. 8211-71

MOTION FOR ORDER THAT BURDEN OF PROOF IS ON THE RESPONDENT UNDER SECTION 534 OF THE INTERNAL REVENUE CODE

Comes now petitioner, by its counsel, and moves this Court:

(1) For an order that the burden of proving that all or any part of petitioner's earnings and profits have been permitted to accumulate beyond the reasonable needs of the business is on the respondent with respect to the grounds set forth in the Statement filed by petitioner under Section 534(c) of the Internal Revenue Code, a copy of which is attached to the petition and marked "Exhibit B,"* and

(2) For an order setting this motion for oral argument at Washington, D.C., prior to the Trial Session at Indianapolis, Indiana, beginning September 18, 1972, preferably on August 23 or August 30, 1972.

*Not reproduced.

In support of this motion, petitioner respectfully shows the Court as follows:

1. This case has been set for trial on the Trial Session beginning September 18, 1972, at Indianapolis, Indiana. Accordingly, petitioner urges that this motion be set for oral argument at Washington, D.C., before the judge assigned to conduct the Indianapolis Trial Session on either August 23 or August 30, 1972, in order that the parties may be appraised of the incidence of the burden of proof sufficiently in advance of trial to properly complete their trial preparation.

2. Lester M. Ponder, counsel for petitioner, will be on vacation and thereafter attending the annual meeting of the American Bar Association at San Francisco, California, to and including August 16, 1972. Accordingly, a date prior to August 23 would be exceedingly inconvenient for petitioner's counsel to be present in view of these prior commitments.

3. Counsel for petitioner has orally notified counsel for respondent of petitioner's intention to file the instant motion and request oral argument thereon in Washington, D.C., in advance of the September 18, 1972, Trial Session, so that respondent has had ample notice of petitioner's intention to resolve the incidence of the burden of proof in advance of this Trial Session.

WHEREFORE, it is prayed that this motion for order that burden of proof is on the respondent under section 534 of the Internal Revenue Code be set for oral argument at Washington, D.C., on either August 23 or August 30, 1972, preferably August 23, and that thereafter the motion be granted and an appropriate order be entered by the Court.

____

COUNSEL FOR PETITIONER

Form N

UNITED STATES TAX COURT

XYZ COMPANY, INC., Petitioner, v. COMMISSIONER OF INTERNAL REVENUE, Respondent.	Docket No. ____________

REQUEST FOR PRODUCTION OF DOCUMENTS AND THINGS UNDER RULE 72

Petitioner requests respondent to respond within thirty days to the following requests:

(1) That respondent produce and permit petitioner to inspect and to copy each of the following documents:

> (Here list the documents either individually or by category and describe each of them.)

(2) That respondent produce and permit petitioner to inspect and to copy, test or sample each of the following objects:

> (Here list the objects either individually or by category and describe each of them.)
>
> (Here state the time, place and manner of making the inspection and performance of any related acts.)

(3) That respondent permit petitioner to enter (here describe property to be entered) and to inspect and to photograph, test or sample (here describe the portion of the real property and the objects to be inspected.) (Here state the time, place and manner of making the inspection and performance of any related acts.)

Signed: ______________________
Attorney for Petitioner

Address: ______________________

____

Form O

UNITED STATES TAX COURT

XYZ COMPANY, INC., Petitioner, v. COMMISSIONER OF INTERNAL REVENUE Respondent.	Docket No. ____________

MOTION FOR JUDGMENT ON THE PLEADINGS

The petitioner, by John Doe, its attorney, hereby moves the Court to enter judgment for the petitioner in accordance with the provisions of Rule 120, on the ground that the pleadings do not raise a genuine issue of material fact, and that the petitioner is entitled to judgment as a matter of law, as set forth in the attached memorandum.

John Doe, Esquire
Attorney for Petitioner

Form P

UNITED STATES TAX COURT

XYZ COMPANY, INC., Petitioner, v. COMMISSIONER OF INTERNAL REVENUE Respondent.	Docket No. ____________

MOTION FOR SUMMARY JUDGMENT

The petitioner, by John Doe, its attorney, hereby moves the Court to enter summary judgment for the petitioner, in accordance with the provisions of Rule 121, on the ground that the pleadings and the stipulation of facts, together with its affixed exhibits heretofore filed in these cases, show that there is no genuine issue as to any material fact and that the petitioner is entitled to judgment as a matter of law, as set forth in the attached memorandum.

John Doe, Esquire
Attorney for Petitioner

Form Q

UNITED STATES TAX COURT

XYZ COMPANY, INC.,

Petitioner,

v. Docket No. ____________

COMMISSIONER OF INTERNAL REVENUE

Respondent.

REQUEST FOR ADMISSION UNDER RULE 90

Petitioner requests respondent, within thirty days after service of this request, to make the following admissions for the purpose of this action only and subject to all pertinent objections to admissibility which may be interposed at the trial:

1. That each of the following documents, exhibited with this request, is genuine.

(Here list the documents and describe each document.)

2. That each of the following statements is true.

(Here list the statements.)

Signed: ____________________________
Attorney for Petitioner

Address: ____________________________

____

TABLE OF CASES

Case *Text Page*

Case *Text Page*

INDEX

I

J

L

M

N

O

P

Q

R

APPENDIX—
Rules of Practice and Procedure of the United States Tax Court

RULES

OF

PRACTICE AND PROCEDURE

OF THE

UNITED STATES TAX COURT

EFFECTIVE JANUARY 1, 1974

TABLE OF CONTENTS

Title I. Scope of Rules; Construction, Effective Date; Definitions

Title II. The Court

Title III. Commencement of Case; Service and Filing of Papers; Form and Style of Papers; Appearance and Representation; Computation of Time

Title IV. Pleadings

Title VIII. Depositions

Title IX. Admissions and Stipulations

Title X. General Provisions Governing Discovery, Depositions, and Requests For Admission

Title XI. Pretrial Conferences

Title XII. Decision Without Trial

Title XIII. Calendars and Continuances

Title XIV. Trials

Title XVIII. Commissioners of the Court

Title XIX. Appeals

Title XX. Practice Before the Court

Title XXI.—Declaratory Judgments—Retirement Plans

Appendices to the Rules

RULES OF PRACTICE AND PROCEDURE OF THE UNITED STATES TAX COURT

TITLE I.—SCOPE OF RULES; CONSTRUCTION; EFFECTIVE DATE; DEFINITIONS.

RULE 1. Scope of Rules and Construction.—(a) Scope. These Rules govern the practice and procedure in all cases and proceedings in the United States Tax Court. Where in any instance there is no applicable rule of procedure, the Court or the Judge before whom the matter is pending may prescribe the procedure, giving particular weight to the Federal Rules of Civil Procedure to the extent that they are suitably adaptable to govern the matter at hand.

(b) Construction. These Rules shall be construed to secure the just, speedy, and inexpensive determination of every case.

Note: The first sentence of Par. (a), and Par. (b), are derived from FRCP 1. The second sentence of Par. (a) is a new provision.

RULE 2. Effective Date.—(a) Initial Adoption. These Rules will take effect on January 1, 1974. They govern all proceedings and cases commenced after they take effect, and also all further proceedings in cases then pending, except to the extent that in the opinion of the Court their application, in a particular case pending when the Rules take effect, would not be feasible or would work injustice, in which event the former procedure applies.

Note: Par. (a) is derived from the last sentence of FRCP 86(a).

(b) Amendments. Amendments to these Rules shall state their effective date. Amendments shall likewise govern all proceedings both in cases pending on or commenced after their effective date, except to the extent otherwise provided, and subject to the further exception provided in paragraph (a) of this Rule.

Note: Par. (b) is derived selectively from the pattern in FRCP 86(b), (c), (d), (e).

RULE 3. Definitions. (a) Division. The Chief Judge may from time to time divide the Court into Divisions of one or more Judges and, in case of a Division of more than one Judge, designate the chief thereof.

Note: Rule 3 is the counterpart of present T.C. Rule 1(f). Par. (a) is a new provision, based on Code Sec. 7444(c).

(b) Clerk. Reference to the Clerk in these Rules means the Clerk of the United States Tax Court.

Note: Par. (b) is a new provision.

(c) Commissioner. Reference to Commissioner in these Rules means the Commissioner of Internal Revenue, unless the context of the particular Rule shows that the intended reference is to a commissioner of the Court as provided in Rule 180.

Note: The first part of Par. (c) is derived from present T.C. Rule 1(f)(2), and the remainder of the paragraph is new.

(d) Time. As provided in these Rules and in orders and notices of the Court, time means standard time in the location mentioned, except when advanced time is substituted therefor by law. For computation of time, see Rule 25.

Note: Par. (d) is derived from present T.C. Rule 1(f)(1).

(e) Business Hours. As to the Court's business hours, see Rule 10(d).

(f) Filing. For requirements as to filing with the Court, see Rule 22.

Note: Pars. (e) and (f), while strictly not definitions, were inserted as helpful guides.

(g) Code: Any reference or citation to the Code relates to the Internal Revenue Code of 1954, as amended.

Note: Par. (g) is derived from present T.C. Rule 1(f)(3).

TITLE II.—THE COURT.

RULE 10. Name, Office and Sessions.—(a) Name. The name of the Court is the United States Tax Court.

Note: Par. (a) is a new provision, based on Code Section 7441.

(b) Office of Court. The principal office of the Court shall be in the District of Columbia, but the Court or any of its Divisions may sit at any place within the United States.

Note: Par. (b) is based on Code Section 7445, replacing present T.C. Rule 1(a), (b), and (c).

(c) Sessions. The time and place of sessions of the Court shall be prescribed by the Chief Judge.

Note: Par. (c) is based on Code Section 7446.

(d) Business Hours. The office of the Clerk at Washington, D.C., shall be open during business hours on all days, except Saturdays, Sundays, and legal holidays, for the purpose of receiving petitions, pleadings, motions, and other papers. Business hours are from 8:45 a.m. to 5:15 p.m. For legal holidays, see Rule X25(b).

Note: Par. (d) is derived from present T.C. Rule 1(d).

RULE 11. Payments to Court. All payments to the Court for fees or charges of the Court shall be made either in cash or in checks, money orders, or other drafts made payable to the order of "Clerk, United States Tax Court," and shall be mailed or delivered to the Clerk of the Court at Washington, D.C. For particular payments, see Rules 12(c) (copies of Court records), 20(b) (filing of petition), 175(a)(2) (small tax cases), and 200(a) (application to practice before Court).

Note: This provision is based on present T.C. Rule 1(e), but specifies cash as a permissible medium of payment.

RULE 12. Court Records. (a) Removal of Records. No original record, paper, document, or exhibit filed with the Court shall be taken from the courtroom or from the offices of the Court or from the custody of a Judge or employee of the Court, except as authorized by a Judge of the Court or except as may be necessary for the Clerk to furnish copies or to transmit the same to other courts for appeal or other official purposes. With respect to return of exhibits after a decision of the Court becomes final, see Rule 143(d)(2).

Note: Par. (a) is the same in substance as present T.C. Rule 53(a).

(b) Copies of Records. After the Court renders its decision in a case, a plain or certified copy of any document, record, entry, or other paper, pertaining to the case and still in the custody of the Court, may be obtained upon application to the Clerk and payment of the required fee. Unless otherwise permitted by the Court, no copy of any exhibit or original document in the files of the Court shall be furnished to other than the parties until the Court renders its decision.

Note: Par. (b) in substance is the same as present T.C. Rule 53(b), except that the dividing line, after which copies of records are available with little restriction, has been shifted to the time the decision is rendered from the time the decision becomes final. While control and convenience of records are important while work is being done on a case up to the time of decision, these considerations do not apply as reasons for continuing the restrictions until the time, often after appeals are taken, when the decision becomes final.

(c) Fees. The fees to be charged and collected for any copies will be determined in accordance with Code section 7474. See Appendix III, p. 67.

Note: Par. (c) is a new provision, inserted for informational purposes.

RULE 13. Jurisdiction.—(a) Notice of Deficiency or of Transferee or Fiduciary Liability Required. In a case commenced in the Court by a taxpayer, the jurisdiction of the Court depends upon the issuance by the Commissioner of a notice of deficiency in income, gift, or estate tax or in the taxes imposed on private foundations under Code Sections 4940 through 4945. In a case commenced in the Court by a transferee or fiduciary, the jurisdiction of the Court depends upon the issuance by the Commissioner of a notice of liability to the transferee or fiduciary. See Code Sections 6212, 6213, 6901.

(b) Timely Petition Required. In all cases, the jurisdiction of the Court also depends on the timely filing of a petition. See Code Sections 6213, 7502.

Note: There is no counterpart to this rule in the present T.C. rules. Pars. (a) and (b) concern the two fundamental requirements for the Court's jurisdiction, the issuance of a notice of deficiency or a notice of liability, and the filing of a timely petition with the Court. Their basic importance requires expression in the rules for the guidance of parties and practitioners.

(c) Contempt of Court. Contempt of the Court may be punished by fine or imprisonment within the scope of Code Section 7456(d).

Note: Par. (c) is a new provision, related to the discharge of the Court's functions in the exercise of its jurisdiction.

TITLE III.—COMMENCEMENT OF CASE; SERVICE AND FILING OF PAPERS; FORM AND STYLE OF PAPERS; APPEARANCE AND REPRESENTATION; COMPUTATION OF TIME.

RULE 20. Commencement of Case.—(a) General. A case is commenced in the Court by filing a petition with the Court to redetermine a deficiency set forth in a notice of deficiency issued by the Commissioner, or to redetermine the liability of a transferee or fiduciary set forth in a notice of liability issued by the Commissioner to the transferee or fiduciary. See Rule 13, Jurisdiction.

Note: Par. (a) is the counterpart of FRCP 3, and is comparable to the initial portion of present T.C. Rule 7(a)(1). The balance of present T.C. Rule 7 deals largely with matters of pleading, which are treated elsewhere in these Rules.

(b) Filing Fee. A fee of $10 shall be paid at the time of filing a petition, unless the petitioner establishes to the satisfaction of the Court that he is unable to make such payment, in which case the Court may waive payment of the fee. For manner of payment, see Rule 11.

Note: Par. (b) is derived from present T.C. Rule 7(b) and Code Section 7451.

RULE 21. Service of Papers.—(a) When Required. Except as otherwise required by these Rules or directed by the Court, all pleadings, motions, orders, decisions, notices, demands, briefs, appearances, or other similar documents or papers relating to a case, also referred to as the papers in a case, shall be served on each of the parties to the case other than the party who filed the paper.

Note: Par. (a) is the counterpart of FRCP 5(a). It continues present practice. Service on other parties to a case is required in the absence of a particular rule, order of the Court, or recognized procedure which clearly departs from this general rule.

(b) Manner of Service. (1) General. All petitions shall be served by the Clerk. All other papers required to be served on a party shall also be served by the Clerk unless otherwise provided in these Rules or directed by the Court, or unless the original paper is filed with a certificate by a party or his counsel that service of that paper has been made on the party to be served or his counsel. For the form of such certificate of service, see Form 13, Appendix I, p. 67. Such service may be made by mail directed to the party or his counsel at his last known address. Service by mail is complete upon mailing, and the date of such mailing shall be the date of such service. As an alternative to service by mail, service may be made by delivery to a party, or his counsel or authorized representative in the case of a party other than an individual (see Rule 24(b)). Service shall be made on the Commissioner by service on, or directed to, his counsel at the office address shown in his answer filed in the case or, if no answer has been filed, on the Chief Counsel,

Internal Revenue Service, Washington, D.C. 20224. Service on a person other than a party shall be made in the same manner as service on a party, except as otherwise provided in these Rules or directed by the Court.

Note: This Rule retains the present practice of requiring service of the petition by the Clerk of the Court. But this Rule expands the present practice as to all other papers, by permitting them to be served by the parties on condition that the original of the paper with a certificate of service be filed with the Clerk. This is an alternative method of permissible service which has been added to present practice, subject to the exceptions indicated in the Rule. While the Court hopes that direct service will be fully utilized, parties are still permitted to file all papers with the Clerk for service by him, in the same manner as heretofore has been done under present T.C. Rule 22(a). Nothing in this Rule relieves any party from the necessity of satisfying any requirement of filing any paper with the Court.

FRCP 5(b) provides that service by mail is complete upon mailing, and the same concept is incorporated here. Service on persons other than a party, such as a nonparty witness to be questioned on deposition, is subject to the same rules and subject to variation by direction of the Court.

(2) Counsel of Record. Whenever under these Rules service is required or permitted to be made upon a party represented by counsel who has entered an appearance, service shall be made upon such counsel unless service upon the party himself is directed by the Court. Where more than one counsel appear for a party, service will be made only on that counsel whose appearance was first entered of record, unless that counsel designates in writing filed with the Court other counsel of record to receive service, in which event service will be made accordingly.

Note: Par. (b)(2) represents present practice and is derived from present T.C. Rule 22(b).

(3) Writs and Process. Service and execution of writs, process, or similar directives of the Court may be made by a United States marshal, by his deputy, or by a person specially appointed by the Court for that purpose, except that a subpoena may be served as provided in Rule 147(c). The person making service shall make proof thereof to the Court promptly and in any event within the time in which the person served must respond. Failure to make proof of service does not affect the validity of the service.

Note: Par. (b)(3) is derived from FRCP 4(c) and (g). Code Section 7456(d) refers to the "writ, process, order, rule, decree or command" of the Court, and Sen. Rep. No. 91-552, 91st Cong., 1st Sess. p. 304 states that "the Tax Court is given the same powers regarding contempt, and the carrying out of its writs, orders, etc. that Congress has previously given to the District Courts." Service by the Clerk may be inappropriate in such instances, and Par. (b)(3) provides another method of service.

RULE 22. Filing. Any pleadings or other papers to be filed with the Court must be filed with the Clerk in Washington, D.C., during business hours, except that the Judge presiding at any trial or hearing may permit or require documents pertaining thereto to be filed at that particular session of the Court, or except as otherwise directed by the Court.

Note: This Rule is basically the same as present T.C. Rule 5. FRCP 5(e) is essentially similar. Code Section 7502 interacts with this Rule where mail is used.

RULE 23. Form and Style of Papers.—(a) Caption, Date, and Signature Required. All papers filed with the Court shall have a caption, shall be dated, and shall be signed as follows:

(1) Caption. A proper caption shall be placed on all papers filed with the Court, and the requirements provided in Rule 32(a) shall be satisfied with respect to all such papers. All prefixes and titles, such as "Mrs." or "Dr.", shall be omitted from the caption. The full name and surname of each individual petitioner shall be set forth in the caption. The name of an estate or trust or other person for whom a fiduciary acts shall precede the fiduciary's name and title, as for example "Estate of John Doe, deceased, Richard Roe, Executor."

(2) Date. The date of signature shall be placed on all papers filed with the Court.

(3) **Signature.** The signature, either of the party or his counsel, shall be subscribed in writing to the original of every paper filed by or for that party with the Court, except as otherwise provided by these Rules. An individual rather than a firm name shall be used, except that the signature of a petitioner corporation or unincorporated association shall be in the name of the corporation or association by one of its active and authorized officers or members, as for example "John Doe, Inc., by Richard Roe, President." The name, mailing address, and telephone number of the party or his counsel shall be typed or printed immediately beneath the written signature. The mailing address of a signatory shall include a firm name if it is an essential part of the accurate mailing address.

Note: This Rule in substance retains the present practice as to the form and style of papers to be filed in the Court. The requirements as to form of caption in Par. (a)(1) are the same as in present T.C. Rule 4(e). Similarly, the requirements as to signature in Par. (a)(3) are the same as in present T.C. Rule 4(f), except that a party or his counsel is required to furnish his telephone number and except that reference has been inserted regarding the unincorporated association. Par. (a)(2), requiring all papers to be dated, is new in the Rules, but reflects the prevailing practice.

(b) **Number Filed.** For each paper filed in Court, there shall be filed four conformed copies together with the signed original thereof, except as otherwise provided in these Rules. Where filing is in more than one case (as a motion to consolidate, or in cases already consolidated), the number filed shall include one additional copy for each docket number in excess of one. As to stipulations, see Rule 91(b).

Note: Par. (b) is in substance the same as present T.C. Rule 4(g).

(c) **Legible Copies Required.** Papers filed with the Court may be prepared by any process, provided that all papers, including copies, filed with the Court are clear and legible.

Note: Par. (c) is in substance the same as present T.C. Rule 4(a)(1) and (h).

(d) **Size and Style.** Typewritten papers shall be typed on only one side, unless produced by offset, mimeograph, multilith, photocopy, or similar process, and shall be on plain white paper, 8½ inches wide by 11 inches long, and weighing not less than 16 pounds to the ream, except that copies other than the original may be made on any weight paper. Printed papers shall be printed in 10-point or 12-point type, on good quality unglazed paper, 5⅞ inches wide by 9 inches long, and with double-leaded text and single-leaded quotations. All papers, whether typed or printed, shall have an inside margin not less than 1¼ inches wide.

Note: Par. (d) is a combination of present T.C. Rule 4(b) and (c) and (h), but enlarges the size of the inside margin and extends it to all papers. It also permits the use of both sides of a sheet in the case of typewritten papers if produced as specified.

(e) **Binding and Covers.** All papers shall be bound together on the left-hand side only, and, except in the case of briefs, shall have no backs or covers.

Note: Par. (e) is substantially the same as present T.C. Rule 4(a)(2).

(f) **Citations.** All citations shall be underscored when typewritten, and shall be in italics when printed.

Note: Par. (f) is the same in substance as present T.C. Rule 4(d).

RULE 24. Appearance and Representation.—(a) Appearance. (1) General. Counsel may enter an appearance either by subscribing the petition or other initial pleading or document in accordance with subparagraph (2) hereof, or thereafter by filing an entry of appearance in accordance with subparagraph (3) hereof.

(2) **Appearance in Initial Pleading.** If the petition or other paper initiating the participation of a party in a case is subscribed by counsel admitted to practice before the Court, that counsel shall be recognized as representing that party and no separate entry of appearance by him shall be necessary, provided that such initial paper shall also contain the mailing address of counsel and other information required for entry of appearance (see subparagraph (3) hereof). Thereafter counsel

shall be required to notify the Clerk of any changes in applicable information to the same extent as if he had filed a separate entry of appearance.

(3) **Subsequent Appearance.** Where counsel has not previously appeared, he shall file an entry of appearance in duplicate, signed by counsel individually, containing the name and docket number of the case, the name, mailing address and telephone number of counsel so appearing, and a statement that counsel is admitted to practice before the Court. A separate entry of appearance, in duplicate, shall be filed for each additional docket number in which counsel shall appear. The entry of appearance shall be substantially in the form set forth in Appendix I, p. 55. The Clerk shall be given prompt written notice, filed in duplicate for each docket number, of any change in the foregoing information.

(4) **Counsel Not Admitted to Practice.** No entry of appearance by counsel not admitted to practice before this Court will be effective until he shall have been admitted, but he may be recognized as counsel in a pending case to the extent permitted by the Court and then only where it appears that he can and will be promptly admitted. For the procedure for admission to practice before the Court, see Rule 200.

Note: This Rule reorganizes the appearance and representation provisions of the present T.C. Rules 23 and 24 into a more logical sequence. The essential nature of the practice in such matters, however, is not changed.

Two methods of appearance by counsel are available, one being by subscribing the initial pleading and the other being the entry of an appearance at a time after the initial pleading was filed. Par. (a)(2) contains the substance of present Tax Court Rule 24(a)(1), but specifies that in addition there shall be contained the information required in the entry of appearance. Par. (a)(3), relating to the entry of appearance, is essentially similar to present T.C. Rule 24(a)(3). Par. (a)(4) is the counterpart of present T.C. Rule 24(a)(4) in regard to counsel not admitted to practice before the Court, but makes clear that counsel will not be permitted to enter an appearance in any case if he is not admitted to practice before the Court.

(b) **Personal Representation Without Counsel.** In the absence of appearance by counsel, a party will be deemed to appear for himself. An individual party may represent himself. A corporation or an unincorporated association may be represented by an authorized officer of the corporation or by an authorized member of the association. An estate or trust may be represented by a fiduciary thereof. Any such person shall state, in the initial pleading or other paper filed by or for the party, his name, address, and telephone number, and thereafter shall promptly notify the Clerk in writing, in duplicate for each docket number involving that party, of any change in that information.

Note: Par. (b) is concerned with pro se appearances, and is the counterpart of present T.C. Rule 3. However, Par. (b) states a rule, not expressed in T.C. Rule 3, that a party is deemed to appear for himself in the absence of appearance by counsel. In such event, the Clerk can make service of papers by directing them by mail to the party, foreclosing any claim of failure to serve counsel. Par. (b) goes beyond T.C. Rule 3 in specifying the information required of the pro se party, and expands the provision on the persons who may act in a representative capacity for a pro se party.

(c) **Withdrawal of Counsel.** Counsel of record desiring to withdraw his appearance, or any party desiring to withdraw the appearance of counsel of record for him, must file a motion with the Court requesting leave therefor, and showing that prior notice of the motion has been given by him to his client, or his counsel, as the case may be. The Court may, in its discretion, deny such motion.

Note: Par. (c) is the same in substance as present T.C. Rule 24(b).

(d) **Death of Counsel.** If counsel of record dies, the Court shall be so notified, and other counsel may enter an appearance in accordance with this Rule.

Note: Par. (d) is a new provision, not in the present T.C. Rules.

(e) **Change in Party or Authorized Representative or Fiduciary.** Where (i) a party other than an individual participates in a case through an authorized representative (such as an officer of a corporation or a member of an association) or through a fiduciary, and there is a change in such representative or fiduciary, or (ii) there is a substitution of parties in a pending case, counsel subscribing the motion resulting in the Court's approval of the change or substitution shall thereafter be deemed first counsel of record for the new representative or party.

Note: Par. (e) is derived from present T.C. Rules 23(a) and (b), and 24(a)(2). The first part of Par. (e) concerns a change in representative through whom a party, other than a natural person, acts, as for example, a change in fiduciaries or corporate officers. The second part of Par. (e) concerns a change in parties, as for example, on the death of a taxpayer and the substitution of his estate as petitioner.

RULE 25. Computation of Time.—(a) Computation. In computing any period of time prescribed or allowed by these Rules or by direction of the Court or by any applicable statute which does not provide otherwise, the day of the act, event, or default from which a designated period of time begins to run shall not be included. In the event of service made by mail, a period of time computed with respect to the service shall begin on the day after the date of mailing. Saturdays, Sundays, and all legal holidays shall be counted; provided, however, that, when the period prescribed or allowed is less than seven days, intermediate Saturdays, Sundays, and legal holidays in the District of Columbia shall be excluded in the computation; and, provided further, that the last day of the period so computed shall be included, unless it is a Saturday, Sunday, or a legal holiday in the District of Columbia, in which event the period runs until the end of the next day which is not a Saturday, Sunday, or such a legal holiday. When such legal holiday falls on a Sunday, the next day shall be considered a holiday; and, when such a legal holiday falls on a Saturday, the preceding day shall be considered a holiday. For computation of the period within which to file a petition with the Court to redetermine a deficiency or liability, see Code Sections 6213, 7502.

Note: Par. (a) is based on FRCP 6(a) and present T.C. Rule 61(a) and (c). A new provision is included which excludes certain days from the computation when the period within which to act is small, e.g., less than seven days and service is made by mail. Often some addition is made, under rules of procedure, to the allowable time when service is made by mail rather than by personal service. Under the procedure of these Rules, service generally is made by mail and that fact has been taken into account in fixing various periods, so that such a provision for further extending the allowable time is unnecessary.

(b) District of Columbia Legal Holidays. The legal holidays within the District of Columbia, in addition to any other day appointed as a holiday by the President or the Congress of the United States, are as follows:

New Year's Day—January 1

Inauguration Day—Every fourth year

Washington's Birthday—Third Monday in February

Memorial Day—Last Monday in May

Independence Day—July 4

Labor Day—First Monday in September

Columbus Day—Second Monday in October

Veterans Day—Fourth Monday in October

Thanksgiving Day—Fourth Thursday in November

Christmas Day—December 25

Note: Par. (b) is derived from present T.C. Rule 61(b), except that a general provision is added to cover Federal holidays established in addition to those specified in the Rule. The list of holidays in the Rule reflects Pub. Law 90-363, 90th Cong., 2d Sess., approved June 18, 1968.

(c) Enlargement or Reduction of Time. Unless precluded by statute, the Court in its discretion may make longer or shorter any period provided by these Rules. As to continuances, see Rule 134. Where a motion is made concerning jurisdiction or the sufficiency of a pleading, the time for filing a response to that pleading shall begin to run from the date of service of the order disposing of the motion by the Court, unless the Court shall direct otherwise. Where the dates for filing briefs are fixed, an extension of time for filing a brief shall correspondingly extend the time for filing any other brief due at the same time and for filing succeeding briefs, unless the Court shall order otherwise. The period fixed by statute, within which to file a petition with the Court to redetermine a deficiency or liability, cannot be extended by the Court.

Note: Par. (c) is the counterpart of present T.C. Rule 20 and FRCP 6(b), and is in more general and flexible form than those rules. Provisions is made in Par. (c) both for shortening as well as enlarging a time period, unlike present T.C. Rule 20. The definitional problems of FRCP 6(b), in using the requirement of "cause shown" or "excusable neglect", are avoided, although the Court, in the exercise of its discretion may take into account the factors involved in those concepts together with any other applicable considerations.

(d) Miscellaneous. With respect to computation of time, see also Rule 3(d) (definition), Rule 10(d) (business hours of the Court), Rule 13(b) (filing of petition), and Rule 134 (continuances).

TITLE IV. PLEADINGS.

RULE 30. Pleadings Allowed. There shall be a petition and an answer, and, where required under these Rules, a reply. No other pleading shall be allowed, except that the Court may permit or direct some other responsive pleading.

Note: This Rule is adapted from FRCP 7(a), to reflect pleading in the Tax Court.

RULE 31. General Rules of Pleading.—(a) Purpose. The purpose of the pleadings is to give the parties and the Court fair notice of the matters in controversy and the basis for their respective positions.

Note: Par. (a) is a new provision, without counterpart in the present Tax Court Rules. It is intended to incorporate, to the extent not inconsistent with Tax Court procedure as reflected in these Rules, the approach of the Federal Rules of Civil Procedure. See *Conley* v. *Gibson,* 355 U.S. 41, 48 (1957). The statement of purpose in this Rule offers a general guide to help resolve conflicts about pleadings. More specific rules for particular pleadings are provided hereafter.

(b) Pleading to be Concise and Direct. Each averment of a pleading shall be simple, concise, and direct. No technical forms of pleading are required.

Note: Par. (b) is a new provision, without counterpart in the present T.C. Rules. It is derived from FRCP 8(e)(1). The obective of simple, concise, and direct pleading is emphasized here, but does not represent a change in Tax Court practice. While no technical forms of pleading are required, there are pleading requirements imposed by these Rules, and a pleading such as a petition must contain allegations covering required areas in order to avoid being defective or insufficient.

(c) Consistency. A party may set forth two or more statements of a claim or defense alternatively or hypothetically. When two or more statements are made in the alternative and one of them would be sufficient if made independently, the pleading is not made insufficient by the insufficiency of one or more of the alternative statements. A party may state as many separate claims or defenses as he has regardless of consistency or the grounds on which based. All statements shall be made subject to the signature requirements of Rules 23(a)(3) and 33.

Note: Par. (c) is a new provision, without counterpart in the present T.C. Rules. It is derived from FRCP 8(e)(2), with some language modification to eliminate the references to "counts" and to "legal, equitable, or maritime" grounds. It is not intended to represent a change in present Tax Court practice.

(d) Construction of Pleadngs. All pleadings shall be so construed as to do substantial justice.

Note: Par. (d) has no counterpart in present T.C. Rules, and is derived from FRCP 8(f).

RULE 32. Form of Pleadings.—(a) Caption; Names of Parties. Every pleading shall contain a caption setting forth the name of the Court (United States Tax Court), the title of the case, the docket number after it becomes available (see Rule 35), and a designation to show the nature of the pleading. In the petition, the title of the case shall include the names of all parties, but in other pleadings it is sufficient to state the name of the first party with an appropriate indication of other parties.

Note: This Rule is derived from FRCP 10. Similar provisions do not appear in the present T.C. Rules. No change in present practice is involved in this Rule. Par. (a) is derived from FRCP 10(a).

(b) Separate Statement. All averments of claim or defense, and all statements in support thereof, shall be made in separately designated paragraphs, the contents of each of which shall be limited as far as practicable to a statement of a single item or a single set of circumstances. Such paragraph may be referred to by that designation in all succeeding pleadings. Each claim and defense shall be stated separately whenever a separation facilitates the clear presentation of the matters set forth.

Note: Par. (b) is derived from FRCP 10(b).

(c) Adoption by Reference; Exhibits. Statements in a pleading may be adopted by reference in a different part of the same pleading or in another pleading or in any motion. A copy of any written instrument which is an exhibit to a pleading is a part thereof for all purposes.

Note: Par. (c) is derived from FRCP 10(c).

Under this Rule, the notice of deficiency attached to the petition is a part of that pleading, although representing only the deficiency notice issued by the Commissioner and the allegations made in that notice when it was issued.

(d) Other Provisions. With respect to other provisions relating to the form and style of papers filed with the Court, see Rule 23.

RULE 33. Signing of Pleadings.—(a) Signature. Each pleading shall be signed in the manner provided in Rule 23. Where there is more than one attorney of record, the signature of only one is required. Except when otherwise specifically directed by the Court, pleadings need not be verified or accompanied by affidavit.

Note: Par. (a) eliminates the requirement, as a general rule, that pleadings be verified. This adopts the rule of FRCP 11. Under present Tax Court Rules, the petition is required to be verified; the answer need not be verified; and the reply is to be verified only on express order made after motion for good cause shown.

(b) Effect of Signature. The signature of counsel or a party constitutes a certificate by him that he has read the pleading; that, to the best of his knowledge, information, or belief, there is good ground to support it; that it is not frivolous; and that it is not interposed for delay. The signature of counsel also constitutes a representation by him that he is authorized to represent the party of parties on whose behalf the pleading is filed. If a pleading is not signed, or is signed with intent to defeat the purpose of this Rule, it may be stricken, and the action may proceed as though the pleading has not been filed. Similar action may be taken if scandalous or indecent matter is inserted. For a willful violation of this Rule, counsel may be subjected to appropriate disciplinary action.

Note: Par. (b) is derived from FRCP 11. A similar provision does not appear in present T.C. Rules.

RULE 34. Petition.—(a) General. The petition shall be substantially in accordance with Form 1 shown in Appendix I, p. 52, and shall comply with the requirements of these Rules relating to pleadings. Ordinarily, a separate petition shall be filed with respect to each notice of deficiency or each notice of liability. However, a single petition may be filed seeking a redetermination with respect to all notices of deficiency or liability directed to one person alone or to him and one or more other persons, except that the Court may require a severance and a separate case to be maintained with respect to one or more of such notices. Where the notice of deficiency or liability is directed to more than one person, each such person desiring to contest it shall file a petition on his own behalf, either separately or jointly with any such other person, and each such person must satisfy all the requirements of this Rule with respect to himself in order for the petition to be treated as filed by or for him. The petition shall be complete, so as to enable ascertainment of the issues intended to be presented. No telegram, cablegram, radiogram, telephone call, or similar communication will be recognized as a petition. Failure of the petition to satisfy applicable requirements may be ground for dismissal of the case. As to the joinder of parties, see Rule 61; and as to the effect of misjoinder of parties, see Rule 62.

Note: Par. (a) of this Rule is a new provision. Rule 20 continues the present practice of starting a case with the petition. Reference to the number of copies to be filed is omitted here, since the general rule is provided in Rule 23(b). The provision of present T.C. Rule 7(c)(3), that certain media for communicating a petition are insufficient, is continued because of the problems of authenticity and definiteness. The dismissal of a petition, for failure to satisfy applicable requirements, depends on the nature of the defect, and therefore is put in the contingent "may" rather than the mandatory "shall" of present T.C. Rule 7(a)(2). Beyond those provisions, Par. (a) is new in its formulation of guides concerned with joinder in a single petition. As a general rule, the extent of joinder is determined initially by the scope of the notice of deficiency and by the identity of the petitioner, subject in any event to separation or severance in the overriding discretion of the Court. The subject of joinder of parties is further considered in Rules 61 and 62. No person can obtain Tax Court review unless a petition is filed by him, thus, a petition filed by a taxpayer, to review a deficiency asserted in a notice against two taxpayers, will not commence a case in the Court for the second taxpayer.

(b) Content of Petition. The petition shall contain (see Form 1, Appendix I, p. 52):

(1) The petitioner's name and legal residence, in the case of a petitioner other than a corporation; in the case of a corporate petitioner, its name and principal place of business or principal office or agency; and, in all cases, the office of the Internal Revenue Service with which the tax return for the period in controversy was filed. The legal residence, principal place of business, or principal office or agency shall be stated as of the date of filing the petition. In the event of a variance between the name set forth in the notice of deficiency or liability and the correct name, a statement of the reasons for such variance shall be set forth in the petition.

(2) The date of mailing of the notice of deficiency or liability, or other proper allegations showing jurisdiction in the Court, and the city and state of the office of the Internal Revenue Service which issued the notice.

(3) The amount of the deficiency or liability, as the case may be, determined by the Commissioner; the nature of the tax; the year or years or other periods for which the determination was made; and, if different from the Commissioner's determination, the approximate amount of taxes in controversy.

(4) Clear and concise assignments of each and every error which the petitioner alleges to have been committed by the Commissioner in the determination of the deficiency or liability. The assignments of error shall include issues in respect of which the burden of proof is on the Commissioner. Any issue not raised in the assignment of errors shall be deemed to be conceded. Each assignment of error shall be separately lettered.

(5) Clear and concise lettered statements of the facts on which petitioner bases the assignments of error, except with respect to those assignments of error as to which the burden of proof is on the Commissioner.

(6) A prayer setting forth relief sought by the petitioner.

(7) The signature of each petitioner or his counsel. If the petition is filed in the name of more than one petitioner, it shall be signed by each such petitioner or his counsel.

(8) A copy of the notice of deficiency or liability, as the case may be, which shall be appended to the petition, and with which there shall be included so much of any statement accompanying the notice as is material to the issues raised by the assignments of error. If the notice of deficiency or liability or a accompanying statement incorporates by reference any prior notices or other material furnished by the Internal Revenue Service, such parts thereof as are material to the issues raised by the assignments of error likewise shall be appended to the petition.

Note: Par. (b) is derived from present T.C Rules 6 and 7(c)(4).

The nature and form of the petition remain basically unchanged from present practice, except that verification of the petition is eliminated.

The requirement of assignment of errors more emphatically indicates that the petitioner must assert all such errors regardless of the party who may have the burden of proof with respect to them. Otherwise, the issue involving such an error is conceded by the taxpayer. Facts relating to an issue as to which the Commissioner has the burden of proof need not be set forth in the petition. No change in practice is made by these provisions.

RULE 35. Entry on Docket. Upon receipt of the petition by the Clerk, the case wll be entered upon the docket and assigned a number, and the parties will be notified thereof by the Clerk. The docket number shall be placed by the parties on all papers thereafter filed in the case, and shall be referred to in all correspondence with the Court.

Note: This paragraph is substantially identical with present T.C. Rule 11.

RULE 36. Answer.—(a) Time to Answer or Move. The Commissioner shall have 60 days from the date of service of the petition within which to file an answer, or 45 days from that date within which to move with respect to the petition. With respect to an amended petition or amendments to the petition, the Commissioner shall have like periods from the date of service of those papers within which to answer or move in response thereto, except as the Court may otherwise direct.

Note: The first sentence of Par. (a) is substantially the same as present T.C. Rule 14(a). The second sentence of Par. (a) is derived from present T.C. Rule 14(d).

(b) Form and Content. The answer shall be drawn so that it will advise the petitioner and the Court fully of the nature of the defense. It shall contain a specific admission or denial of each material allegation in the petition; however, if the Commissioner shall be without knowledge or information sufficient to form a belief as to the truth of an allegation, he shall so state, and such statement shall have the effect of a denial. If the Commissioner intends to qualify or to deny only a part of an allegation, he shall specify so much of it as is true and shall qualify or deny only the remainder. In addition, the answer shall contain a clear and concise statement of every ground, together with the facts in support thereof, on which the Commissioner relies and has the burden of proof. Paragraphs of the answer shall be designated to correspond to those of the petition to which they relate.

Note: Par. (b) is based on present T.C. Rule 14(b). More detailed requirements, based on FRCP 8 and on the underlying approach to pleading in Rule 31(a), have been inserted with objective of obtaining an answer which is informative to the petitioner and the Court of the nature of the defense and the facts on which it is founded. Thus, if there is insufficient knowledge or belief, that should be asserted rather than a denial; and, if matter in the petition is partially true or can be taken as true if qualified, the answer should pursue that approach rather than a denial.

Present T.C. Rule 14(b) refers to affirmative defenses or issues as to which the Commissioner has the burden of proof by statute. However, there may be other issues as to which he has the burden of proof, and that restriction therefore has been deleted.

The last sentence of present T.C. Rule 14(b) is omitted, in view of the general signature rule in 23(a)(3).

(c) Effect of Answer. Every material allegation set out in the petition and not expressly admitted or denied in the answer shall be deemed to be admitted.

Note: Par. (c) is derived from present T.C. Rule 18(a), except that it is made applicable to all allegations, including those in the assignments of error, and not just to allegations of fact.

RULE 37. Reply.—(a) Time to Reply or Move. The petitoner shall have 45 days from the date of service of the answer within which to file a reply, or 30 days from that date within which to move with respect to the answer. With respect to an amended answer or amendments to the answer, the petitioner shall have like periods from the date of service of those papers within which to reply or move in response thereto, except as the Court may otherwise direct.

(b) Form and Content. In response to each material allegation in the answer and the facts in support thereof on which the Commissioner has the burden of proof, the reply shall contain a specific admission or denial; however, if the petitioner shall be without knowledge or information sufficient to form a belief as to the truth of an allegation, he shall so state, and such statement shall have the effect of a denial. In addition, the reply shall contain a clear and concise statement of every ground, together with the facts in support thereof, on which the petitioner relies affirmatively or in avoidance of any matter in the answer on which the Commissioner has the burden of proof. In other respects the requirements of pleading applicable to the answer provided in Rule 36(b) shall apply to the reply. The paragraphs of the reply shall be designated to correspond to those of the answer to which they relate.

(c) Effect of Reply or Failure Thereof. Where a reply is filed, every affirmative allegation set out in the answer and not expressly admitted or denied in the reply, shall be deemed to be admitted. Where a reply is not filed, the affirmative allegations in the answer will be deemed denied unless the Commissioner, within 45 days after expiration of the time for filing the reply, files a motion for an order that specified allegations in the answer be deemed admitted. That motion will be noticed for a hearing, at which the motion may be granted unless on or before the date thereof the required reply has been filed.

(d) New Material. Any new material contained in the reply shall be deemed to be denied.

Note: This Rule retains the time pattern for a reply and the substance of the requirements which appear in present T.C. Rules 15(a) and (b) and 18(b) and (c). The approach to the reply taken in this Rule is the same as is taken with respect to the answer in Rule 36.

RULE 38. Joinder of Issue. A case shall be deemed at issue upon the filing of the answer, unless a reply is required under Rule 37, in which event it shall be deemed at issue upon the filing of a reply or the entry of an order disposing of a motion under Rule 37(c) or the expiration of the period specified in Rule 37(c) in case the Commssioner fails to move.

Note: This Rule expands the provision in present T.C. Rule 16.

RULE 39. Pleading Special Matters. A party shall set forth in his pleading any matter constituting an avoidance or affirmative defense, including res judicata, collateral estoppel, estoppel, waiver, duress, fraud, and the statute of limitations. A mere denial in a responsive pleading will not be sufficient to raise any such issue.

Note: This Rule is a new provision, not in the present T.C. Rules. It is suggested by FRCP 8(c).

RULE 40. Defenses and Objections Made by Pleading or Motion. Every defense, in law or fact, to a claim for relief in any pleading shall be asserted in the responsive pleading thereto if one is required, except that the following defenses may, at the option of the pleader, be made by motion: (a) lack of jurisdiction; and (b) failure to state a claim upon which relief can be granted. If a pleading sets forth a claim for relief to which the adverse party is not required to serve a responsive pleading, he may assert at the trial any defense in law or fact to that claim for relief. If, on a motion asserting failure to state a claim on which relief can be granted, matters outside the pleading are to be presented, the motion shall be treated as one for summary judgment and disposed of as provided in Rule 121, and the parties shall be given an opportunity to present all material made pertinent to a motion under Rule 121.

Note: This is a new rule, derived selectively from FRCP 12(b).

RULE 41. Amended and Supplemental Pleadings.—(a) Amendments. A party may amend his pleading once as a matter of course at any time before a responsive pleading is served. If the pleading is one to which no responsive pleading is permitted and the case has not been placed on a trial calendar, he may so amend it at any time within 30 days after it is served. Otherwise a party may amend his pleading only by leave of court or by written consent of the adverse party; and leave shall be given freely when justice so requires. No amendment shall be allowed after expiration of the time for filing the petition, however, which would involve conferring jurisdiction on the Court over a matter which otherwise would not come within its jurisdiction under the petition as then on file. A motion for leave to amend a pleading shall state the reasons for the amendment and shall be accompanied by the proposed amendment. See Rules 36(a) and 37(a) for time for responding to amended pleadings.

Note: The provisions on amendment of pleadings are derived largely from the Federal Rules, but in essence do not represent a change in present practice.

The first three sentences of Par. (a), are derived from FRCP 15(a), and reflect a liberal attitude toward amendment of pleadings. The next-to-last sentence of Par. (a), regarding a motion to amend, is derived from present T.C. Rule 17(a).

While normally pleadings are amended at the initiative of the parties, the Court may direct amendment upon its own motion, and the Rule is not intended to limit the latitude of the Court.

The rule of liberal amendment provided here applies to all pleadings, except for certain areas relating to the petition which concern the jurisdiction of the Court. The Court's jurisdiction is limited with respect to (a) the taxpayers whose tax deficiency or liability may be redetermined; (b) the years for which such redetermination may pertain. In these respects, a case is fixed by the petition as originally filed or as amended within the statutory period for filing the petition, and thereafter may not be altered by amendment as to any of these areas. *Miami Valley Paper Co.* v. *Commissioner,* 211 F.2d 422 (C.A. 6, 1954); *Estate of Frank M. Archer,* 47 B.T.A. 228 (1942); *Citizens Mutual Investment Association,* 46 B.T.A. 48 (1942); *Percy N. Powers,* 20 B.T.A. 753 (1930); *John R. Thompson Co.,* 10 B.T.A. 57 (1928); *Louis Wald,* 8 B.T.A. 1003 (1927).

Within the limits which apply to permissible amendments, see paragraph (d) of this Rule as to the relation back of the amendment to the initial date of filing of the pleading.

(b) Amendments to Conform to the Evidence.—(1) Issues Tried by Consent. When issues not raised by the pleadings are tried by express or implied consent of the parties, they shall be treated in all respects as if they had been raised in the pleadings. The Court, upon motion of any party at any time, may allow such amendement of the pleadings as may be necessary to cause them to conform to the evidence and to raise these issues; but failure to amend does not affect the result of the trial of these issues.

(2) Other Evidence. If evidence is objected to at the trial on the ground that it is not within the issues raised by pleadings, the Court may receive the evidence and at any time allow the pleadings to be amended to conform to the proof, and shall do so freely when justice so requires and the objecting party fails to satisfy the Court that the admission of such evidence would prejudice him in maintaining his position on the merits.

(3) Filing. The amendment or amended pleadings permitted under this paragraph (b) shall be filed with the Court at the trial or shall be filed with the Clerk at Washington, D.C., within such time as the Court may fix.

Note: Par. (b) is derived from FRCP 15(b) and present T.C. Rule 17(d).

(c) Supplemental Pleadings. Upon motion of a party, the Court may, upon such terms as are just, permit him to file a supplemental pleading setting forth transactions or occurrences or events which have happened since the date of the pleading sought to be supplemented. Permission may be granted even though the original pleading is defective in its statements of a claim for relief or defense. If the Court deems it advisable that the adverse party plead to the supplemental pleading, it shall so direct, specifying the time therefor.

Note: Par. (c) is substantially the same as FRCP 15(d). The present T.C. Rules do not have such a provision.

(d) Relation Back of Amendments. When an amendement of a pleading is permitted, it shall relate back to the time of filing of that pleading, unless the Court shall order otherwise either on motion of a party or on its own initiative.

Note: Par. (d) is a new provision, without counterpart in the present T.C. Rules. See the note to Par. (a) of this Rule.

TITLE V.—MOTIONS.

RULE 50. General Requirements.—(a) Form and Content of Motion. An application to the Court for an order shall be by motion in writing, which shall state with particularity the grounds therefor and shall set forth the relief or order sought. If there is no objection to a motion in whole or in part, the absence of such objection shall be stated on the motion, preferably over the signature of the other party or his counsel. Unless the Court directs otherwise, motions made during a hearing or trial need not be in writing. The rules applicable to captions, signing, and other matters of form and style of pleadings apply to all motions. See Rules 23, 32, and 33.

Note: Par. (a) represents the present practice before the Court, although the provisions of Par. (a) are based on FRCP 7(b) and revisions of present T.C. Rule 19. The first sentence of Par. (a) is derived from FRCP 7(b)(1). The second sentence of Par. (a) is derived from present T.C. Rule 19(b). The third sentence is derived from present T.C. Rule 19(d). The last sentence of Par. (a) is derived from FRCP 7(b)(2).

(b) Disposition of Motions. A motion may be disposed of in one or more of the following ways, in the discretion of the Court:

(1) The Court may take action after directing that a written response be filed. In that event, the motion shall be served upon the opposing party, who shall file such response within such period as the Court may direct. Written response to a motion shall conform to the same requirements of form and style as apply to motions.

(2) The Court may take action after directing a hearing, which normally will be held in Washington, D.C. The Court may, on its own motion or upon the written request of any party to the motion, direct that the hearing be held at some other location which serves the convenience of the parties and the Court.

(3) The Court may take such action as the Court in its discretion deems appropriate, on such prior notice, if any, which the Court may consider reasonable. The action of the Court may be taken with or without written response, hearing, or attendance of a party to the motion at the hearing.

Note: Par. (b) is a new provision, which largely reflects present practice. Such a provision does not appear in the present T.C. Rules. Three main procedures for disposing of a motion are indicated here, dependent on the nature of the motion and the discretion of the Court. The Court may defer disposition until a written response is made, without providing for a hearing. The Court may hold a hearing, with or without a written response. The Court may dispose of a motion without a written response and without a hearing. Cf. present T.C. Rule 17(c)(2). In the discretion of the Court, the procedure followed in particular instances may consist of combinations or variations of these methods. They are not intended to be alternatives or exclusive.

Hearings on motions have been held mainly at Washington. Where convenient and feasible, this Rule permits them to be held elsewhere upon written application.

(c) Attendance at Hearings. If a motion is noticed for hearing, a party to the motion may, prior to or at the time for such hearing, submit a written statement of his position together with any supporting documents. Such statement may be submitted in lieu of or in addition to attendance at the hearing.

Note: Par. (c) is derived in part from present T.C. Rule 27(a)(2). It illustrates a combination of the procedures indicated in Par. (b), involving both a hearing and the filing of a written response. It further enables a party, who is unable to attend a hearing, to submit a written statement without being present at the hearing. However, such a hearing may proceed with only his adversary being heard. Moreover, this provision is not intended to preclude the Court, where it deems it beneficial to have a party or his counsel present for the purpose of discussing the matter involved, from directing that he be present at a hearing.

(d) Defects in Pleading. Where the motion or order is directed to defects in a pleading, prompt filing of a proper pleading correcting the defects may obviate the necessity of a hearing thereon.

Note: This provision is substantially the same as present T.C. Rule 27(a)(3).

(e) Postponement of Trial. The filing of a motion shall not constitute cause for postponement of a trial. With respect to motions for continuance, see Rule 134.

Note: This provision is substantially the same as present T.C. Rule 19(c).

(f) Service of Motions. The rules applicable to service of pleadings apply to service of motions. See Rule 21.

RULE 51. Motion for More Definite Statement.—(a) General. If a pleading to which a responsive pleading is permitted or required is so vague or ambiguous that a party cannot reasonably be required to frame a responsive pleading, he may move for a more definite statement before interposing his responsive pleading. The motion shall point out the defects complained of and the details desired. See Rules 70 and 90 for procedures available to narrow the issues or to elicit further information as to the facts involved or the positions of the parties.

Note: The "more definite statement" involved in this Rule is the counterpart of the "further and better statement" under present T.C. Rule 17(c)(1). The use of the reference "more definite statement" is derived from FRCP 12(e), on which Par. (a) of this Rule is based.

In determining whether a pleading should be made more definite, the basic standard in Rule 31(a) should be applied. Whether the pleading will be ordered to be made more definite is a matter within the discretion of the Court.

A pleading may be sufficiently definite or represent a sufficient statement, and yet the adverse party may be entitled to further information for other reasons. In that event, other procedures, such as those to which cross-reference is made in this Rule, should be used rather than the motion for a more definite statement.

(b) Penalty for Failure of Response. The Court may strike the pleading to which the motion is directed or may make such other order as it deems just, if the required response is not made within such period as the Court may direct.

Note: Par. (b) is based upon present T.C. Rule 17(c)(3).

RULE 52. Motion to Strike. Upon motion made by a party before responding to a pleading or, if no responsive pleading is permitted by these Rules, upon motion made by a party within 30 days after the service of the pleading, or upon the Court's own initiative at any time, the Court may order stricken from any pleading any insufficient claim or defense or any redundant, immaterial, impertinent, frivolous, or scandalous matter. In like manner and procedure, the Court may order stricken any such objectionable matter from briefs, documents, or any other papers or responses filed with the Court.

Note: This Rule is derived from FRCP 12(f), but has been enlarged, in the last sentence, to extend beyond pleadings. There is no comparable rule in the present T.C. Rules.

RULE 53. Motion to Dismiss. A case may be dismissed for cause upon motion of a party or upon the Court's initiative.

Note: This Rule is the same in substance as present T.C. Rule 21.

RULE 54. Timely Filing and Joinder of Motions. Motions must be made timely, unless the Court shall permit otherwise. Generally motions shall be separately stated and not joined together, except that motions under Rules 51 and 52 directed to the same pleading or other paper may be joined.

Note: The first sentence of this Rule is derived from present T.C. Rule 19(a). The second sentence generally represents present practice, although it does not appear in the present T.C. Rules.

RULE 55. Miscellaneous. For reference in the Rules to other motions, see Rules 25(c) (extension of time), 40 (defenses made by motion), 41 (amendment of pleadings), 63 (substitution of parties), 71(c) (answers to interrogatories), 81(b) (depositions), 90(d) (requests for admissions), 91(f) (stipulations), 121(a) (summary judgment), 123(c) (setting aside default or dismissal), 134 (continuances), 140(d) (place of trial), 141 (consolidation and separation), 151(c) (deliquent briefs), 161 (reconsideration), and 162 (vacating or revising decision).

TITLE VI.—PARTIES.

RULE 60. Proper Parties; Capacity.—(a) Petitioner. A case shall be brought by and in the name of the person against whom the Commissioner determined the deficiency (in the case of a notice of deficiency) or liability (in the case of a notice of liability), or by and with the full descriptive name of the fiduciary entitled to institute a case on behalf of such person. See Rule 23(a)(1). A case timely brought shall not be dismissed on the ground that it is not properly brought on behalf of a party until a reasonable time has been allowed after objection for ratification by such party of the bringing of the case; and such ratification shall have the same effect as if the case had been properly brought by such party. Where the deficiency or liability is determined against more than one person in the notice by the Commissioner, only such of those persons who shall duly act to bring a case shall be deemed a party or parties.

Note: Par. (a) is patterned after FRCP 17(a). The first sentence of Par. (a) is derived from present T.C. Rule 6. The second sentence of Par. (a) is adapted from FRCP 17(a). Where the intention is to file a petition on behalf of a party, the scope of this provision permits correction of errors as to the proper party or his identity made in a petition otherwise timely and correct. The last sentence is a new provision which ties in to Rule 34(a).

(b) Respondent. The Commissioner shall be named the respondent.

Note: Par. (b) is derived from present T.C. Rule 6.

(c) Capacity. The capacity of an individual, other than one acting in a fiduciary or other representative capacity, to engage in litigation in the Court shall be determined by the law of his domicile. The capacity of a corporation to engage in such litigation shall be determined by the law under which it was organized. The capacity of a fiduciary or other representative to litigate in the Court shall be determined in accordance with the law of the jurisdiction from which he derives his authority.

Note: Par. (c) is derived from FRCP 17(b). There is no counterpart provision in present T.C. Rules.

(d) Infants or Incompetent Persons. Whenever an infant or incompetent person has a representative, such as a general guardian, committee, conservator, or other like fiduciary, the representative may bring a case or defend in the Court on behalf of the infant or incompetent person. If an infant or incompetent person does not have a duly appointed representative, he may act by his next friend or by a guardian ad litem. Where a party attempts to represent himself and, in the opinion of the Court, there is a serious question as to his competence to do so, the Court, if it deems justice so requires, may continue the case until appropriate steps have been taken to obtain an adjudication of the question by a court having jurisdiction so to do, or may take such other action as it deems proper.

Note: Par. (d) is derived in part from FRCP 17(c). There is no counterpart provision in present T.C. Rules.

RULE 61. Permissive Joinder of Parties.—(a) Permissive Joinder. Any person, to whom a notice of deficiency or notice of liability has been issued, may join with any other such person in filing a petition in the Court which is timely with respect to the notice issued to each joining party. After a petition has been filed, any such person may join therein with the consent of all the petitioners and the permission of the Court. Joinder is permitted only where all or part of each participating party's tax liability arises out of the same transaction, occurrence, or series of transactions and occurrences and, in addition, there is a common question of law or fact relating to those parties. As to the filing of a joint petition, see also Rule 34.

(b) Severance or Other Orders. The Court may make such orders as will prevent a party from being embarrassed, delayed, or put to expense by the inclusion of a party; or may order separate trials or make other orders to prevent delay or prejudice; or may limit the trial to the claims of one or more parties, either dropping other parties from the case on such terms as are just or holding in abeyance the proceedings with respect to them. Any claim by or against a party may be severed and proceeded with separately. See also Rule 141(b).

Note: This Rule provides for permissive joinder of parties petitioner, under specified conditions, to whom separate notices of deficiency have been sent. No such practice is permitted under present T.C. Rules.

The approach of this Rule is to allow joinder within the terms of the Rule, but to give the Court ultimate, very broad discretion to sever the parties or their claims to the extent it considers appropriate. That overriding discretion is expressed in Par. (b). Such severance or separation may be made by the Court in its discretion, with or without a motion.

Pars. (a) and (b) have been adapted from FRCP 20(a) and (b).

RULE 62. Misjoinder of Parties. Misjoinder of parties is not ground for dismissal of a case. The Court may order a severance on such terms as are just. See Rule 61(b).

Note: This Rule is derived from FRCP 21. The present T.C. Rules do not have such a provision.

RULE 63. Substitution of Parties; Change or Correction in Name.—(a) Death. If a petitioner dies, the Court, on motion of a party or the decedent's successor or representative or on its own initiative, may order substitution of the proper parties.

Note: Par. (a) is derived from present T.C. Rule 23(d). Similar provision is made in substance in FRCP 25(a)(1).

(b) Incompetency. If a party becomes incompetent, the Court, on motion of a party or the incompetent's representative or on its own initiative, may order his representative to proceed with the case.

Note: Par. (b) is adapted from FRCP 25(b). Such a provision is not contained in the present T.C. Rules.

(c) Successor Fiduciaries or Representatives. On motion made where a fiduciary or representative is changed, the Court may order substitution of the proper successors.

Note: Par. (c) is based on present T.C. Rule 23(a). However, the mandatory requirement of a certificate is eliminated.

(d) Other Cause. The Court, on motion of a party or on its own initiative, may order the substitution of proper parties for other cause.

Note: Par. (d) is derived from present T.C. Rule 23(d).

(e) Change or Correction in Name. On motion of a party or on its own initiative, the Court may order a change of or correction in the name or title of a party.

Note: Par. (e) is derived from present T.C. Rule 23(b) and (d). The mandatory requirement of supporting evidence, now in present T.C. Rule 23(b), has been eliminated.

TITLE VII.—DISCOVERY.

RULE 70. General Provisions.—(a) General. (1) Methods and Limitations of Discovery. In conformity with these Rules, a party may obtain discovery by written interrogatories (Rule 71) or by production of documents or things (Rules 72 and 73). However, the Court expects the parties to attempt to attain the objectives of discovery through informal consultation or communication before utilizing the discovery procedures provided in these Rules. Discovery is not available under these Rules through depositions, which may be taken only for the limited purpose and under the conditions provided in Title VIII. See Rules 91(a) and 100 regarding relationship of discovery to stipulations.

(2) Time for Discovery. Discovery shall not be commenced, without leave of Court, before the expiration of 30 days after joinder of issue (see Rule 38), and shall be completed, unless otherwise authorized by the Court, no later than 75 days prior to the date set for call of the case from a trial calendar.

Note: The discovery procedures adopted by these Rules consist of interrogatories and of production and inspection of papers and other things. In that respect, the Federal Rules have been followed in essence. Depositions have not been adopted in these Rules as a discovery device. In that respect, these Rules do not follow the Federal Rules.

The new procedures introduced into Tax Court practice by these Rules are deemed sufficient to enable a party to obtain information needed to prepare for trial. Whatever additional benefits might be obtained by the use of discovery depositions would appear to be outweighed by the problems and burdens they entail for the parties as well as the Court. Provision for discovery depositions in conformity with the Federal Rules at this time would represent too drastic a departure from present Tax Court practice, with uncertain effect in view of the context of Tax Court litigation.

The present Tax Court Rules have no provisions on discovery. While there are provisions in the present Rules on depositions, they have not seen extensive use, and in practice generally have been limited to special circumstances, as were witnesses have not otherwise been available.

Par. (a) sets forth the allowable methods of discovery and the limitations discussed above. No similar provision appears in the present T.C. Rules.

(b) Scope of Discovery. The information or response sought through discovery may concern any matter not privileged and which is relevant to the subject matter involved in the pending case. It is not ground for objection that the information or response sought will be inadmissible at the trial, if that information or response appears reasonably calculated to lead to discovery of admissible evidence, regardless of the burden of proof involved. If the information or response sought is otherwise proper, it is not objectionable merely because the information or response involves an opinion or contention that relates to fact or to the application of law to fact. But the Court may order that the information or response sought need not be furnished or made until some designated time or a particular stage has been reached in the case or until a specified step has been taken by a party.

Note: Par. (b) outlines in general the scope of allowable discovery, and is adapted from FRCP 26(b)(1). There is no counterpart provision in present T.C. Rules. The inclusion, of "an opinion or contention that relates to fact or to the application of law to fact," is derived from FRCP 33(b). In this connection, the Advisory Committee's Explanatory Statement, Proposed Amendments to the Rules of Civil Procedure for the U.S. District Courts, House Doc. No. 91-291, 91st Cong., 2d Sess., stated at p. 46-47:

"There are numerous and conflicting decisions on the question whether and to what extent, interrogatories are limited to matters 'of fact' or may elicit opinions, contentions, and legal conclusions. * * *

"Rule 33 is amended to provide that an interrogatory is not objectionable merely because it calls for an opinion or contention that relates to fact or the application of law to fact. Efforts to draw sharp lines between facts and opinions have invariably been unsuccessful, and the clear trend of the cases is to permit 'factual' opinions. As to requests for opinions or contentions that call for the application of law to fact, they can be most useful in narrowing and sharpening the issues, which is a major purpose of discovery. * * * On the other hand, under the new language interrogatories may not extend to issues of 'pure law', i.e. legal issues unrelated to the facts of the case."

With respect to discovery of an opponent's materials which may be used for impeachment purposes, the same Advisory Committee observed (House Doc. No. 91-291, supra, p. 25-26) that "the courts have in appropriate circumstances protected materials that are primarily of an impeaching character." The Committee concluded that this type of materials is one illustration of "the many situations, not capable of governance by precise rule, in which the courts must exercise judgement. The new subsections in Rule 26(b) do not change existing law with respect to such situations."

With certain exceptions and subject to the limitations of these Rules, the scope of allowable discovery under these Rules is intended to parallel the scope of allowable discovery under the Federal Rules. With respect to experts, the scope of allowable discovery is indicated by Rule 71(d). The other areas, i.e., the "work product" of counsel and material prepared in anticipation of litigation or for trial, are generally intended to be outside the scope of allowable discovery under these Rules, and therefore the specific provisions for disclosure of such materials in FRCP 26(b)(3) have not been adopted. Cf. *Hickman* v. *Taylor,* 329 U.S. 495 (1947).

(c) Party's Statements. Upon request to the other party and without any showing except the assertion in writing that he lacks and has no convenient means of obtaining a copy of a statement made by him, a party shall be entitled to obtain a copy of any such statement which has a bearing on the subject matter of the case and is in the possession or control of another party to the case.

Note: Par. (c) is derived from FRCP 26(b)(3). There is no counterpart provision in present T.C. Rules. The purpose is to enable a party, as a matter of fairness, to obtain his statement without any special showing.

(d) Use in Case. The answers to interrogatories, things produced in response to a request, or other information or responses obtained under Rules 71, 72, and 73, may be used at trial or in any proceeding in the case prior or subsequent to trial, to the extent permitted by the rules of evidence. Such answers or information or responses will not be considered as evidence until offered and received as evidence. No objections to interrogatories or the answers thereto, or to a request to produce or the response thereto, will be considered unless made to the Court within the time prescribed, except that the objection that an interrogatory or answer would be inadmissible at trial is preserved even though not made prior to trial.

Note: The rule in Par. (d), that answers to interrogatories and other responses may be used at trial to the extent permitted by the rules of evidence is derived from FRCP 33(b). The next sentence of Par. (d), requiring an offer and receipt in evidence, is derived from present T.C. Rule 31(c). The last sentence emphasizes that objections must be timely made, in accordance with the provisions of these Rules, rather than waiting until the matter is introduced at trial. Except as indicated above, present T.C. Rules do not have such provisions.

(e) Other Applicable Rules. For Rules concerned with the frequency and timing of discovery in relation to other procedures, supplementation of answers, protective orders, effect of evasive or incomplete answers or responses, and sanctions and enforcement action, see Title X.

Note: Par. (e) provides a cross-reference to certain Rules generally applicable to these discovery methods. A comparable provision does not exist in the present T.C. Rules.

RULE 71. Interrogatories.—(a) Availability. Any party may, without leave of Court, serve upon any other party written interrogatories to be answered by the party served or, if the party served is a public or private corporation or a partnership or association or governmental agency, by an officer or agent who shall furnish such information as is available to the party.

Note: As a method of discovery, interrogatories consist of written questions submitted by a party, to which the other side files written answers. No testimony is taken, as in the course of a deposition. Notwithstanding its caption and language, present T.C. Rule 46 does not provide for interrogatories, but rather for depositions taken on written questions instead of on oral questions, referring to those written questions as "interrogatories".

Par. (a) is derived from FRCP 33(a). There are two prominent characteristics of this provision. First, it is limited to discovery by one party from another party. Interrogatories under this provision cannot be served on third persons. Second, the procedure is initiated without involvement of the Court, but rather by action between the parties. The Court becomes involved only if objecions are filed by the responding party or there is some other source of complaint as the procedure develops. Both of these elements are found in the procedure under the Federal Rules.

(b) Answers. All answers shall be made in good faith and as completely as the answering party's information shall permit. However, the answering party is required to make reasonable inquiry and ascertain readily obtainable information. An answering party may not give lack of information or knowledge as an answer or as a reason for failure to answer, unless he states that he has made reasonable inquiry and that information known or readily obtainable by him is insufficient to enable him to answer the substance of the interrogatory.

Note: Par. (b) is adapted from FRCP 36(a), which concerns answers to requests for admissions. Provision for such requests is made in Rule 90.

There is no similar provision in the present T.C. Rules.

(c) Procedure. Each interrogatory shall be answered separately and fully under oath, unless it is objected to, in which event the reasons for the objection shall be stated in lieu of the answer. The answers are to be signed by the person making them, and the objections shall be signed by the party or his counsel. The party, on whom the interrogatories have been served, shall serve a copy of his answers, and objections if any, upon the propounding party within 45 days after service of the interrogatories upon him. The Court may allow a shorter or longer time. The burden shall be on the party submitting the interrogatories to move for an order with respect to any objection or other failure to answer an interrogatory, and in that connection the moving party shall annex to his motion the interrogatories, with proof of service on the other party, together with the answers and objections if any.

Note: Par. (c) is derived from FRCP 33(a), with some modification in the time requirement considered desirable. A similar provision does not appear in the present T.C. Rules.

(d) Experts. By means of written interrogatories in conformity with this Rule, a party may require any other party (i) to identify each person whom the other party expects to call as an expert witness at the trial of the case, giving his name, address, vocation or occupation, and a statement of his qualifications, and (ii) to state the subject matter and the substance of the facts and opinions to which the expert is expected to testify, and give a summary of the grounds for each such opinion.

Note: Par. (d) is a new provision, without counterpart in the present T.C. Rules. The complex discovery provisions relating to experts in the Federal Rules, in FRCP 26(b)(4), are considered inappropriate for purposes of litigation in this Court.

(e) Option to Produce Business Records. Where the answer to an interrogatory may be derived or ascertained from the business records of the party upon whom the interrogatory has been served, or from an examination, audit or inspection of such business records, or from a compilation, abstract or summary based thereon, and the burden of deriving or ascertaining the answer is substantially the same for the party serving the interrogatory as for the party served, it is sufficient answer to such interrogatory to specify the records from which the answer may be derived or ascertained and to afford to the party serving the interrogatory reasonable opportunity to examine, audit or inspect such records and to make copies, compilations, abstracts or summaries.

Note: Par. (e) is derived from FRCP 33(c). No counterpart provision appears in the present T.C. Rules. The purpose of this provision is to limit the burden on the responding party of searching and extracting information from available materials. On the other hand, the responding party is expected reasonably to narrow the materials to be examined. For the work involved in assembling and making them more effectively accessible, the Court may require the responding party to be reimbursed by the interrogating party. See Rule 103(a)(9).

RULE 72. Production of Documents and Things.—(a) Scope. Any party may, without leave of Court, serve on any other party a request to:

(1) Produce and permit the party making the request, or someone acting on his behalf, to inspect and copy, any designated documents (including writings, drawings, graphs, charts, photographs, phono-records, and other data compilations from which information can be obtained, translated, if necessary, by the responding party through detection devices into reasonably usable form), or to inspect and copy, test, or sample any tangible things, to the extent that any of the foregoing items are in the possession, custody or control of the party on whom the request is served; or

(2) Permit entry upon designated land or other property in the possession or control of the party upon whom the request is served for the purpose of inspection and measuring, surveying, photographing, testing, or sampling the property or any designated object or operation thereon.

Note: This discovery method is derived from FRCP 34. Par. (a) is derived from FRCP 34(a). There is no comparable provision in the present T.C. Rules.

(b) Procedure. The request shall set forth the items to be inspected, either by individual item or by category, and describe each item and category with reasonable particularity. It shall specify a reasonable time, place, and manner of making the inspection and performing the related acts. The party upon whom the request is served shall serve a written response within 30 days after service of the request. The Court may allow a shorter or longer time. The response shall state, with respect to each item or category, that inspection and related activities will be permitted as requested, unless the request is objected to in whole or in part, in which event the reasons for objection shall be stated. If objection is made to part of an item or category, that part shall be specified. To obtain a ruling on an objection by the responding party, the requesting party shall file an appropriate motion with the Court.

Note: Par. (b) is derived from FRCP 34(b). No comparable provision appears in present T.C. Rules. This procedure, as in the case of interrogatories, operates without participation of the Court, and also requires motion to the Court by the requesting party in the event of objection to, failure of, or inadequate response.

(c) Foreign Petitioners. For production of records by foreign petitioners, see Code section 7456(b).

RULE 73. Examination By Transferees.—(a) General. Upon application to the Court and subject to these Rules, a transferee of property of a taxpayer shall be entitled to examine before trial the books, papers, documents, correspondence, and other evidence of the taxpayer or of a preceding transferee of the taxpayer's property, provided that the transferee making the application is a petitioner seeking redetermination of his liability in respect of the taxpayer's tax liability (including interest, additional amounts, and additions provided by law). Such books, papers, documents, correspondence, and other evidence may be made available to the extent that the same shall be within the United States, will not result in undue hardship to the taxpayer or preceding transferee, and in the opinion of the Court is necessary in order to enable the transferee to ascertain the liability of the taxpayer or preceding transferee.

(b) Procedure. A petitioner desiring an examination permitted under paragraph (a), shall file an application with the Court, showing that he is entitled to such an examination, describing the documents and other materials sought to be examined, giving the names and addresses of the persons to produce the same, and stating a reasonable time and place where the examination is to be made. If the Court shall determine that the applicable requirements are satisfied, it shall issue a subpoena, signed by a judge, directed to the appropriate person and ordering the production at a designated time and place of the documents and other materials involved. If the person to whom the subpoena is directed shall object thereto or to the production involved, he shall file his objections and the reasons therefor in writing with the Court, and serve a copy thereof upon the applicant, within 10 days after service of the subpoena or on or before such earlier time as may be specified in the subpoena for compliance. To obtain a ruling on such objections, the applicant for the subpoena shall file an appropriate motion with the Court. In all respects not inconsistent with the provisions of this Rule, the provisions of Rule 72(b) shall apply where appropriate.

(c) Scope of Examination. The scope of the examination authorized under this Rule shall be as broad as is authorized under Rule 72(a), including, for example, the copying of such documents and materials.

Note: This Rule is a new provision, without counterpart in the present T.C. Rules or in the Federal Rules. It is based on Code Section 6902(b). It is intended to be cumulative rather than exclusive of other pretrial procedures. Except for the requirement of prior application to the Court, its procedure follows Rule 72.

TITLE VIII. DEPOSITIONS.

RULE 80. General Provisions.—(a) General. On complying with the applicable requirements, depositions may be taken in a pending case before trial (Rule 81), or in anticipation of commencing a case in this Court (Rule 82), or in connection with the trial (Rule 83). Depositions may be taken only for the purpose of making testimony or any document or thing available as evidence in the circumstances herein authorized by the applicable Rules. These Rules do not provide for taking depositions for discovery purposes.

(b) Other Applicable Rules. For Rules concerned with the timing and frequency of depositions, supplementation of answers, protective orders, effect of evasive or incomplete answers or responses, and sanctions and enforcement action, see Title X.

Note: Depositions are adopted in these Rules only for the purpose of perpetuating or preserving evidence. They are not adopted for discovery purposes. Although, for example, the examination of a witness may result in disclosure, a deposition is not authorized unless it can be linked sufficiently with the object of perpetuating evidence.

The use of depositions under these Rules generally is not favored, unless it can be shown that the required objective exists. To control the use of depositions, these Rules require that a deposition can be taken only after application to and approval by the Court. The notice procedure of the Federal Rules, in FRCP 30, is not adopted in these Rules.

The deposition is not limited to an adverse party. It may be used with respect to any person, if the other applicable conditions are satisfied.

Depositions, for the authorized purpose, are permitted at three stages—before trial in a pending case, in advance of commencement of a case, and after trial has begun.

Par. (a) is an introductory provision, and Par. (b) is a cross-reference to other Rules applicable to depositions. Neither provision has a counterpart in the present T.C. Rules or the Federal Rules.

RULE 81. Depositions in Pending Case.—(a) Depositions to Perpetuate Testimony. A party to a case pending in the Court, who desires to perpetuate his own testimony or that of any other person or to preserve any document or thing, shall file an application pursuant to these Rules for an order of the Court authorizing such party to take a deposition for such purpose. Such depositions shall be taken only where there is a substantial risk that the person or document or thing involved will not be available at the trial of the case, and shall relate only to testimony or document or thing which is not privileged and is material to a matter in controversy.

Note: Par. (a) is a new provision. The present T.C. Rules do not have any provision as to the purpose of the deposition.

(b) The Application.—(1) Content of Application. The application to take a deposition pursuant to paragraph (a) of this Rule shall be signed by the party seeking the deposition or his counsel, and shall show the following:

(i) the names and addresses of the persons to be examined;

(ii) the reasons for deposing those persons rather than waiting to call them as witnesses at the trial;

(iii) the substance of the testimony which the party expects to elicit from each of those persons;

(iv) a statement showing how the proposed testimony or document or thing is material to a matter in controversy;

(v) a statement describing any books, papers, documents, or tangible things to be produced at the deposition by the persons to be examined;

(vi) the time and place proposed for the deposition;

(vii) the officer before whom the deposition is to be taken;

(viii) the date on which the petition was filed with the Court, and whether the pleadings have been closed and the case placed on a trial calendar; and

(ix) any provision desired with respect to payment of expenses, fees, and charges relating to the deposition (see paragraph (g) of this Rule, and Rule 103). The application shall also have annexed to it a copy of the questions to be propounded, if the deposition is to be taken on written questions. For the form of application to take a deposition, see Appendix I, p. 58.

(2) Filing and Disposition of Application. The application may be filed with the Court at any time after the case is docketed in the Court, but must be filed at least 45 days prior to the date set for the trial of the case. The deposition must be completed and filed with the Court at least 10 days prior to the trial date. The application and a conformed copy thereof, together with an additional conformed copy for each additional docket number involved and an additional conformed copy for each person to be served, shall be filed with the Clerk of the Court, who shall serve a copy on each of the other parties to the case as well as on such other persons who are to be examined pursuant to the application. Such other parties or persons shall file their objections or other response, with the same number of copies, within 15 days after such service of the application. A hearing on the application will be held only if directed by the Court. Unless the Court shall determine otherwise for good cause shown, an application to take a deposition will not be regarded as sufficient ground for granting a continuance from a date or place of trial theretofore set. If the Court approves the taking of a deposition, it will issue an order which will include in its terms the name of the person to be examined, the time and place of the deposition, and the officer before whom it is to be taken.

Note: Par. (b)(1) sets forth the requirements, for an application to take a deposition, in the context of the purpose of the Rule. It therefore diverges from present T. C. Rule 45(a). Since the Federal practice is based on a notice procedure, the Federal Rules do not have a comparable provision.

Par. (b)(2) is a new provision, derived in part from present T.C. Rule 45(a), (b), and (d). The Federal Rules do not have such a provision.

(c) Designation of Person to Testify. The party seeking to take a deposition may name, as the deponent in his application, a public or private corporation or a partnership or association or governmental agency, and shall designate with reasonable particularity the matters on which examination is requested. The organization so named shall designate one or more officers, directors, or managing agents, or other persons who consent to testify on its behalf, and may set forth, for each person designated, the matters on which he will testify. The persons so designated shall testify as to matters known or reasonably available to the organization.

Note: Par. (c) is derived from FRCP 30(b)(6). The present T.C. Rules do not have a comparable provision.

(d) Use of Stipulation. The parties or their counsel may execute and file a stipulation to take a deposition by agreement instead of filing an application as hereinabove provided. Such a stipulation shall be filed with the Court in duplicate, and shall contain the same information as is required in items (i), (vi), (vii), and (ix) of Rule 81(b)(1), but shall not require the approval or an order of the Court unless the effect is to delay the trial of the case. A deposition taken pursuant to a stipulation shall in all respects conform to the requirements of these Rules.

Note: Par. (d) is derived from present T.C. Rule 45(e). A stipulation provision also appears in FRCP 29.

(e) Person Before Whom Deposition Taken.—(1) Domestic Depositions. Within the United States or a territory or insular possession subject to the dominion of the United States, depositions shall be taken before an officer authorized to administer oaths by the laws of the United States (see Code Section 7622) or of the place where the examination is held, or before a person appointed by the Court. A person so appointed has power to administer oaths and to take such testimony.

(2) Foreign Depositions. In a foreign country, depositions may be taken on notice (i) before a person authorized to administer oaths or affirmations in the place in which the examination is held, either by the law thereof or by the law of the United States, or (ii) before a person commissioned by the Court, and a person so commissioned shall have the power, by virtue of his commission, to administer any necessary oath and take testimony, or (iii) pursuant to a letter rogatory. A commission or a letter rogatory shall be issued on application and notice and on terms that are just and appropriate. It is not requisite to the issuance of a commission or a letter rogatory that the taking of the deposition in any other manner is impracticable or inconvenient; and both a commission and a letter rogatory may be issued in proper cases. A notice or commission may designate the person before whom the deposition is to be taken either by name or descriptive title. A letter rogatory may be addressed "To The Appropriate Authority in [here name the country]." Evidence obtained by deposition or in response to a letter rogatory need not be excluded merely for reason that it is not a verbatim transcript or that the testimony was not taken under oath or for any similar departure from the requirements for depositions taken within the United States under these Rules.

(3) Disqualification for Interest. No deposition shall be taken before a person who is a relative or employee or counsel of any party, or is a relative or employee or associate of such counsel, or is financially interested in the action. However, on consent of all the parties or their counsel, a deposition may be taken before such person, provided that the relationship of that person and the waiver shall be set forth in the certificate of return to the Court.

Note: Par. (e) is derived from FRCP 28, and is subdivided in the same manner as FRCP 28. It was adopted in place of present T.C. Rule 45(c).

The circumstances, disqualifying a person from being one before whom a deposition may be taken, are adopted as they appear in FRCP 28(c). However, such a person may qualify upon consent of the parties, as suggested by present T.C. Rule 45(c), although there is eliminated the condition of Rule 45(c) that no other officer be available.

Depositions taken abroad present many problems as to arrangements and procedure, and may involve additional expense and greater hardship than if taken in the United States. Foreign depositions are discouraged and normally a deposition should be taken within the United States whenever possible.

(f) Taking of Deposition.—(1) Arrangements. All arrangements necessary for taking of the deposition shall be made by the party filing the application or, in the case of a stipulation, by such other persons as may be agreed upon by the parties.

(2) Procedure. Attendance by the persons to be examined may be compelled by the issuance of a subpoena, and production likewise may be compelled of exhibits required in connection with the testimony being taken. The officer before whom the deposition is taken shall first put the witness on oath (or affirmation) and shall personally, or by someone acting under his direction and in his presence, record accurately and verbatim the questions asked, the answers given, the objections made, and all matters transpiring at the taking of the deposition which bear on the testimony involved. Examination and cross-examination of witnesses, and the marking of exhibits, shall proceed as permitted at trial. All objections made at the time of examination shall be noted by the officer upon the deposition. Evidence objected to, unless privileged, shall be taken subject to the objections made. If an answer is improperly refused and as a result a further deposition is taken by the interrogating party, the objecting party or deponent may be required to pay all costs, charges, and expenses of that deposition to the same extent as is provided in paragraph (g) of this Rule where a party seeking to take a deposition fails to appear at the taking of the deposition. At the request of either party, a prospective witness at the deposition, other than a person acting in an expert or advisory capacity for a party, shall be excluded from the room in which, and during the time that, the testimony of another witness is being taken; and if such person remains in the room or within hearing of the examination after such request has been made, he shall not thereafter be permitted to testify, except by the consent of the party who requested his exclusion or by permission of the Court.

Note: Par. (f) is adapted from FRCP 30(a) and (c), and from present T.C. Rule 45(d), (f) and (g).

(g) Expenses.—(1) General. The party taking the deposition shall pay all the expenses, fees, and charges of the witness whose deposition is taken by him, any charges of the officer presiding at or recording the deposition other than for copies of the deposition, and any expenses involved in providing a place for the deposition. The party taking the deposition shall pay for a copy of the deposition to be filed in Court; and, upon payment of reasonable charges therefor, the officer shall also furnish a copy of the deposition to any party or the deponent. By stipulation between the parties or on order of the Court, provision may be made for any costs, charges, or expenses relating to the deposition.

(2) Failure to Attend or to Serve Subpoena. If the party authorized to take a deposition fails to attend and proceed therewith and another party attends in person or by attorney pursuant to the arrangements made, the Court may order the former party to pay to such other party the reasonable expenses incurred by him and his attorney in attending, including reasonable attorney's fees. If the party authorized to take a deposition of a witness fails to serve a subpoena upon him and the witness because of such failure does not attend, and if another party attends in person or by attorney because he expects the deposition of that witness to be taken, the Court may order the former party to pay to such other party the reasonable expenses incurred by him and his attorney attending, including reasonable attorney's fees.

Note: Par. (g) is a new provision, without counterpart in the present T.C. Rules. It is adapted in part from FRCP 30(f)(2) and (g).

(h) Execution and Return of Deposition.—(1) Submission to Witness; Changes; Signing. When the testimony is fully transcribed, the deposition shall be submitted to the witness for examination and shall be read to or by him, unless such examination and reading are waived by the witness and by the parties. Any changes in form or substance, which the witness desires to make, shall be entered upon the deposition by the officer with a statement of the reasons given by the witness for making them. The deposition shall then be signed by the witness, unless the parties by stipulation waive the signing or the witness is ill or cannot be found or refuses to sign. If the deposition is not signed by the witness within 30 days of its submission to him, the officer shall sign it and state on the record the fact of the waiver or of the illness or absence of the witness or the fact of the refusal to sign together with the reason, if any, given therefor; and the deposition may then be used as fully as though signed unless the Court determines that the reasons given for the refusal to sign require rejection of the deposition in whole or in part. As to correction of errors see Rules 85 and 143(c).

(2) **Form.** The deposition shall show the docket number and caption of the case as they appear in the Court's records, the place and date of taking the deposition, the name of the witness, the party by whom called, the names of counsel present and whom they represent. The pages of the deposition shall be securely fastened. Exhibits shall be carefully marked, and when practicable annexed to, and in any event returned with, the deposition, unless, upon motion to the Court, a copy shall be permitted as a substitute after an opportunity is given to all interested parties to examine and compare the original and the copy. The officer shall execute and attach to the deposition a certificate in accordance with Form 7 shown in Appendix I, p. 60.

(3) **Return of Deposition.** Unless otherwise authorized or directed by the Court, the officer shall enclose the original deposition and exhibits, together with such other copies for the parties and deponent as to which provision for payment therefor shall have been made, in a sealed packet with registered or certified postage or same to the Clerk of the Court or shall direct and forward the same to the United States Tax Court, Box 70, Washington, D.C. 20044. Upon written request of a party or his counsel, the officer may deliver a copy to him or his representative in lieu of sending it to the Court, in which event the officer shall attach to his return to the Court that written request and shall state in his certificate the fact of delivery by him of such copy or copies.

Note: Par. (h)(1) is derived from FRCP 30(e). A brief provision appears in present T.C. Rule 45(h).

Par. (h)(2) is derived from present T.C. Rule 45(i). The same matter is treated in FRCP 30(f)(1).

Par. (h)(3) is derived from present T.C. Rule 45(j). The same matter is treated in FRCP 30(f)(1).

(i) **Use of Deposition.** At the trial or in any other proceeding in the case, any part or all of a deposition, so far as admissible under the rules of evidence applied as though the witness were then present and testifying, may be used against any party who was present or represented at the taking of the deposition or who had reasonable notice thereof, in accordance with any of the following provisions:

(1) The deposition may be used by any party for the purpose of contradicting or impeaching the testimony of deponent as a witness.

(2) The deposition of a party may be used by an adverse party for any purpose.

(3) The deposition may be used for any purpose if the Court finds: (A) that the witness is dead; or (B) that the witness is at such distance from the place of trial that it is not practicable for him to attend, unless it appears that the absence of the witness was procured by the party seeking to use the deposition; or (C) that the witness is unable to attend or testify because of age, illness, infirmity, or imprisonment; or (D) that the party offering the deposition has been unable to obtain attendance of the witness at the trial, as to make it desirable in the interests of justice, to allow the deposition to be used; or (E) that such exceptional circumstances exist, in regard to the absence of the witness at the trial, as to make it desirable in the interests of justice, to allow the deposition to be used.

(4) If only part of a deposition is offered in evidence by a party, an adverse party may require him to introduce any other part which ought in fairness to be considered with the part introduced, and any party may introduce any other parts.

As to introduction of deposition in evidence, see Rule 143(c).

Note: Par. (i) is derived from FRCP 32(a). A comparable provision does not appear in the present T.C. Rules.

RULE 82. Depositions Before Commencement of Case. A person, who desires to perpetuate his own testimony or that of another person or to preserve any document or thing regarding any matter that may be cognizable in this Court, may file an application with the Court to take a deposition for such purpose. The application shall be entitled in the name of the applicant, shall otherwise be in the same style and form as apply to a motion filed with the Court, and shall show the following: (1) The facts showing that the applicant expects to be a party to a case cognizable in this Court but is at present unable to bring it or cause it to be brought. (2) The subject matter of the expected action and his interest therein. (3) All matters required to be shown in an application under paragraph (b)(1) of Rule 81 except item (viii) thereof. Such an application will be entered upon a special docket, and service thereof and pleading with respect thereto will proceed subject to the requirements otherwise applicable to a motion. A hearing on the application may be required by the Court. If the Court is satisfied that the perpetuation of the testimony or the preservation of the document or thing may prevent a failure or delay of justice, it will make an order authorizing the deposition and including such other terms and conditions as it may deem appropriate consistently with these Rules. If the deposition is taken, and if thereafter the expected case is commenced in this Court, the deposition may be used in that case subject to the Rules which would apply if the deposition had been taken after commencement of the case.

Note: This Rule is derived from FRCP 27(a). A comparable provision does not appear in the present T.C. Rules. *Louisville Builders Supply Co.* v. *Commissioner,* 294 F.2d 333 (C.A. 6th, 1961), is not considered to prevent the promulgation and operation of this Rule.

RULE 83. Depositions After Commencement of Trial. Nothing in these Rules shall preclude the taking of a deposition after trial has commenced in a case, upon approval or direction of the Court. The Court may impose such conditions to the taking of the deposition as it may find appropriate and, with respect to any aspect not provided for by the Court, Rule 81 shall govern to the extent applicable.

Note: This is a new rule, not derived either from the present Tax Court Rules or the Federal Rules. Cf. FRCP 27(b). It is intended to reflect present practice in the Court.

RULE 84. Depositions Upon Written Questions.—(a) Use of Written Questions. A party may make an application to the Court to take a deposition, otherwise authorized under Rules 81, 82, or 83, upon written questions rather than oral examination. The provisions of those Rules shall apply in all respects to such a deposition except to the extent clearly inapplicable or otherwise provided in this Rule. Unless there is special reason for taking the deposition on written questions rather than oral examination, the Court will deny the application, without prejudice to seeking approval of the deposition upon oral examination. The taking of depositions upon written questions is not favored, except when the deposition is to be taken in a foreign country, in which event the deposition must be taken on written questions unless otherwise directed by the Court for good cause shown.

Note: A procedure for taking a deposition by submitting written questions, which are asked by the supervising official and the answers to which are recorded by him or at his direction, is allowed by present T.C. Rule 46 and FRCP 31.

The procedure is continued in the present Rules, although its use is narrowly restricted. Par. (a) is a new provision, which incorporates the present restrictions. Even within those narrow limits, moreover, the other requirements applicable to the purpose and scope of depositions under these Rules must be satisfied, including the fundamental one of perpetuating evidence.

This Rule changes the terminology from "interrogatories" to "questions", in conformity with FRCP 31.

(b) Procedure. An application under Paragraph (a) hereof shall have the written questions annexed thereto. With respect to such application, the 15-day period for filing objections prescribed by paragraph (b)(2) of Rule 81 is extended to 20 days, and within that 20-day period the objecting or responding party shall also file with the Court any cross-questions which he may desire to be asked at the taking of the deposition. The applicant shall then file any objections to the cross-questions, as well as any redirect questions, within 15 days after service on him of the cross-questions. Within 15 days after service of the redirect questions on the other party, he shall file with the Court any objections to the redirect questions, as well as any recross questions which he may desire to be asked. No objection to a written question will be considered unless it is filed with the Court within such applicable time. An original and five copies of all questions and objections shall be filed with the Clerk of the Court, who will make service thereof on the opposite party. The Court for good cause shown may enlarge or shorten the time in any respect.

Note: Par. (b) is adapted from present T.C. Rules 46(a) and 47(b). The procedure is intended to conform, to the extent feasible, to that used for oral depositions. Par. (b) enlarges the present Rule by providing for redirect questions as well as cross-questions, as is permitted under FRCP31(a), and emphasizes the requirement of timely objection if it is to be considered. Here, as in the case of oral depositions, prior approval of the Court is required in order to take the deposition.

(c) Taking of Deposition. The officer taking the deposition shall propound all questions to the witness in their proper order. The parties and their counsel may attend the taking of the deposition but shall not participate in the deposition proceeding in any manner.

Note: Par. (c) is derived from present T.C. Rule 46(b), but modifies the present provision in allowing the parties and counsel to attend the deposition.

(d) Filing. The execution and filing of the deposition shall conform to the requirements of paragraph (h) of Rule 81.

Note: Par. (d) incorporates the execution and filing requirements applicable to oral depositions, and is comparable to present T.C. Rule 46(c).

RULE 85. Objections, Errors, and Irregularities.—(a) As to Initiating Deposition. All errors and irregularities in the procedure for obtaining approval for the taking of a deposition are waived, unless made in writing within the time for making objections or promptly where no time is prescribed.

Note: Par. (a) is adapted from FRCP 32(d)(1). A similar provision is not contained in the present T.C. Rules.

(b) As to Disqualification of Officer. Objection to taking a deposition because of disqualification of the officer before whom it is to be taken is waived, unless made before the taking of the deposition begins or as soon thereafter as the disqualification becomes known or could be discovered with reasonable diligence.

Note: Par. (b) is adopted verbatim from FRCP 32(d)(2). A similar provision is not contained in the present T.C. Rules.

(c) As to Use. In general, an objection may be made at the trial or hearing to use of a deposition, in whole or in part as evidence, for any reason which would require the exclusion of the testimony as evidence if the witness were then present and testifying. However, objections to the competency of a witness or to the competency, relevancy, or materiality of a testimony are waived by failure to make them before or during the taking of the deposition, if the ground of the objection is one which might have been obviated or removed if presented at that time.

Note: Par. (c) is a combination of FRCP 32(b) and FRCP 32(d)(3)(A). The latter, however, has been reworded to assert an affirmative rather than a negative rule. The counterpart provision appears in present T.C. Rule 47(a)(1).

(d) As to Manner and Form. Errors and irregularities occurring at the oral examination in the manner of taking the deposition, in the form of the questions or answers, in the oath or affirmation, or in the conduct of the parties, and errors of any kind which might have been obviated, removed, or cured if promptly presented, are waived unless seasonable objection thereto is made at the taking of the deposition.

Note: Par. (d) is derived from FRCP 32(d)(3)(B). A similar provision appears in present T.C. Rule 47(a)(2).

(e) As to Errors by Officer. Errors or irregularities in the manner in which testimony is transcribed or the deposition is prepared, signed, certified, sealed, endorsed, transmitted, filed, or otherwise dealt with by the presiding officer, are waived unless a motion to correct or suppress the deposition or some part thereof is made with reasonable promptness after such defect is, or with due diligence might have been, ascertained. See also Rule 143(c).

Note: Par. (e) is derived from present T.C. Rule 47(a)(3) and FRCP 32(d)(4).

TITLE IX.—ADMISSIONS AND STIPULATIONS.

RULE 90. Requests for Admission.—(a) Scope and Time of Request. A party may serve upon any other party a written request for the admission, for purposes of the pending action only, of the truth of any matters which are not privileged and are relevant to the subject matter involved in the pending action, provided such matters are set forth in the request and relate to statements or opinions of fact or of the application of law to fact, including the genuineness of any documents described in the request. Requests for admission must be commenced and completed within the same period provided in Rule 70(a)(2) for commencement and completion of discovery.

Note: The request for admission is a procedure contained in FRCP 36. There is no counterpart provision in the present T.C. Rules.

Such requests are principally a means of establishing matters which are not disputed, whether of fact or of the application of law to fact, and are intended to avoid the time and effort needed to prove them at trial. Such requests may also aid the discovery efforts of a party, or they may assist in arriving at stipulations under Rule 91. In a larger context, therefore, such requests may promote the narrowing of issues and the settlement of cases. Their effective operation, however, requires a succinct and clear statement of the request, and an answer which is not evasive.

Par. (a) is derived essentially from the first paragraph of FRCP 36(a), except that the last sentence of Par. (a) has been added in order to correlate this provision with the scope of the discovery permitted by Rule 70(b).

See also Note to Rule 70(b).

(b) The Request. The request may, without leave of Court, be served by any party to a pending case. Each matter of which an admission is requested shall be separately set forth. Copies of documents shall be served with the request unless they have been or are otherwise furnished or made available for inspection and copying. The party making the request shall serve a copy thereof on the other party, and shall file the original with proof of service with the Court.

Note: Par. (b) is derived from the first paragraph, and the first sentence of the second paragraph, of FRCP 36(a).

(c) Response to Request. Each matter is deemed admitted unless, within 30 days after service of the request or within such shorter or longer time as the Court may allow, the party to whom the request is directed serves upon the requesting party (i) a written answer specifically admitting or denying the matter involved in whole or in part, or asserting that it cannot be truthfully admitted or denied and setting forth in detail the reasons why this is so, or (ii) an objection, stating in detail the reasons therefor. The response shall be signed by the party or his counsel, and the original thereof, with proof of service on the other party, shall be filed with the Court. A denial shall fairly meet the substance of the requested admission; and, when good faith requires that a party qualify his answer or deny only a part of a matter, he shall specify so much of it as is true and deny or qualify the remainder. An answering party may not give lack of information or knowledge as a reason for failure to admit or deny unless he states that he has made reasonable inquiry and that the information known or readily obtainable by him is insufficient to enable him to admit or deny. A party who considers that a matter, of which an admission has been requested, presents a genuine issue for trial may not, on that ground alone, object to the request; he may, subject to the provisions of paragraph (f) of this Rule, deny the matter or set forth reasons why he cannot admit or deny it. An objection on the ground of relevance may be noted by any party but is not to be regarded as just cause for refusal to admit or deny.

Note: Par. (c) is derived from the second paragraph of FRCP 36(a), except that the period for response has been changed.

The request for an admission is served by one party on another party, and the response likewise is served by the parties on each other. Here, as in the case of interrogatories, the burden is on the requesting party to obtain a sufficient response, as provided in Par. (d).

(d) Motion to Review. The party who has requested the admissions may move to determine the sufficiency of the answers or objections. Unless the Court determines that an objection is justified, it shall order that an answer be served. If the Court determines that an answer does not comply with the requirements of this Rule, it may order either that the matter is admitted or that an amended answer be served. In lieu of any such order, the Court may determine that final disposition of the request shall be made at some later time which may be more appropriate for disposing of the question involved.

Note: Par. (d) is derived from the third paragraph of FRCP 36(a). The provision in FRCP 36(a), for the award of the expenses involved in such a motion, has not been adopted, since a broad sanctions provision is adopted in Par. (f).

(e) Effect of Admission. Any matter admitted under this Rule is conclusively established unless the Court on motion permits withdrawal or modification of the admission. Subject to any other orders made in the case by the Court, withdrawal or modification may be permitted when the presentation of the merits of the case will be subserved thereby, and the party who obtained the admission fails to satisfy the Court that the withdrawal or modification will prejudice him in prosecuting his case or defense on the merits. Any admission made by a party under this Rule is for the purpose of the pending action only and is not an admission by him for any other purpose, nor may it be used against him in any other proceeding.

Note: Par. (e) is derived from FRCP 36(b).

(f) Sanctions. If any party unjustifiably fails to admit the genuineness of any document or the truth of any matter as requested in accordance with this Rule, the party requesting the admission may apply to the Court for an order imposing such sanction on the other party or his counsel as the Court may find appropriate in the circumstances, including but not limited to the sanctions provided in Title X. The failure to admit may be found unjustifiable unless the Court finds that (1) the request was held objectionable pursuant to this Rule, or (2) the admission sought was of no substantial importance, or (3) the party failing to admit had reasonable ground to doubt the truth of the matter or the genuineness of the document in respect of which the admission was sought, or (4) there was other good reason for failure to admit.

Note: The sanctions provision in Par. (f) is a new provision. Its intention is to apprise the parties of the broad discretion in the Court to enforce the requirements of this Rule. The remainder of Par. (f), concerned with justification, is derived from FRCP 37(c).

With respect to the award of expenses against the Commissioner, cf. FRCP 37(f).

(g) Other Applicable Rules. For Rules concerned with frequency and timing of requests for admissions in relation to other procedures, supplementation of answers, effect of evasive or incomplete answers or responses, protective orders, and sanctions and enforcements, see Title X.

RULE 91. Stipulations for Trial.—(a) Stipulations Required. (1) General. The parties are required to stipulate, to the fullest extent to which complete or qualified agreement can or fairly should be reached, all matters not privileged which are relevant to the pending case, regardless of whether such matters involve fact or opinion or the application of law to fact. Included in matters required to be stipulated are all facts, all documents and papers or contents or aspects thereof, and all evidence which fairly should not be in dispute. Where the truth or authenticity of facts or evidence claimed to be relevant by one party is not disputed, an objection on the ground of materiality or relevance may be noted by any other party but is not to be regarded as just cause for refusal to stipulate. The requirement of stipulation applies under this Rule without regard to where the burden of proof may lie with respect to the matters involved. Documents or papers or other exhibits annexed to or filed with the stipulation shall be considered to be part of the stipulation.

(2) **Stipulations To Be Comprehensive.** The fact that any matter may have been obtained through discovery or requests for admission or through any other authorized procedure is not ground for omitting such matter from the stipulation. Such other procedures should be regarded as aids to stipulation, and matter obtained through them which is within the scope of paragraph (1), must be set forth comprehensively in the stipulation, in logical order in the context of all other provisions of the stipulation.

Note: The stipulation process, under present T.C. Rule 31(b), has been a mainstay of practice in the Tax Court. The intention of this Rule is to strengthen and clarify that process, and to continue its central function as an instrument for the more expeditious trial of cases as well as for purposes of settlement.

A comparable rule is not contained in the Federal Rules. However, the stipulation process, while not given the prominence and emphasis it has in Tax Court practice, nevertheless is woven through other procedures such as the pretrial conference.

Requests to admit, as provided in Rule 90, and the stipulation procedure in this Rule, may overlap to some extent. The stipulation procedure is more comprehensive, supported by affirmative action of the Court, and mandatory in all cases. The request for admissions is elective, dependent on the action of a requesting party, and is relatively rigid. The stipulation process is more flexible, based on conference and negotiation between parties, adaptable to statements on matters in varying degrees of dispute, susceptible of defining and narrowing areas of dispute, and offering an active medium for settlement. The request for admissions, typically used before the stipulation stage occurs, should reinforce the stipulation process.

Par. (a) is the counterpart of present Rule 31(b)(1) and (2), but has been recast and enlarged beyond the terms of the present provisions. Par. (a) is drafted in the broadest terms, and is not confined to stipulation of "facts" or "evidence". Par. (a) also makes it clear that certain commonly asserted contentions, for refusing to stipulate, are not proper grounds under the Rule. One of these, based on materiality or relevance, is adapted from the second paragraph of present Rule 31(b)(5). The intention is to give the stipulation process very broad scope, to encompass any matter with a bearing on the disposition of an issue in the case.

See also Note to Rule 70(b).

(b) **Form.** Stipulations required under this Rule shall be in writing, signed by the parties thereto or by their counsel, and shall observe the requirements of Rule 23 as to form and style of papers, except that the stipulation shall be filed with the Court in duplicate and only one set of exhibits shall be required. Documents or other papers, which are the subject of stipulation in any respect and which the parties intend to place before the Court, shall be annexed to or filed with the stipulation. The stipulation shall be clear and concise. Separate items shall be stated in separate paragraphs, and shall be appropriately lettered or numbered. Exhibits attached to a stipulation shall be numbered serially, i.e., 1, 2, 3, etc., if offered by the petitioner; shall be lettered serially i.e., A, B, C, etc., if offered by the respondent; and shall be marked serially, i.e., 1-A, 2-B, 3-C, etc., if offered as joint exhibits.

Note: Par. (b) is derived in part from present T.C. Rule 31(b)(3) and (d). No change is made here in present practice.

(c) **Filing.** Executed stipulations prepared pursuant to this Rule, and related exhibits, shall be filed by the parties at or before commencement of the trial of the case, unless the Court in the particular case shall otherwise specify. A stipulation when filed need not be offered formally to be considered in evidence.

Note: Par. (c) is the same in substance as the first sentence in present T.C. Rule 31(b)(3).

(d) **Objections.** Any objection to all or any part of a stipulation should be noted in the stipulation, but the Court will consider any objection to a stipulated matter made at the commencemnt of the trial or for good cause shown made during the trial.

Note: Par. (d) is the same in substance as present T.C. Rule 31(b)(4), except that it refines the time at which an objection may be heard even though not asserted in the stipulation.

(e) **Binding Effect.** A stipulation shall be treated, to the extent of its terms, as a conclusive admission by the parties to the stipulation, unless otherwise permitted by the Court or agreed upon by those parties. The Court will not permit a party to a stipulation to qualify, change, or contradict a stipulation in whole or in part, except that it may do so where justice requires. A stipulation and the admissions therein shall be binding and have effect only in the pending case and not for any other purpose, and cannot be used against any of the parties thereto in any other case or proceeding.

Note: Par. (e) is derived in part from present T.C. Rule 31(b)(6), and in part is adapted from FRCP 36(b).

(f) Noncompliance by a Party.—(1) Motion to Compel Stipulation. If, at the date of issuance of trial notice in a case, a party has refused or failed to confer with his adversary with respect to entering into a stipulation in accordance with this Rule, or he has refused or failed to make such a stipulation of any matter within the terms of this Rule, the party proposing to stipulate may, at a time not earlier than 75 days and not later than 50 days prior to the date set for call of the case from a trial calendar, file a motion with the Court for an order directing the delinquent party to show cause why the matters covered in the motion should not be deemed admitted for the purposes of the case. The motion shall (i) show with particularity and by separately numbered paragraphs each matter which is claimed for stipulation; (ii) set forth in express language the specific stipulation which the moving party proposes with respect to each such matter and annex thereto or make available to the Court and the other parties each document or other paper as to which the moving party desires a stipulation; (iii) set forth the sources, reasons, and basis for claiming, with respect to each such matter, that it should be stipulated; (iv) show that opposing counsel or the other parties have had reasonable access to those sources or basis for stipulation and have been informed of the reasons for stipulation; and (v) show proof of service of a copy of the motion on opposing counsel or the other parties.

(2) Procedure. Upon the filing of such a motion, an order to show cause as moved shall be issued forthwith, unless the Court shall direct otherwise. The order to show cause will be served by the Clerk of the Court, with a copy thereof sent to the moving party. Within 20 days of the service of the order to show cause, the party to whom the order is directed shall file a response with the Court, with proof of service of a copy thereof on opposing counsel or the other parties ,showing why the matters set forth in the motion papers should not be deemed admitted for purposes of the pending case. The response shall list each matter involved on which there is no dispute, referring specifically to the numbered paragraphs in the motion to which the admissions relate. Where a matter is disputed only in part, the response shall show the part admitted and the part disputed. Where the responding party is willing to stipulate in whole or in part with respect to any matter in the motion by varying or qualifying a matter in the proposed stipulation, the response shall set forth the variance or qualification and the admission which the responding party is willing to make. Where the response claims that there is a dispute as to any matter in part or in whole, or where the response presents a variance or qualification with respect to any matter in the motion, the response shall show the sources, reasons and basis on which the responding party relies for that purpose. The Court, where it is found appropriate, may set the order to show cause for a hearing or conference at such time as the Court shall determine.

(3) Failure of Response. If no response is filed within the period specified with respect to any matter or portion thereof, or if the response is evasive or not fairly directed to the proposed stipulation or portion thereof, that matter or portion thereof will be deemed stipulated for purposes of the pending case, and an order will be entered accordingly.

(4) Matters Considered. Opposing claims of evidence will not be weighed under this Rule unless such evidence is patently incredible. Nor will a genuinely controverted or doubtful issue of fact be determined in advance of trial. The Court will determine whether a genuine dispute exists, or whether in the interests of justice a matter ought not be deemed stipulated.

Note: Par. (f) is the counterpart of present T.C. Rule 31(b)(5), and is the enforcement section of the Rule. It uses the technique of a show cause order to compel observance of the stipulation process. Failure to respond, or an insufficient response, results in the Court's concluding that the assertions of the moving party are to be treated as stipulated for the particular case.

Par. (f)(1) is derived from the first paragraph of present Rule 31(b)(5). However, it sets up more extensive requirements for the contents of the motion for the show cause order, and it also changes the time for the motion.

Par. (f)(2) is the counterpart of the second paragraph of present Rule 31(b)(5), but treats in greater detail the requirements for the response to the show cause order. The time, within which to respond, is also changed.

Under this procedure, the initial motion and the response are served by the parties. But the show cause order is served by the Clerk. The show cause order is issued ex parte.

The provision for a hearing, after a response to the show cause order, is left in more flexible form in Par. (f)(2) than in the last paragraph of present Rule 31(b)(5).

Par. (f)(3) is a new provision, not contained in present Rule 31(b)(5). It is intended to articulate present practice.

Par. (f)(4) is also a new provision, not contained in present Rule 31(b)(5). It furnishes some standards for resolving objections or disagreements under this Rule.

TITLE X.—GENERAL PROVISIONS GOVERNING DISCOVERY, DEPOSITIONS, AND REQUESTS FOR ADMISSION.

RULE 100. Applicability. The Rules in this Title apply according to their terms to written interrogatories (Rule 71), production of documents or things (Rule 72), examination by transferees (Rule 73), depositions (Rules 81, 82, 83, and 84), and requests for admissions (Rule 90). Such procedures may be used in anticipaton of the stipulation of facts required by Rule 91, but the existence of such procedures or their use does not excuse failure to comply with the requirements of that Rule. See Rule 91(a)(2).

Note: This Rule indicates the procedures to which the succeeding Rules apply, and emphasizes the continuing obligation to observe the stipulation requirements of Rule 91. Present T.C. Rules do not contain such a provision.

RULE 101. Sequence, Timing and Frequency. Unless the Court orders otherwise for the convenience of the parties and wtnesses and in the interests of justice, and subject to the provisions of the Rules herein which apply more specifically, the procedures set forth in Rule 100 may be used in any sequence, and the fact that a party is engaged in any such method or procedure shall not operate to delay the use of any such method or procedure by any other party. However, none of these methods or procedures shall be used in a manner or at a time which shall delay or impede the progress of the case toward trial status or the trial of the case on the date for which it is noticed, unless in the interests of justice the Court shall order otherwise. Unless the Court orders otherwise under Rule 103, the frequency of use of these methods or procedures is not limited.

Note: This Rule is derived from FRCP 26(d) and the last sentence of FRCP 26(a). There is no counterpart in present T.C. Rules.

RULE 102. Supplementation of Responses. A party who has responded to a request for discovery (under Rules 71, 72, or 73 or to a request for admission (under Rule 90) in a manner which was complete when made, is under no duty to supplement his response to include information thereafter acquired, except as follows:

(1) A party is under a duty seasonably to supplement his response with respect to any matter directly addressed to (A) the identity and location of persons having knowledge of discoverable matters, and (B) the identity of each person expected to be called as an expert witness at trial, the subject matter on which he is expected to testify, and the substance of his testimony.

(2) A party is under a duty seasonably to amend a prior response if he obtains information upon the basis of which he knows that (A) the response was incorrect when made, or (B) the response, though correct when made, is no longer true and the circumstances are such that a failure to amend the response is in substance a knowing concealment.

(3) A duty to supplement responses may be imposed by order of the Court, agreement of the parties, or at any time prior to trial through new requests for supplementation of prior responses.

Note: This Rule is derived from FRCP 26(e). There is no counterpart in present T.C. Rules.

RULE 103. Protective Orders.—(a) Authorized Orders. Upon motion by a party or any other affected person, and for good cause shown, the Court may make any order which justice requires to protect a party or other person from annoyance, embarrassment, oppression, or undue burden or expense, including but not limited to one or more of the following:

(1) That the particular method or procedure not be used.

(2) That the method or procedure be used only on specified terms and conditions, including a designation of the time or place.

(3) That a method or procedure be used other than the one selected by the party.

(4) That certain matters not be inquired into, or that the method be limited to certain matters or to any other extent.

(5) That the method or procedure be conducted with no one present except persons designated by the Court.

(6) That a deposition or other written materials, after being sealed, be opened only by order of the Court.

(7) That a trade secret or other information not be disclosed or be disclosed only in a designated way.

(8) That the parties simultaneously file specified documents or information enclosed in sealed envelopes to be opened as directed by the Court.

(9) That expense involved in a method or procedure be borne in a particular manner or by specified person or persons.

(10) That documents or records be impounded by the Court to insure their availability for purpose of review by the parties prior to trial and use at the trial.

(b) Denials. If a motion for a protective order is denied in whole or in part, the Court may, on such terms or conditions it deems just, order any party or person to comply or to respond in accordance with the procedure involved.

Note: This Rule is derived from FRCP 26(c). There is no counterpart in present T.C. Rules. It is an essential adjunct to the methods or procedures to which it applies.

RULE 104. Enforcement Action and Sanctions.—(a) Failure to Attend Deposition or to Answer Interrogatories or Respond to Request for Inspection or Production. If a party or an officer, director or managing agent of a party or a person designated in accordance with Rule 81(c) to testify on behalf of a party fails (1) to appear before the officer who is to take his deposition pursuant to Rules 81, 82, 83 or 84, or (2) to serve answers or objections to interrogatories submitted under Rue 71, after proper service thereof, or (3) to serve a written response to a request for production or inspection submitted under Rules 72 or 73 after proper service of the request, the Court on motion may make such orders in regard to the failure as are just, and among others it may take any action authorized under paragraphs (b) or (c) of this Rule. If any person, after being served with a subpoena or having waived such service, willfully fails to appear before the officer who is to take his deposition or refuses to be sworn, or if any person willfully fails to obey an order requiring him to answer designated interrogatories or questions, such failure may be considered contempt of court. The failure to act described in this paragraph (a) may not be excused on the ground that the deposition sought, or the interrogatory submitted, or the production or inspection sought, is objectionable, unless the party failing to act has theretofore raised the objection, or has applied for a protective order under Rule 103, with respect thereto at the proper time and in the proper manner, and the Court has either sustained or granted or not yet ruled on the objection or the application for the order.

Note: Par. (a) is adapted from FRCP 37(d). There is no counterpart in present T.C. Rules.

(b) Failure to Answer. If a person fails to answer a queston or interrogatory propounded or submitted in accordance with Rules 71, 81, 82, 83 or 84, or fails to respond to a request to produce or inspect or fails to produce or permit the inspection in accordance with Rules 72 or 73, or fails to make a designation in accordance with Rule 81(c), the aggrieved party may move the Court for an order compelling an answer, response, or compliance with the request, as the case may be. When taking a deposition on oral examination, the examination may be completed on other matters or the examination adjourned, as the proponent of the question may prefer, before he applies for such order.

Note: Par. (b) is adapted from FRCP 37(a)(2). There is no counterpart in present T.C. Rules.

(c) Sanctions. If a party or an officer, director, or managing agent of a party or a person designated in accordance with Rule 81(c) fails to obey an order made by the Court with respect to the provisions of Rules 71, 72, 73, 81, 82, 83, 84, or 90, the Court may make such orders as to the failure as are just, and among others the following:

(1) An order that the matters regarding which the order was made or any other designated facts shall be taken to be established for the purposes of the case in accordance with the claim of the party obtaining the order.

(2) An order refusing to allow the disobedient party to support or oppose designated claims or defenses, or prohibiting him from introducing designated matters in evidence.

(3) An order striking out pleadings or parts thereof, or staying further proceedings until the order is obeyed, or dismissing the case or any part thereof, or rendering a judgment by default against the disobedient party.

(4) In lieu of any of the foregoing orders or in addition thereto, an order treating as a contempt of the Court the failure to obey any such order.

Note: Par. (c) is derived from FRCP 37(b)(2). The references to physical or mental examination are omitted, see FRCP 37(b)(2)(D) and (E), since a rule on that subject has not been adopted. With respect to the award of expenses, see the comment under Rule 90(f).

There is no counterpart in present T.C. Rules.

(d) Evasive or Incomplete Answer or Response. For purposes of this Rule and Rules 71, 72, 73, 81, 82, 83, 84, and 90, an evasive or incomplete answer or response is to be treated as a failure to answer or respond.

Note: Par. (d) is derived from FRCP 37(a)(3). There is no counterpart in present T.C. Rules.

TITLE XI. PRETRIAL CONFERENCES.

RULE 110. Pretrial Conferences.—(a) General. In appropriate cases, the Court will undertake to confer with the parties in pretrial conferences with a view to narrowing issues, stipulating facts, simplifying the presentation of evidence, or otherwise assisting in the preparation for trial or possible disposition of the case in whole or in part without trial.

Note: Par. (a) is the same as present T.C. Rule 28(a).

(b) Cases Calendared. Either party in a case listed on any trial calendar may request of the Court, or the Court on its own motion may order, a pretrial conference. The Court may, in its discretion, set the case for a pretrial conference during the trial session. If sufficient reason appears therefor, a pretrial conference will be scheduled prior to the call of the calendar at such time and place as may be practicable and appropriate.

Note: Par. (b), while more complete, is derived from present T.C. Rule 28(b).

(c) Cases Not Calendared. If a case is not listed on a trial calendar, the Chief Judge, in his discretion, upon motion of either party or upon his own motion, may list such case for a pretrial conference upon a calendar in the place designated for trial, or may assign the case for a pretrial conference either in Washington, D. C., or in any other convenient place.

Note: Par. (c) is the same in substance as present T.C. Rule 28(c).

(d) Conditions. A request or motion for a pretrial conference shall include a statement of the reasons therefor. Pretrial conferences will in no circumstances be held as a substitute for the conferences required between the parties in order to comply with the provisions of Rule 91, but a pretrial conference, for the purpose of assisting the parties in entering into the stipulations called for by Rule 91, will be held by the Court where the party requesting such pretrial conference has in good faith attempted without success to obtain such stipulation from his adversary. Nor will any pretrial conference be held where the Court is satisfied that the request therefor is frivolous or is made for purposes of delay.

Note: Par. (d) is the same in substance as present T.C. Rule 28(d).

(e) **Order.** The Court may, in its discretion, issue appropriate pretrial orders.

Note: Par. (e) is substantially the same as present T.C. Rule 28(e).

TITLE XII.—DECISION WITHOUT TRIAL.

RULE 120. Judgment On The Pleadings.—(a) General. After the pleadings are closed but within such time as not to delay the trial, any party may move for judgment on the pleadings. The motion shall be filed and served in accordance with the requirements otherwise applicable. See Rules 50 and 54. Such motion shall be disposed of before trial unless the Court determines otherwise.

Note: The motion for judgment on the pleadings, as adopted in this Rule, is based on the same procedure under the Federal Rules. Par. (a) is derived, almost verbatim, from portions of FRCP 12(c) and (d). There is no comparable provision in the present T.C. Rules.

This motion is not to be made until the pleadings are closed. It is appropriate only where the pleadings do not raise a genuine issue of material fact, but rather involve only issues of law. The motion is to be granted only if, on the admitted facts, the moving party is entitled to a decision.

(b) **Matters Outside Pleadings.** If, on a motion for judgment on the pleadings, matters outside the pleadings are presented to and not excluded by the Court, the motion shall be treated as one for summary judgment and shall be disposed of as provided in Rule 121, and all parties shall be given reasonable opportunity to present all material made pertinent to such a motion by Rule 121.

Note: Par. (b) is derived, almost verbatim, from FRCP 12(c). There is no comparable provision in the present T.C. Rules.

RULE 121. Summary Judgment.—(a) General. Either party may move, with or without supporting affidavits, for a summary adjudication in his favor upon all or any part of the legal issues in controversy. Such motion may be made at any time commencing 30 days after the pleadings are closed but within such time as not to delay the trial.

Note: This Rule provides for a summary judgment procedure of the type employed under the Federal Rules. Par. (a) is adapted from FRCP 56(a) and (b). There are no counterpart provisions in the present T.C. Rules.

A summary judgment, like a judgment on the pleadings under Rule 120, is available only if there is no genuine issue of a material fact. However, the summary judgment procedure is available even though there is a dispute as to fact under the pleadings, but, through materials outside the pleadings, it is shown that there is no geneuine issue of material fact. Such outside materials may consist of affidavits, interrogatories, admissions, documents, or other materials which demonstrate the absence of such an issue of fact despite the pleadings.

(b) **Motion and Proceedings Thereon.** The motion shall be filed and served in accordance with the requirements otherwise applicable. See Rules 50 and 54. Any opposing written response, with or without supporting affidavits, shall be filed not later than 10 days prior to the date set for hearing. A decision shall thereafter be rendered if the pleadings, answers to interrogatories, depositions, admissions, and any other acceptable materials, together with the affidavits, if any, show that there is no genuine issue as to any material fact and that a decision may be rendered as a matter of law. A partial summery adjudication may be made which does not dispose of all the issues in the case.

Note: Par. (b) is derived from FRCP 56(c). There is no counterpart provision in the present T.C. Rules.

(c) **Case Not Fully Adjudicated on Motion.** If, on motion under this Rule, decision is not rendered upon the whole case or for all the relief asked and a trial is necessary, the Court may ascertain, by examining the pleadings and the evidence before it and by interrogating counsel, what material facts exist without substantial controversy and what material facts are actually and in good faith controverted. It may thereupon make an order specifying the facts that appear to be without substantial controversy, including the extent to which the relief sought is not in controversy, and directing such further proceedings in the case as are just. Upon the trial of the case, the facts so specified shall be deemed established, and the trial shall be conducted accordingly.

Note: Par. (c) is derived from FRCP 56(d). There is no counterpart provision in the present T.C. Rules.

(d) Form of Affidavits; Further Testimony; Defense Required. Supporting and opposing affidavits shall be made on personal knowledge, shall set forth such facts as would be admissible in evidence, and shall show affirmatively that the affiant is competent to testify to the matters stated therein. Sworn or certified copies of all papers or parts thereof referred to in an affidavit shall be attached thereto or filed therewith. The Court may permit affidavits to be supplemented or opposed by answers to interrogatories, depositions, further affidavits, or other acceptable materials, to the extent that other applicable conditions in these Rules are satisfied for utilizing such procedures. When a motion for summary judgment is made and supported as provided in this Rule, an adverse party may not rest upon the mere allegations or denials of his pleading, but his response, by affidavits or as otherwise provided in this Rule, must set forth specific facts showing that there is a genuine issue for trial. If he does not so respond, a decision, if appropriate, may be entered against him.

Note: Par. (d) is derived, almost verbatim, from FRCP 56(e). There is no counterpart provision in the present Tax Court Rules.

(e) When Affidavits Are Unavailable. Should it appear from the affidavits of a party opposing the motion that he cannot for reasons stated present by affidavit facts essential to justify his opposition, the Court may deny the motion or may order a continuance to permit affidavits to be obtained or other steps to be taken or may make such other order as is just. Where it appears from the affidavits of a party opposing the motion that his only legally available method of controverting the facts set forth in the supporting affidavits of the moving party is through cross-examination of such affiants or the testimony of third parties from whom affidavits cannot be secured, such a showing may be deemed sufficient to establish that the facts set forth in such supporting affidavits are genuinely disputed.

Note: The first sentence of Par. (e) is derived, almost verbatim, from FRCP 56(f). The second sentence is new. Its purpose is self-explanatory. There is no counterpart provision in the present T.C. Rules.

(f) Affidavits Made In Bad Faith. Should it appear to the satisfaction of the Court at any time that any of the affidavits presented pursuant to this Rule are presented in bad faith or for the purpose of delay, the Court may order the party employing them to pay to the other party the amount of the reasonable expenses which the filing of the affidavits caused him to incur, including reasonable counsel's fees, and any offending party or counsel may be adjudged guilty of contempt or otherwise disciplined by the Court.

Note: Par. (f) is derived from FRCP 56(g). There is no counterpart provision in the present T.C. Rules. Par. (f) authorizes, as a consequence of the conduct described here, disciplinary and other action against a party or his counsel.

RULE 122. Submission Without Trial.—(a) General. Any case not requiring a trial for the submission of evidence (as, for example, where sufficient facts have been admitted, stipulated, established by deposition, or included in the record in some other way), may be submitted at any time by notice of the parties filed with the Court. The parties need not wait for the case to be calendared for trial and need not appear in Court. The Chief Judge will assign such a case to a Division, which will fix a time for filing briefs or for oral argument.

Note: This Rule continues the procedure, in present T.C. Rule 30, for submission of a case where the normal trial process is unnecessary because the parties have agreed upon a complete statement of the facts or evidence. There may be genuine issues of fact to be decided, but their determination is to be made on the record thus presented.

Par. (a) is substantially the same as present T.C. Rule 30(a).

(b) Burden of Proof. The fact of submission of a case, under paragraph (a) of this Rule, does not alter the burden of proof, or the requirements otherwise applicable with respect to adducing proof, or the effect of failure of proof.

Note: Par. (b) is adapted from present T.C. Rule 31(g).

RULE 123. Default and Dismissal.—(a) Default. When any party has failed to plead or otherwise proceed as provided by these Rules or as required by the Court, he may be held in default by the Court either on motion of another party or on the initiative of the Court. Thereafter, the Court may enter a decision against the defaulting party, upon such terms and conditions as the Court may deem proper, or may impose such sanctions (see, e.g., Rule 104) as the Court may appropriate. The Court may, in its discretion, conduct hearings to ascertain whether a default has been committed, to determine the decision to be entered or the sanctions to be imposed, or to ascertain the truth of any matter.

Note: Par. (a) is a new rule, without counterpart in the present T.C. Rules. Cf. FRCP 55(a) and (b).

(b) Dismissal. For failure of a petitioner properly to prosecute or to comply with these Rules or any order of the Court or for other cause which the Court deems sufficient, the Court may dismiss a case at any time and enter a decision against the petitioner. The Court may, for similar reasons, decide against any party any issue as to which he has the burden or proof; and such decision shall be treated as a dismissal for purposes of paragraphs (c) and (d) of this Rule.

Note: Par. (b) is likewise a new rule, without counterpart in the present T.C. Rules. Cf. FRCP 41. As to a motion to dismiss, see Rule 53.

(c) Setting Aside Default or Dismissal. For reasons deemed sufficient by the Court and upon motion expeditiously made, the Court may set aside a default or dismissal or the decision rendered thereon.

Note: Par. (c) is adapted from FRCP 55(c). There is no counterpart in the present T.C. Rules.

(d) Effect of Decision on Default or Dismissal. A decision rendered upon a default or in consequence of a dismissal, other than a dismissal for lack of jurisdiction, shall operate as an adjudication on the merits.

Note: Par. (d) is adapted from the last sentence of FRCP 41(b). There is no counterpart in present T.C. Rules. Cf. Code Section 7459(d).

TITLE XIII. CALENDARS AND CONTINUANCES.

RULE 130. Motions and Other Matters.—(a) Calendars. If a hearing is to be held on a motion or other matter, apart from a trial on the merits, such hearing ordinarily will be held at Washington, D.C., on a motion calendar called on Wednesday throughout the year, unless the Court, on its own motion or on the motion of a party, shall direct otherwise. As to hearings at other places, see Rule 50(b)(2). The parties will be given notice of the place and time of hearing.

(b) Failure to Attend. The Court may hear a matter ex parte where a party fails to appear at such a hearing. With respect to attendance at such hearings, see Rule 50(c).

Note: Par. (a) is derived from present T.C. Rule 27(a)(1).
Par. (b) is derived from present T.C. Rule 27(a)(2).

RULE 131. Report Calendars. On a calendar specifically set for the purpose or on a trial calendar, and after notice to the parties of the time and place, any case at issue may be listed and called, first, for report as to whether the case is to be tried or otherwise disposed of, and if the latter, for report as to its status; and, secondly, if it is to be tried, for report on the status of preparations for trial, with particular reference to the stipulation requirements of Rule 91. With respect to any case on such a calendar, the Court may consider other matters and take such action as it deems appropriate.

Note: This Rule is derived from present Rule 27(b). The last sentence was added to indicate that any appropriate steps may be taken by the Court in response to the report rendered.

RULE 132. Trial Calendars.—(a) General. Each case, when at issue, will be placed upon a calendar for trial at the place designated in accordance with Rule 140. Not less than 90 days in advance unless otherwise authorized by the Chief Judge, the Clerk shall notify the parties of the place and time for which the calendar is set.

Note: Par. (a) is substantially the same as present T.C. Rule 27(c)(1).

(b) Calendar Call. Each case appearing on a trial calendar will be called at the time and place scheduled. At the call, counsel or the parties shall indicate their estimate of the time required for trial. The cases for trial will thereupon be tried in due course, but not necessarily in the order listed.

Note: Par. (b) is derived from present T.C. Rule 27(c)(2).

RULE 133. Special or Other Calendars. Special or other calendars may be scheduled by the Court, upon motion or at its own initiative, for any purpose which the Court may deem appropriate. The parties involved shall be notified of the place and time of such calendars.

Note: This a new rule, not in the present T.C. Rules. It reflects existing practice.

RULE 134. Continuances. A case or matter scheduled on a calendar may be continued by the Court upon motion or at its own initiative. Court action, on cases or matters set for hearing or trial or other consideration, will not be delayed by a motion for continuance unless it is timely, sets forth good and sufficient cause, and complies with all applicable Rules. Conflicting engagements of counsel or employment of new counsel will not be regarded as ground for continuance unless the motion for continuance, in addition to otherwise satisfying this Rule, is filed promptly after notice is given of the hearing or trial or other scheduled matter, or unless extenuating circumstances for later filing are shown which the Court deems adequate. A motion for continuance, filed 30 days or less prior to the date to which it is directed, may be set for hearing on that date. As to extensions of time, see Rule 25(c).

Note: This Rule is derived from present T.C. Rule 27(d)(1) and (2).

TITLE XIV. TRIALS.

RULE 140. Place of Trial.—(a) Requests for Place of Trial. The petitioner, at the time of filing the petition, shall file a request showing the place at which he would prefer the trial to be held. If the petitioner has not filed such request, the respondent, at the time he files his answer, shall file a request showing the place of trial preferred by him. For a list of places at which the Court has held trial sessions, see Appendix IV, p. 68.

Note: Par. (a) is substantially the same as present T.C. Rule 26(a).

(b) Form. Such request shall be filed separately from the petition or answer, shall be subject to the requirements of form applicable to motions, see Rule 50(a), and shall consist of an original and two copies. See Form 4, Appendix I, p. 56.

Note: Par. (b) is derived from present T.C. Rule 26(b).

(c) Designation of Place of Trial. The Court will designate a place of trial which involves as little inconvenience and expense to taxpayers as is practicable. The parties will be notified of the place at which the trial will be held.

Note: Par. (c) is the same in substance as present T.C. Rule 26(c).

(d) Motion to Change Place of Trial. If either party desires a change in the designation of the place of trial, he shall file a motion to that effect, stating fully his reasons therefor. Such motions, made after the notice of the time of trial has been issued, will not be deemed to have been timely filed.

Note: Par. (d) is derived from present T.C. Rule 26(d).

RULE 141. Consolidation; Separate Trials.—(a) Consolidation. When cases involving a common question of law or fact are pending before the Court, it may order a joint hearing or trial of any or all the matters in issue; it may order all the cases consolidated; and it may make such orders concerning proceedings therein as may tend to avoid unnecessary costs or delay or duplication. Similar action may be taken where cases involve different tax liabilities of the same parties, notwithstanding the absence of a common issue. As to joinder of parties, see Rule 61(a).

Note: Par. (a) is derived from FRCP 42(a). It conforms to present Tax Court practice.

(b) Separate Trials: The Court, in furtherance of convenience or to avoid prejudice, or when separate trials will be conducive to expedition or economy, may order a separate trial of any one or more claims or defenses or issues, or of the tax liability of any party or parties. The Court may enter appropriate orders or decisions with respect to any such claims, defenses, issues, or parties that are tried separately. As to severance of parties or claims, see Rule 61(b).

Note: Par. (b) is derived from FRCP 42(b). It conforms to present Tax Court practice.

RULE 142. Burden of Proof.—(a) General. The burden of proof shall be upon the petitioner, except as otherwise provided by statute or determined by the Court; and except that, in respect of any new matter, increases in deficiency, and affirmative defenses, pleaded in his answer, it shall be upon the respondent. As to affirmative defenses, see Rule 39.

Note: Par. (a) is derived from present T.C. Rule 32.

(b) Fraud. In any case involving the issue of fraud with intent to evade tax, the burden of proof in respect of that issue is on the respondent, and that burden of proof is to be carried by clear and convincing evidence. Code section 7454(a).

Note: Par. (b) is a new provision, not in the present T.C. Rules. It is based on Code section 7454(a).

(c) Foundation Managers. In any case involving the issue of the knowing conduct of a foundation manager as set forth in the provisions of Code sections 4941, 4944, or 4945, the burden of proof in respect of such issue is on the respondent, and such burden of proof is to be carried by clear and convincing evidence. Code section 7454(b).

Note: Par. (c) is a new provision, not in the present T.C. Rules. It is based on Code section 7454(b). Sen. Rep. No. 91-552, 91st Cong., 1st Sess., p. 32, stated that the Code intends, in section 7454(b), to impose "upon the Service the same burden of proof where such sanction is being considered as is required in cases of civil fraud—that is, proof by clear and convincing evidence."

(d) Transferee Liability. The burden of proof is on the respondent to show that a petitioner is liable as a transferee of property of a taxpayer, but not to show that the taxpayer was liable for the tax. Code section 6902(a).

Note: Par. (d) is a new provision, not in present T.C. Rules. It is based on Code section 6902(a).

(e) Accumulated Earnings Tax. Where the notice of deficiency is based in whole or in part on an allegation of accumulation of corporate earnings and profits beyond the reasonable needs of the business, the burden of proof with respect to such allegation is determined in accordance with Code section 534. If the petitioner has submitted to the respondent a statement which is claimed to satisfy the requirements of Code section 534(c), the Court will ordinarily on timely motion filed after the case has been calendared for trial, rule prior to the trial on whether such statement is sufficient to shift the burden of proof to the respondent to the limited extent set forth in Code section 534(a)(2).

Note: Par. (e) is a new provision, not in the present T.C. Rules. It is based on Code section 534. See *The Shaw-Walker Company*, 39 T.C. 293 (1962); *Chatham Corp.*, 48 T.C. 145 (1967).

RULE 143. Evidence.—(a) General. Trials before the court will be conducted in accordance with the rules of evidence applicable in trials without a jury in the United States District Court for the District of Columbia. See Code Section 7453. To the extent applicable to such trials, those rules include the rules of evidence in the Federal Rules of Civil Procedure and any rules of evidence generally applicable in the Federal courts (including the United States District Court for the District of Columbia).

Note: The first sentence of Par. (a) is substantially the same as the first sentence of present T.C. Rule 31(a). The second sentence is a new provision, not in the present T.C. Rules. The reference in that sentence to the Federal Rules of Civil Procedure only embodies present practice. The remainder of the second sentence, although not thus restricted in its scope, at this time is mainly intended to call attention to the proposed Federal Rules of Evidence, prescribed by the Supreme Court in its order of November 20, 1972, pursuant to 18 U.S.C. §§ 3402, 3771 and 3772, and 28 U.S.C. §§ 2072 and 2075. However, the adoption of these proposed rules has been suspended by Congressional action, to permit legislative consideration of certain controversial changes incorporated in the proposed rules. See Public Law 93-12, 87 Stat. 9. The proposed rules appear in 56 F.R.D. 183.

(b) Ex Parte Statements. Ex parte affidavits, statements in briefs, and unadmitted allegations in pleadings, do not constitute evidence. As to allegations in pleadings not denied, see Rules 36(c), 37(c) and (d).

Note: Par. (b) is substantially the same as present T.C. Rule 31(f).

(c) Depositions. Testimony taken by deposition shall not be treated as evidence in a case until offered and received in evidence. Error in the transcript of a deposition may be corrected by agreement of the parties, or by the Court on proof it deems satisfactory to show an error exists and the correction to be made, subject to the requirements of Rules 81(h)(1) and 85(e). As to the use of a deposition, see Rule 81(i).

Note: The first sentence of Par. (c) is substantially the same as present T.C. Rule 31(c). The second sentence is a new provision, not in the present T.C. Rules.

(d) Documentary Evidence. (1) Copies. A *clearly legible* copy of any book, record, paper, or document may be offered directly in evidence in lieu of the original, where there is no objection, or where the original is available but admission of a copy is authorized by the Court; however, unless impractical, the Court may require the submission of the original. Where the original is admitted in evidence, a *clearly legible* copy may be substituted later for the original or such part thereof as may be material or relevant, upon leave granted in the discretion of the Court.

(2) Return of Exhibits. Exhibits may be disposed of as the Court deems advisable. A party desiring the return at his expense of any exhibit belonging to him, shall, after decision of the case by the Court has become final, make prompt written application to the Clerk, suggesting a practical manner of delivery.

Note: Par. (d)(1) is expanded from present T.C. Rule 31(e)(1). While a copy may be authorized in lieu of an original, the Court may nevertheless require submission of the original. The emphasis, with respect to all copies, is that they be *clearly legible.*

Par. (d)(2) is substantially the same as present T.C. Rule 31(e)(2).

(e) Interpreters. The Court may appoint an interpreter of its own selection and may fix his reasonable compensation, which compensation shall be paid by one or more of the parties or otherwise as the Court may direct.

Note: Par. (e) is without counterpart in the present T.C. Rules. Ordinarily, the parties will be expected to make their own arrangements in respect of obtaining and compensating their interpreters, without resort to Par. (e).

RULE 144. Exceptions Unnecessary. Formal exceptions to rulings or orders of the Court are unnecessary. It is sufficient that a party at the time the ruling or order of the Court is made or sought, makes known to the Court the action which he desires the Court to take or his objection to the action of the Court and his grounds therefor; and, if a party has no opportunity to object to a ruling or order at the time it is made, the absence of an objection does not thereafter prejudice him.

Note: This Rule is derived from FRCP 46, and reflects present Tax Court practice.

RULE 145. Exclusion of Proposed Witnesses.—(a) Exclusion. On its own motion or on motion of a party, the Court may exclude from the courtroom any or all persons, other than parties, whom the parties expect or intend to call as witnesses in the case. In connection with any such exclusion, the Court may issue to witnesses (actual or potential), counsel, and parties such instructions as it may deem appropriate in the circumstances. In the discretion of the Court, it may refuse to apply this paragraph to a person acting in an advisory capacity to counsel for either party. Undue delay in moving for such exclusion of a person may be treated by the Court as sufficient ground for denying the motion.

(b) Contempt. Among other measures which the Court may take in the circumstances, it may punish as for a contempt (i) any witness who remains within hearing of the proceedings after such exclusion has been directed, that fact being noted in the record; and (ii) any person (witness, counsel, or party) who willfully violates instructions issued by the Court with respect to such exclusion.

Note: This is a new Rule, without counterpart in the present T.C. Rules.

RULE 146. Determination of Foreign Law. A party who intends to raise an issue concerning the law of a foreign country shall give notice in his pleadings or other reasonable written notice. The Court, in determining foreign law, may consider any relevant material or source, including testimony, whether or not submitted by a party or otherwise admissible. The Court's determination shall be treated as a ruling on a question of law.

Note: This Rule is taken almost verbatim from FRCP 44.1. There is no similar provision in present T.C. Rules.

RULE 147. Subpoenas.—(a) Attendance of Witnesses; Form; Issuance. Every subpoena shall be issued under the seal of the Court, shall state the name of the Court and the caption of the case, and shall command each person to whom it is directed to attend and give testimony at a time and place therein specified. A subpoena, including a subpoena for the production of documentary evidence, signed and sealed but otherwise in blank, shall be issued to a party requesting it, who shall fill it in before service. Subpoenas may be obtained at the Office of the Clerk in Washington, D.C., or from a deputy clerk at a trial session. See Code Section 7456(a).

Note: Par. (a) is derived from FRCP 45(a). Counterpart provisions appear in present T.C. Rule 44(a) and (b).

(b) Production of Documentary Evidence. A subpoena may also command the person to whom it is directed to produce the books, papers, documents, or tangible things designated therein; but the Court, upon motion made promptly and in any event at or before the time specified in the subpoena for compliance therewith, may (1) quash or modify the subpoena if it is unreasonable and oppressive, or (2) condition denial of the motion upon the advancement by the person in whose behalf the subpoena is issued of the reasonable cost of producing the books, papers, documents, or tangible things.

Note: Par. (b) is substantially the same as FRCP 45(b). A counterpart provision appears in present T.C. Rule 44(c).

(c) Service. A subpoena may be served by a United States marshal, or by his deputy, or by any other person who is not a party and is not less than 18 years of age. Service of a subpoena upon a person named therein shall be made by delivering a copy thereof to such person and by tendering to him the fees for one day's attendance and the mileage allowed by law. When the subpoena is issued on behalf of the Commissioner, fees and mileage need not be tendered. See Rule 148 for fees and mileage payable. The person making service of a subpoena shall make his return thereon in accordance with the form appearing in the subpoena.

Note: Par. (c) is substantially the same as FRCP 45(c). A counterpart provision appears in present T.C. Rule 44(d).

(d) Subpoena for Taking Depositions.

(1) Issuance and Response. The order of the Court approving the taking of a deposition pursuant to Rule 81(b)(2), or the executed stipulation pursuant to Rule 81(d), constitutes authorization for issuance of subpoenas for the persons named or described therein. The subpoena may command the person to whom it is directed to produce and permit inspection and copying of designated books, papers, documents, or tangible things, which come within the scope of the order or stipulation pursuant to which the deposition is taken. Within 10 days after service of the subpoena or such earlier time designated therein for compliance, the person to whom the subpoena is directed may serve upon the party on whose behalf the subpoena has been issued written objections to compliance with the subpoena in any or all respects. Such objections should not include objections made, or which might have been made, to the application to take the deposition pursuant to Rule 81 (b)(2). If an objection is made, the party serving the subpoena shall not be entitled to compliance therewith to the extent of such objection, except as the Court may order otherwise upon application to it. Such application for an order may be made, with notice to the other party and to any other objecting persons, at any time before or during the taking of the deposition, subject to the time requirements of Rule 81(b)(2). As to availability of protective orders, see Rule 103; and, as to enforcement of such subpoenas, see Rule 104.

(2) Place of Examination. The place designated in the subpoena for examination of the deponent shall be the place specified in the order of the Court referred to in Rule 81(b)(2) or in the executed stipulation referred to in Rule 81(d). With respect to a deposition to be taken in a foreign country, see Rules 81(e)(2) and 84(a).

Note: Par. (d)(1) is a new provision, designed to tie in with the provisions in these Rules on depositions. Counterpart provisions appear in FRCP 45(d)(1).

Par. (d)(2) is a new provision, likewise cast to fit in with the deposition provisions. Present T.C. Rules have no counterpart provision.

(e) Contempt. Failure by any person without adequate excuse to obey a subpoena served upon him may be deemed a contempt of the Court.

Note: Par. (e) is substantially the same as FRCP 45(f). No counterpart provision appears in the present T.C. Rules.

RULE 148. Fees and Mileage.—(a) Amount. Any witness summoned to a hearing or trial, or whose deposition is taken, shall receive the same fees and mileage as witnesses in the United States District Courts. For such amounts, see Appendix III, p. 67.

Note: Par. (a) is substantially the same as present T.C. Rule 60(a).

(b) Tender. No witness, other than one for the Commissioner, shall be required to testify until he shall have been tendered the fees and mileage to which he is entitled according to law. With respect to witnesses for the Commissioner, see Code section 7457(b)(1).

Note: Par. (b) is substantially the same as the last paragraph in present T.C. Rule 60.

(c) Payment. The party at whose instance a witness appears shall be responsible for the payment of the fees and mileage to which that witness is entitled.

Note: Par. (c) is a new provision. A counterpart provision appears in present T.C. Rule 60(b).

RULE 149. Failure to Appear or to Adduce Evidence.—(a) Attendance at Trials. The unexcused absence of a party or his counsel when a case is called for trial will not be ground for delay. The case may be dismissed for failure properly to prosecute, or the trial may proceed and the case be regarded as submitted on the part of the absent party or parties.

Note: Par. (a) is substantially the same as present T.C. Rule 27(c)(3).

(b) Failure of Proof. Failure to produce evidence, in support of an issue of fact as to which a party has the burden of proof and which has not been conceded by his adversary, may be ground for dismissal or for determination of the affected issue against that party. Facts may be established by stipulation in accordance with Rule 91, but the mere filing of such stipulation does not relieve the party, upon whom rests the burden of proof, of the necessity of properly producing evidence in support of facts not adequately established by such stipulation. As to submission of a case without trial, see Rule 122.

Note: Par. (b) is derived from present T.C. Rule 31(g).

RULE 150. Record of Proceedings.—(a) General. Hearings and trials before the Court shall be stenographically reported or otherwise recorded, and a transcript thereof shall be made if, in the opinion of the Court or the Judge presiding at a hearing or trial, a permanent record is deemed appropriate. Transcripts shall be supplied to the parties and other persons at such charges as may be fixed or approved by the Court.

Note: Par. (a) is based upon present T.C. Rule 40.

(b) Stenographic Transcript as Evidence. Whenever the testimony of a witness at a trial or hearing which was stenographically reported or otherwise recorded is admissible in evidence at a later trial or hearing, it may be proved by the transcript thereof duly certified by the person who reported the testimony.

Note: Par. (b) is substantially the same as FRCP 80(c). There is no counterpart provision in present T.C. Rules.

RULE 151. Briefs.—(a) General. Briefs shall be filed after trial or submission of a case, except as otherwise directed by the presiding Judge. In addition to or in lieu of briefs, the presiding Judge may permit or direct the parties to make oral argument or file memoranda or statements of authorities.

Note: Par. (a) is adapted from present T.C. Rule 35(a). Par. (a) reduces the emphasis on the making of oral argument at the end of a case.

(b) Time for Filing Briefs. Briefs may be filed simultaneously or seriatim, as the presiding Judge directs. The following times for filing briefs shall prevail in the absence of any different direction by the presiding Judge:

(1) *Simultaneous briefs:* Opening briefs within 45 days after the conclusion of the trial, and answering briefs 30 days thereafter.

(2) *Seriatim briefs:* Opening brief within 45 days after the conclusion of the trial, answering brief within 30 days thereafter, and reply brief within 20 days after the due date of the answering brief.

A party who fails to file an opening brief is not permitted to file an answering or reply brief except on leave granted by the Court. A motion for extension of time for filing any brief shall be made not less than five days prior to the due date and shall recite that the moving party has advised his adversary and whether or not he objects to the motion. As to the effect of extensions of time, see Rule 25(c).

Note: Par. (b) is derived from present T.C. Rule 35(b). Express provision is made in Par. (b) for seriatim briefs, which are not covered by present Rule 35(b). In addition, Par. (b) adopts a period of 20 days for filing reply briefs.

(c) Service. Each brief will be served by the Clerk promptly upon the opposite party after it is filed, except where it bears a notation that it has already been served by the party submitting it, and except that, in the event of simultaneous briefs, such brief will not be served until the corresponding brief of the other party has been filed, unless the Court directs otherwise. Delinquent briefs will not be accepted unless accompanied by a motion setting forth reasons deemed sufficient by the Court to account for the delay. In the case of simultaneous briefs, the Court may refuse to receive a delinquent brief from a party after his adversary's brief has been served upon him.

Note: Par. (c) is adapted from present T.C. Rule 35(c). New provisions are adopted regarding delinquent briefs.

(d) Number of Copies. Two copies of each brief, plus an additional copy for each person to be served, shall be filed.

Note: Par. (d) changes the requirements of present T.C. Rule 35(d) as to the number of copies of briefs to be filed. The requirement of additional copies of briefs where they are printed has been eliminated.

(e) Form and Contents. All briefs shall contain the following in the order indicated:

(1) On the first page, a table of contents with page references, followed by a list of all citations arranged alphabetically as to cited cases and stating the pages in the brief at which cited. Citations shall be in italics when printed and underscored when typewritten.

(2) A statement of the nature of the controversy, the tax involved, and the issues to be decided.

(3) Proposed findings of fact (in the opening brief or briefs), based on the evidence, in the form of numbered statements, each of which shall be complete and shall consist of a concise statement of essential fact and not a recital of testimony nor a discussion or argument relating to the evidence or the law. In each such numbered statement, there shall be inserted references to the pages of the transcript or the exhibits or other sources relied upon to support the statement. In an answering or reply brief, the party shall set forth his objections, together with his reasons therefor, to any proposed findings of any other party, showing the numbers of the statements to which his objections are directed; in addition, he may set forth alternative proposed findings of fact.

(4) A concise statement of the points on which the party relies.

(5) The argument, which sets forth and discusses the points of law involved and any disputed questions of fact.

(6) The signature of counsel or the party submitting the brief. As to signature, see Rule 23(a)(3).

Note: Par. (e) is derived from present T.C.Rule 35(e). Subparagraph (3), regarding the filing of proposed findings of fact, has been revised, so that the filing of such proposed findings is not confined to the party having the burden of proof. Moreover, a responding brief must set out any objections to proposed findings, correlated with the findings. Filing of counter-findings or alternative findings is not sufficient to satisfy this requirement.

TITLE XV. DECISION.*

RULE 155. Computations by Parties For Entry of Decision.—(a) Agreed Computations. Where the Court has filed its opinion determining the issues in a case, it may withhold entry of its decision for the purpose of permitting the parties to submit computations pursuant to the Court's determination of the issues, showing the correct amount of the deficiency, liability, or overpayment to be entered as the decision. If the parties are in agreement as to the amount of the deficiency or overpayment to be entered as the decision pursuant to the findings and conclusions of the Court, they or either of them shall file promptly with the Court an original and two copies of a computation showing the amount of the deficiency, liability, or overpayment and that there is no disagreement that the figures shown are in accordance with the findings and conclusions of the Court. The Court will then enter its decision.

(b) Procedure in Absence of Agreement. If, however, the parties are not in agreement as to the amount of the deficiency, liability, or overpayment to be entered as the decision in accordance with the findings and conclusions of the Court, either of them may file with the Court a computation of the deficiency, liability, or overpayment believed by him to be in accordance with the Court's findings and conclusions. The Clerk will serve a copy thereof upon the opposite party, will place the matter upon a motion calendar for argument in due course, and will serve notice of the argument upon both parties. If the opposite party fails to file objection, accompanied or preceded by an alternative computation, at least 5 days prior to the date of such argument or any continuance thereof, the Court may enter decision in accordance with the computation already submitted. If in accordance with this Rule computations are submitted by the parties which differ as to the amount to be entered as the decision of the Court, the parties will be afforded an opportunity to be heard in argument thereon on the date fixed, and the Court will determine the correct deficiency, liability, or overpayment and will enter its decision accordingly.

(c) Limit on Argument. Any argument under this Rule will be confined strictly to consideration of the correct computation of the deficiency, liability, or overpayment resulting from the findings and conclusions made by the Court, and no argu-

* For statutory provisions relating to entry, date, and finality of decision, see Code Sections 7459, 7463(b), and 7481.

ment will be heard upon or consideration given to the issues or matters disposed of by the Court's findings and conclusions or to any new issues. This Rule is not to be regarded as affording an opportunity for retrial or reconsideration.

Note: This Rule is substantially the same as present T.C. Rule 50.

RULE 156. Estate Tax Deduction Developing At or After Trial. If the parties in an estate tax case are unable to agree under Rule 155, or under a remand, upon a deduction involving expenses incurred at or after the trial, any party may move to reopen the case for further trial on that issue.

Note: This Rule is an expansion of present T.C. Rule 51. It has been extended to apply to cases on remand, and no longer requires that the petition or an amendment thereto raise the issue.

TITLE XVI. POST-TRIAL PROCEEDINGS.

RULE 160. Harmless Error. No error in either the admission or exclusion of evidence, and no error or defect in any ruling or order or in anything done or omitted by the Court or by any of the parties, is ground for granting a new trial or for vacating, modifying, or otherwise disturbing a decision or order, unless refusal to take such action appears to the Court inconsistent with substantial justice. The Court at every stage of a case will disregard any error or defect which does not affect the substantial rights of the parties.

Note: This Rule is substantially the same as FRCP 61. There is no counterpart provision in present T.C. Rules.

RULE 161. Motion for Reconsideration of Findings or Opinion. Any motion for reconsideration of an opinion or findings of fact, with or without a new or further trial, shall be filed within 30 days after the opinion has been served, unless the Court shall otherwise permit.

Note: This Rule is derived from present T.C. Rule 19(e).

RULE 162. Motion to Vacate or Revise Decision. Any motion to vacate or revise a decision, with or without a new or further trial, shall be filed within 30 days after the decision has been entered, unless the Court shall otherwise permit.

Note: This Rule is derived from present T.C. Rule 19(f).

RULE 163. No Joinder of Motions Under Rules 161 and 162. Motions under Rules 161 and 162 shall be made separately from each other and not joined to or made part of any other motion.

Note: This Rule is derived from the last paragraph of present T.C. Rule 19.

TITLE XVII. SMALL TAX CASES.

RULE 170. General. The Rules of this Title XVII, referred to herein as the "Small Tax Case Rules," set forth the special provisions which are to be applied to small tax cases as defined in Rule 171. See Code Section 7463 (Appendix II p. 67). Except as otherwise provided in these Small Tax Case Rules, the other rules of practice of the Court are applicable to such cases.

Note: This Rule is derived from present T.C. Rule 36(a).

RULE 171. Small Tax Case Defined. The term "small tax case" means a case in which:

(a) Neither the amount of the deficiency, nor the amount of any claimed overpayment, placed in dispute (including any additions to tax, additional amounts, and penalties) exceeds—

(1) $1,500 for any one taxable year in the case of income or gift taxes, or

(2) $1,500 in the case of estate taxes;

(b) The petitioner has made a request in accordance with Rule 172 to have the proceedings conducted under Code section 7463; and

(c) The Court has not entered an order in accordance with Rule 172(d) or Rule 173, discontinuing the proceedings in the case under Code section 7463.

Note: This Rule is substantially the same as present T.C. Rule 36(b), except for the increase of the jurisdictional limit from $1,000 to $1,500, as required by the Federal-State Tax Collection Act of 1972. Public Law 92-512, 86 Stat. 919,945.

RULE 172. Election of Small Tax Case Procedure. With respect to classification of a case as a small tax case under Code section 7463, the following shall apply:

(a) A petitioner who wishes to have the proceedings in his case conducted under Code section 7463 may so request at the time he files his petition. See Rule 175.

(b) If the Commissioner opposes the petitioner's request to have the proceedings conducted under Code section 7463, he shall at the time he files his answer submit an accompanying motion in which he shall set forth the reasons for his opposition.

(c) A petitioner may, at any time after the petition is filed and before trial, request that the proceedings be conducted under Code section 7463. Upon the filing of such request, the Commissioner will be given due time in which to indicate whether he is opposed to it, and he shall state his reasons therefor in the event of such opposition.

(d) If such request is made in accordance with the provisions of this Rule 172, the case will be docketed as a small tax case. The Court, on its own motion or on the motion of a party to the case, may, at any time before the trial commences, enter an order directing that the small tax case designation shall be removed and that the proceedings shall not be conducted under the Small Tax Case Rules. If no such order is entered, the petitioner will be considered to have exercised his option and the Court shall be deemed to have concurred therein, in accordance with Code section 7463, at the commencement of the trial.

Note: This Rule is the same in substance as present T.C. Rule 36(c), except that unlike present T.C. Rule 36(c)(3), a petitioner may make his request at any time before trial without leave of Court.

RULE 173. Discontinuance of Proceedings. After the commencement of a trial of a small tax case, but before the decision in the case becomes final, the Court may order that the proceedings be discontinued under Code section 7463, and that the case be tried under the rules of practice other than the Small Tax Case Rules, but such order will be issued only if (1) there are reasonable grounds for believing that the amount of the deficiency, or the claimed overpayment, in dispute will exceed $1,500 and (2) the Court finds that justice requires the discontinuance of the proceedings under Code section 7463, taking into consideration the convenience and expenses for both parties that would result from the order.

Note: This Rule is substantially the same as present T.C. Rule 36(d), except for the increase in the jurisdictional limit from $1,000 to $1,500, as required by Section 203(b) of the Federal-State Tax Collection Act of 1972, Public Law 92-512, 86 Stat. 919,945.

RULE 174. Representation. A petitioner in a small tax case may appear for himself without representation or may be represented by any person admitted to practice before the Court. As to representation, see Rule 24.

Note: This Rule is derived from present T.C. Rule 36(g).

RULE 175. Pleadings.—(a) Petition. (1) Form and Content. The petition in a small tax case shall be substantially in accordance with Form 2 shown in Appendix I, p. 53, or shall, in the alternative, comply with the requirements of Rule 34(b), and contain additionally (A) the office of the Internal Revenue Service which issued the deficiency notice, (B) the taxpayer identification number (e.g., social security number) of each petitioner, and (C) a request that the proceedings be conducted under Code Section 7463.

(2) Filing Fee. The fee for filing a petition shall be $10, payable at the time of filing. The Court may waive payment of the fee if the petitioner establishes to the satisfaction of the Court that he is unable to make such payment.

(3) Verification Not Required. The petition need not be verified, unless the Court directs otherwise.

(b) Answer. The provisions of Rule 36 shall apply to answers filed by the Commissioner in small tax cases.

(c) Reply. A reply to the answer shall not be filed unless the Court, on its own motion or upon motion of the Commissioner, shall otherwise direct. Any reply shall conform to the requirements of Rule 37(b). In the absence of a requirement of a reply, the provisions of the second sentence of Rule 37(c) shall not apply and the affirmative allegations of the answer will be deemed denied.

Note: This Rule is substantially the same as present T.C. Rule 36(h), (i), and (j).

RULE 176. Preliminary Hearings. If, in a small tax case, it becomes necessary to hold a hearing on a motion or other preliminary matter, the parties may submit their views in writing and may, but shall not ordinarily be required to, appear personally at such hearing. However, if the Court deems it advisable for the petitioner or his counsel to appear personally, the Court will so notify the petitioner or his counsel and will make every effort to schedule such hearing at a place convenient to them.

Note: This Rule is identical with present T.C. Rule 36(f).

RULE 177. Trial.—(a) Place of Trial. At the time of filing the petition, the petitioner may, in accordance with Form 4 in Appendix I, page 56, or by other separate writing, request the place where he would prefer the trial to be held. If the petitioner has not filed such a request, the respondent, at the time he files his answer, shall file a request showing the place of trial preferred by him. The Court will make every effort to designate the place of trial at the location most convenient to that requested where suitable facilities are available.

(b) Conduct of Trial and Evidence. Trials of small tax cases will be conducted as informally as possible consistent with orderly procedure, and any evidence deemed by the Court to have probative value shall be admissible.

(c) Briefs. Neither briefs nor oral arguments will be required in small tax cases, but the Court on its own motion or upon request of either party may permit the filing of briefs or memorandum briefs.

Note: The Rule is substantially the same as present T.C. Rule 36(k), (l), and (m).

RULE 178. Transcripts of Proceedings. The hearing in, or trial of, a small tax case shall be stenographically reported or otherwise recorded but a transcript thereof need not be made unless the Court otherwise directs.

Note: This Rule is substantially the same as present T.C. Rule 36(n).

RULE 179. Number of Copies of Papers. Only an original and two conformed copies of *any* paper need be filed in a small tax case. An additional copy shall be filed for each additional docketed case which has been, or is requested to be, consolidated.

Note: This Rule is identical with present T.C. Rule 36(e).

TITLE XVIII. COMMISSIONERS OF THE COURT.

RULE 180. Assignment. The Chief Judge may from time to time designate a commissioner, appointed under section 7456(c) of the Code, to deal with any matter pending before the Court in accordance with these Rules and such directions as may be prescribed by the Chief Judge.

Note: This Rule makes clear that a commisioner's assignments and duties are determined by the Chief Judge.

RULE 181. Powers and Duties. Subject to the specifications and limitations in the order designating a commissioner and in accordance with the applicable provisions of these Rules, the commissioner has and shall exercise the power to regulate all proceedings in any matter before him, including the conduct of trials, pretrial conferences, an hearings on motions, and to do all acts and take all measures necessary or proper for the efficient performance of his duties. He may require the production before him of evidence upon all matters embraced within his assignment, including the production of all books, papers, vouchers, documents, and writings applicable thereto, and he has the authority to put witnesses on oath and to examine them. He may rule upon the admissibility of evidence, in accordance with provisions of Code sections 7453 and 7463, and may exercise such further and incidental authority, including ordering the issuance of subpoenas, as may be necessary for the conduct of trials or other proceedings.

Note: This Rule is derived from present T.C. Rule 48(b) and FRCP 53(c).

RULE 182. Post-Trial Procedure. Except in small tax cases (see Rule 183) or as otherwise provided, the following procedure shall be observed in cases tried before a commissioner:

(a) Proposed Findings and Briefs. Each party shall file his initial brief, including his proposed findings of fact and legal argument, within 60 days after the date on which the trial is concluded, unless otherwise directed. A party thereafter desiring to file a responsive brief shall do so, including any objections to any proposed findings of fact, within 30 days after the expiration of the period for filing the initial brief, unless otherwise directed. With respect to the content, form, number of copies, and other applicable requirements, the proposed findings of fact and the briefs shall conform to the provisions of Rule 151.

(b) Commissioner's Report. After all the briefs have been filed by all the parties or the time for doing so has expired, the commissioner shall file his report, including his findings of fact and opinion. A copy of the report shall forthwith be served on each party.

(c) Exceptions. Within 45 days after service of the commissioner's report, a party may file with the Court a brief setting forth any exceptions of law or of fact to that report. Within 30 days of service upon him of such brief, any other party may file a brief in response thereto. In any brief filed pursuant to this paragraph, a party may rely in whole or in part upon the briefs previously submitted by him to the commissioner under paragraph (a) of this Rule 182. Unless a party shall have proposed a particular finding of fact, or unless he shall have objected to another party's proposed finding of fact, the Court may refuse to consider his exception to the commissioner's report for failure to make such a finding desired by him or for inclusion of such finding proposed by the other party, as the case may be.

(d) Oral Argument and Decision. The Division to which the case is assigned may, upon motion of any party, or its own motion, direct oral argument. The Division inter alia may adopt the commissioner's report or may modify it or may reject it in whole or in part, or may receive further evidence, or may recommit it with instructions. Due regard shall be given to the circumstance that the commissioner had the opportunity to evaluate the credibility of witnesses; and the findings of fact recommended by the commissioner shall be presumed to be correct.

Note: This Rule represents a revision of present T.C. Rule 48(c). The commissioner's function is expanded to include matters of both law and fact and the preparation of an opinion, to the extent deemed appropriate in the particular case, and is limited only by the scope of his assignment.

Briefs on both the facts and the law, as well as all objections thereto, are to be filed with the commissioner. Exceptions to the commissioner's report and any arguments in support of those exceptions, may be filed with the Court, but the parties are encouraged to limit their briefs to such exceptions and arguments in order to avoid duplication. The parties may request the opportunity to present oral argument before the Court in order to focus on claims or points already presented.

The decision of a case is made by a Judge, and the Rule expands the alternatives available in reviewing the determinations of the commissioner as embodied in his report. The Judge, to whom the case is assigned, may take any action he deems appropriate for a proper disposition of the case, even with respect to the commissioner's findings of fact, although they are accorded special weight insofar as those findings are determined by the opportunity to hear and observe the witnesses. In this regard, see Court of Claims Rule 147(b).

Similarly, a range of alternatives are available in the disposition of a case after the report has been made by the commissioner. The Judge, on the one hand, may prepare new findings accompanied by a new opinion, or, on the other hand, he may note review of the commissioner's findings and opinion and direct entry of a decision accordingly.

This Rule is intended to make the use of commissioners more effective, and to provide procedures more comparable to those which obtain in the Court of Claims.

RULE 183. Small Tax Cases. Rule 182 shall not apply to small tax cases, as defined in Rule 171. A commissioner who conducts the trial of such a small tax case shall, as soon after such trial as shall be practicable, prepare a summary of the facts and reasons for his proposed disposition of the case, which then shall be submitted promptly to the Chief Judge or to a Judge or division of the Court, if the Chief Judge shall so direct.

Note: This Rule is substantially the same as present T.C. Rule 48(h).

TITLE XIX. APPEALS.

RULE 190. How Appeal Taken.—(a) General. Review of a decision of the Court by a United States Court of Appeals is obtained by filing a notice of appeal with the Clerk of the Tax Court within 90 days after the decision is entered. If a timely notice of appeal is filed by one party, any other party may take an appeal by filing a notice of appeal within 120 days after the Court's decision is entered. Code Section 7483. For other requirements governing such an appeal, see Rules 13 and 14 of the Federal Rules of Appellate Procedure. A suggested form of the notice of appeal is contained in Appendix I, p. 61. See Code Section 7482(a).

(b) Venue. For the circuit of the court of appeals to which the appeal is to be taken, see Code Section 7482(b).

Note: This Rule is derived from Section 13(a) of the Federal Rules of Appellate Procedure. No such rule appears in the present T.C. Rules.

RULE 191. Preparation of the Record on Appeal. The Clerk will prepare the record on appeal and forward it to the Clerk of the Court of Appeals pursuant to the notice of appeal filed with the Court, in accordance with Rules 10 and 11 of the Federal Rules of Appellate Procedure. In addition, at the time the Clerk forwards the record on appeal to the Clerk of the Court of Appeals, he shall forward to each of the parties a copy of the index to the record on appeal.

Note: This Rule is a new provision, without counterpart in the present T.C. Rules.

RULE 192. Bond to Stay Assessment and Collection. The filing of a notice of appeal does not stay assessment or collection of a deficiency determined by the Court unless, on or before the filing of the notice of appeal, a bond is filed with the Court in accordance with Code Section 7485. For forms of bonds, see Appendix I, pp. 62, 63; for forms of power of attorney used with United States Bonds as collateral, see Appendix I, pp. 65, 66.

Note: This Rule is a new provision, without counterpart in the present T.C. Rules.

TITLE XX. PRACTICE BEFORE THE COURT.

RULE 200. Admission to Practice.—(a) Qualifications. (1) General. An applicant for admission to practice before the Court must establish to the satisfaction of the Court that he is a citizen of the United States, of good moral character and repute, and is possessed of the requisite qualifications to represent others in the preparation and trial of cases. In addition, the applicant must satisfy the further requirements of this Rule 200.

(2) Attorneys. An attorney at law may be admitted to practice upon filing with the Admissions Clerk a completed application accompanied by a fee of $10 and a current certificate from the Clerk of the Appropriate court, showing that the applicant has been admitted to practice before and is a member in good standing of the Bar of the Supreme Court of the United States, or of the highest or appropriate court of any State, or Territory, or of the District of Columbia. A current court certificate is one executed within 60 calendar days preceding the date of the filing of the application.

(3) Other Applicants. An applicant, not an attorney at law, must file with the Admissions Clerk a completed application accompanied by a fee of $10. In addition, such an applicant, as a condition of being admitted to practice, must give evidence of his qualifications satisfactory to the Court by means of a written examination given by the Court, and the Court may require such person, in addition, to give similar evidence by means of an oral examination. Any person who has thrice failed to give such evidence by means of such written examination shall not thereafter be eligible to take another examination for admission.

(b) Application. An application for admission to practice before the Court must be on the form provided by the Court. Application forms and other necessary information will be furnished upon request addressed to the Admissions Clerk, United States Tax Court, Box 70, Washington, D. C. 20044.

(c) Sponsorship. An applicant for admission by examination must be sponsored by at least three persons theretofore admitted to practice before this Court, and each sponsor must send a letter of recommendation directly to the Admissions Clerk of the Court, where it will be treated as a confidential communication.. The sponsor shall send his letter promptly, stating therein fully and frankly the extent of his acquaintance with the applicant, his opinion of the moral character and repute of the applicant, and his opinion of the qualifications of the applicant to practice before this Court. The Court may in its discretion accept such an applicant with less than three such sponsors.

(d) Written Examinations. Written examinations, for applicants other than attorneys at law, will be held in Washington, D. C., on the last Wednesday in October of each year, and at such other times and places as the Court may designate. The Court will notify each applicant, whose application is in order, of the time and place at which he is to present himself for examination, and the applicant must present that notice to the examiner as his authority for taking an examination.

(e) Checks and Money Orders. Where the application fee is paid by check or money order, it shall be made payable to the order of the "Treasurer of the United States."

(f) Admission. Upon approval of an application for admission and satisfaction of the other applicable requirements, an applicant will be admitted to practice before the Court upon taking and subscribing the oath or affirmation prescribed by the Court. Such an applicant shall thereupon be entitled to a certificate of admission.

(g) Change of Address. Each person admitted to practice before the Court shall promptly notify the Admissions Clerk of any change in office address for mailing purposes.

(h) Corporations and Firms Not Eligible. Corporations and firms will not be admitted to practice or recognized before the Court.

Note: Par. (a) is derived from present T.C. Rule 2. A uniform application fee of $10 is adopted both for attorneys at law and other applicants.

Pars. (b), (c), (d), (e), (f), (g), and (h), are substantially the same as the counterpart provisions in present T.C. Rule 2.

RULE 201. Conduct of Practice Before the Court.—(a) General. Practitioners before the Court shall carry on their practice in accordance with the letter and spirit of the Code of Professional Responsibility of the American Bar Association.

(b) Statement of Employment. The Court may require any practitioner before it to furnish a statement, under oath, of the terms and circumstances of his employment in any case.

Note: This Rule is substantially the same as the counterpart provisions in present T.C. Rule 2. In keeping with the revision made by the American Bar Association, reference is made to the new designation of its code of ethics.

RULE 202. Disqualification, Suspension, or Disbarment. The Court may deny admission to, suspend, or disbar any person who in its judgment does not possess the requisite qualifications to represent others, or who is lacking in character, integrity, or proper professional conduct. Upon the conviction of any practitioner admitted to practice before this Court for a criminal violation of any provision of the Internal Revenue Code or for any crime involving moral turpitude, or where any practitioner has been suspended or disbarred from the practice of his profession in any State or the District of Columbia, the Court may, in the exercise of its discretion, forthwith suspend such practitioner from the Bar of This Court until further order of Court; but otherwise no person shall be suspended for more than 60 days or disbarred until he has been afforded an opportunity to be heard. A Judge of the Court may immediately suspend any person for not more than 60 days for contempt or misconduct during the course of any trial or hearing.

Note: This Rule is derived from a counterpart provision in present T.C. Rule 2, except that the provision for immediate suspension upon criminal conviction has been added.

TITLE XXI.–DECLARATORY JUDGMENTS–RETIREMENT PLANS

Prefatory Note[1]

Section 1041 of the Employee Retirement Income Security Act of 1974 adds Section 7476 to the Internal Revenue Code and provides for jurisdiction of the United States Tax Court to issue declaratory judgments with respect to the qualification of retirement plans. The procedures set forth in the statute are "applicable to pleadings filed more than 1 year after the date of the enactment of this Act," which occurred on September 2, 1974. The accompanying new Title XXI of the Rules of Practice and Procedure of the United States Tax Court contains the procedural rules which will govern this declaratory judgment litigation. The following material outlines the principal considerations which influenced the formulation of these rules and discusses the major provisions which should be kept in mind:

(1) The focus of the declaratory judgment procedure in respect of qualification of retirement plans is review of an administrative determination (or failure to make such a determination) and thus has a much narrower scope than exists in respect of declaratory judgment litigation of the United States District Courts. Consequently, much of the practice and procedure involved in such litigation is not applicable to the declaratory judgment procedures of the Court. However, to the extent pertinent, such practice and procedure may be used as guidelines for the application of the within Rules.

(2) The entire declaratory judgment procedure is predicated upon the existence of an "actual controversy" as required by Section 7476(a). Thus the inclusion in Rule 211 of the provisions of the Rule relating to the content of petitions to be filed by certain persons does not necessarily indicate such a person is entitled to commence an action under Section 7476–to be so entitled an "actual controversy" must exist.

(3) As is the case with Title XVII relating to Small Tax Cases, Title XXI makes clear that, except as otherwise provided, the other Rules of Practice and Procedure of the Court, to the extent pertinent, are applicable to declaratory judgment litigation. See Rule 210(a).

(4) The requirements contained in Rule 211 that a party allege in his petition that he has given notice to other interested parties, that he has exhausted his administrative remedies, and that the retirement plan has been put into effect prior to the filing of a petition for a declaratory judgment are of critical importance. See Rule 211(c)(1), (2),

---

[1]This note was prepared by the Rules Committee and is reproduced here for such assistance as it may provide for the bar. It is not officially part of the Rules. Cf. 60 T.C. 1057, 1058.

and (3) and (e)(2). It is anticipated that the Secretary of the Treasury will issue regulations in regard to qualification as an interested party for purposes of the administrative proceeding and in regard to the administrative remedies which will be available.

(5) Declaratory judgment cases will usually be decided on the basis of the administrative record made in the proceedings within the Internal Revenue Service in connection with a request for a determination on the qualification of a retirement plan or amendment thereto. See Rule 217. The parties will normally be able to stipulate the contents of the administrative record. To facilitate this stipulation process, the respondent is expected to retain the administrative record in his field office for at least 30 and not more than 45 days after the filing of his answer in order to afford petitioner an opportunity to examine it. To facilitate further the stipulation process, the respondent is required to file with his answer an index to the administrative record. See Rule 213(a)(3). Similarly, the requirement that the petitioner *shall* file a reply (and that his failure to do so will be deemed an admission of the affirmative allegations of the answer), which is the reverse of the situation obtaining under Rule 37, is designed as a further tool for assuring that the administrative record will be complete or that any differences between the parties will be brought to the attention of the Court. See Rule 213(b). It should be noted that the definition of "administrative record" (see Rule 210(b)(3)) is not intended to be all-inclusive but it is essential that such record contain all the material upon which the Commissioner based his determination. See Rule 217(b)(1).

(6) It is contemplated that after the administrative record has been filed and the issue joined (see Rule 214), the case will be placed on a calendar for submission to the Court (see Rule 212). Representations and other information contained in the administrative record will be assumed to be true for the purpose of decision. See Rule 217(b)(1). Ordinarily a trial will be held only with respect to a factual dispute in the administrative record or to resolve disagreement between the parties as to whether a particular item is a part of such record.

(7) Provision is made for joinder of other parties under certain circumstances. See Rule 215. It should be noted that where a party moves to have another party joined, he is responsible for causing personal service to be made on such other party. See Rule 215(b). This is to be contrasted with the provisions for service by mail either by the party or the Clerk of the Court as provided in Rule 21. Provisions for intervention are also included. See Rule 216. In developing these provisions for joinder and intervention, the corresponding provisions of the Federal Rules of Civil Procedure were considered, but since the parties who may join or intervene in a declaratory judgment action in the Tax Court and the circumstances under which they may do so are more limited, the Tax Court Rules are not nearly as broad as those provisions of the FRCP.

(8) Provisions relating to the burden of proof are included. See Rule 217(c). These pertain primarily to the burden of proving that a retirement plan does or does not qualify, since, in the usual case, all of the facts will be contained in the agreed administrative record and will be assumed for the purposes of decision.

RULE 210. General. (a) Applicability: The Rules of this Title XXI set forth the special provisions to be applied to actions for declaratory judgments with respect to the qualification of retirement plans. Except as otherwise provided in this Title, the other Rules of Practice and Procedure of the Court, to the extent pertinent, are applicable to actions for declaratory judgments. The Rules of this Title shall take effect on September 2, 1975.

(b) Definitions: As used in the Rules in this Title–

(1) "Retirement plan" has the meaning provided by Code Section 7476(d).

(2) A "determination" means a determination with respect to the initial qualification of a retirement plan, or with respect to the continuing qualification of such a plan.

(3) "Administrative record" includes the request for determination, the retirement plan and any related trust instruments, any written modifications thereof made by the applicant during the proceedings within the Internal Revenue Service, all other documents submitted to the Internal Revenue Service by the applicant in respect of the request for determination, all written correspondence between the Internal Revenue Service and the applicant in respect of his request for determination, and all written comments (and correspondence in respect thereto) submitted to the Internal Revenue Service in the administrative proceedings in respect of the request for determination. See Section 3001(b) of the Employee Retirement Income Security Act of 1974.

(4) "Party" includes a petitioner, a respondent, and any intervenor.

(5) "Declaratory judgment" is the decision of the Court in an action for declaratory judgment.

(c) Jurisdictional Requirements: The Tax Court does not have jurisdiction of an action for declaratory judgment unless the Commissioner has issued a notice of determination with respect to the initial or continuing qualification of a retirement plan or unless he has been requested to make a determination—

(1) With respect to the initial qualification of such a plan, or

(2) With respect to the continuing qualification of such a plan if the controversy arises as a result of an amendment or termination of such a plan, and fails to do so for a period of at least 270 days. If the Commissioner has issued a notice of determination which may be the subject of an action for declaratory judgment, a petition for such a judgment must be filed within the period specified by Code Section 7476(b)(5). See also Code Section 7502. For other jurisdictional requirements, see Code Section 7476(a) and (b).

(d) Form and Style of Papers: All papers filed in an action for declaratory judgment, with the exception of documents included in the administrative record, shall be prepared in the form and style set forth in Rule 23; except that whenever any party joins or intervenes in the action, then thereafter, in addition to the number of copies required to be filed under such rule, an additional copy shall be filed for each party who joins or intervenes in the action.

RULE 211. Commencement of Action for Declaratory Judgment. (a) Commencement of Action: An action for declaratory judgment shall be commenced by filing a petition with the Court. See Rule 22, relating to the place and manner of filing the petition, and Rule 32 relating to form of pleadings.

(b) Contents of Petition: Every petition, which shall be entitled "Petition for Declaratory Judgment," shall contain:

(1) The petitioner's name and address, and the name and principal place of business, or principal office or agency of the employer at the time the petition is filed; and

(2) The office of the Internal Revenue Service with which the request for determination was filed and the date of such filing.

(c) Employer Petitions: In addition to including the information specified in paragraph (b) of this Rule, a petition filed by an employer shall also contain:

(1) A separate numbered paragraph setting forth a statement that he has complied with the requirements of the regulations issued under Code Section 7476(b)(2) with respect to notice to other interested parties;

(2) A separate numbered paragraph setting forth a statement that he has exhausted his administrative remedies within the Internal Revenue Service in accordance with Code Section 7476(b)(3);

(3) A separate numbered paragraph setting forth a statement that the retirement plan has been put into effect in accordance with Code Section 7476(b)(4);

(4) Where the Commissioner has issued a notice of determination that the retirement plan does not qualify—

(i) the date of mailing of the notice of his determination,

(ii) a copy of such notice of determination, and

(iii) in a separate numbered paragraph, a clear and concise assignment of each error, set forth in a separate lettered subparagraph, which he alleges to have been committed by the Commissioner in the determination and the facts on which he relies in support of his claim;

(5) Where the Commissioner has not issued a notice of determination with respect to the qualification of the retirement plan, a separate numbered paragraph setting forth the statements—

(i) that a request for a determination with respect to the qualification of such plan has been made,

(ii) that the requested determination is of the type described in Rule 210(c)(1) or (2),

(iii) that no such determination has been made by the Commissioner, and

(iv) that the retirement plan does qualify;

(6) An appropriate prayer for relief; and

(7) The signature of each petitioner or his counsel. If the petition is filed in the name of more than one petitioner, it shall be signed by each petitioner or his counsel.

(d) Petitions Filed by Plan Administrators: In addition to including the information specified in paragraph (b) of this Rule, a petition filed by a plan administrator shall contain:

(1) The name, address, and principal place of business, or principal office or agency, of each employer who is required to contribute under the plan; and

(2) In separate numbered paragraphs, the statements described in subparagraphs (1), (2), (3), (4), (5), (6), and (7) of paragraph (c) of this Rule.

(e) Employee Petitions: In addition to including the information specified in paragraph (b) of this Rule, a petition filed by an employee shall also contain:

(1) A separate numbered paragraph setting forth a statement that he has qualified as an interested party in accordance with the regulations issued under Code Section 7476(b)(1);

(2) In separate numbered paragraphs, the statements described in subparagraphs (2) and (3) of paragraph (c) of this Rule;

(3) Where the Commissioner has issued a notice of determination that the retirement plan does not qualify, a copy of such notice of determination, and in separate numbered paragraphs, the statements described in paragraph (c)(4)(i) and (iii) of this Rule;

(4) Where the Commissioner has issued a notice of determination that a retirement plan does qualify, a copy of such notice of determination, and in separate numbered paragraphs, the date of mailing of such notice of determination, and a clear and concise statement of each ground, set forth in a separate lettered subparagraph, upon which he relies to assert that such plan does not qualify and the facts to support each ground;

(5) Where the Commissioner has not issued a notice of determination with respect to the qualification of the retirement plan, in a separate numbered paragraph, a statement (a) that the retirement plan does qualify or (b) that the retirement plan does not qualify—

(i) if he alleges that the retirement plan does qualify, such paragraph shall also include the statements described in paragraph (c)(5) of this Rule, or

(ii) if he alleges that the retirement plan does not qualify, in addition to the statements described in paragraph (c)(5)(i), (ii), and (iii) of this Rule, such paragraph shall also include a clear and concise statement of each ground, set forth in a separate lettered subparagraph, upon which he relies to support his allegation that such plan does not qualify and the facts upon which he relies to support each ground; and

(6) In separate numbered paragraphs, the statements described in subparagraphs (6) and (7) of pagagraph (c) of this Rule.

(f) Petitions Filed by the Pension Benefit Guaranty Corporation: In addition to including the information specified in paragraph (b) of this Rule, a petition filed by the Pension Benefit Guaranty Corporation shall also contain in separate numbered paragraphs the statements described in subparagraphs (2), (3), (4), (5), and (6) of paragraph (e) of this Rule.

(g) Service: For the provisions relating to service of the petition and other papers, see Rule 21.

RULE 212. Request for Place for Submission to the Court. At the time of filing a petition for a declaratory judgment, a request for place for submission to the Court shall be filed in accordance with Rule 140, and the provisions of that Rule shall be applied in designating such place. In addition to including in the request the information specified in Rule 140, the petitioner shall also include the date on which he believes the action will be ready for submission to the Court and his estimate of the time required therefor. After the action becomes at issue (see Rule 214), it will ordinarily, without any further request by the Court for information as to readiness for submission, be placed on a calendar for submission to the Court. (See also Rule 217(b)(2).)

RULE 213. Other Pleadings. (a) Answer: (1) Time to Answer or Move: The Commissioner shall have 60 days from the date of service of the petition within which to file an answer, or 45 days from that date within which to move with respect to the petition. With respect to an amended petition or amendments to the petition, the Commissioner shall have like periods from the date of service of those papers within which to answer or move in response thereto, except as the Court may otherwise direct.

(2) Form and Content: The answer shall be drawn so that it will advise the petitioner and the Court fully of the nature of the defense. It shall contain a specific admission or denial of each material allegation in the petition; however, if the Commissioner shall be without knowledge or information sufficient to form a belief as to the truth of an allegation he shall so state, and such statement shall have the effect of a denial. If the Commissioner intends to qualify or to deny only a part of an allegation, he shall specify so much of it as is true and shall qualify or deny only the remainder. In addition, the answer shall contain a clear and concise statement of every ground, together with the facts in support thereof, on which the Commissioner relies and has the burden of proof. Paragraphs of the answer shall be designated to correspond to those of the petition to which they relate.

(3) Index to Administrative Record: In addition, the answer shall contain a statement that attached thereto is a complete index of the contents of the administrative record to be filed with the Court. (See Rule 217(b).) There shall be attached to the answer such complete index.

(4) Effect of Answer: Every material allegation set out in the petition and not expressly admitted or denied in the answer shall be deemed to be admitted.

(b) Reply: Each petitioner shall file a reply in every action for declaratory judgment.

(1) Time to Reply or Move: The petitioner shall have 60 days from the date of service of the answer within which to file a reply, or 30 days from that date within which to move with respect to the answer. With respect to an amended answer or amendments to the answer, the petitioner shall have like periods from the date of service of those papers within which to reply or move in response thereto, except as the Court may otherwise direct.

(2) Form and Content: In response to each material allegation in the answer and the facts in support thereof on which the Commissioner has the burden of proof, the reply shall contain a specific admission or denial; however, if the petitioner shall be without knowledge or information sufficient to form a belief as to the truth of an allegation, he shall so state, and such statement shall have the effect of a denial. In addition, the reply shall contain a clear and concise statement of every ground, together with the facts in support thereof, on which the petitioner relies affirmatively or in avoidance of any matter in the answer on which the Commissioner has the burden of proof. In other respects the requirements of pleading applicable to the answer provided in paragraph (a)(2) of this Rule shall apply to the reply. The paragraphs of the reply shall be designated to correspond to those of the answer to which they relate.

(3) Effect of Reply or Failure Thereof: Where a reply is filed, every affirmative allegation set out in the answer and not expressly admitted or denied in the reply, shall be deemed to be admitted. Where a reply is not filed, the affirmative allegations in the answer will be deemed admitted.

(4) New Material: Any new material contained in the reply shall be deemed to be denied.

RULE 214. Joinder of Issue in Action for Declaratory Judgment. An action for declaratory judgment shall be deemed at issue upon the filing of the reply or at the expiration of the time for doing so.

RULE 215. Joinder of Parties. (a) Permissive Joinder: Any person who under Code Section 7476(b)(1) is entitled to commence an action for a declaratory judgment with respect to the qualification of a retirement plan may join in filing a petition with any other such person in such an action with respect to the same plan. After a petition has been filed, any such person may join therein with the consent of all the petitioners and the permission of the Court. If the Commissioner has issued a notice of determination with respect to the qualification of the plan, any person joining in the petition must do so within the period specified in Code Section 7476(b)(5). If more than one petition is filed with respect to the qualification of the same retirement plan, see Rule 141 (relating to the possibility of consolidating the actions with respect to the plan).

(b) Joinder of Additional Parties: Any party to an action for declaratory judgment with respect to the qualification of a retirement plan may move to have joined in the action any employer who established or maintains the plan, plan administrator, or any person in whose absence complete relief cannot be accorded among those already parties. Unless otherwise permitted by the Court, any such motion must be filed not later than 30 days after joinder of issue (see Rule 214). Such motion shall be served on the parties to the action (other than the movant). See Rule 21(b)(1). The movant shall cause personal service to be made on each person sought to be joined by a United States marshal, or by his deputy, or by any other person who is not a party and is not less than 18 years of age, who shall make a return of service, see Form 13, Appendix I. Such return of service shall be filed with the motion, but failure to do so, or otherwise to make proof of service does not affect the validity of the service. Unless otherwise permitted by the Court, any objection to such motion shall be filed within 30 days after the service of the motion. The motion will be granted whenever the Court finds that in the interests of justice such person should be joined. If the motion is granted, such person will thereupon become a party to the action, and the Court will enter such orders as it deems appropriate as to further pleading and other matters. See Rule 50(b) with respect to actions on motions.

(c) Nonjoinder of Necessary Parties: If the Court determines that any person described in paragraph (b) of this Rule is a necessary party to an action for declaratory judgment and that such person has not been joined, the Court may, on its own motion or on the motion of any party, dismiss the action on the ground that the absent person is indispensable and that justice cannot be accomplished in his absence. An order dismissing a case for nonjoinder of a necessary party may be conditional or absolute.

RULE 216. Intervention. (a) Who May Intervene: The Pension Benefit Guaranty Corporation and, if entitled to intervene pursuant to the provisions of Section 3001(c) of the Employees Retirement Income Security Act of 1974, the Secretary of Labor, or either of them, shall be permitted to intervene in an action for declaratory judgment brought under Code Section 7476 in accordance with the provisions of such section.

(b) Procedure: If either of the persons mentioned in paragraph (a) of this Rule desires to intervene, he shall file a pleading, either a petition in intervention or an answer in intervention, not later than 30 days after joinder of issue (see Rule 214), unless the Court directs otherwise. All new matters of claim or defense in a pleading in intervention shall be deemed denied.

RULE 217. Disposition of Actions for Declaratory Judgment. (a) General: Disposition of an action for declaratory judgment will ordinarily be made on the basis of the administrative record, as defined in Rule 210(b)(3). Only with the permission of the Court, upon good cause shown, will any party be permitted to introduce before the Court any evidence other than that presented before the Internal Revenue Service and contained in the administrative record as so defined.

(b) Procedure: (1) Disposition on the Administrative Record: The Court expects that within 30 days after service of the answer the parties will file with the Court the entire administrative record (or so much thereof as either party may deem necessary for a complete disposition of the action for declaratory judgment), stipulated as to its genuineness. If, however, the parties are unable to file such a stipulated administrative record, then not sooner than 30 days nor later than 45 days after service of the answer the respondent shall file with the Court the entire administrative record, as defined in Rule 210(b)(3), appropriately certified as to its genuineness by the Commissioner or by an official authorized to act for him in such situation. See Rule 212, as to the time and place for submission of the action to the Court. The Court will thereafter issue an opinion and declaratory judgment with respect to the qualification of the retirement plan, based upon the assumption that the facts as represented in the administrative record as so stipulated or so certified are true and upon any additional facts as found by the Court if the Court deems that a trial is necessary. See subparagraph (3) of this paragraph.

(2) Other Dispositions Without Trial: In addition, an action for declaratory judgment may be decided on a motion for a judgment on the pleadings under Rule 120 or on a motion for summary judgment under Rule 121, or such an action may be submitted at any time by notice of the parties filed with the Court in accordance with Rule 122.

(3) Disposition Where Trial is Required: Whenever a trial is required in an action for declaratory judgment, such trial shall be conducted in accordance with the Rules contained in Title XIV, except as otherwise provided in this Title.

(c) Burden of Proof: (1) Parties Petitioner: The burden of proof shall be upon the petitioner, and upon any party joining or intervening on his side, as to those grounds set forth in the respondent's notice of determination that a retirement plan does not qualify. Where the respondent has determined that a retirement plan does qualify, the petitioner, and any party joining or intervening on his side, shall bear the burden of proof as to every ground on which he relies to sustain his position that such plan does not qualify. Where the Commissioner has failed to issue a notice of determination described in Rule 210(c)(1) or (2)–

(i) the petitioner who contends that the retirement plan does qualify, and any party joining or intervening on his side, shall bear the burden of proof as to the statements contained in paragraph (c)(5) or (e)(5)(i) with the exception of the statement required by paragraph (c)(5)(iv), of Rule 211, if such statements are denied by the respondent in his answer; but

(ii) the petitioner who contends that the retirement plan does not qualify, and any party joining or intervening on his side, shall bear the burden of proof as to the grounds described in paragraph (e)(5)(ii) of Rule 211.

(2) Parties Respondent: The burden of proof shall be upon the respondent, and upon any party joining or intervening on his side, as to any ground not stated in the notice of determination upon which either relies to sustain the respondent's determination that a retirement plan does not qualify. If the respondent has not issued a notice of determination described in Rule 210(c)(1) or (2), he, and any party joining or intervening on his side, shall bear the burden of proof as to every ground upon which either relies to sustain his position that such plan does not qualify. But see also subparagraph (1)(ii) of this paragraph.

RULE 218. Procedure in Actions Heard by a Commissioner of the Court. (a) Where Commissioner Is to Make the Decision: When an action for declaratory judgment is assigned to a commissioner and he is authorized in the order of assignment to make the decision, the opinion of the commissioner and his proposed decision shall be submitted to and approved by the Chief Judge, or by another Judge designated by the Chief Judge for that purpose, prior to service of the opinion and decision upon the parties.

(b) Where Commissioner Is Not to Make the Decision: When an action for declaratory judgment is assigned to a commissioner but he is not authorized in order of assignment to make the decision, the procedure provided in Rule 182 shall be followed.

APPENDIX I.

Forms

Page

The following forms are listed in this Appendix:

The forms marked by an asterisk (*) (Forms 2, 3, 4, 5, and 6) have been printed and are available upon request from the Clerk of the Court. All the forms may be typewritten, except that the subpoena (Form 5) must be obtained from the Court. When preparing papers for filing with the Court, attention should be given to the applicable requirements of Rule 23 in regard to form, size, type, and number of copies, as well as to such other Rules of the Court as may apply to the particular item.

FORM 1

PETITION (OTHER THAN IN SMALL TAX CASE)

SEE RULES 30 THROUGH 34

UNITED STATES TAX COURT

.... Petitioner, v. COMMISSIONER OF INTERNAL REVENUE, Respondent.	Docket No.

PETITION

The petitioner hereby petitions for a redetermination of the deficiency (or liability) set forth by the Commissioner of Internal Revenue in his notice of deficiency (or liability) [Service symbols] dated ...., 19.., and as the basis for his case alleges as follows:

1. The petitioner is [set forth whether an individual, fiduciary, corporation, etc., as provide in Rule 60] with legal residence (or principal office) now at

....
(Street)

....
(City) (State) (Zip Code)

The return for the period here involved was filed with the Office of the Internal Revenue Service at ....
(City) (State)

2. The notice of deficiency (or liability) (a copy of which, including so much of the statement and schedules accompanying the notice as is material, is attached and marked Exhibit A) was mailed to the petitioner on ...., 19...,
and was issued by the Office of The Internal Revenue Service at ....
City and State

3. The deficiencies (or liabilities) as determined by the Commissioner are in income (estate, gift, or certain excise) taxes for the calendar (or fiscal) year 19...,
in the amount of $.............., of which $.............., is in dispute.

4. The determination of tax set forth in the said notice of deficiency (or liability) is based upon the following errors: [Here set forth specifically in lettered subparagraphs the assignments of error in a concise manner and avoid pleading facts which properly belong in the succeeding paragraph.]

5. The facts upon which the petitioner relies, as the basis of his case, are as follows: [Here set forth allegations of fact, but not the evidence, sufficient to inform the Court and the Commissioner of the positions taken and the bases therefor, in orderly and logical sequence, with subparagraphs lettered, so as to enable the Commissioner to admit or deny each allegation. See Rules 31(a) and 34(b)(5).]

Wherefore, petitioner prays that [here set forth the relief desired.]

(Signed) ....
(Petitioner or Counsel)

....
(Post Office Address)

Dated: ...., 19...

....
Telephone No. (include area code)

FORM 2

PETITION (SMALL TAX CASE)

(AVAILABLE—ASK FOR FORM 2)

(SEE RULES 170 THROUGH 179)

UNITED STATES TAX COURT

.... Petitioner(s) v. COMMISSIONER OF INTERNAL REVENUE Respondent	Docket No.

PETITION

1. Petitioner(s) request(s) the Court to redetermine the tax deficiency(ies) for the year(s) ...., as set forth in the notice of deficiency dated ...., A COPY OF WHICH IS ATTACHED. The notice was issued by the Office of the Internal Revenue Service at ....
City and State

2. Petitioner(s) taxpayer identification (e.g. social security) number(s) is (are) ....

3. Petitioner(s) make(s) the following claims as to his tax liability:

Year	Amount of Deficiency Disputed	Amount of Addition to Tax, if any, Disputed	Amount of Overpayment Claimed
.....	....	....	....
.....	....	....	....
.....	....	....	....

4. Set forth those adjustments, i.e., changes, in the notice of deficiency with which you disagree and why you disagree.

....

....

....

....

....

....

....

....

....

....

Petitioner(s) request(s) that the proceedings in this case be conducted as a "small tax case" under section 7463 of the Internal Revenue Code of 1954, as amended, and Rule *172* of the Rules of Practice of the United States Tax Court.* [See pages .... and .... of the enclosed booklet.] A decision in a "small tax case" is final and cannot be appealed by either party.

---

* If you do not want to make this request, you should place an "X" in the following box. ☐

....
Signature of Petitioner (Husband)

....
Present Address

....
Signature of Petitioner (Wife)
(If joint return was filed)

....
Present Address

....
Signature and address of counsel, if retained by petitioner(s)

FORM 3

ENTRY OF APPEARANCE
(AVAILABLE—ASK FOR FORM 3)

(SEE RULE 24)

UNITED STATES TAX COURT

.... Petitioner,	
v.	Docket No.
COMMISSIONER OF INTERNAL REVENUE, Respondent.	

ENTRY OF APPEARANCE

The undersigned, being duly admitted to practice before the United States Tax Court, hereby enters his appearance for the petitioner in the above-entitled case.

....
(Signed)

Dated:

....
(Type signature)

....
(Office address)

....
(City)

....
Telephone No. (include area code)

A SEPARATE ENTRY OF APPEARANCE MUST BE FILED IN DUPLICATE FOR EACH DOCKET NUMBER.

FORM 4

REQUEST FOR PLACE OF TRIAL
(AVAILABLE—ASK FOR FORM 4)

(SEE RULE 140)

UNITED STATES TAX COURT

.... Petitioner(s) v. COMMISSIONER OF INTERNAL REVENUE, Respondent.	Docket No.

REQUEST FOR PLACE OF TRIAL

Petitioner(s) hereby request(s) that trial of this case be held at ....
(City and State)

Dated: ...., 19....

....
Signature of petitioner or counsel

FORM 5

SUBPOENA
(AVAILABLE—ASK FOR FORM 5)

(SEE RULE 147)

UNITED STATES TAX COURT

.... Petitioner,		
v.		Docket No.
COMMISSIONER OF INTERNAL REVENUE, Respondent.		

SUBPOENA

To ....

....

YOU ARE HEREBY COMMANDED to appear before the United States Tax Court

....
(or the name and official title of a person authorized to take depositions)

at .... on the .... day of .... at ....
(Time) (Date) (Month)

....
(Place)

then and there to testify on behalf of ....
(Petitioner) or

.... in the above-entitled case, and to bring
(Respondent)

with you ....
....
....
(Use reverse if necessary)

and not to depart without leave of the Court.

Date .... [Seal of Court]

....

Attorney for (Petitioner) (Respondent) (Name) (Title)

RETURN ON SERVICE

The above-named witness was summoned on the .... day of........., 19...... at .... by delivering a copy of this subpoena to h......, and, if a witness for the petitioner, by tendering fees and mileage to h...... pursuant to Rule 148 of the Rules of Practice of the Tax Court.

Dated .... Signed ....

Subscribed and sworn to before me this .... day of............, 19.......

..................[SEAL]
(Name and Title)

FORM 6

APPLICATION FOR ORDER TO TAKE DEPOSITION*
(AVAILABLE—ASK FOR FORM 6)

(SEE RULES 81 THROUGH 84)

UNITED STATES TAX COURT

.... Petitioner, v. COMMISSIONER OF INTERNAL REVENUE, Resondent.	Docket No.

Application For Order To Take Deposition*

To the United States Tax Court:

1. Application is hereby made by the above-named ....
(Petitioner or respondent)
for an order to take the deposition .. of the following-named person ..:

Name of witness	*Post-office address*
(a)	....
(b)	....
(c)	....
(d)	....

* Applications must be filed at least 45 days prior to the date set for trial. When the application seeks to take depositions upon written questions, the title of the application shall so indicate and the application shall be accompanied by an original and five copies of the proposed questions. The taking of depositions upon written questions is not favored, except when the depositions are to be taken in foreign countries, in which case any depositions taken *must* be upon written questions, except as otherwise directed by the Court for cause shown. (See Rule 84(a)). If the parties so stipulate, depositions may be taken without application to the Court. (See Rule 81(d)).

2. It is desired to take the deposition .. of the above-named person .. for the following reasons (With respect to each of the above-named persons, set forth the reasons for taking the depositions rather than waiting until trial to introduce the testimony or other evidence):

3. The substance of the tesimony, to be obtained through the deposition .., is as follows (With respect to each of the above-named persons, set forth briefly the substance of the expected testimony or other evidence):

4. The following books, papers, documents, or other tangible things to be produced at the deposition, are as follows (With respect to each of the above-named persons, describe briefly all things which the applicant desires to have produced at the deposition):

5. The expected testimony or other evidence is material to one or more matters in controversy, in the following respect:

6. (a) This deposition (will) (will not) be taken on written questions (see Rule 84).

(b) All such written questions are annexed to this application (attach such questions pursuant to Rule 84).

7. The petition in this case was filed with the Court on ....
(month, day, year)
The pleadings in this case (are) (are not) closed. This case (has) (has not) been placed on a trial calendar.

8. An arrangement as to payment of fees and expenses of the deposition is desired which departs from the Rules 81(g) and 103, as follows:

9. It is desired to take the testimony of ....

on the .... day of ...., 19.., at the hour of .... o'clock ... M.,* at.....................................
(state room number, street number,

.... before ....
street name, city and state) (state name and official title)

---

* (A deposition in a pending case, under Rule 81, must be completed and filed with the Court at least 10 days prior to trial.)

10. .... is a
(name of person before whom deposition is to be taken)
is a person who is authorized to administer an oath, in his capacity as .... Such person is not a relative or employee or counsel of any party, or a relative or employee or associate of such counsel, nor is he financially interested in the action. (For possible waiver of this requirement, see Rule 81(e)(3).)

Dated ...., 19.....

(Signed) ....
(Petitioner or counsel)

....
(Post-office address)

FORM 7

CERTIFICATE ON RETURN
UNITED STATES TAX COURT

.... Petitioner, v. COMMISSIONER OF INTERNAL REVENUE, Respondent.	Docket No.

CERTIFICATE ON RETURN OF DEPOSITION

To the United State Tax Court:

I, ..., the person named in an order of this Court dated ...., to take depositions in this case, hereby certify:

1. I proceeded, on the .... day of ...., A.D. 19..., at the office of ...., in the city of ...., State of ...., at ...... o'clock ...m., under the said order and in the presence of .... and .... the counsel of the respective parties, to take the following depositions, viz:

.................., a witness produced on behalf of the ....;
(Petitioner or respondent)

.................., a witness produced on behalf of the ....;
(Petitioner or respondent)

.................., a witness produced on behalf of the ....
(Petitioner or respondent)

2. Each witness was examined under oath at such times and places as conditions of adjournment required, and the testimony of each witness (or his answers to the questions filed) was taken stenographically or otherwise recorded and reduced to typewriting by me or under my direction.

3. After the said testimony of each witness was reduced to writing, the transcript of the testimony was read and signed by the witness and was acknowledged by him to be his testimony, in all respects truly and correctly transcribed except as otherwise stated.

4. All exhibits introduced during the deposition are transmitted herewith, except to the following extent agreed to by the parties or directed by the Court (state disposition of exhibits if not transmitted with the deposition):

5. This deposition (was) (was not) taken on written questions pursuant to Rule 84 of the Rules of Practice and Procedure of the United State Tax Court. All such written questions are annexed to the deposition.

6. After the signing of the deposition, no alterations or changes were made therein.

7. I am not a relative or employee or counsel of any party, or a relative or employee or associate of such counsel, nor am I financially interested in the action.

....
(Signature of person taking deposition)

....
(Official title)

Note.—This form, when properly executed, should be attached to and bound with the transcript preceding the first page thereof. It should then be enclosed in a sealed packet, with registered or certified postage or other transportation charges prepaid, and directed and forwarded to the United States Tax Court, P.O. Box 70, Washington, D.C. 20044.

FORM 8

NOTICE OF APPEAL TO COURT OF APPEALS

(SEE RULES 190 AND 191)

UNITED STATES TAX COURT

...., Petitioner, v. COMMISSIONER OF INTERNAL REVENUE, Respondent.	Docket No.

NOTICE OF APPEAL

Notice is hereby given that .... hereby appeals to the United States Court of Appeals for the .... Circuit from [that part of] the decision of this court entered in the above captioned proceeding on the .... day of ...., 19... [relating to ....].

....
Party or Counsel

....
Post office Address

FORM 9
APPEAL BOND, CORPORATE SURETY

(SEE RULE 191)

The following is a satisfactory form of bond for use in case bond with a corporate surety approved by the Treasury Department is to be furnished to stay the assessment and collection of tax involved in an appeal from a decision of the Tax Court. The original bond and one copy are required. There are no printed forms. Each petitioner must execute the bond, and the corporate seal or a designation of seal in the case of individuals must be affixed:

UNITED STATES TAX COURT

...., Petitioner, v. COMMISSIONER OF INTERNAL REVENUE, Respondent.	Docket No.

BOND

KNOW ALL MEN BY THESE PRESENTS that we .... as principal, and ...., as surety, are held and firmly bound unto the above-named COMMISSIONER OF INTERNAL REVENUE and/or the UNITED STATES OF AMERICA, in the sum of $..........., (double the deficiency or such sum as the Tax Court has fixed upon petitioner's prior motion), to be paid to the said Commissioner of Internal Revenue and/or the United States of America for the payment of which well and truly to be made we bind ourselves and each of us and our successors and assigns jointly and severally firmly by these presents.

Signed, sealed, and dated this ...... day of ...., 19....

WHEREAS, the above named .... is filing or is about to file with the United States Tax Court, an appeal from the said Court's decision in respect of the tax liability of the above petitioner for the taxable year or years .... by the United States Court of Appeals for the .... Circuit to reverse the decision rendered in the above-entitled cause.

NOW, THEREFORE, the condition of this Obligation is such that if the above-named .... shall file its appeal and shall prosecute said appeal to effect and shall pay the deficiency as finally determined, together with any interests, additional amounts or additions to the tax provided for by law, then this obligation shall be void, otherwise the same shall be and remain in full force and virtue.

[SEAL]

....
(for an individual petitioner)

....
(for a corporate petitioner)

By ....
Title

....
(Corporate Seal) Surety

Attest: By ....
Title (surety corporate seal)

....
Secretary

FORM 10

APPEAL BOND, APPROVED COLLATERAL

(SEE RULE 191)

A satisfactory form of bond for use in case an appellant desires to furnish approved collateral (Treasury Department Circular No. 154, Revised), instead of furnishing a corporate surety bond, and also forms of powers of attorney covering the pledged collateral are shown below. The original and one copy are required in either case. There are no printed forms. Each petitioner must execute the bond, and the corporate seal or a designation of seal in the case of individuals must be affixed.

UNITED STATES TAX COURT

.... Petitioner, v. COMMISSIONER OF INTERNAL REVENUE, Respondent.	Docket No.

BOND

KNOW ALL MEN BY THESE PRESENTS that .... is held and firmly bound unto the above-named Commissioner of Internal Revenue and/or the United States of America in the sum of .... ($..........) Dollars, to be paid to the said COMMISSIONER OF INTERNAL REVENUE, and/or the UNITED STATES OF AMERICA, for the payment of which, well and truly to be made, the .... binds itself and its successors, firmly by these presents.

Signed, sealed, and dated this .... day of ...., 19....

WHEREAS, the above-named .... is filing or is about to file with the United States Tax Court, an appeal from the said Court's decision in respect of the tax liability of the above petitioner for the taxable year or years .... by the United States Court of Appeals for the .... Circuit to reverse the decision rendered in the above-entitled cause.

NOW, THEREFORE, the condition of this obligation is such that if the above-named .... shall file its appeal and shall prosecute said appeal to effect and shall pay the deficiency as finally determined, together with any interest, additional amounts or additions to the tax provided for by law, then this obligation shall be void, otherwise the same shall be and remain in full force and virtue.

The above-bounden obligor, in order for more fully to secure the Commissioner of Internal Revenue and/or the United States in the payment of the aforementioned sum, hereby pledges as security therefor bonds/notes of the United States in a sum equal at their par value to the aforementioned sum, to wit: .... dollars ($...........), whch said bonds/notes are numbered serially and are in the denominations and amounts, and are otherwise more particularly described as follows: ....

....

....

which said bonds/notes have this day been deposited with the Clerk of the United States Tax Court and his receipt taken therefor.

Contemporaneously herewith the undersigned has also executed and delivered an irrevocable power of attorney and agreement in favor of the Clerk of the United States Tax Court, authorizing and empowering him, as such attorney to collect or sell or transfer or assign, the above-described bonds/notes so deposited, or any part thereof, in case of any default in the performance of any of the above-named conditions or stipulations.

[SEAL]

....

(for an individual petitioner)

(Corporate Seal) ....

Attest: (for a corporate petitioner)

.... By..

Secretary Title

FORM 11

POWER OF ATTORNEY AND AGREEMENT BY CORPORATION

(SEE RULE 191)

KNOW ALL MEN BY THESE PRESENTS: That ...., a corporation duly incorporated under the laws of the State of .... and having its principal office in the city of ...., State of ...., in pursuance of a resolution of the Board of Directors of said corporation, passed on the .... day of ...., 19...., a duly certified copy of which resolution is hereto attached, does hereby constitute and appoint the Clerk of the United States Tax Court as attorney for said corporation, for and in the name of said corporation to collect or to sell, assign, and transfer certain United States Liberty bonds or other bonds or notes of the United States, the property of said corporation, described as follows:

Title of bonds/notes	Total face amount	Denomi- nation	Serial No.	Interest dates
....	....	....	....	....
....	....	....	....	....
....	....	....	....	....

such bonds/notes having been deposited by it, pursuant to the Act of July 30, 1947, c. 390, 61 Stat. 646, as security for the faithful performance of any and all of the conditions or stipulations of a certain obligation entered into by it with (here enter "the Comissioner of Internal Revenue and/or the United States") under date of ...., which is hereby made a part thereof, and the undersigned agrees that, in case of any default in the performance of any of the conditions and stipulations of such undertaking, its said attorney shall have full power to collect said bonds/notes or any part thereof, or to sell, assign, and transfer said bonds/notes or any part thereof without notice, at public or private sale, or to transfer or assign to another for the purpose of effecting either public or private sale, free from any equity of redemption and without appraisement or valuation, notice and right to redeem being waived, and the proceeds of such sale or collection, in whole or in part to be applied to the satisfaction of any damages, demands, or deficiency arising by reason of such default, as may be deemed best, and the undersigned further agrees that the authority herein granted is irrevocable.

And said corporation, hereby for itself, its successors and assigns, ratifies and confirms whatever its said attorney shall do by virtue of these presents.

In witness whereof, the ...., the corporation hereinabove named, by .... (Name and title of officer), duly authorized to act in the premises, has executed this instrument and caused the seal of the corporation to be hereto affixed this .... day of ...., 19.....

Attest:

....

(Corporate seal) Secretary By ....

Title

State of ....)
) SS:
County of ....)

Before me, the undersigned, a notary public within and for the said county and State, personally appeared .... (Name and title of officer), and for and in behalf of said ...., corporation, acknowledged the execution of the foregoing power of attorney.

Witness my hand and notarial seal this .... day of ...., 19.. ..

[Notarial seal] ....

Notary Pubic

My Commission expires..............................

FORM 12

POWER OF ATTORNEY AND AGREEMENT BY INDIVIDUALS

(SEE RULE 191)

KNOW ALL MEN BY THESE PRESENTS: That I (we) ...., do hereby constitute and appoint the Clerk of the United States Tax Court as attorney for me (us), and in my (our) name to collect or to sell, assign, and transfer certain United States Liberty bonds, or other bonds or notes of the United States, being my (our) property described as follows:

Title of bonds/notes	Total face amount	Denomination	Serial No.	Interest dates
....	....	....	......	......
....	....	....	......	......
....	....	....	......	......

such bonds/notes having been deposited by me (us) pursuant to the Act of July 30, 1947, c. 390, 61 Stat. 646, as security for the faithful performance of any and all of the conditions or stipulations of a certain obligation entered into by me (us) with (here enter "the Commissioner of Internal Revenue and/or the United States") under date of ...., which is hereby made a part thereof, and I (we), agree that, in case of any default in the performance of any of the conditions and stipulations of such undertaking, my (our) said attorney shall have full power to collect said bonds/notes or any part thereof, or to sell, assign, and transfer said bonds/notes or any part thereof without notice, at public or private sale, or to transfer or assign to another for the purpose of effecting either public or private sale, free from any equity of redemption and without appraisement or valuation, notice and right to redeem being waived, and the proceeds of such sale or collection, in whole or in part to be applied to the satisfaction of any damages, demands, or deficiency arising by reason of such default, as may be deemed best, and I (we) further agree that the authority herein granted is irrevocable.

And for myself (ourselves), my (our several) administrators, executors, and assigns, I (we) hereby ratify and confirm whatever my (our) said attorney shall do by virtue of these presents.

In witness whereof, I (we) hereinabove named, have executed this instrument and affixed my (our) seal this .... day of ...., 19....

....[SEAL]

State of ....)
) SS:
County of ....)

Before me, the undersigned, a notary public within and for the said county and State, personally appeared .... (Name of obligor), and acknowledged the execution of the foregoing power of attorney.

Witness my hand and notarial seal this .... day of ...., 19....

[Notarial seal]

....

Notary Public

My Commission expires ....

FORM 13

CERTIFICATE OF SERVICE

(SEE RULE 21)

This is to certify that a copy of the foregoing paper was served on .... by (delivering the same to him at .... on ....) or (mailing the same on .... in a postage paid wrapper addressed to him at ....).

Dated:

....
Party or Counsel

APPENDIX II

CODE SECTION 7463

DISPUTES INVOLVING $1,500 OR LESS

(SEE RULES 170 THROUGH 179)

(a) In General.—In the case of any petition filed with the Tax Court for a redetermination of a deficiency where neither the amount of the deficiency placed in dispute, nor the amount of any claimed overpayment, exceeds—

(1) $1,500 for any one taxable year, in the case of the taxes imposed by subtitle A and chapter 12, or

(2) $1,500 in the case of the tax imposed by chapter 11, at the option of the taxpayer concurred in by the Tax Court or a division thereof before the hearing of the case, proceedings in the case shall be conducted under this section. Nonwithstanding the provisions of section 7453, such proceedings shall be conducted in accordance with such rules of evidence, practice, and procedure as the Tax Court may prescribe. A decision, together with a brief summary of the reasons therefor, in any such case shall satisfy the requirements of sections 7459(b) and 7460.

(b) Finality of Decisions.—A decision entered in any case in which the proceedings are conducted under this section shall not be reviewed in any other court and shall not be treated as a precedent for any other case.

(c) Limitation of Jurisdiction.—In any case in which the proceedings are conducted under this section, notwithstanding the provisions of sections 6214(a) and 6512(b), no decision shall be entered redetermining the amount of a deficiency, or determining an overpayment, except with respect to amounts placed in dispute within the limits described in subsection (a) and with respect to amounts conceded by the parties.

(d) Discontinuance of Proceedings.—At any time before a decision entered in a case in which the proceedings are conducted under this section becomes final, the taxpayer or the Secretary or his delegate may request that further proceedings under this section in such case be discontinued. The Tax Court, or the division thereof hearing such case, may, if it finds that (1) there are reasonable grounds for believing that the amount of the deficiency placed in dispute, or the amount of an overpayment, exceeds the applicable jurisdictional amount described in subsection (a), and (2) the amount of such excess is large enough to justify granting such request, discontinue further proceedings in such case under this section. Upon any such discontinuance, proceedings in such case shall be conducted in the same manner as cases to which the provisions of sections 6214(a) and 6512(b) apply.

(e) Amount of Deficiency in Dispute.—For purposes of this section, the amount of any deficiency placed in dispute includes additions to the tax, additional amounts, and penalties imposed by chapter 68, to the extent that the procedures described in subchapter B of chapter 63 apply.

APPENDIX III

FEES AND CHARGES

(SEE RULE 148)

(a) Fees and charges payable to the Court:

1. Filing petition $10.00

2. Application for admission to practice 10.00
3. Photocopies (plain)—per page .... .25
4. Photocopies (certified)—per page .... .50
5. Transmitting record on appeal .... *

* Actual cost of insurance and postage

(b) Fees and mileage payable to witnesses, as provided for by 28 U.S.C. § 1821:

Witness fee (per day)	$20.00
Per diem in lieu of subsistence	16.00
Mileage (per mile)	.10

Note: The Attorney General of the United States has adopted the Rand-McNally Standard Mileage Guide as the table of distances under 28 U.S.C. § 1821.

(c) Charges for copies of transcripts of proceedings:

Transcripts of proceedings before the Tax Court are supplied to the parties and to the public by the official reporter at such rates as may be fixed by contract between the Court and the reporter. Information as to those rates may be obtained from the Clerk of the Court or from the deputy clerk at a trial session.

APPENDIX IV

PLACES OF TRIAL

(SEE RULES 140 AND 177)

A partial list of cities in which regular sessions of the Court are held appears below.* This list is published to assist parties in making requests under Rules X140 and X177. If sufficient cases are not ready for trial in a city requested by a taxpayer, or if suitable courtroom facilities are not available in that city, the Court may find it necessary to calendar cases for trial in some other city within reasonable proximity of the designated place.

List

ALABAMA:
Birmingham.
Mobile.
ALASKA:
Anchorage.
ARIZONA:
Phoenix.
ARKANSAS:
Little Rock.
CALIFORNIA:
Los Angeles.
San Francisco.
COLORADO:
Denver.
CONNECTICUT:
New Haven.
DISTRICT OF COLUMBIA:
Washington.
FLORIDA:
Jacksonville.
Miami.
Tampa.
GEORGIA:
Atlanta.
HAWAII:
Honolulu.
IDAHO:
Boise.
ILLINOIS:
Chicago.
INDIANA:
Indianapolis.
IOWA:
Des Moines.
KANSAS:
Kansas City.
KENTUCKY:
Louisville/Frankfort.
LOUISIANA:
New Orleans.
MARYLAND:
Baltimore.
MASSACHUSETTS:
Boston.
MICHIGAN:
Detroit.
MINNESOTA:
St. Paul.
MISSISSIPPI:
Biloxi.
Jackson.

* The Court sits in about 35 other cities to hear Small Tax Cases. A list of such cities is contained in a pamphlet entitled "Election of Small Tax Case Procedure and Preparation of Petitions," a copy of which may be obtained from the Clerk of the Court.

MISSOURI:
- Kansas City.
- St. Louis.

MONTANA:
- Helena.

NEBRASKA:
- Omaha.

NEVADA:
- Las Vegas/Reno.

NEW JERSEY:
- Newark.

NEW MEXICO:
- Albuquerque.

NEW YORK:
- Buffalo.
- New York City.

NORTH CAROLINA:
- Greensboro/Durham.

OHIO:
- Cleveland.
- Cincinnati.
- Columbus.

OKLAHOMA:
- Oklahoma City.
- Tulsa.

OREGON:
- Portland.

PENNSYLVANIA:
- Philadelphia.
- Pittsburgh.

SOUTH CAROLINA:
- Columbia.

TENNESSEE:
- Knoxville.
- Memphis.
- Nashville.

TEXAS:
- Dallas.
- El Paso.
- Houston.
- Lubbock.
- San Antonio.

UTAH:
- Salt Lake City.

VIRGINIA:
- Richmond.

WASHINGTON:
- Seattle.
- Spokane.

WEST VIRGINIA:
- Charleston/Huntington.

WISCONSIN:
- Milwaukee.